A SPIRIT OF SERVICE

THE FOUNDERS SERIES

The Founders Series publishes books on and about Purdue University, whether the physical campus, the University's impact on the region and world, or the many visionaries who attended or worked at the University.

OTHER TITLES IN THIS SERIES

Purdue Memorial Union: The First 100 Years, 1924–2024
Robert L. Mindrum

Forging the Future: A History of the John Martinson Honors College, 2013–2023
Emily Allen, Jannine Huby, and Pulkit Manchanda (Eds.)

Boiler Up: A University President in the Public Square
Mitchell E. Daniels, Jr.

The Rocket Lab: Maurice Zucrow, Purdue University, and America's Race to Space
Michael G. Smith

Planting the Seeds of Hope: Indiana County Extension Agents During the Great Depression and World War II
Frederick Whitford

Queen of American Agriculture: A Biography of Virginia Claypool Meredith
Frederick Whitford, Andrew G. Martin, and Phyllis Mattheis

WBAA: 100 Years as the Voice of Purdue
Angie Klink

Pledge and Promise: Celebrating the Bond and Heritage of Fraternity, Sorority, and Cooperative Life at Purdue University
Angie Klink

Wings of Their Dreams: Purdue in Flight, Second Edition
John Norberg

Ever True: 150 Years of Giant Leaps at Purdue University
John Norberg

Purdue at 150: A Visual History of Student Life
David M. Hovde, Adriana Harmeyer, Neal Harmeyer, and Sammie L. Morris

Memories of Life on the Farm: Through the Lens of Pioneer Photographer J. C. Allen
Frederick Whitford and Neal Harmeyer

A Purdue Icon: Creation, Life, and Legacy
James L. Mullins (Ed.)

A SPIRIT OF SERVICE

Purdue University® and the United States Military

John Norberg

Purdue University Press • West Lafayette, Indiana

Printed in the United States of America.

Cataloging-in-Publication data is on file at the Library of Congress.
978-1-61249-976-5 (hardcover)
978-1-61249-977-2 (paperback)
978-1-61249-978-9 (epub)
978-1-61249-979-6 (epdf)

For all photographs, information about individuals, places, events, and dates has been provided to the extent it is known. Cover images courtesy of: USAF Col. (ret.) Dave Hankins (top left); Gabrielle Trent (top center); Christina S. Peterson (top right); Lt. Col. Kevin White (center left); 2d Lt. Thomas McLean (center right); Gabrielle Schmidt (bottom left); Eric Dietz (bottom, 2nd from left); Lt. Cdr. Joseph "Summer" Camp, Jr. (bottom, 3rd from left); and Purdue NROTC (bottom right).

Dedicated with thanks to the men and women of Purdue University, educated in a spirit of service to the nation, whose patriotism, leadership, and heroism have preserved human life, liberty, and the pursuit of happiness for generations of Americans— past, present, and future.

In Honor of John Francis (Jack) Babbitt, IV

June 24, 1923–July 22, 2024

An international businessman and entrepreneur, decorated WWII B-17 pilot, talented chemical engineer, and distinguished Purdue alumnus whose philanthropy and service created conditions for the graduate education success of hundreds of military officers at Purdue University.

No other university has a higher responsibility to the nation than Purdue. Purdue, and others of like kind, was conceived and born in a spirit of service to the nation. . . .

PURDUE UNIVERSITY PRESIDENT
WINTHROP STONE, MAY 30, 1917

CONTENTS

FOREWORD

Martin Luther King Jr. stated that "the arc of the moral universe is long, but it bends toward justice." History has shown that time is required to make this journey, that it must be free from tyranny, and that knowledge is an essential companion.

To play a role along this arc, Purdue University was born of the Morrill Land Grant Act in 1869 to teach military tactics as well as engineering, agriculture, and any other subjects of its choosing. On the eve of the 150th anniversary of Purdue Engineering, a story that began with the first classes in 1874, we are reminded of the critical work that universities do to better our world.

A Spirit of Service describes the intersection of Purdue with the United States military. We see the consequential role that Purdue Boilermakers have played in defending the Declaration of Independence's aspirations of "life, liberty, and the pursuit of happiness" during times of war when freedom was under great duress.

Purdue contributions have often been pioneering ones, such as participating in the Manhattan Project, learning how to better cool machine gun barrels, making radar practical, leading the transition from vacuum tubes to semiconductors, Dorothy Stratton advancing the role of women in the military, the founding of the National Society of Black Engineers, establishing the first School of Engineering Education, building the first university airport, and, most famously, Neil Armstrong—a Navy officer—being the first to set foot on the moon.

Today Purdue is at the forefront of drones, hypersonics, energetics, artificial intelligence, space exploration, cybersecurity, and much more. In fact, approximately one-third of U.S. space flights have included a Purdue astronaut and many of those alumni have served in the military. This large number of astronauts partially stems from a Purdue-Air Force Academy program to provide advanced degrees to graduating officers.

Purdue ROTC programs, including Army, Navy, Marine Corps, Air Force, and Space Force, consistently number among the largest and most successful programs in our nation. The Purdue Military Research Institute (PMRI) continues this leadership into the twenty-first century and expands it to citizen-soldier active-duty officers from all services, with more than two hundred presently on campus or already graduated. These officers, who live and learn among those they protect, are role models for Purdue students from all over the United States and the world.

We have a number of faculty who have stated that their students continue to benefit from the example of these military officers long after they graduate. Their hard work, ingenuity, humility, sense of humor, discipline, maturity, and tenacity inspire everyone to perform at a higher level.

A Purdue education provides our military students with the knowledge to protect freedom, but alumni such as Jack Babbitt show that the true power is using this ingenuity and knowledge to do good. On his final military mission, Captain Babbitt dropped food to starving people at the end of World War II. Then, after graduating from Purdue with an engineering degree, he pioneered the manufacture of ammonia which is used in fertilizer that helps to feed the world.

We are proud that Purdue spans the entire spectrum of engineering education, from the Purdue Polytechnic Institute to the College of Engineering. Collectively we have graduated thousands of military veterans who have served all branches and at all ranks from private to four-star general.

I trust you will enjoy reading *A Spirit of Service* and learning the many ways that Purdue has served the cause of freedom on our planet and beyond.

Boiler Up and Hail Purdue.

Arvind Raman
Dean of Engineering, Purdue University
West Lafayette, Indiana
October 2023

PREFACE

The wording is awkward, almost like it was added as an afterthought.

It was.

In 1859, the United States Congress passed "An Act Donating Public Lands to the Several States and Territories which may provide Colleges for the Benefit of Agriculture and the Mechanic Arts." "Mechanic Arts" was later termed "engineering," which many people of the time confused with operating a locomotive engine.

This land grant act was vetoed by President James Buchanan.

When the act was reintroduced and again approved by Congress in 1862, there were three changes. First, the Southern states that had originally opposed the bill had seceded and were at war with the Union. Second, there was a new President, Abraham Lincoln, who understood the need for learning, especially in the frontier states where he was born, lived, and received little formal education. Third, there was a requirement that a new field of study be added in addition to agriculture and mechanic arts: military tactics.

By 1862, the states that remained in the Union were coming to the realization that this would be a long and bloody conflict. They also realized they were woefully short of trained officers to lead their men in battle.

Nothing Congress could do would impact the number of trained officers in the Civil War of 1861–1865. But people recognized there would be more wars and more need for trained officers who could be called into service. Representative Justin Morrill, a Republican from Vermont and sponsor of the Land Grant Act, added training in military tactics to the bill to meet an important need and to gain support for his new universities. The 1862 act, approved by Congress and signed by Lincoln, gave states public lands to be sold for the support of universities "where the leading object shall be, without excluding other scientific and classical studies, and including military tactics, to teach such branches of learning as are related to agriculture and the mechanic arts."

Purdue University in West Lafayette is one of the great land grant schools of the nation. Its thirteen colleges and schools are national and world leaders in education, research, and outreach. But not all people are aware that land-grant universities are required by federal law to teach military tactics.

Purdue has excelled in military support, from its modest opening in 1874 with 39 students (only 13 of whom were found prepared for college studies), to nearly 52,000 students and 2,000 faculty in the twenty-first century.

In 2023 Purdue includes:

- About 500 male and female students enrolled in Reserved Officers Training Corps (ROTC);
- About 2,100 additional military-connected students studying for degrees on university campuses;
- An office created to assist military-connected students with their unique needs and G.I. Bill benefits;
- A Purdue Global online school that enrolls more than 30,000 students, nearly 10,000 of them with connections to the military and growing;
- An additional Purdue Online program with about 1,000 military connected students;
- A Purdue Military Research Institute (PMRI) providing more active military officers with graduate degrees than any non-military school in the nation;
- And with a strategic initiative on teaching, research and partnerships focused on national security and technology, Purdue in the twenty-first century is a leader in hypersonic, semiconductors, and more.

In the summer of 2021, Dr. J. Eric Dietz, a professor of computer and information technology, director of the Purdue Military Research Institute, and director of the Purdue Homeland Security Institute along with Dr. Joseph Pekny, a professor of chemical engineering, came to me with the idea of a book focused on the history of the University and the military.

A committee was formed, including Dietz, Pekny, Dr. Arvind Raman (who in 2023 became Dean of Engineering), Professor of Electrical and Computer Engineering and Associate Dean of Graduate Education Dr. Dana Weinstein, Executive Assistant to the Dean of Engineering Jill Vigar, and Engineering Lead Administrative Assistant Stephanie Porter.

The committee supported the book for publication working with Purdue University Press. I started research in the Virginia Kelly Karnes Archives and Special Collections where the history of the University comes alive. Through research there and piecing together information from books and publications along with many interviews, an incredible story emerged, including:

- A crude Corps of Cadets formed in 1876 and led by an incredible professor and researcher, born in a log cabin in southern Indiana, who would one day be known as the "Father of the Pure Food and Drug Act," and the first head of the Food and Drug Administration. He knew far more about food adulteration and roosters than he did about military tactics.
- The 1889–91 Purdue Register announced military training would be required by all male freshmen and sophomores at Purdue unless they played in the band, which was considered a military organization. ROTC became voluntary at Purdue for male students in 1965.
- In 1916, Purdue cadets were called into active service by President Woodrow Wilson and spent a hot summer at the southern tip of Texas guarding the border from raids by Pancho Villa.
- In 1918, during the Great War, Purdue looked like a military camp with men living in barracks while they studied and trained. During the Great War, more Purdue men died in military service from the flu pandemic than from battlefield injuries.
- The Purdue Airport became the first in the nation to train students as pilots before the United States' entry into World War II.
- At the peak of World War II, there were twice as many military personnel and civilian men and women preparing for defense industry jobs at Purdue than there were traditional degree-seeking students.
- An African American receiving training at Purdue late in the war went on to become the first Black Marine officer.
- More than one hundred Purdue professors worked on the Manhattan Project during World War II.
- ROTC and the Purdue Airport played an important role in attracting students to the University, especially those who would later become astronauts.
- A Purdue military drill team in the 1950s and 1960s won six national championships. It was the best team in the University's history. Judges stopped scoring them in the middle of one contest and just sat down and enjoyed it.
- Between 1958 and 2005, more than nine hundred Navy enlisted men and women were sent to Purdue to receive a college education and a commission as an officer.

- ROTC had a lifelong impact on its students. More than 180 men and women have been named to the Purdue ROTC Hall of Fame as of 2023.
- A Purdue woman was among the first six female U.S. Navy pilots.
- In addition to the Purdue Military Research Institute, Purdue provides graduate education to officers in the Royal Australian Air Force.

A Spirit of Service tells the stories of men and women who lived this history, from ROTC students to a Medal of Honor recipient, from soldiers at the front during the Great War to a man who witnessed the December 7, 1941 attack on Pearl Harbor, from a pilot who led thousands of planes in bombing missions over Germany during World War II to military astronauts, from trailblazing female officers and pilots to twenty-first-century teachers and researchers who are creating the future. This volume records the stories of Purdue men and women whose patriotism, leadership, and heroism have preserved life, liberty, and the pursuit of happiness for generations of Americans—past, present, and future.

My thanks to J. Eric Dietz and Joseph Pekny for bringing this book to me and guiding me through it. Thanks also to the committee, including Purdue Chemical Engineering Professor of Practice and Army Brigadier General (retired) Dr. Leon L. Robert Jr., for its advice and support. Purdue Military Research Institute (PMRI) Senior Project Manager David Hankins, Davidson School of Chemical Engineering Project Manager Chris Murray, and David Tate, chair of the Purdue ROTC Hall of Fame, helped often during this project. Thanks to Neil Harmeyer and all the incredible people at Virginia Kelly Karnes Archives and Special Collections who guided me to wonderful stories, understanding that in addition to creating the future, the university plays a key role in preserving the past. Thanks to Kelly Lippe, Tippecanoe County Historical Association curator of collections and memberships, and to everyone at the TCHA archives. Special thanks to Tara Saunders, production editor at Purdue University Press, for her guidance and excellent editing that greatly improved this book. And thanks to everyone at Purdue University Press, including Justin Race, Kelley Kimm, Chris Brannan, Katherine Purple, and Bryan Shaffer. Thanks to everyone who spent time answering my endless questions and telling me their incredible life stories.

And most of all, thank you to my wife Jeanne always and for everything.

John Norberg
October 2023

PART 1

1862–1918

1

LEGISLATION TO BUILD A NATION

> *. . . the leading object shall be, without excluding other scientific and classical studies and including military tactics, to teach such branches of learning as are related to agriculture and the mechanic arts . . .*
>
> MORRILL LAND GRANT ACT (1862)

On a fresh spring day in 1877, camping in a wooded area along the Wabash River with Purdue University students who were there to learn military tactics, Professor Harvey Wiley awoke at dawn with a start when he felt something strange beneath his pillow.

He was the first person named captain of Purdue's Corps of Cadets, and this was their first campout after being organized in the fall of 1876—two years after Purdue opened its doors to students. Wiley had slept well until awakened by the strange object. Still half asleep, he grabbed the offending item and held it to his face.

He was a young man that morning. He lived to be eighty-five years old, and to the end of his life he never forgot what was under his pillow on that campout.

Wiley, who would become one of the most prominent Americans of the early twentieth century, and whose work would impact the lives of millions of people, was the youngest member of the faculty at the new land-grant university near the little town of Chauncey, across the Wabash River from Lafayette, Indiana. He was one month short of his thirtieth birthday when Purdue opened in September 1874—not much older than some of the students.

Educated at Hanover College in southern Indiana, Harvard University in Massachusetts, and the Indiana Medical College in Indianapolis, he was a medical doctor and a professor of chemistry and physics at Purdue. He also taught classes at the medical school seventy miles to the south.

Wiley was not only the youngest member of the faculty, he was also unmarried. So, the offer to become one of the first six members of the faculty came with free living accommodations, if he so desired. The accommodations were in the university men's dorm, where he would be placed in charge of boys and young men out on their own and away from parental authority for the first time in their lives. Wiley accepted the offer—or perhaps it should be called a challenge. He received no additional pay for keeping order in the residence hall, only free accommodation.

The residence hall was quickly dominated by a group of boys who eventually called themselves the "Dorm Devils." They initiated and terrorized new residents, raised havoc whenever they could, and made use of the indoor plumbing and buckets to make certain that everyone and everything was soaking wet from time to time. Wiley found that the best way to handle the sometimes-chaotic situations was to become deaf and blind to the antics. He chose to ignore the chaos rather than fight it. Boys will be boys, after all. Worth Reed, of Covington, Indiana, entered Purdue in 1874. He remembered those days in a 1919 *Alumnus* magazine: "Professor Wiley roomed in the dormitory the first year or so in order to keep these wild and wooly embryonic students in order. But Wiley was a big, jolly boy himself and so we had a good time."[1]

On opening day of the University in 1874, the Purdue Board of Trustees expected two hundred prospective students to apply. Only thirty-nine showed up and only thirteen of those were deemed qualified for college studies. The rest were placed in a preparatory school where the faculty worked to bring them up to college standards.

"The course of study was still crude," Wiley would remember in his autobiography fifty-six years later, a book that showed he could easily find humor in everyday life. "Most of the boys who came from the country to join Purdue Agricultural School were not even well enough trained to enter high school," he wrote. "In addition to this, the bad boys of the city who were expelled from the high schools sought a more congenial environment at Purdue. We had for that reason a number of boys who were modestly described as being 'tough.'"[2]

By and large these were students who did not have the money and the education to find their way to private universities such as Ivy League schools on the East Coast. So, they enrolled in the start-up state university, named for wealthy Lafayette businessman John Purdue, who had provided $150,000 to get the school up and running in his home county. He also promised to find the state one hundred acres of land for the school at no cost to taxpayers. Purdue was an entrepreneur whose main activity during the Civil War was selling pork to the Union

Army. He spent most of the war years in New York City. Fifty-eight years old when the war started, he did not serve in the military. But in 1862, he spent his own money to create a volunteer force named Purdue Rifles to protect Lafayette from any possible attack or sabotage. In 1863, the Purdue Rifles were sent to southern Indiana along the Ohio River where they reportedly captured nineteen Confederate troops and forty horses. At another time the men were sent to Alabama to guard railroads.

MORRILL LAND GRANT ACT

Purdue University was part of the Morrill Land Grant Act approved by the U.S. Congress in 1862. Considered one of the greatest pieces of federal legislation ever enacted, the Morrill Act would change higher education and it would change the United States—which is exactly what it was designed to do.

It would also change U.S. military training and ultimately lead to Reserve Officer Training Corps (ROTC) programs that thrive on more than 1,700 U.S. college campuses in the twenty-first century.

U.S. Army ROTC was created by the National Defense Act of 1916. As of 2023, more than 600,000 men and women have earned a commission through the U.S. Army ROTC—the military's oldest and largest officer producing program. According to Brigadier General Sean A. Gainey, writing for the U.S. Army Cadet Command, among those who have earned ROTC commissions nationally are "two chairmen of the joint chiefs of staff, seven Army chiefs of staff, two cabinet secretaries and a sitting Supreme Court Justice."[3]

At Purdue, military training would grow from twenty-six students in a cadet corps in the fall of 1876 to more than five hundred ROTC students in 2023, with opportunities to serve in the Air Force, Space Force, Navy, Marines, and Army.

There were years when the number of ROTC students at Purdue exceeded two thousand. In addition to ROTC, in 2023 about 2,100 military-connected veterans and their families were studying for undergraduate degrees at Purdue, benefiting from programs specifically intended to foster their success. Another 10,000 military-connected students were studying in Purdue Global, an online school, also with extensive support. Finally, another 1,000 students were enrolled in Purdue Online, a separate program that includes support for military personnel, veterans, and their families.

In 2023, the Purdue Military Research Institute (PMRI) program provided more active military officers with graduate degrees than any non-military school in the nation. Sixty-eight active military service personnel were enrolled in the fall of 2023. And with a strategic initiative on research and partnerships focused on national security and technology, Purdue became a hypersonics research center for the nation, partnering with the military and industry in chip manufacturing, and much more.

How did all of this happen since 1874, when Purdue opened its doors?

It all started with the Morrill Land Grant Act of 1862.

The purpose of the act was to open higher education to the masses—not just to the wealthy and elite who studied the classics and liberal arts. The focus of the schools created by the Morrill Act was to be practical and career-oriented, with a strong emphasis on agriculture, engineering, and ultimately military training.

The Act was named for its principal sponsor, United States Representative (and later Senator) Justin Morrill from Vermont. The act provided public land for states to sell, and the proceeds from the land sale were used to start universities. Each state was given thirty thousand acres of public land for each of its senators and representatives. Since many states, including Indiana, did not have that much available public land within their borders, and since they could not directly sell land in other states, certificates called scrip were issued. The states auctioned the scrip, and the buyers used it to buy land west of the Mississippi. The states could use up to ten percent of the money raised to buy land for a university. The rest was to be invested and the interest used to help support the school.

There were three overriding goals of the Morrill Act. First, it was approved to increase the number of people seeking higher education. Only about one percent of the population of the day attended college. The second goal was to use these educated young people to build the nation. The states and the nation needed roads, factories, bridges, and much more. To build and design these structures, it needed engineers. The third goal was agriculture. The nation needed young people who could apply science to agriculture. Americans were still farming the way their fathers and grandfathers had taught them. Meanwhile, Europeans were advancing. As they applied science to their farming, they began to outproduce the United States.

The Land Grant Act was initially approved by Congress in 1859 over the objections of southern states who said it was a federal intrusion on states' rights. President James Buchanan vetoed the bill and there was not enough support to override the veto. When it came up again in 1862, the southern states had seceded, so there was less opposition. There was also a new president, Abraham Lincoln, who was born in Kentucky and who had grown up in rural southern Indiana.

With very little formal schooling himself, Lincoln understood the value of education. Moreover, he knew how few opportunities there were, especially in the frontier areas of the nation, for young men and women to seek a college degree.

Land-grant schools were always intended for men, women, and people of all races, although people of color were sometimes excluded, resulting in the development of Historically Black Colleges and Universities (HBCUs). Women also faced challenges that began to be addressed in the 1970s with Title IX legislation that prohibited discrimination based on sex in educational institutions that received federal funds. U.S. Senator Birch Bayh of Indiana authored Title IX and is called its "Father." Bayh graduated from Purdue in 1951, after serving with the U.S. Army in occupied Germany from 1946 to 1948 following World War II. Purdue has admitted women since 1875, and African Americans began to apply and were enrolled in small numbers beginning in the 1890s.

In 1862, there was more to the Land Grant Act than agriculture and engineering. The Civil War had begun, and Morrill added a provision that military train ing be taught at the land-grant schools. The addition of military training brought stronger support for the Morrill Act.

With the Civil War in its second year, people realized it would not end quickly as many had initially hoped. It would be long, bloody, and horrible. There would be more than 600,000 deaths before it ended in 1865.

In a 2012 *New York Times* opinion piece, Michael David Cohen, then an assistant research professor of history at the University of Tennessee, Knoxville (later with American University, in Washington, D.C.), noted the Union Army was not prepared for the war when it began.

> The peacetime Army had been tiny.... Volunteers rallied to defend the Union, but what they brought in enthusiasm they lacked in experience. Many were too young to have fought in the Mexican War and, since most military academies were located in the South, few Northern youths had formal training in combat. To win the war, the Army had to create citizen-soldiers from scratch.... Bemoaning the unreadiness of Northern men to fight the rebels a year earlier, he [Morrell] blamed politicians in Washington for having "long assumed that military discipline" was as "spontaneous" as patriotism. That assumption, he said, had cost many lives. Had Congress earlier passed a law like the one he now proposed, "The young men might have had more of fitness for their sphere of duties, whether on the farm, in the workshop, or in the battlefield."[4]

The Morrill Act would be too late to have an impact on the Civil War. It would take years to get most of the land-grant universities started and young men trained. But a provision was added to the Act, if somewhat parenthetically, that would prepare the nation for the future. It was decided the teaching of military tactics would be required at the land-grant universities, along with the emphasis on agriculture and engineering. It's important to note, while the Morrill Act required land-grant schools to provide military training, it did not mandate the students to take part.

In June 1862 Morrill said:

> Something of military instruction has been incorporated in the bill in consequence of the new conviction of its necessity forced upon the attention of the loyal states by the history of the past year. A total unpreparedness presents too many temptations even to a foe otherwise weak. The national school at West Point may suffice for the regular Army in ordinary years of peace, but it is wholly inadequate when a large Army is to be suddenly put into service. If we ever expect to reduce the Army to its old dimensions and again rely on the volunteer system for defense, each state must have the means within itself to organize and officer [provide officers for] its own forces. With such a system as that here offered—nurseries in every state—an efficient force would at all times be ready to support the cause of the nation and secure that wholesome respect which belongs to people whose power is always equal to its pretensions.[5]

Congress soon added more laws supporting military training in higher education. In 1866 it authorized Army officers to do the teaching. In 1870 it authorized loaning weapons including artillery to schools in an effort to prepare young men for military service when needed.

HARVEY WILEY: AN UNLIKELY TEACHER OF MILITARY TACTICS

Indiana decided to participate in the Land Grant Act, and in March 1865, the state received $212,238.50 from the sale of its scrip. The state invested the money while it recovered from the Civil War and considered where to locate the new university.

In June 1875, about nine months after classes started at Purdue, the Board of Trustees requested that the Indiana governor ask the U.S. Army for an officer to be detailed to the University as a military professor. However, no one was sent in response. So, in the fall of 1876, Harvey Wiley volunteered to teach military tactics. He was far from a professional soldier, having served only one hundred days in the Union Army during the Civil War.

Wiley was born and grew up near the village of Kent, in southern Indiana's Jefferson County, near the Ohio River. "Southern Indiana was peopled almost exclusively by settlers from the South," Wiley wrote in his autobiography. "And it was in this part of the state that the greatest number of sympathizers with the new Confederacy were found."[6] The family of Abraham Lincoln moved from Kentucky to Indiana in 1816 and the future president grew up there from the age of seven to twenty-one. The Lincoln family home was only about one hundred miles west of Kent.

Wiley's father, Preston, was a very strict Christian. He believed that celebrations such as those associated with Christmas were pagan and he lived strictly by the Bible. He was strongly opposed to slavery and a supporter of Lincoln. "My father was the original abolitionist of Jefferson County," Wiley wrote.[7] He was a conductor on the Underground Railroad who helped runaway slaves as they came across the Ohio River. Knowing his convictions, when Preston Wiley went to vote some of his neighbors lined up on either side of him as he passed, shouting racial slurs. There was no question which side of the war Wiley and his son would be on.

When the war started in 1861, Harvey Wiley was between his sixteenth and seventeenth birthdays—too young to enlist. He was a big man. Throughout his life in group photos, he usually was the tallest. "Had I allowed my own ardor to guide me, I should have been among the first volunteers, provided I had the conscience to deny my age," Wiley wrote. "I was a big, husky youth, and could easily have passed for eighteen. But because of my parental training in truthfulness, I would not swear falsely as to my age."[8]

He decided to join the Indiana Home Guards, who were less strict about the age of recruits. His father joined him and enlisted as well. "They took one look at my tall robust physique and decided that anyone who could grow that much in less than seventeen years was needed in defense of the state," Wiley wrote.[9]

Wiley and his father joined a local cavalry company guarding the Indiana side of the Ohio River to fight off any raids coming up through Kentucky. There was little for these Indiana Home Guards to do during the first two years of the war, until Confederate Brigadier General John Hunt Morgan led raids into Indiana and Ohio throughout June and July 1863. Wiley did not see any fighting, as he was an orderly. "But I had a fine speedy horse and carried messages with dispatch and certainty," he said.[10]

In 1863, he enrolled at Hanover College in nearby Madison, Indiana and became acquainted with the Bruner family who lived nearby. Years later an old oaken bucket was taken from the Bruner farm to become the trophy for the Purdue-IU football game. Wiley walked to the Bruner home twice a week to get fresh baked bread and on hot summer days might have quenched his thirst from that old oaken bucket.[11]

In 1864, President Lincoln authorized enlistments in the Union Army for one hundred days. These recruits, who had little training, were used for routine duty, thereby freeing the experienced soldiers to move to the front lines of the battles. Hanover had no female students at that time, and nearly all the men left school for the military, including Wiley. He came down with measles, was nursed back to health, and eventually was involved in one minor skirmish. At the end of one hundred days, he was discharged with the rank of fourth corporal.

While he had little military experience, as a boy growing up in rural nineteenth-century Indiana, he had experience with guns. And he had a horrible tragedy in his family from a gun accident. When Wiley was ten, his older brother James Edward, whom he idolized, took part in a shooting contest. "He had forgotten that he had reloaded his piece, after it had been fired, and was blowing into the muzzle of the gun to rid it of the smoke when his foot slipped, the gun fired and he fell dead upon the ground," Wiley wrote. "From that day on all kinds of firearms were banished from our home, except during the Civil War."[12] He had reoccurring nightmares about the accident his entire life.

Such was the military background of the man who became the first instructor of military tactics at Purdue.

When the company of cadets was first organized at the new University, it was entirely voluntary. In the fall of 1876, out of a total enrollment of 140 students (including a handful of women and boys in the preparatory school), twenty-six young men signed up for the company. Cadets were formally sworn into the Indiana militia, which added strict discipline to the training.

Although Wiley said "the influence of this organization on the 'tough' boys was most marked," they weren't all "tough" boys.[13] A few were the sons of some of the most prominent people in the county. One of them was Frank Levering, the son of Colonel John Levering, who made a fortune in the real estate and loan business in Lafayette. Another was the son of August Thieme, who in 1863 founded the Thieme and Wagner Brewing Company at Fourth and Union

Streets. At its peak it produced 100,000 barrels of beer each year and was the sixth-largest brewery in Indiana. Drinking by Purdue students was forbidden, but rules were broken.

A third student, Orth Stein, was the son of Lafayette attorney John Stein, who as a state senator guided the legislation that accepted a $150,000 gift from John Purdue and brought the University to his home county. Stein also served as secretary of the Purdue Board of Trustees. Orth Stein was only fourteen years old in 1876. By the time he reached adulthood, Lafayette historian Robert C. Kriebel called Stein "a mystic and amazing wanderer, perhaps the most brilliant yet erratic of the genius-tinged family; a writer of fiction, poet, newspaper reporter, editor, illustrator; and also, a convicted and acquitted murderer, forger, and confidence man who died obscurely in a New Orleans hotel" in 1901.[14]

Wiley sought the concurrence of the faculty in making the military training part of the college curriculum. As part of the curriculum, any student who joined the corps had to gain the permission of the faculty before withdrawing.

At a faculty meeting on September 27, 1876, four resolutions were approved:

- "That military tactics be taught to such students as desired instruction in the same;
- "That students entering this class shall be required to observe attendance and deportment as in the other college classes during the year;
- "That the time for this exercise shall be from 1:15 to 2 o'clock P.M. of each school day;
- "That the uniform of the company be for the present year the regulation blouse and cap of the U.S. Army."[15]

The regulations and the appointment of Wiley as military instructor without additional pay were approved by the Board of Trustees in December of 1876. The Trustees also asked the Governor of Indiana to provide arms for the company, and the weapons were received in November of 1877.

Among the six buildings on campus when it opened, including a barn, was a military hall/gymnasium. On January 13, 1874, before the University opened the following September, the Board had passed a resolution to construct a wood-frame building it would need to fulfill the Morrill Act—an armory. The building would be fifty feet by one hundred feet, without heat. The price was $6,410.

The first use of the building would be as a gymnasium that featured exercise equipment. From early in the morning until chapel time, the gym was open to students who did not live on campus. It was closed during class hours and open in the afternoon for students who lived on campus. It was also closed on Sundays.

Wiley was not one for exercise. The big man loved to eat, became round as he aged, and could remember in detail the menus at banquets he had attended years earlier. But the wood-frame building provided an excellent space for drilling during inclement weather, and that's where the students trained.

"Our company of cadets was probably the best-trained company in the state, and especially among college students," Wiley wrote. "They took great pride in their military exercises."[16]

In the fourth annual University Register of 1877–1878, it was reported that more than sixty students were taking military training. The total enrollment that year, including a handful of women, was 166 in the university and the preparatory school. Most of the men taking the training had purchased a cap and blouse at their own expense, $1.60 for both. "It is believed that the drill is an excellent exercise and that all who take it are greatly benefited," the Register reported.[17]

Wiley's prize cadet was George W. McCoy. He was the grandson of Indiana Governor James "Blue Jeans" Williams, a southern Indiana Democrat and farmer. He picked up his nickname by always wearing denim, including suits made by his wife. While serving as governor, Williams spoke at the 1877 Purdue commencement and gave perhaps the most memorable message ever given at the event. He was a tall man, and when he stood up to speak, it seemed to take forever to get his entire body erect. He stood for a moment silently looking at his audience and then finally made his opening statement with a notable mispronunciation: "Edicate a boy and he won't work."

"This was his theme, and he launched forth into a bitter denunciation of higher education for a boy, after affirming it would unfit him for any useful vocation in life," Wiley wrote.[18]

Williams later began to support Purdue and sent two grandsons to the University, including McCoy. Both were among Wiley's cadets. McCoy advanced to first lieutenant and was placed in command during exercises when Wiley could not attend. McCoy went on to become a lawyer in Terre Haute, Indiana, where he organized a company of the Indiana militia.

In 1909, McCoy was named adjutant general of the state. His rank was brigadier general. "Naturally I attributed his success in military matters to the instruction which he had received in my company of cadets," Wiley wrote.[19]

Beginning in the spring of 1878, Wiley took a one semester leave of absence from Purdue and traveled in Europe. In 1880 he purchased a nickel-plated

Harvard roadster bicycle with a huge front wheel and a very small rear one. It was difficult to ride, especially when a person was new to the experience, and bicycles were very new in 1880 Lafayette.

"Sitting on this vehicle made one feel as if one were riding through thin air," Wiley said. "Striking a stone or stump meant disaster, for an undignified fall was the result. I acquired a bicycle uniform with knee breeches and I rode daily through the streets of Lafayette, over the bridge across the Wabash and up to the University, frightening horses, attracting attention, and grieving the hearts of the staid president and professors as well as members of the board of trustees."[20]

Wiley enjoyed riding his bicycle around the Oval in front of University Hall, where President Emerson White had his office. This gave him a good view of his professor recruiting military students to hold the bicycle for him while he mounted it. Wiley then rode it until he was ready to stop, a feat he accomplished by ramming it into the University's well-manicured prize hedgerow. The cadets then pulled their military instructor out of the hedge and set him off riding again.

In short time, Wiley received an invitation to appear before the Board of Trustees. His research, teaching, and leadership of the cadet corps had been so successful he thought he might be getting a raise in salary. But when he entered the room there was dead silence. Finally, Trustee John Doublebower spoke:

> The disagreeable duty has been assigned to me to tell Professor Wiley the cause of his appearance before us. We have been greatly impressed with the excellence of his instruction and are pleased with the popularity he enjoys among his pupils. We are deeply grieved, however, at his conduct. He has put on a uniform and played baseball with the boys, much to the discredit of the dignity of a professor. But the most grave offense of all has lately come to our attention. Professor Wiley has bought a bicycle. Imagine my feelings and those of other members of the board on seeing one of our professors dressed up like a monkey and astride a cartwheel riding along our streets. Imagine my feelings when some astonished observer says to me, "who is that?" And I am compelled to say, "He is a professor in our University." It is with the greatest pain that I feel it my duty to make these statements in his presence and before the board.[21]

In response, Wiley wrote and signed his letter of resignation and handed it to Board Secretary John Stein. He quickly received a response: the board unanimously refused the resignation.

Meanwhile, Wiley was gaining respect statewide for his work at Purdue, if not for his bicycle riding. In 1880, Indiana Governor Albert Porter appointed James R.

Carnahan as adjutant general with the rank of brigadier general. Carnahan had served as a Union Army officer during the Civil War and took part in the Battle of Nashville, which was a decisive Union victory. Carnahan lived in Lafayette and offered Wiley the position of major on his staff. Wiley accepted and enjoyed it.

"We all looked very handsome, I suppose, in our brilliant uniforms and on our prancing steeds on occasions of review of the military forces in the state," Wiley wrote. "The most important function we were called upon to perform was to accompany Governor Porter to Cleveland to attend the funeral of President Garfield. The governors and their staffs from many states, the vast concourse of military representatives, and a crowd so dense and numerous as to be practically uncountable, paid their last respect to the martyred president."[22]

In 1883, Purdue needed a new president. White resigned, as had the first two University presidents before him, mostly over differences with founding donor John Purdue. But White resigned after a dispute with members of the Indiana General Assembly concerning fraternities left the University with no state appropriation.[23]

Wiley was considered for the position of university president. In fact, some said he campaigned for it. But instead, he left Purdue and was named chief chemist in the U.S. Department of Agriculture. James Smart, a native of New Hampshire who had served as Indiana Superintendent of Public Instruction, was named to lead Purdue. He continued in the position until his death in February 1900.

At Purdue, Wiley's research had focused on food adulteration and lack of accurate labeling. In Washington, D.C., he became involved in researching chemical preservatives that were being used in foods. He believed these were harmful to people, and to prove it, he recruited a group of young men and fed them just enough of the chemicals to make them a little ill. Knowing how to attract attention to his research, he invited newspaper reporters to observe. They named the young men "the poison squad." Borax was one of the first substances tested, and the reporters dubbed Wiley "Old Borax."[24] It drew attention from around the nation to Wiley's work.

Wiley played a key role in passage of the 1906 Pure Food and Drug Act, which prohibited the sale of misbranded or adulterated food and drugs in interstate commerce. It also laid the foundation for the Food and Drug Administration, which Wiley would later lead as its first commissioner.

The 1906 Food and Drug Act was a precursor to future legislation further protecting people from harmful food additives and addictive drugs. Wiley later worked at the laboratories of the Good Housekeeping Institute, where the *Good Housekeeping* seal of approval was bestowed on deserving products, and he campaigned against cigarette smoking forty years before a government finding that connected cigarettes to cancer.

He married for the first time at the age of sixty-six, explaining that he was so engrossed with his work that he "quite neglected affairs of the heart" until he coincidentally ran into a woman on a streetcar in Washington, D.C. He had known her ten years earlier and throughout that time carried a photograph of her in his pocket watch, clearly longing to see her again but too busy to contact her—or too afraid she was already married to a man less obsessed with his job. She was younger than Wiley, born during the time that he was teaching military cadets at Purdue.[25]

Anna Kelton and Harvey Wiley married in 1911 soon after their chance remeeting. They had two sons together. Harvey Wiley took care of the young boys six years later when his wife was arrested for demonstrating in front of the White House and spent fifteen days in jail. She was a suffragette, campaigning for women's right to vote.

Wiley died June 30, 1930—the twenty-fourth anniversary of the signing of the Pure Food and Drug Act. He is buried at Arlington National Cemetery beneath a gravestone that reads "Father of the Pure Food Law."

He never forgot his time in Lafayette, nor his service forming the first military company at Purdue. He especially remembered that first camp experience away from campus in 1877. "In addition to our military exercises we indulged freely in bathing in the Wabash," he wrote in his autobiography, published the year of his death. "I was a fairly good swimmer, but I was not acquainted with the treacherous character of the Wabash current, and when I struck out vigorously for the center of the river was caught in a very swift current which was more than a match for my skill."[26] He nearly drowned. One of his cadets rescued him.

Strict rules were maintained during the campout, and there was even a guardhouse. Wiley noted in spite of everything, "there were some depredations in nearby chicken coops."[27]

So, what had he found under his pillow that morning in the spring of 1877, carefully placed there by one of his cadets?

It was a rooster. A dead rooster. A dead rooster he remembered his entire life as being "very attractive"[28] to this brilliant scientist who grew up on a farm and never lost his sense of humor and easygoing ways. If he ever disciplined his boys for the "depredations" and the dead rooster under his pillow, he never reported it.

From his telling of the story, it sounds like he found it all rather humorous. He always found it best to be deaf and blind to the antics of his boys.

Military training at Purdue continued after Wiley left. And the cadets soon helped create a group on campus that would become known worldwide as "All-American!"

2

AN "ALL-AMERICAN" MILITARY BAND

The military company has bought a new bugle. It is a copper one, and its melodious tones will be heard on the campus in the spring.

THE PURDUE STUDENT NEWSPAPER, JANUARY 1886

Purdue University student Edward Barnes only stood up and said "no" to his band director once. The director of the Purdue Marching Band was caustic, tough, and "had a temper like an elephant with an impacted molar," as one former student explained.[1]

But in the fall of 1946, Barnes had heard enough.

Barnes participated in the band during his early years at Purdue, then joined the Marines and spent the next three years serving in World War II.

When he returned to campus, he walked into the office of band director Paul Spotts Emrick and asked to be part of the band again. Emrick was happy to have him back, and he didn't need to seek other opinions before reinstating Barnes.

Emrick *was* the Purdue Band. He had first led it as a student in 1905 and, except for a few years after his graduation, continued as director until he was forced to retire in 1954.

His brilliance was the inspiration for the band being branded "All-American" by famed radio sportscaster Ted Husing in 1935, following a football halftime performance at the Northwestern University stadium that included lights on the band members' uniforms.[2]

Emrick commissioned the Big Bass Drum, and initiated college marching band formations that were copied then and are still used at Purdue and other universities around the nation in the twenty-first century.[3]

Emrick didn't go quietly when his time to retire arrived. At his last concert during Purdue Mother's Day weekend on Sunday, May 9, 1954, he turned to the audience at the end of the performance and announced he wasn't leaving voluntarily. He said he was being forced to retire because of his age. He was seventy years old.[4]

This was the man World War II Marine veteran Barnes, a Purdue band drum major, challenged during a rehearsal before the Ohio State football game in 1946. OSU Marching Band drum majors were known for strutting around the field during performances and bending backwards until the plumes of their tall hats sometimes touched the ground.

"The only time he and I tangled was in the fall of 1946 when we were preparing for a performance at Ohio State," Barnes said. "He wanted me to prance around like the drum major at Ohio State. I refused and told him we were an ROTC unit and I had more class than that. He guffawed through his famous microphone and replied, 'Damn it, you're right.'"[5]

Emrick probably knew Barnes would refuse to do it. Maybe he just brought it up to make a point. And the point was this: the Purdue "All-American" Marching Band was and always had been a military band attached to ROTC.

The band was started in 1886—not by the University, but by students who had a love for music. In the early days of Purdue, students came mostly from small towns dotted all around Indiana. Those towns had community parks and bandstands, and on Sunday summer afternoons, community bands performed to the delight of people sitting on benches or on blankets carefully placed upon the ground.

It was a time when the lives of people were not interrupted by computers, iPhones, iPads, computer games, or online meetings. In the evenings, people gathered in parlors around pianos. Others joined in with their own instruments, and they entertained one another with the joy of music. "Sailing, Sailing," and "Blow the Man Down" were popular, as were selections from *The Pirates of Penzance*, and "Love's Old Sweet Song."

That tradition of music came to Purdue from all around Indiana and the nation. Students who loved playing trumpets, clarinets, trombones, drums, and other instruments quickly found one another and began making music together. And the students soon found the perfect partner for their talents in Purdue's military training.

Musicians and marching have a centuries-old history together, and in 1886 the Purdue Band became part of military training. At first it was drums and bugles, but it expanded from there. In its earliest days it was called the Cadet Drum Corps.

Purdue football began in 1887, a year after the band was created, and another quick bond was formed. Band performances at football games immediately became part of the festivities of autumn Saturday afternoons.

But wherever it performed, the band at Purdue was a military unit, wore military uniforms, and marched mostly in military formations. This continued until 1954, when Al G. Wright took over the directing duties from Emrick and introduced a popular, free-flowing, entertainment style of music and marching.

The uniforms changed with the arrival of Wright, as did the music and marching, but it was still considered a military band.

From its simple beginnings, performing on campus during military drills with only a handful of musicians playing brass and drum instruments, the "All-American" Marching Band has since played for millions of people around the world.

A NEW LEADER OF MILITARY TACTICS AT PURDUE

Purdue Professor Harvey Wiley served as captain of the Purdue cadets from the fall of 1876 to the fall of 1880, although he was on sabbatical in the fall of 1878. Student officers were in charge of drill during his absence. In the fall of 1880, Wiley was teaching chemistry and physics and was also serving as state chemist. He was a busy man, and he was not and never had been an Army officer.

In November 1880 the Board of Trustees hired Lieutenant W. R. Hamilton to handle military tactics at Purdue. The U.S. War Department had assigned Hamilton to Asbury College, soon to be renamed DePauw, in Greencastle, Indiana. Hamilton divided his time between the two schools and provided two days of instruction each week at Purdue.[6] By the fall of 1882, Hamilton was listed in the Purdue Annual Register as an instructor of engineering and military tactics, working full time for the University.[7]

The year 1882 also marked the start of a new student newspaper simply titled *The Purdue*. Volume 1, Number 1 of *The Purdue* included a column about military training called "Bugle Notes." As much as the cadets loved Wiley's easygoing manner, students also enjoyed working with Hamilton. The first issue of *The Purdue* student newspaper said "Hamilton makes a good drillmaster. He is very generally liked by the boys and his wishes are obeyed with alacrity."[8]

The students not only received military training, they also were given physical training. "Lieutenant Hamilton, our drill master, allowed the boys to try a run around the elliptical driveway on the campus" in front of University Hall, *The Purdue* reported in that first issue. "It was the first run of any worth taken by them, and some of the raw men were pretty well 'blown' when they halted. The time was two minutes and fifty seconds."[9]

"The Military Hall [the armory] is a fine place to drill," the report continued. "It was built as a gymnasium and thus has a very solid, firm floor. It is large and airy. Forty men, shoulder to shoulder, will about reach across it and it is fully two-thirds longer. The armory is neatly fitted up, and the gun racks are usually kept in good order. With these opportunities there is no reason that the cadets should not succeed and become proficient in military tactics."[10]

It's one of the first mentions of the word "Military Hall" on the Purdue campus. It was often called the "Gymnasium."

"The boys think double quick is lots of fun," *The Purdue* said, and added some sarcasm. "Just wait 'till we trot around fifteen or twenty miles under a June sun. The fun will have emigrated then. We have a good company of cadets this year. They all seem to take an interest in the work. For a short time, the drill was as well, if not better, than any of the former companies. The campus is an excellent drill ground, twenty acres surrounded with good high fence to make the boys climb over, plenty of trees and in summertime, high grass making it very *pleasant?* for double quick movements. It may look easy to manipulate a Springfield rifle but that rifle usually weighs about twenty-five pounds at the end of a drill."[11]

By the spring of 1883, things were not going as well. On Saturday, April 21, the Lafayette *Journal* said, "There were only seven members of the cadet company at drill Thursday and four of them were officers. Lt. Hamilton was disgusted, mad, hot."[12]

An April 1883 issue of *The Purdue* reported that "a misunderstanding between Hamilton and University President Emerson White caused the Lieutenant to lock up the Armory and take the keys. This put the boys in a bad fix." The cadets were planning to use guns stored in the Armory in a "Union Fix," a military exercise on campus. "A committee waited upon President White and secured an order for the keys," *The Purdue* reported. "[Hamilton] was evidently ruffled, as he didn't treat the boys very nicely, in fact quite harshly, but we trust things will run more smoothly now."[13]

Things did not run more smoothly. Hamilton quit military training at Purdue in June, and by that autumn, he was no longer an instructor in engineering, nor listed in the Purdue Register.[14] There was no further explanation of the "misunderstanding" or if Hamilton departed because of it. White also left in 1883 following a controversy over his attempts to keep fraternities off the campus. He was replaced as Purdue president by James Smart.

With no one from the faculty to lead military drilling at the University, student officers took over the training. In October 1883, *The Purdue* reported the cadet corps for the new school year "promises to be a grand success. Last year the company did very well but was greatly deficient in numbers. This year it is hoped that the company will not only make good the deficiency in quantity but also in quality. The matter of buying suits seemed for a while to be the main difficulty in getting students to join the company, but the difficulty has been partially met by an agreement with President Smart whereby suits, full uniform, can be had for $12. Certainly no one will allow the expense of a suit to prevent his joining the company." In twenty-first century money, that $12 was equal to about $300.[15]

CORPS OF CADETS GOES TO CAMP

Military training on campus continued, and from May 12 to May 15, 1886, the student cadets were given a leave of absence to camp at Aroma, Illinois, located on the Kankakee River about eighty miles from Lafayette. It was located on a railroad line, so transportation was easy. They camped on an island in the Kankakee, and all was going well until a huge storm blew in. The tents were blown down and the student soldiers were drenched by rain. The river rose and ultimately they were forced off the island.

Before leaving, they pulled themselves together and staged a drill for the people of the community. There was a particular group of people in the community the cadets were especially hoping to impress: "The natives out there are nice folks," *The Purdue* reported. "Especially the young ladies."

FIRST FULL-TIME MILITARY INSTRUCTOR AT PURDUE

On April 1, 1887, the Purdue faculty passed a resolution recommending that the Board of Trustees make military drilling compulsory if an instructor could be found.

He wasn't found. He was sent—by the U.S. Army, in September 1888. He was Lieutenant Abner Pickering, a graduate of the U.S. Military Academy, and he was the first full-time military instructor at Purdue officially dispatched by the

U.S. Army. He arrived with one hundred Springfield rifles and two three-inch rifled cannons supplied by the government. The year 1888 marked the beginning of real military training at Purdue. In earlier years, the cadets were mostly trained in drilling. With the arrival of Pickering, Purdue had an officer sent by the Army and he taught a military tactics course. In addition, Pickering served as an instructor in mathematics.

The cadets were organized into an infantry battalion, a light artillery company, a drum corps, and a signal corps. By 1890 the drum corps had ten members. There were 260 men enrolled at Purdue and ninety-two had joined the Cadet Corps. The Purdue yearbook *Debris* later reported in those early days "aptitude was good, interest great, and discipline moderately good."[16]

"It is not compulsory upon the part of any student to join any of the military organizations," the University Register for 1888 states. "Yet all male students are urged to do so. Having once joined any one of them, regular attendance upon regular drills is required."[17]

CADET CORPS CONTINUES TO REORGANIZE

Female students were not included in the military training. However, they were provided with opportunities for exercise in the gym/military hall.

With the growing number of women on the campus, in 1889 Pickering asked the Purdue faculty to approve a military ball for the students. He was no doubt amazed when the faculty refused him.

The first issue of the Purdue yearbook *Debris* was published in the spring of 1889—the end of Pickering's first academic year on campus. The *Debris* report on the infantry gives the impression that military training at Purdue was basically starting from scratch. The students were untrained at marching and disorganized, the yearbook said. But "from out of that deformed and misshapen humanity has emanated the pride of the University," it reported.[18]

The students had not reached a decision on what uniforms to wear when they arrived on campus in September 1889. But they soon chose regular U.S. Army colors. The uniforms apparently didn't fit well. "The cap and blouses are dark blue in color, the latter being well padded wherever there seems to be a lack of man on the interior," the yearbook stated.[19]

There were ninety men in the entire company, "including a drum corps, whose music if we may judge from appearances, is exceedingly hard to beat," the *Debris* said.[20]

An 1889 yearbook report on the artillery battalion stated that "like the infantry, the [artillery] company at first presented an extremely dilapidated appearance, but when fitted? with the regulation uniform the transformation was complete."[21] The editors put that question mark after the word "fitted," indicating that the "fitting" wasn't that great.

"CO-ED CADET CORPS"

Early issues of the *Debris* were never short on humor and sarcasm and the first issue was no exception. The issue included a report on "The Co-Ed Cadet Corps." They were the young women who were given their own time in the gymnasium/military hall for exercise.

The male students lived on campus in a residence hall on the north side of the campus. Some female students lived in Art Hall, also named Ladies Hall, to the south. "The military spirit, so contagious during the first part of the year, could not be confined to the north part of the campus," the 1889 *Debris* reported. "Regardless of the rules to the contrary, it crossed the line and invaded the sacred precincts on the south."[22]

The report said the women were provided with ten-pound weights at the gymnasium "which constitute the only weapons [they] used. . . . Visitors are excluded from the drill room so it is impossible to know much of the work they are doing, but it is rumored that great skill has already been acquired in the use of the dumb bells. They can be hurled with great force and precision and in the hands of a practiced cadet they are no mean weapon. In all probability they will supersede the paternal ancestor . . . as an ejector of unwelcome suitors."[23]

MILITARY TRAINING MANDATED FOR MALE STUDENTS DURING FRESHMAN AND SOPHOMORE YEARS

With the arrival of Pickering from the U.S. Army, the Purdue Board of Trustees made a decision that would impact male students on the campus for the next seventy-six years.

The Autumn 1889–91 Purdue Annual Register stated that "all male students who hereafter enter the preparatory or freshman classes will be expected to join the military company and remain in it for two years, unless excused therefrom for good and sufficient reasons by the President. Experience has shown us that the drill of two hours per week has a beneficial effect on both discipline and health."[24]

From its inception in 1876 until the 1889–90 school year, participation in military training was voluntary. The University made clear that the musicians were considered part of military training by listing them in the Officers of Military Organizations chart in the Registry.[25]

In the twentieth century, the Registry became the Catalogue. Catalogues listed "other societies" including "the Purdue band which is subject to the orders of the Military Department."[26] Compulsory participation of freshmen and sophomore men in military training continued at Purdue until 1965, and throughout that time, participation in the military band fulfilled that obligation.[27]

At first many of the students thought they would be excused from this. They were not. The 1891 *Debris* said:

> When the catalogue announced that all the Preparatory students and freshmen would hereafter be expected to join the military company, a smile passed over their faces, as they thought it would be expected in the same sense of the word as it is used in regard to attendance at Sunday Chapel. Quite a different expression came over the same faces when it was interpreted at the office as being compulsory. Many were the excuses and physicians' testimonials that were handed in concerning the physical ability of various pupils, but they availed nothing.[28]

The Register stated that a uniform, including a cap, must be purchased by the student and that the $15 cost was actually less expensive than an "ordinary suit of clothes." The course of study included practical and theoretical tactics in infantry, artillery, and signal branches. The Register also explained that "it may be stated that the Purdue Cadet Corps is an independent organization and is simply required to drill. It cannot be called out for military service."[29]

That's the way it was in 1898. But when the sons of those nineteenth-century students enrolled at Purdue, the world would be a far different place.

"YOU CARRY YOUR GUN LIKE A BEAR CARRIES A CUB"

The Army often moved its people to different assignments. Pickering was transferred in the fall of 1893 and was succeeded in October by Lieutenant David Johnson. Johnson left in January of 1894 and was succeeded by Lieutenant Samuel Miller.

Miller was popular with the students. Now mandatory for all freshman and sophomore men, the Corps had grown to 257 students. Total Purdue enrollment in 1894, including women, was 595. Miller was a dashing looking man with close-cropped hair and a well-trimmed mustache. He looked like a strict, by-the-rules, military officer.

Years later, after Miller left Purdue, students remembered his quips in an issue of the *Debris:*

> "Mr. Vandervort, you carry your gun like a bear carries a cub."
>
> "Mr. Morey, step two paces to the front. (Morey steps to front). Scratch your nose (Morey scratches his nose) Step back to your place, sir. No man can scratch his nose standing in the ranks."
>
> "You are present, Mr. Ernst. You are not 'here.'"
>
> To Slimp, [who stepped out of ranks to get a drink] "Mr. Slimp, you are gross, disgracefully gross, and bad. If one man can go to the pail for a drink, the next man can go to the dormitory, another man can go over to the city, and the next man can go to Indianapolis."
>
> "Wake up! Wake up, Mr. Kelsey. We must have life and snap or we cannot have military drill."
>
> "Mr. Anderson, stop that laughing! The gross man must not laugh. The perfect man may laugh but he does not."
>
> "That was bad, bad. Why, the Baptist Boys Brigade can drill better than you men."
>
> "Mr. Vandervort, your belt is crooked. You might as well come with your pants on crooked as your belt."
>
> "Mr. Gordon, if you are tired we will get you a couch."
>
> "There are men in this company who have not two consecutive ideas about military drill."[30]

Under Miller, a twenty-five-man Bicycle Corps was added to the corps, which would have pleased Harvey Wiley, who had been disciplined for his bike rides.

In the 1895 *Debris* a student noted the physical strain of military training:

> Almost hidden away among the evergreens between the dormitory and the athletic field stands the Military Hall. One stoops to avoid the low-hanging limbs as he passes to the entrance. Before him stands a building antiquated, unadorned, uninviting to the eyes. Yet its echoes have responded to the footsteps of nearly every student who has sought an education at Purdue. Yes, everyone except those who are conscientiously opposed or are physically unable to stand the strains of military drill. . . . The company . . . executes many movements with such uniformity and rhythm as to rouse immediately the military aspirations of the uninitiated. After donning the uniform, this charm soon disappears. The new soldier soon finds that these movements become very monotonous by frequent repetitions and that his arms and back become very tired before the command 'break ranks' is given.[31]

One day each year was set aside as Military Day with drilling in the morning and a practice "battle" in the afternoon. On Military Day in 1895, the Purdue artillery students set a world record for dismantling a three-inch muzzle-loading rifled cannon.

The male cadets believed they were attracting an admiring audience to their drilling, and perhaps they were. "The department is growing in general favor to such an extent that many ladies visit the evergreen-hidden armory each Saturday to witness the battalions drill and hear the military music," the *Debris* said in 1891.[32] The 1897 *Debris* was the first to include a photo of the Military Band with thirteen members, including a clarinet, cornets, tenor and baritone horns, cymbals, a base drum, and a snare drum.

In the 1897–98 academic year, more than two hundred students were enrolled in the military department, mostly from the freshmen and sophomore classes. Total Purdue enrollment was 699. There were two hours of drilling on Saturdays and a one-hour lecture during the week.

A student working for the *Debris* wrote:

> When we consider that at no time has our country enjoyed forty years of continual peace, it is absurd to believe that the age of war was to be a thing of the past. It is far more probable that arms may yet be called upon to save the nation from destruction. At such a time a man well-drilled in even the rudiments of military tactics would be of inestimable value to the government. While this military training gives young men a taste of the glories of war, it also gives

them an insight to the horrors of war. It brings before the thoughtful ones as nothing else can, the sacrifices of our ancestors in establishing and maintaining our great government.[33]

SPANISH-AMERICAN WAR

The report in the *Debris* that the United States had not gone forty years without a war proved ominous. In 1898, war broke out between the United States and Spain, thirty-three years after the end of the U.S. Civil War.

The war ended with a treaty December 10, 1898, but not before six Purdue students and alumni enlisted in the war effort. They were the first Boilermakers to serve the United States at war. The 1899 *Debris* listed them:

> Parker Hitt enlisted July 1, 1898 and served in the Second U.S. Volunteer Engineers. They reached Havana on November 27 and became the first company of the Army of occupation to land in Cuba. He became a second lieutenant on March 13, 1899.
>
> [Private] Earnest Von Der Lippe enlisted in June of 1898 in Battery D of the Fifth Light Artillery immediately entering active service at Santiago [Cuba], after the surrender of which he proceeded with General Miles to Puerto Rico. [He] was present at the taking of Ponce [Cuba], at the battle of Mayaguez [Puerto Rico], August 10, and also at Los Maria [Puerto Rico], August 13, engaging in occasional skirmishes until ordered home November 24, 1898.
>
> [Private] J. T. Nichols enlisted in Company D, Second U.S. Volunteer Engineers soon after school closed in June [1898]. Went immediately into camp at Fort Sheridan. Soon removed to Camp Wikoff where most of the time was spent in putting the camp in first class order. Obtained discharge October 30, 1898 and returned to school.
>
> [Corporal] C. E. Parker enlisted in May [1898] with the First Kentucky Volunteers. After being in camp at Bradley and Thomas, he proceeded to Puerto Rico with the regiment in August, where, after a few skirmishes, his company was engaged in putting the camp in first class order. Obtained discharge October 30, 1898 and returned to school.
>
> [Private] D. W. Smith enlisted at Fort Wayne with a battery of artillery which, April 12, was mustered into the United States service as the Twenty-

Eighth Battery Light Artillery going into Camp Chickamauga from where they were mustered out of service October 31, 1898.

Edwin Lenox, member of the Hospital Corps, Fourth Indiana Infantry, afterward 160th Indiana Infantry with headquarters at Indianapolis.[34]

MILITARY TRAINING GROWS AS LEADERS CONTINUE TO COME AND GO

During the 1898–99 academic year, the Army did not send a commandant. Cadet Major F. B. Jenks took charge at Purdue until the end of the fall semester.

"This year's drill has been discontinued since the War Department failed to detail an officer to serve as commandant," the 1899 *Debris* said. "We trust that the time may not be far distant when the cadet corps will be reorganized and once more brought to that degree of proficiency where it is a credit both to the students and to the University."[35]

But it was far distant. It would be three years before the Army sent a new commandant to Purdue, and military training would be suspended throughout that time. There was no mention of the military corps in the 1900, 1901, or 1902 *Debris* yearbooks. However, by 1905 Captain William Lutz was in charge at Purdue, and the University cadet corps was recognized as the largest in the United States.[36] Lutz had graduated from Purdue in 1889 and had served as cadet captain of light artillery.

Lutz introduced grades to the military program and put the course on par with others at the University required for graduation. During his years as head of the corps, a special military diploma was introduced, cadet officers were given small cash scholarships, and the band was reported to be "united more closely to the corps of cadets than it had been."[37]

Lutz left in 1909 and was replaced by Benjamin H. Watkins until 1910. The period from 1910 to 1913 is called "the worst in the military history of Purdue University," according to a scrapbook titled "A History of Military Training At Purdue University," written by Army ROTC students.[38] The corps was led at that time by Captain Harrison J. Price. Price remained as commandant until October 1, 1913, when he was replaced by First Lieutenant Robert Kirkwood. Kirkwood had graduated from Purdue in 1908. He majored in chemical engineering, was nicknamed "Kirk," and was active in the cadet corps, serving as a lieutenant, a captain, and finally a major. He also belonged to the Athletic Association. He had actually enrolled with the Class of 1907 but took a year off from his studies.[39]

MILITARY BALL

In 1889, the faculty had refused to approve a military ball. But in the 1895–96 school year, the first military ball was held on campus. It would become an annual event and one of the highlights of the campus social year well into the twentieth century, when it was sometimes called the Cadet Hop.

"The military ball was a brilliant social feature, and many will be the years before the memory of it dies out," the 1896 *Debris* reported. "In fact, the military training affords everyone who has been connected with it some of the most pleasant recollections of his college days."[40]

The cadet corps became an important part of campus academic and social life. In the fall of 1912, three hundred couples attended the Military Ball. "Promptly at eight o'clock Captain and Mrs. H. J. Price opened the dance by leading the grand march," the 1913 *Debris* reported. "The unusually long line of couples which followed made a very impressive sight. Refreshments were served after the twelfth dance in buffet style."[41]

The event was held in the new Memorial Gymnasium built in honor of the seventeen people, fourteen of them students, who died in the 1903 train wreck when the Purdue team and fans were bound for Indianapolis for a football game against Indiana University. There were seventeen steps leading into the building, some outside and some inside, one for each person who died.

For the Military Ball in 1912, the Memorial Gymnasium was decorated with American flags and black and gold bunting. There was a twelve-piece orchestra selected from the Purdue Band. Students had dance cards and arranged dances with one another early in the evening.

"A very noticeable feature was the fact that all four classes were well represented," the *Debris* reported. "The rule this year of excluding from the floor all men not in uniform added much to the military aspect of the dance. As well as being a social success the hop also proved to be financially profitable. Enough money was netted above all expenses to place the band entirely out of debt, and at the same time gave it a very comfortable sum for defraying future expenses."[42]

"THE BOYS WOULD GO TO TOWN ON SATURDAY NIGHT AND RAISE CAIN"

James Roberts graduated from Purdue in the spring of 1913. A native of Lafayette, his father was Police Commissioner and his family lived in Highland Park. In 1978, Roberts returned to campus for alumni activities, sixty-five years after he graduated, and reminisced about his time at Purdue in the early twentieth century.

The dormitory that had housed men when the University first opened was converted to classrooms and offices in 1903. In 1913, male students such as Roberts lived at their family homes, in fraternity houses, or in boardinghouses.

"A bunch of us would walk into campus every morning and if we had a couple hours at noon would walk home for lunch," Roberts said in a *Journal and Courier* newspaper interview in April 1978. "If we decided to eat on campus you could get a big bowl of beans for a dime and a glass of milk for a nickel."[43]

He had military drilling two days a week and continued in the corps through his junior and senior years. "We had old blue uniforms, like they wore in '98," Roberts said. "The Springfields [rifles] were 1878 models. We'd drill and carry on. When I graduated I was a second lieutenant."[44] But he was not in the Army. If he joined the Army, he would have entered at the lowest enlistee rank.

It was a "man's" school in his days. He remembered only one woman studying in engineering, which was his major. "We had fun," he said. "The Purdue boys would go into town [Lafayette] on a Saturday night and raise Cain. The police couldn't handle us. We'd push a trolley car driver off and drive the thing back ourselves so we didn't have to pay the fare. Oh yes, it was a lot of fun. I liked Purdue then and I still like it today."[45]

A LEGEND NAMED "OLLIE"

In the spring of 1914, at the end of his senior year at Purdue, the name Elmer "Ollie" Oliphant appeared an astounding twenty-eight times in the school's *Debris* yearbook.

"Everybody knows 'Ollie' as an athlete," the yearbook stated. "But only his closer friends can appreciate what a good heart and generous disposition he has. He is just a great, big, unaffected boy who has too broad a mind to let the 'praise of the press' make him even the least bit conceited."

More than one hundred years later, the Purdue and U.S. Military Academy graduate and Great War veteran is still remembered and praised in the media as one of the greatest all-around athletes in the history of college sports.

Reports on the number of varsity letters Oliphant received at Purdue have varied widely through the years. According to his senior profile in the 1914 *Debris* and a Purdue *Exponent* newspaper article from October 16, 1915, Oliphant won nine varsity letters: three in football and two each in basketball, baseball, and track. The 1912 *Debris* shows him playing intramural basketball and baseball in his sophomore year. But in 1958, through an intermediary, he told Lafayette *Journal and Courier* sports columnist Gordon Graham that he won eleven letters with the two additional in basketball and baseball.[46]

Whether nine or eleven, it was a lot, and in four different sports, which had never been accomplished previously at Purdue. He also competed in swimming, boxing, and wrestling, but at the time Purdue didn't give varsity letters in those sports.[47] He scored forty-three points in a Boilermaker football victory in 1912, in which he also set school records of five touchdowns and thirteen extra points in a single game. He blocked, ran, and passed on offense, played defense, kicked, and punted. He broke his ankle in a football victory against the University of Illinois and still kicked an extra point. In basketball, during the fifth overtime against the University of Wisconsin, he shot the winning basket as time ran out while seated on the floor after a fall.

For the Boilermakers one spring, he competed against the University of Chicago in baseball and track events on adjacent fields at the same time. When he did not bat during innings, he changed into track shoes and won the mile and low hurdle races, took second in the pole vault, and was a member of the winning relay team.[48] Purdue also won the baseball game, which was held up a few minutes waiting for his return.

There were no athletic scholarships in those days. Oliphant worked his way through Purdue with seven different jobs[49] and earned his degree in 1914 in mechanical engineering. In accordance with University requirements, he also took part in the Corps of Cadets at Purdue.

U.S. Military Academy rules state that a person can be admitted if he ("he or she," since 1976) is not twenty-three years old or older on July 1 of the year they apply. No matter what their previous education, the students must enter as "plebes" (freshmen) and complete four years.

Oliphant turned twenty-two on July 9, 1914. He entered West Point that fall. In contemporary times, NCAA regulations prohibit an athlete from competing for four years in a sport at one university and then going to another to compete for four more years. However, in the early 1900s eligibility regulations were different, and not always strictly enforced. Moreover, Army was an independent, and therefore not subject to any conference rules. The organization that would later be renamed the NCAA had just been formed in 1906. When Oliphant entered the Academy, it actively and openly recruited players who had exhausted their years of eligibility at other universities and continued doing so for many years. At that time most schools limited player eligibility to three years, making freshmen ineligible for varsity sports. The 1928 and 1929 Army-Navy games were canceled because of a dispute concerning West Point's position on eligibility.[50]

At West Point, the Academy's Hall of Fame states Oliphant earned eleven varsity letters in football, basketball, track, and baseball. He was also the heavyweight boxing champion at five feet, seven inches tall and weighing 175 pounds. Muscular, blond, and handsome, equipped with a leather helmet (but no face guard or nose guard), and a menacing expression, Oliphant was captain of the Academy's football team. He scored forty-five points in one game. He was remembered for running down the field carrying the ball with opponents hanging on to him, unable to bring him down to the ground. His Army team was undefeated and considered the national champion in 1914 and 1916.

Oliphant was also captain of the baseball and track teams and a member of the hockey, swimming, and boxing teams. In his "plebe" year in the spring of 1915, he broke the Academy's record in the 220-yard hurdles. The record had been held by George Patton, who graduated in 1909 and became a World War II four-star general. At Army, Oliphant established a world record time in the 220-yard hurdles on grass. In 1914, he played on the West Point national champion football team with Omar Bradley, who graduated in 1915, became a World War II general, and in 1949 became the first chairman of the Joint Chiefs of Staff. At the academy Oliphant was also a friend of Dwight Eisenhower, who graduated in 1915, became a five-star general, and served as Supreme Commander of the Allied Expeditionary Force in Europe during World War II, before becoming the 34th president of the United States in 1952.[51]

Oliphant won "All-America" honors and was inducted in many halls of fame, including the National Football Hall of Fame, the College Football Hall of Fame, the Leroy Keyes Purdue Athletics Hall of Fame, the Army Sports Hall of Fame at West Point, and the Knute Rockne All-Time All-American team. He was the first person at Purdue and the Academy to receive varsity letters in four sports. In 1969, on the hundredth anniversary of the beginning of college football, the Football Writers Association of America named two All-Time All-American teams, one from 1869 to 1919, and one from 1919 to 1969. Oliphant was named to the earlier team. He was the only member of the early team still living, and he attended the ceremony.

After graduating from the Academy in 1918, he served in the Army, including service in the United States during the Great War. He played two years of professional football for the Rochester Jeffersons and the Buffalo All-Americans at the birth of what became the National Football League and was named to All-Pro honors before retiring from the game. He went to work for Metropolitan Life Insurance, where he became a senior executive in the New York region, retiring in 1957.

Oliphant died on July 3, 1975, six days before his eighty-third birthday. In his obituary, the *New York Times* called him a "legend."[52]

THE ARMORY BURNS

In 1916, the forty-two-year-old armory that Purdue students had declared "entirely inadequate" fourteen years earlier burned to the ground. The wood-frame structure, one of the original buildings when the University opened in 1874, had been moved from its first location north of University Hall to a spot near what is now the intersection of Third Street and University Street, where the rebuilt Armory still stands in the twenty-first century.

The fire in the early morning hours of Thursday, February 24 quickly consumed the building. According to the *Indianapolis Star*, "when the fire was discovered . . . the side of the building was a mass of flames."[53]

In 1916, many faculty owned houses on the west edge of campus. Professor Arthur Cole was awakened that morning by smoke pouring in his open window at 224 Waldron Street, about two blocks southwest of the armory. He sprang from his bed and looked out the window but could see no flames, so he assumed a barn behind the Armory was on fire. He called the West Lafayette Fire Department and then he woke up Herbert Glass, a Purdue junior who boarded in the professor's home. Glass grabbed an axe and headed for the barn where a much-loved horse named John Purdue was stabled.

"As Glass ran along the street he awakened a number of people and the alarm spread through that section of the town," the Lafayette *Courier* reported.

> As Glass neared the armory he noticed the blaze through the windows of the building. He ran to the front door and broke it in with an axe but great billows

of smoke rolled through the door and prevented entrance. By this time the flames were bursting through the roof and in less than a minute after the arrival of the young man the entire building was a mass of seething flames while sparks shot skyward by the detonation of several thousand rounds of ammunition in the building.

The West Side fire department arrived at the scene of the fire promptly but as the entire inside of the building was in flames at the time of the discovery it was impossible to do more than save the surrounding property.

Heroic work on the part of the students and firemen saved the [nearby football] grandstand on Stuart Field. As soon as a number of students had collected on campus they went to the power plant where three tanks of chemicals are kept and taking these to the top of the grandstand they poured them over the wood. Later the fireman stationed themselves in the narrow alley [that separated the armory and the grandstand] less than ten feet in width and with the scorching flames at their backs continued to pour water on the grandstand until the flames had died away. It was impossible to save any of the small arms in the building or the three-inch light artillery piece.[54]

There were more than one thousand rifles in the building and hundreds of rounds of ammunition, some of it "blanks." "The boxes containing this ammunition were stored at different places in the armory and during the fire a continuous rattle of detonations was audible," the *Courier* newspaper said.

The steady noise of the small cartridges would be punctuated at times with an explosion of greater violence as an entire box would go off. The explosions caused millions of sparks, varying in size to rise from the building and rift westward over the town and on every roof for squares around students were perched with buckets and lines of garden hose to prevent further conflagration.

One of the most thrilling incidents of the affair was the heroic rescue of the horse John Purdue who was stabled in the barn at the rear of the armory. Shortly after arriving at the blaze, Herbert Glass went to the barn to get the animal. At the time he entered the barn it was blazing on the outside and the horse was kicking frantically at the sides of the large box stall and his shrill cries filled the night with horror. After a battle lasting more than five minutes, Glass succeeded in throwing a burlap sack over the head of the horse and he was then led from the stable.[55]

The West Lafayette Fire Department only had a single one-horse wagon. At 4:40 a.m. a horse wagon from Lafayette arrived to assist.

The cause of the fire was never determined. "A series of fires within the last month has aroused a great deal of comment," the Indianapolis *Star* reported.[56] Just two weeks earlier the Sigma Psi Epsilon fraternity house had been destroyed by a 4:00 a.m. fire. Another fire was discovered at a fraternity house shortly after, but it was extinguished before doing much damage.

The Armory was valued at $20,000 and covered by insurance. Also lost in the fire were rifles that were on loan from the U.S. War Department, valued at $15,000, and the three-inch field gun owned by Company B of the Indiana National Guard, valued at $3,000. ROTC commander Robert Kirkwood told the newspapers it would probably be seven months before new rifles would be available from the War Department.

On March 29, 1916, the Purdue Board of Trustees voted unanimously to build a new $150,000 armory. The final cost would be $200,000.

That spring, as the academic year at Purdue neared its end, the Great War was underway in Europe. Since its beginning in 1914, there had been concern among Americans—including the young men and women at Purdue—that the United States would be drawn into the fight, while some wanted to join the war. Purdue's commencement was held on Wednesday, June 7, 1916, in Fowler Hall. Commencement is a day when there is much excitement about the future, but this was a day of great anxiety about what was to come.

A call to arms would come. And it would come much sooner than expected.

3

PURDUE BATTERY B, "PANCHO" VILLA, AND THE TEXAS-MEXICAN BORDER

Under no condition can the Purdue Cadet Corps be called out for active service. It is an independent organization for instructional purposes only.

THE PURDUE UNIVERSITY CATALOGUE, 1915–16

On June 23, 1916, Purdue students in Battery B got the shock of their young lives. The President of the United States called them to active duty.

For years the University Register/Catalogue had stated that the Purdue Cadet Corps was an independent organization that could not be called into military service. Even if a man spent four years in the Purdue military unit, he did not graduate and enter the Army as an active or reserve duty officer. He graduated into civilian life.

The statement was true for most members of the Cadet Infantry Regiment. But it was not true for the men in Purdue Artillery Battery B.

Lieutenant Robert Kirkwood, Purdue's military leader since the fall of 1913, was an artillery officer. He pushed to have an artillery battery at Purdue at a time when the federal government was interested in establishing the units at state universities. By 1940, nearly one-sixth of the Field Artillery Reserve officers in the U.S. Army had been produced by Purdue. But the initial establishment of the battery required some clever strategy on the part of Kirkwood and his men.

In the spring of 1914, Kirkwood brought a group of students, staff, and faculty together to discuss forming the artillery unit. But the Purdue Cadet Corps was not able to get the artillery guns and horses needed for the battery. So, they looked at a supply tactic being used elsewhere.

On October 18, 1914, the student newspaper *The Exponent* reported:

> The cadet corps of the University has expanded so greatly in the last few years that those in charge have been impelled to seek a channel into which it might branch. Some of the companies have nearly one hundred men on their roll, which number is considered too large and unwieldy for a cadet infantry company. In looking for different means of enlarging their field of work it was found that the field artillery battery presented an ideal addition.
>
> The University of Minnesota in the last year has acquired a duplicate of the battery which may be acquired by Purdue. This battery is a regular United States battery of field artillery of the same type used by the National Guard of all the states. The students who belong to the battery are all members of the Minnesota state National Guard and come under the rules and regulations of that organization.[1]

Purdue followed Minnesota's lead and formed an artillery battery that became part of the Indiana National Guard. Members of Purdue's Battery B were sworn into the Indiana National Guard on November 14, 1914.[2]

By December the artillery battery was already coming together at Purdue. On December 18, the *Exponent* reported the work of the unit would begin after Christmas break. Equipment valued at $107,000 arrived, including four three-inch field guns, carts for the guns, wagons, seventy-two sets of harness, thirty-five saddles, and blacksmith tools for repair work. Some of the equipment, stored in a West Lafayette building near the Wabash River, would be damaged by a flood in 1915. The University hoped to increase the number of men enrolled in the battery to one hundred sixty-six.[3]

In the second decade of the twentieth century, the world was in a perilous state. Mexico was in the middle of a revolution that would last from 1910 to 1920. And in July 1914, the Great War (later known as World War I) broke out in Europe, threatening to pull the United States into the conflict.

FRANCISCO "PANCHO" VILLA

Francisco "Pancho" Villa was a key figure in the Mexican Revolution. He initially was a bandit, but when the armed rebellion against the Mexican government began, he joined it, at times leading hundreds of men as a revolutionary and guerrilla fighter. He understood publicity and fought some battles, real or faked, with an American camera crew recording all the action. He posed for photos sometimes wearing a sombrero or other wide-brimmed hats. His full mustache was often curved upward at the tips, and he wore bandoliers—leather ammunition belts—strapped across his chest. His image and assumed name were well-known in Mexico and the United States.

For years, violence from the Mexican Revolution in the northern part of the country took place only miles from U.S. communities, and sometimes spilled over the border. According to the McAllen (Texas) *Monitor* newspaper, "Panic erupted in 1915 with revelation of the Plan of San Diego, a revolutionary manifesto calling for liberation of Texas, New Mexico, California, Arizona and Colorado, and death to all Anglos. A series of raids beginning in July 1915 inaugurated a period known locally as the Bandit Wars. Bands of ten to one hundred men launched more than seventy raids into Texas attacking ranches, bridges, irrigation pumps and stores. Valley citizens blamed criminal activity on the bandits and there was indiscriminate killing."[4]

Some of these early attacks on Texas were believed to be led by Villa. The bands of men were also looking for supplies, and some believed they were being encouraged by Germans to keep American forces occupied and out of the European war. There are reports of Villa's men killing Americans who were in Mexico.[5]

On March 9, 1916, Villa's men raided the border town of Columbus, New Mexico. Columbus, a town of about four hundred people, was home to U.S. Army Camp Furlong and the Thirteenth Cavalry. Eighteen Americans were killed in the battle: ten civilians and eight soldiers.[6] Part of the town was burned, and an unknown but large number of Villa's forces died. A famous newspaper editorial cartoon about that raid showed Uncle Sam stepping over a border fence into Mexico, and saying, "I've had just about enough of this," as Villa ran away.[7]

U.S. President Woodrow Wilson moved swiftly. The day after the Columbus raid, he telegraphed the War Department and said, "I urgently recommend that American troops be given authority to pursue into Mexican territory hostile Mexican bandits who raid American territory. So long as the border is a shelter for them they will continue to harass our ranches and towns to our chagrin."[8]

Brigadier General John "Blackjack" Pershing, who was based in El Paso, Texas, was given command of five thousand soldiers and sent into Mexico to capture Villa and scatter his forces. It was called the Punitive Expedition of 1916. Pershing's forces quickly grew to more than ten thousand regular Army troops, and with so many regular Army soldiers in Mexico chasing Villa, the U.S. border with Mexico was left unguarded.

At this time, the U.S. Congress was debating what would become the National Defense Act of 1916. In a May 2016 article for the U.S. Army Center of Military History, historian Glenn Williams wrote, "The bill may have remained under debate in the House had not Pancho Villa raided the town of Columbus, New Mexico, in March of 1916. With the small Regular Army not capable of mounting the so-called 'Punitive Expedition' in pursuit of Villa and adequately [protecting] the entire length of the U.S. border against continued attacks, the two houses of Congress reached a compromise."[9]

As part of the provisions of the National Defense Act of 1916, the size of the regular U.S. Army was increased. The National Guard was increased fourfold, to four hundred thousand men. Members of the National Guard units in the states also had to follow federal standards, and they had to respond when the President of the United States called them to active duty. The 1916 National Defense Act also created the Reserve Officers Training Corps. Rather than a Corps of Cadets, ROTC was an officer training program that was standardized nationally and put under federal control.

Wilson signed the act into law on June 3, 1916. The Indiana National Guard was called into service along the Mexican border on June 23, 1916, and joined roughly one hundred thousand other men from state national guards watching the border from the Gulf of Mexico to California.

Certainly, some members of Purdue's Battery B had not seen this coming. But rumors on campus had started soon after the raid on Columbus, New Mexico. On March 31, 1916, the *Exponent* reported: "When questioned as to the authority of the report that Battery B had been ordered to Mexico—or to the border, as has been rumored during the past week—Captain H. E. McIvor made the following statement: 'Uninterested persons are apparently circulating false reports among the members of Battery B and the community to the effect that Battery has been ordered to Mexico, or to the border. No call has yet been received and the reports which have been circulated are entirely without foundation. In case a call does come members of the battery will receive official notice from the proper source.'"[10]

The rumors continued and on May 14 the *Exponent* reported:

> Lieutenant Kirkwood was unable to either confirm or deny the report that the local battery would be taken to the Mexican border instead of their usual

> summer encampment, owing to the fact that no official report regarding the matter has been sent out by the War Department. It is quite likely according to reports last night that both the summer volunteer camps and the militia camps will be postponed indefinitely because of the insufficiency of regular officers to give instructional work. When asked upon short notice [if] Battery B could entrain for the border if called Lieutenant Kirkwood said: "Battery B could leave in thirty-six to forty-eight hours with what equipment it has at present, but rations, horses and wagons along with certain other equipment would have to be issued at once to bring them up to the strength necessary to go into action. Adjutant General Ben W. Hough and Colonel W. H. Duffy, assistant quartermaster general of the Ohio National Guard were in Washington this week and it is reported, were convinced that more national guard organizations would be called out unless matters at the border changed considerably in a short time."[11]

Purdue commencement in 1916 was on June 6th. So, most of the men of Battery B had left campus and gone home before they were called to protect the southern border. Some of the men had graduated and were finished with Purdue—but they were still in the Indiana National Guard. Indiana University Company One, comprised of students and a few faculty, was also called to active duty and sent to the Mexican border, as was Battery C of Tippecanoe County, with many Purdue graduates.

When the call mobilizing the National Guard units went out, newspaper front pages across the nation were filled with stories about the men heading south. On June 24, 1916, the Indianapolis *Star* reported ten thousand people in Lafayette had gathered to send the young men of Battery B off to serve their country.

The *Star* said:

> The citizens of Lafayette and West Lafayette turned out tonight to honor Battery B, the Purdue University branch of the Indiana National Guard which left here [Lafayette] shortly after 8 o'clock [p.m.] for Fort Benjamin Harrison. The members of the battery were cheered by more than 10,000 persons as they passed through the streets. The parade started from the top of State Street in West Lafayette and more than 4,000 West Lafayette and Lafayette men, women and children marched to the railroad station [with the men]. Dr. W. E. Stone, president of Purdue, and R. M. Southworth [a West Lafayette

> bookstore owner] were the grand marshals. A large number of Boy Scouts were in line. The Purdue bell was featured in the procession.
>
> In the afternoon members of Battery B were entertained at a dinner at the Fowler Hotel. President Stone spoke in praise of the students who are ready to go to the front. Purdue yells were given. The men sang "Hail to Old Purdue" and stood at attention as the orchestra played "America" and other patriotic pieces.[12]

The men were dressed in their olive-green uniforms, which included breeches and a waist length coat. They wore broad-rimmed campaign hats with four creases. Some wore puttees—cloth wrapped around their lower legs.

During the ceremonies, citizens of West Lafayette presented the men with an American flag to take with them. The flag went to the border and was brought home, preserved, and officially presented to the University on November 11, 1941—Armistice Day. The flag has been displayed in the Great Hall of the Memorial Union ever since.

Battery B became the only Purdue military unit called into service as a group by the President of the United States. There were about 163 men in the battery. At the border, the captain of the Purdue Battery was Harry E. McIvor, University purchasing agent. McIvor had graduated from Purdue in 1913. The senior first lieutenant was H. C. Mahin, a professor of German, and the first lieutenant was Frank D. Dexter, an instructor in the machine shops. All the other men were students, except a first sergeant, a stable sergeant, and the company cook. McIvor along with Mahin and Kirkwood were credited with forming the unit at Purdue in 1914.

They left from Fort Benjamin Harrison in Indianapolis and traveled to Texas by train. White paint across the side of their rail car proudly proclaimed them "Purdue University Battery B." They arrived at their destination on July 10 and found themselves among the early arrivals to what would become Camp Llano Grande. But first, they would have to clear the land and build that camp in the summer heat, humidity, and rain at the southernmost point of Texas near the Rio Grande River at Mercedes. They arrived in their wool uniforms to find temperatures often above 100 degrees.

Llano Grande is Spanish for "big plain." The area was given that name in an eighteenth-century royal land grant awarded to Juan Jose Hinojosa, military captain and chief justice of Reynosa, Nueva Santander (now Tamaulipas), Mexico. The camp was part of the central section of the grant. In 1916, there was a railroad water stop nearby named Llano Grande, but not many other signs of permanent settlement.

At its peak, about eleven thousand men were camped at Llano Grande on two hundred acres rented by the War Department. They came from Indiana, Nebraska, Minnesota, and North Dakota. Also at Camp Llano Grande was Dr. A. C. Arnett, of Lafayette. The cofounder of the Arnett Clinic in Lafayette, he was a 1907 graduate of the Purdue Medical School in Indianapolis before it was given to Indiana University. Arnett was part of the medical team at the camp.

The first troops had arrived at Llano Grande on July 6, only four days before Battery B. More National Guardsmen continued to arrive for the rest of July. As they stepped off the train, the men were handed picks and shovels to clear brushland. Some wooden buildings went up, but the men slept in tents with wood floors. Piles of mesquite logs kept the fires in the kitchen stoves burning.

The McAllen *Monitor* newspaper described the camp in an article that appeared many years later:

> Linemen set up additional telephone and telegraph wires in late July, and a mess hall to replace sheds was under construction. They had walls six feet high with screens above the base and with a portioned-off kitchen.
>
> After the July rains when several Army motor trucks and mule wagons were mired, mile seven north between Llano Grande and Mercedes was oiled heavily and the bridge strengthened. Two jitneys [small buses] did a big business and more autos were pressed into service. However, when the road was muddy, troops had to walk the tracks to town.[13]

The campsite was home to some things that the boys from Indiana didn't often see. Among the rattlesnakes was one that was said to be more than seven feet long. The ground was sandy soil covered with mesquite and cactuses. There were other poisonous snakes, scorpions, tarantulas, flies, and sand fleas. Roaming the area were deer, wildcats, armadillos, and some longhorn cattle.

"Ditches were dug to bring in water from irrigation ditches," the McAllen *Monitor* said. "But the water was by no means sanitary. The water and lack of screens on floors brought dysentery and other diseases, the worst of which was dengue fever."[14]

The men worked hard. Fifty years later, preparing for the fiftieth reunion of Battery B on the Purdue campus, Edwin L. McMahan noted he was bugler for the Battery, blowing revelry at 5:30 every morning. He hoped none of his fellow

National Guardsmen still held fifty-year grudges against his rude awakenings.[15] Minnesota Company Commander Harold Nelson said, "While on the border we went out on patrols along the Rio Grande, placed guards at pumping stations, established outposts and took measures to ensure that no invaders would take them by surprise."[16]

Only once did the National Guardsmen exchange fire with a foe on the other side of the river. A detachment from Minnesota guarding a pumping station on the banks of the Rio Grande exchanged brief gunfire with someone from the Mexican side. No one from Minnesota was injured. It was not known if there were Mexican casualties.

The men trained often, in addition to patrols. But there was a lot of downtime and the camp included YMCA buildings, open-air theaters, a soda fountain, a barber shop, a restaurant, a poolroom, and canteens.[17] Much of the camp had been developed by the soldiers.

Just south of the camp were stock pens for beef cattle and corrals for horses and mules. The McAllen *Monitor* noted this was the area where living quarters for African American cavalry men were placed.

As July turned to August, and August to September, the mobilized college students began to worry about continuing their university classes. They petitioned President Wilson, who had been president of Princeton University. He understood their concerns.

While Camp Llano Grande remained open until mid-February 1917, Purdue and other students received permission to return home early. Purdue Battery B arrived at Fort Benjamin Harrison on September 16, 1916. On September 28, they returned to campus, and when they signed up for classes, they sent the total enrollment at Purdue to 2,226—a record number.

There was a huge celebration to mark the return of Battery B. Stacked headlines in the *Exponent* said, "Streets Are Thronged With People Eager to Welcome the Soldier Boys. Concert by Purdue Band. Thrilling Strains of 'Back to Old Purdue' Sound As the Boys Disembark."[18]

> When the much-delayed special train pulled slowly into the Big Four station [in Lafayette] at 8:40 last night, bearing the members of Battery B back to Purdue, a great cheer burst from the throng of patriots who crowded the platform and blockaded the streets in all directions. As the cars, whose windows were crowded with the faces of soldier boys came to a rest, the strains of "Back to Old Purdue," led by the Purdue band, burst forth, welcoming the boys home.

> At an early hour a large crowd had already gathered at the station. The tolling of the historic old Purdue Bell, as it was drawn by the students across the levee, attracted many more to the scene. The bell, preceded by the band, and followed by about six hundred students, four abreast, halted near the station. The Purdue band, composed of about fifty pieces, congregated beneath the nearest arc light and thrilled the crowd with a fine concert of martial and national airs interspersed with popular hits, which added to the jubilance of the great mass. Just before the arrival of the train, D. A. Weber, yell leader, mounted a box car and demanded "Rahs for Battery." He got them.
>
> As soon as the boys had disembarked an alley was forced through the crowd, and Battery B assembled in the street and was formally welcomed by President Stone. Captain McIvor accepted the welcome and Professor Babson spoke a few words after which the Battery joined with the crowd in singing "Hail Purdue." Weber then led the "Purdue Series" and the Battery was invited to the Family theater.
>
> The spirit of welcome and celebration continued after the battery and the band had made their way to the Family theater where they were the guests of Manager Maurice. The commandant, Lieut. R. G. Kirkwood, and his wife were heartily applauded when they appeared and took seats in the section reserved for the military contingent. It chanced that the "Stars and Stripes" appeared several times in the moving picture preliminary and at each appearance the entire audience rose to its feet and cheered. The orchestra caught the spirit and played "Hail Purdue," all the students singing and several members of the band aiding in the accompaniment. The talent extended itself in the program of vaudeville and was repeatedly cheered. As a fitting climax the Gallerini Four in a novelty orchestra act, played "Hail Purdue" and several national and military airs which were received with wild bursts of applause.[19]

Pershing pulled out of Mexico in February 1917, ending the Punitive Expedition. He never captured Villa, but he did disperse Villa's men. And Pershing and the Army learned much about modern combat, including the use of airplanes, that would prove very helpful very soon when the United States entered World War I, where Pershing served as commander of the American Expeditionary Forces in Europe. There were no major attacks on the U.S. southern border while the National Guard units were in place. The widely published presence of the troops was enough to deter any problems.

The men of Battery B were mustered out of the Indiana National Guard on January 12, 1917. They received medals and discharge papers. Hundreds of people watched the ceremony in the Purdue Memorial Gymnasium (now Felix Haas Hall), built near where the original 1874 armory had once stood after being moved from its original location. (After it was relocated, the original Armory stood directly in front of where the second Armory still stands in 2023.) By the following spring some of these young men would be in the Army serving in the Great War. Among them was McIvor, who enlisted in May 1917, attained the rank of major, and served at a field artillery school at Fort Sill, Oklahoma. He did not return to Purdue after the war and instead engaged in the oil business in Lawton, Oklahoma. He died October 15, 1919, from typhoid fever, at the South Bend home of his parents.

In the *Exponent*'s coverage of the mustering out of Battery B, it noted that the group "was subjected to many setbacks during its short existence, among which were lack of equipment, the flooding of the temporary armory by the Wabash River, and the loss of the Purdue armory by fire." At the event, "Dean Coulter was called upon to represent the university. He said that everyone connected with or interested in Purdue, was proud of the work of the students at the border. The work of Battery B, he stated, would occupy a place, and no small place, in the history of the university. Captain McIvor then distributed the discharge papers and, following the last bugle call, the final command, 'Battery B, Disband!' was given, and the organization which has made such a remarkable record for Purdue passed out of existence."[20]

But it did not pass out of memory. For Purdue students such as Benjamin Franklin Wolfe, from Columbia City, Indiana, the summer of 1916 on the U.S. southern border in Texas became a part of their lives never to be forgotten.

PROFILE

BENJAMIN FRANKLIN WOLFE

IN JULY 1916, LEWIS AND PHILENA WOLFE OF NEAR LOON LAKE IN NOBLE COUNTY, INDIANA, north of Ft. Wayne, received a letter from their son, Benjamin Franklin Wolfe, a handsome young man with light hair and light blue eyes stationed with Purdue University Battery B along the Mexican border in south Texas.

The letter was printed in a local newspaper and is preserved in Purdue University's Virginia Kelly Karnes Archives with information about Battery B.

Battery B First Indiana Field Artillery
Mercedes, Texas, Llano Grande

Dear father, well we are now in camp in the land of sand, cactus, tarantulas, scorpions, ants, mosquitos, rattle snakes . . . etc. We arrived here Monday night July 10 after a very pleasant trip through Illinois, Missouri, Oklahoma, and Texas. At Springfield, Missouri they gave us sleepers [railroad cars] so the trip was pretty good in that respect. The people along the route gave us papers, sandwiches, post cards and pencils. We received permission to go swimming in the Gasconade River, Missouri and then again in San Marcos, Texas.

In Texas from Fort Worth down to San Antonio is fine, but from San Antonio southward there is much sand and many cactus plants. The brush is thicker than I ever dreamed of and the Mexicans are almost as thick as mesquite, which is about the only kind of tree and brush in this part of the state. The land around Mercedes is irrigated and is valued from $50 to $400 per acre but I'd rather have a few acres in Indiana where the mosquitos are not so numerous nor so large. I actually have seen mosquitos here as big as those "gallinippers" [enormous mosquitos]. I guess they won't be so thick after it quits raining—the raining season here has just begun and the natives say it is the first rain in eighteen months and that it is likely to rain for *two months. It rains continually, that is several hours daily. It is not so warm today but it is so muddy that everything is quite disagreeable.*

Back to arrival, we unloaded Monday night and our tents were in the A battery's train. We had to sleep on the platform. The mosquitoes were so bad we couldn't sleep, so we built a couple fires to smoke them away. Slept a short while, then it began raining so we had to seek shelter. Cutler and I took one of the paulins [coverings] from a caisson and put it over one of the escort wagons of the Nebraska troops. Tuesday morning everyone was swelled up from bites. We pitched tents in the forenoon and cleaned up the campground. Today we have been gathering up trash around the camp.

We are in among the mesquite trees so we have some shade. This afternoon we went down to the lake about two miles from camp and went swimming and washed our dirty clothing.

The U.S. government has leased [the land] and a bunch of Mexicans are employed to clean up the brush and provide a clear space for our camp. When the entire bunch of soldiers arrive, there will be about 15,000 here.

The water is of such quality that it makes me homesick. It tastes like cistern water only not so cold. We have ice, though, so we have it fairly good. Shower baths are to be constructed and water supplying them will be piped from someplace and I understand electric lights will be installed in the company streets. Power will be furnished from Mercedes, Texas which is about three miles down the road.

The men on guard have ammunition issued to them, since there was a large amount of cartridges shipped in today. We will have it issued to us tomorrow. The captain said a telegram had been sent in today for about 4,000 rounds of shrapnel for the battalion guns. That will give us 1,333 rounds. The above ammunition will be used for target practice. We have not yet received the horses. It will take one hundred fifty-two horses and twenty mules for each battery. We are six miles north of the Rio Grande and about forty miles west of Brownsville so we are about as far south in the U. S. as we can get, and eighteen feel above sea level.

The men in congress who voted down the bill to give the soldier "privates" thirty dollars a month should have to come down here and spend a few months, then I'm sure they would be willing to reconsider the proposition. If a man had to work for a firm and eat the food we get and be in all kinds of weather and under all conditions he sure would revolt or give up his job.

If Mr. Wilson were to depend upon soldiers for re-election he would never again see the job and maybe not the U.S. Everyone thinks this is just a political move. We will likely be here for six months. Still, the experience will be good for a fellow, if

I had a job. The fellows in the battery who had jobs got full pay until January 1. If anyone asks how things are here let them read this letter then I won't have to write so much. I'm broke now so I can't buy any more stamps until August 1 when we get our fifty cents per day.

Sincerely your son B. F. Wolfe.
P.S.—one of the fellows who had breakfast just now says the lunch on a free lunch counter is a banquet compared to this.

Born in Columbia City, Indiana, on November 17, 1892, Wolfe had seven siblings and five half-siblings. He enrolled at Purdue in the fall of 1913. When he returned to Purdue in September 1916, he was beginning his junior year as an agriculture major.

In June 1917, he completed his junior year. In April 1917, the United States entered the Great War in Europe, and Wolfe registered for the draft in Columbia City.

On his registration form, he said he worked with his father on the farm and that he'd served as a private in an artillery unit. He answered the question "Do you claim exemption from draft?" by saying, "Yes, I conscientiously believe I am needed more at home; [I have] school funds to pay. Will serve if needed."

Wolfe was drafted in August 1917, and was with the expeditionary forces as an Air Service Officer. During the war he received a serious leg fracture. He returned to Purdue in the fall of 1919 and left campus in the winter of 1920 for surgery on his leg. During his senior year he was president of the Purdue Aero Club, which was trying to acquire a plane.

When he graduated in June 1920, the *Debris* yearbook said, "Bennie as he is known to his many friends, [was] an Air Service officer who spent most of his time with the Texas Expeditionary Force. He and his cane have been inseparable during the year for two reasons—sick leave and at first because he needed it. Bennie specialized in education but is going to Texas as a landscape artist and we know he will succeed."

Wolfe had three marriages, the last to a woman named Ona, who was a pediatrician. In addition to graduating from Purdue, he earned degrees from Harvard University and Massachusetts Institute of Technology.

He lived in Evansville, Indiana at the start of World War II and registered for the draft. At 48 years old when the war started, he was not called into the armed services.

His wife Ona Wolfe died in 1981 on her 82nd birthday. Benjamin Wolfe died in 1986 at the age of 93. No children are listed in their obituaries.

He did what he said he was going to do when he graduated from Purdue. He served as a landscape architect for the Indianapolis Civic Plan Commission, and he was an instructor in landscape architecture at the University of Oklahoma. And in September 1933, he purchased Crescent Landscape Nurseries, Inc., in Evansville—and operated it for the next forty years.

4

THE GREAT WAR

Sad news received—Glossop, football captain in 1913, a fine athlete and popular fellow, dies.

PURDUE ALUMNUS NEWS LETTER AND WAR BULLETIN, DECEMBER 1918

In the spring of 1917, the Purdue yearbook *Debris* carried a drawing of a young man, suitcase in hand, tipping his hat goodbye to a drawing of the campus including the Heavilon Hall bell tower.

"At last, an alumnus," the caption read. "Now to solve the problems of life. The trunks are packed, friends are bade farewell, and with one last glance at the campus and towers, he seeks his way in the world. Godspeed alumnus."[1]

The problems of life faced by the Class of 1917 were immediate and overwhelming. On April 6, probably not long after that drawing was completed, the United States entered the Great War in Europe. The Class of 1917 went from the quiet of the Purdue campus headlong into combat noted for artillery bombardments that went on continuously for eight hours or more, and men leaving deep trenches and "going over the top" to venture into "no man's land," encountering deadly hand-to-hand bayonet combat, with shells exploding all around them.

4,006 Purdue men and women, including alumni and faculty, entered the military service during the Great War. That was more than one-third of the total number who had enrolled in the University from its opening in 1874 to 1917.[2]

They were men like twenty-two-year-old James Byron Manson, 22, of Crawfordsville, Indiana, who graduated from Purdue in the spring of 1917 with a degree in civil engineering. His grandfather, Mahlon Dickenson Manson, had been a Civil War general and president of the Purdue Board of Trustees from 1877 to 1879. Tall, with dark brown hair and blue eyes, James Manson had served with

Purdue Artillery Battery B at the Texas border in the summer of 1916 and returned to school that fall for his senior year. By August 1917 he had graduated, married, and was in the Army. He shipped out to France in January 1918, leaving his young bride Catharine at home with his parents. On Monday, July 1 at a military camp more than 4,000 miles away, he read a letter from home and learned of Catharine's "brave fight to keep from losing our baby girl."[3]

Their baby girl was stillborn.

They were men like Maxwell Erwin McDowell, 23, an instructor in English at Purdue, a six-foot tall young man with blond hair and blue-gray eyes, who, in September 1917, two days after arriving at the front in France to serve with a French ambulance service, wrote his parents in Troy, New York: "A human being mashed and seeping in a dozen places and then left lying all thru the night in a patch of barbed wire until he turns pea green from cold and loss of blood isn't a pretty sight."[4]

They were men like Julius Leopold Born, 26, a 1913 Purdue graduate with a degree in mechanical engineering, who on November 25, 1917, in France waiting to be sent to the front, wrote his parents, "I am mighty glad to know you are making three more [pairs of] socks, mother. The three pairs I have are simply great and I am wearing them every day. They keep my feet very warm and comfortable and I count them among my treasured possessions."[5] He was of medium height and build with brown hair and blue eyes. He signed every letter home "Your loving son Jul."

The Great War was to be the "war to end all wars." It was not, and it would later be named World War I. It began in 1914 following the assassination of Archduke Franz Ferdinand of Austria, which began a chain of events in Europe that pitted Germany, Austria-Hungary, Bulgaria, and the Ottoman Empire against Great Britain, France, Russia, Italy, Romania, Canada, Japan, and eventually the United States. By the time the war ended with an armistice on November 11, 1918, more than sixteen million people—civilians and soldiers—were dead, and towns, cities, and countryside lay in ruins.

Lieutenant Charles R. Brouse, 25, of Rockford, Illinois, left Purdue in May 1917, before his commencement ceremony in June. His degree in electrical engineering would be granted, but he immediately entered the Army and in March 1918 was with an artillery battery in France. He combed his hair straight back and wore frameless glasses. He wrote of the carnage of battle: "The awfulness and completeness of the German destruction is almost inconceivable. One must actually be there to see it in order to believe it and sense what it means to the

French people. I happened to be talking to a French lieutenant one day and we were standing on a road among some ruins of houses when I asked him where a certain town was. He said, 'you're standing right in the middle of it now.' Nothing was left, not one stone left above another, nothing but broken rock and shell holes, not a tree, not a bush, not a blade of grass. He didn't know anything about his sister, father, and mother for they had been driven from their home while he was away fighting."[6]

THE GREAT WAR COMES TO PURDUE

The year 1917 began quietly on the Purdue campus. Similar to many people of his time, Purdue University President Winthrop Stone kept a diary of his activities and thoughts throughout most days of the year. The 1917 diary book was given to him by his wife and fellow mountain climber, Margaret. "May there be much happiness recorded for the year," she wrote on the cover.[7]

Instead of happiness, what was recorded for the year was stress, upheaval, uncertainty, injury, and death: war.

Prior to 1917 there was mounting pressure on U. S. President Woodrow Wilson to enter the war in Europe. He resisted. However, in early 1917 Germany resumed unrestricted warfare against U.S. shipping, and the pressure on Wilson became more intense. The final event that drew the United States into the war came with revelation of the Zimmerman Telegram. In January 1917, Germany sent a coded telegram to Mexico proposing a military alliance. It proposed that if Mexico would enter the war on the side of Germany and it resulted in victory, Mexico would get Texas, New Mexico, and Arizona.

The telegram was intercepted and decoded by the British. On March 3, 1917, the Germans admitted that they had in fact tried to recruit Mexico into the war. Mexico rejected the overture. But Wilson decided to respond, and his cabinet unanimously called for a declaration of war.

On April 2, 1917, President Stone, a man who stood very straight and whose hair and finely trimmed mustache were turning white, wrote in his diary: "Congress assembles to a special call to hear the President's message on a state of war with Germany. Great excitement throughout the country. Special [Purdue] committee meeting for directing students in enlistment and a special faculty meeting this evening at the library. All present signed a statement of allegiance."[8]

In April 1917, immediately after the U.S. declaration of war, a field artillery regiment of nearly 1,300 Purdue men was offered to the War Department. It was declined because the government planned to use conscription to bring men into the military.[9]

Lt. Robert Kirkwood had arrived on the Purdue campus in 1913 and quickly transformed cadet training, including creation of Artillery Battery B, which had served at the country's southern border. A Purdue graduate, "he knew the men and he knew military affairs in large and in detail and he knew how to work," according to the 1917 *Debris*. "The cadet officers began to realize that they knew too little about commanding, about drill, regulations, and the execution of commands, and about military courtesy.... It has been said that at the close of Lieutenant Kirkwood's connection with the corps the [student] sergeants have a more thorough knowledge of military work than did the [student] captains when he came."[10]

In an essay written for the 1917 *Debris* before the United States joined the Great War in April, Kirkwood said the National Defense Act of 1916 had "opened the way for material improvement in military instruction. The part effecting our cadet corps is that which authorizes the establishment of units of the Reserve Officers Training Corps at colleges and universities. Purdue has obtained permission to establish an infantry unit. This put the corps on the basis of a federal organization. Although it cannot be called out for active service in time of war or other emergency, it is furnished equipment for instruction purposes. The object is to fit graduates who have had four years of university military training to become reserve officers who will be used in time of war to officer volunteer organizations and to replace losses among officers in the regular Army."[11]

The National Defense Act of 1916 standardized military training on university campuses across the country. Those students who continued military training in their junior and senior years were paid $9 per month. Universities were given more military instructors. At Purdue in the spring of 1917 there were two commissioned officers and three non-commissioned officers, all regular Army.

While the United States Army Reserve Officers' Training Corps dates from the National Defense Act of 1916, the Great War delayed the full development of the program.

Kirkwood believed it would take time and work by Purdue and the federal government to complete the corps reorganization. Purdue had lost its armory to a fire and was building a new one. He believed by the fall of 1917 the Purdue regiment would be "a military asset to the nation."[12]

But all this was said before the U.S. entered the war. In fact, in anticipation of the coming war, in March 1917 Kirkwood was transferred from Purdue to Fort Sam Houston, Texas. He was replaced by Assistant Commandant of Cadets First Lieutenant Robert Donaldson, who had arrived at Purdue in 1916. Donaldson would be transferred away from Purdue himself in September 1917.

Purdue historian H. B. Knoll, an English professor on campus, wrote *The Story of Purdue Engineering* in 1963. He noted, "World War I brought exciting, swiftly changing times to the campus and foreshadowed the end of an older, more conservative Purdue. Through official policy, every resource of the University was placed at the government's disposal."[13]

Purdue Librarian William Murry Hepburn and History Professor Louis Martin Sears wrote a history of the University in 1925: *Purdue University: Fifty Years of Progress.* In the book they included a condensed narrative by Elmer Andrews of the Purdue History Department, written for the Indiana Historical Commission, which detailed Purdue's response to the war effort.

"As an important unit in the field artillery service of the peace establishment, it was inevitable that Purdue should figure weightily in the government's war time plans," Hepburn and Sears wrote, based on Andrews's research. "In addition to routine and drill, the Military Department [at Purdue] constituted itself an information bureau for the service of students and alumni who sought to ascertain their field of greatest usefulness. It expediated enlistment and assembled information concerning the eligibility and training of alumni for certain offices—a service of importance in view of the obvious need for trained technicians."[14]

In May 1917 an ambulance corps was organized, and Purdue and Lafayette men rushed to volunteer. Nearly three times as many men volunteered as could be accepted. Fifty were chosen and they served in Italy in 1918. "Their service was altogether glorious," Hepburn and Sears said.[15]

"MEN MUST FACE DEATH ON SEA AND LAND"

On May 27, 1917, Stone gave an early Memorial Day address in West Lafayette. He did not mince words about what lay ahead. He said, "Our young men must lay down their peaceful pursuits and face death on sea and land. This is the lesson of the day, the necessity of sacrifice for the preservation of all that we value."[16]

War with Germany had personal significance for Stone. He had studied chemistry and biology at Boston University before moving to Germany and the University of Göttingen, where he received his PhD in 1888.

In July 1888, Stone returned to the United States, joined by Victoria Heitmuller. They met in Göttingen where she was born; they married in Nashville, Tennessee in 1889, the same year that Stone became a professor of chemistry at Purdue. They had two sons, David and Richard, before Victoria abandoned the family in 1907, eventually returning to Germany. Both sons would serve in the war, and no doubt Stone thought about what their sacrifice might mean to him and his family. Stone's second wife, Margaret, was also born in Germany.

On May 30, 1917, Stone gave another Memorial Day address, this time on campus: "To no class of people does this hour appeal so deeply as to us of the University," he said. "It is for us to set an example of practical patriotism not for any self-glorification, but as our plain duty as American citizens.... No other university has a higher responsibility to the nation than Purdue. Purdue, and others of like kind, was conceived and born in a spirit of service to the nation.... There can be no doubt that the institutions thus created were intended to be bulwarks of defense in time of war."[17] While he stated that Purdue and its people must play a major role in the battles ahead, he also urged students not to enlist until they were called. He wanted them to continue their studies as long as possible. "Do not desert your classes half trained," he said. "The war will last a long time and the need for trained men and women will steadily increase.... Chemists, physicists, biologists, nurses, pharmacists, engineers, and farmers, in short exponents of every kind of teaching given at Purdue, will be greatly needed, but not in half developed stages."[18]

Hepburn and Sears later wrote, "To render the maximum of service every effort was made to detain men in college so as to prepare themselves for tasks requiring training. British experience was, in this respect, an object lesson, the college youth of England having sacrificed itself in vain in the early months of the war. But when President Stone declared with reference to the call for 10,000 officers in the latter part of April that 'The time has come for Purdue men to act,' the response was eager. Two hundred eighty-five men enlisted before the summer's close, one hundred fifty-eight of whom entered the ROTC camp at Ft. Benjamin Harrison [Indianapolis]. During these stirring days the faculty gave twenty-four of its members to the same cause."[19]

"The excitement and agitation to join one of the officers' training corps became very intense," Purdue senior Charles Brouse wrote explaining his decision to leave campus in May and join the military.[20] Seventy seniors attended the June 1917 commencement wearing military uniforms.[21]

The opening of the school year in the fall of 1917 brought continued enthusiasm for the war effort. Because of enlistments and conscription, enrollment dropped from 2,226 in 1916 to 1,687, the lowest since 1904.

Some men, such as Lieutenant Julius Born, were already in Europe. In a letter to his parents written on November 25, 1917, somewhere in France, he said: "I have . . . taken out $10,000 worth of government insurance which is payable to you for twenty years at the rate of $41 a month. The insurance has only recently been available to us and is a fine thing as it is not very expensive."[22]

Those who remained on campus were focused on the war effort in their own ways. The School of Agriculture helped increase food production in Indiana. Home Economics faculty, under the leadership of Mary Matthews, stressed the importance of food conservation in meetings with people throughout the state. Purdue's Lella Gaddis was state leader of home demonstration, and she went to work hiring agents to help women in Indiana learn to conserve food. Some members of the Purdue faculty took positions with the federal and state governments.

"Particularly did Purdue girls count in their cooperation with the Lafayette Chapter of the Red Cross," Hepburn and Sears wrote. "They made surgical dressings, knitted sweaters, and wristlets [wool wrist and hand warmers], served meatless and wheatless meals at the dormitory and boarding houses and gave generously of time and money to the success of the campus drives for war funds."[23]

Many students on campus had been taking German language courses. In the fall of 1917, the majority switched to French. "Special courses were organized in wireless telegraphy, bayonet practice, semaphore practice [a system of sending messages by holding arms, two flags or poles in certain positions], field service regulations, the service remount for cavalry finding horses, the care of gas motors in aviation, and more ominously in first aid and general field practice," Hepburn and Sears wrote.[24]

During the 1917–18 academic year, nearly four hundred male students withdrew to join the military or to serve in essential industries. According to Hepburn and Sears, men at Purdue were also in the Naval Reserves: "They remained at the University until the semester closed and were then assigned to duty at the Great Lakes Training Station."[25] Also during the school year an ROTC unit—as opposed to a student cadet corps—was established with a quota of nine hundred men.[26] The stories from the front were horrific, but most people didn't hear them until the war had ended. Men from Purdue entered the service with far more patriotism than knowledge of what they would experience.

LIEUTENANT MAXWELL MCDOWELL

Lieutenant Maxwell McDowell, with the French Army ambulance service, wrote:

> I shall never forget my first load. The bearers came shuffling out of a trench with two things on stretchers that looked more like heaps of dirt than like men. The worst patients go in first. By the first star shell I saw one hobnailed shoe sticking out and where the other should have been a mass of reddish rags. Then I had to get inside to arrange the stretcher holders and as they slid him in beside me another flash revealed his face. One eye and most of the cheek was gone. A shell had mashed him. I didn't watch while they loaded the other poor devil who had been slashed with a bayonet. As we started back two explosions came just off the road to the rear. My guide, a man of about fifty years, lost his nerve, pulled his mask down over his eyes and grabbed me by the arm until he nearly pulled us off the road and kept repeating one of the few English words he knew, "hurry, hurry, hurry." I am afraid I forgot all about the groaning wrecks inside for believe me, we did hurry . . . I made six trips by 9 a.m. In my last load was a young lad with a lung full of gas inflammation.[27]

LIEUTENANT JAMES MANSON

Lieutenant James Manson wrote of his experiences somewhere in France during July of 1918:

> As I stood beside one of our guns . . . I saw a French officer coming slowly down the hill. An American soldier, stripped of all equipment save his gas mask, without a helmet, his left arm exposed to his shoulder where the sleeve of his blouse had been cut away wrapped in a dirty, blood stained bandage, was walking alongside the Frenchman holding a folded wad of gauze against the back of the officer's neck. Both were covered with mud and walked slowly

> and unsteadily as they half supported one another. When they emerged from the path one of our boys came up and offered to help. I stepped forward to see what I could do. The doughboy simply said, "get first aid for this officer. He's badly hurt." As he said this he moved the gauze pad a little and I glanced at the Frenchman's head. My stomach almost turned a somersault. A shell splinter had caught the man just under his helmet and behind his ear and a piece of his skull as large as a dollar was gone, revealing a spot of tissue which moved with every heartbeat.... [Looking through binoculars at valley ahead.] The floor of the valley, especially in the swampy area, looked like the surface of the moon as literally thousands of shell holes dotted what seemed to be every square foot of the surface .... No burial squads had worked their way this far forward as yet and I had never yet seen so many Americans dead as my binoculars discovered in that valley. They lay as thick as stumps in a woods where all the trees have been cut down and they were many bayonets sticking up out of the swamp grass which hid the bodies of the fallen soldiers.[28]

By March 1918 it was estimated that 1,700 Purdue men were serving in the military, including current students and alumni.[29]

PURDUE ARMORY

When Purdue's original 1874 Armory was destroyed by fire in 1916, the University Trustees immediately began plans for a new building. It was dedicated on April 26, 1918, and the cost had risen from the original budget of $150,000 to $200,000. At 169,814 gross square feet, it was enormous. It was the most expensive building constructed on the Purdue campus at that time, and it was completed in the nick of time. Nearly 2,600 Army men on active duty started arriving on campus the next day for special training in maintaining automobiles and trucks, and they were housed in the new Armory.

"Tonight, the Armory will be the scene of social gayety, the occasion being the dedication hop, a military dance. Tomorrow the building will be given over to the grim task of preparing men for winning the war against Germany and Austria," the *Indianapolis News* reported on the day of the dedication. Purdue University President Stone declared the building the finest armory on any college campus in the west.[30]

In addition to the Armory, Purdue allocated about $25,000 for a mess hall, kitchens, latrines, and other facilities the Army school required.

The 2,600 Army men who came to Purdue to study autos and live in the armory were just the beginning. According to Hepburn and Sears, when the Armory opened, "many detachments were assigned for special training courses. These were offered by a special faculty which in the summer months included many of the Purdue permanent staff, their compensation being reimbursed under a system of contracts entered into with the War Department. Under these arrangements, prior to the armistice, 1,634 auto mechanics, 1,278 truck-masters, 750 radio operators, and 201 concrete workers received instruction. . . . These men were soldiers and not students but every effort was exerted to make them feel at home and give them a share in campus life."[31]

The Memorial Gymnasium, dedicated in 1909 and built to remember the seventeen football players and adults killed in the Purdue train wreck of 1903, was also used as a barracks to house military men.

STUDENT ARMY TRAINING CORPS

The U.S. Selective Service Act of 1917, enacted May 18, required all men between the ages of twenty-one and thirty to register for a draft by June 5, 1917. In 1918, the War Department announced that in the fall, as the United States hurried to get more soldiers to the front, the law would change, setting the draft ages for men at age eighteen through forty-five. And, the government announced, when the new draft ages went into effect, it planned to draft all men of eligible age.

That had the potential for a huge impact on universities such as Purdue. It meant the entire male student body as well as a significant part of the faculty would be drafted for the war effort. Since there were not enough female students and older faculty to keep the University open, Purdue and other schools like it would be forced to close.

"A restless, nervous feeling of indifference pervaded the campus last September when school opened and studies once more were resumed," the Purdue *Debris* reported in the spring of 1919. "The cause of the abnormality was the new selective service legislation which included all men from the ages of 18 to 45. As the law stood, it meant the doom of universities and colleges within a short period, as it would eventually have drafted all the physically fit students."[32]

To encourage young men to continue their education and receive military training at the same time, the U.S. War Department created the Student Army Training Corps (SATC). The SATC would save higher education and train men for victory in Europe.

Young men who enlisted in the program were assigned to universities and given the rank of private, but those who did particularly well would have an opportunity for officer training. The men were issued military uniforms and lived according to military rules: for example, they were not allowed to leave campus without permission. Moreover, they were subject to being called to active duty in the draft.

On August 15, 1918, the Lawrence, Kansas *Daily Journal-World* quoted Army Major Bruno T. Schér as saying: "While the SATC is being established primarily to prevent the country from being robbed of its educated young men and to prevent the wrecking of the institutions of learning by the calls to the Army, it is essential that the men bear in mind that they are being schooled because they are of more use to the government educated." Purdue President Stone had made a similar statement in the spring of 1917.

The SATC began on the Purdue campus and others across the nation on October 1, 1918. ROTC at the University was suspended from June 30, 1918 to January 1, 1919, while the SATC took over military training.

With only a month remaining before the SATC became a reality, the school activities were existing more or less in a state of coma and some activities were not resumed in the least at the opening of the school year, due to the uncertain trend of affairs," the 1919 *Debris* reported.

> The Exponent did not consider it advisable to issue newspapers for one month only, and so the staff arranged to work in cooperation with the Lafayette Journal and the Courier to publish the daily news of the University. . . . Departmental societies and clubs did not hold meetings during the short period . . . and their organizations were allowed to drift along. Debating and literary societies for the most part held only one or two meetings and then decided to disband temporarily until the war was over and until normal conditions were again restored at the University. The same was true of dancing clubs. . . . The social fraternities were facing an acute situation. Not to initiate early meant the death of the organizations if the war had lasted very long.[33]

Purdue entered a contract with the War Department and pledged to house, feed, and train 1,500 men in the SATC. The government gave the University one dollar per day per man for housing and food, and twelve cents per day for tuition. In 1918, there were no male residence halls and no cafeterias on the Purdue campus. Some men lived in fraternities that had about twenty-five members, but the rest lived in boardinghouses or at their family homes. They were fed mostly in private eating clubs or in the boardinghouses.

The SATC changed that. The men would be crowded in large, wood-frame barracks eating, sleeping, studying, and marching together, day and night.

The buildings each housed 250 men. The program also required sheds for storing equipment, including one that sheltered twenty-six Army trucks. The wood barracks, always considered temporary, were put up on vacant land east of the Armory. One of the buildings to house equipment was longer than a football field.

"The existence of the SATC at Purdue was responsible for a great increase in the enrollment," Hepburn and Sears wrote in their 1925 campus history. "About 1,400 new students were received in September [1918] preliminary to their enrollment in the corps, yet the influx caused no case representing a lowering of standards. In addition to these 1,400 men there were special student groups in no sense affiliated with the SATC. These were members of the Naval Reserves, also persons who . . . were subject to the draft. A third group consisted of men physically disqualified for full service but permitted to join the SATC for limited service. Finally, there was a considerable body of students under eighteen years of age. These men pursued a regular college course and were not connected with the soldiers' organizations."[34]

Enrollment jumped from 1,687 in the fall of 1917 to 2,549 in the fall of 1918—and that did not include the active-duty soldiers receiving special training such as auto mechanics. At the height of enrollment on the campus, there were 5,071 in the Purdue community in the fall of 1918, including 1,208 in the SATC and 200 Navy Reservists.[35] There were only 260 women enrolled at the University.

The University was now called Camp Purdue, and it was a military camp. Everywhere men were walking through the campus and taking classes in uniform.

On October 1, 1918, when the SATC program officially began nationwide, about 3,000 soldiers and SATC students were in formation on the Stuart Field football field to take the Oath of Allegiance. At about the same time 150,000 students at more than 500 SATC programs at other universities in colleges across the nation also took the oath.

The transfer of so many men to SATC barracks resulted in many vacant rooms in West Lafayette boardinghouses. Some fraternities combined. Unmarried, commissioned officers leased the Phi Kappa Psi house and hired a caretaker to keep things clean and prepare their meals. The Phi Delta Theta fraternity house became a hostess house for the soldiers. Dances were held there, and wives and mothers were temporarily housed there during visits to campus.

"The order of the day was severe," Hepburn and Sears wrote. "From first call at 6 a.m., to reveille at 6:10, to supervised study at 7 p.m., and taps at 9:45 p.m. Life was a constant alternation of drill and classroom, and sleep at night was interrupted by frequent calls to first drill."[36]

This was not the lifestyle these men had enjoyed on campus in earlier years.

Everything on campus was affected, including football. Some members of the 1917 team still eligible for the 1918 season had enlisted or been drafted and were not on campus. Other members of the football team were in the SATC, where military rules allowed the men to have only one hour per day for athletics and recreation, so practice was very limited. The rules also required men in the SATC to remain on campus during October, with their only break from noon to taps on Saturday. So, games that required long travel were impossible.

In 1918, Purdue only played five official games and one special contest against Wabash. That game was played in Indianapolis with all money from ticket sales going to the United War Work campaign to provide entertainment for troops abroad. The biggest victory of the season was defeating Chicago 7-3 on Stuart Field east of the Armory at Purdue. The overall record was 3-3. Its worst loss was 27-0 against Great Lakes Naval Station. The station drew sailors from all around the country and included three future Pro Football Hall of Famers, one of them George Halas, who would found and own the Chicago Bears.

INFLUENZA PANDEMIC

There was one other problem with the 1918 football season: flu.

The year 1918 was marked by a flu pandemic. No one knows how many people died in the pandemic. Estimates have a huge range, from fifty million to perhaps one hundred million people worldwide.[37] Historical estimates are that 675,000 Americans died during the worst fifteen months of the pandemic.[38] The pandemic lasted several years, but the worst of it was in the fall of 1918 when as many as two-thirds of the deaths might have taken place.

It is also unknown where the pandemic began. It was commonly called the "Spanish flu," but it did not begin in Spain. In 1918, Spain was not a combatant in the Great War and newspapers worldwide were free to report its flu cases. American newspapers and others across the world did not report the severity of the pandemic in their own countries, since that was considered information that could aid the enemy. Although newspapers at the time did report that "Spanish flu" was a misnomer, this term has persisted even into the twenty-first century.

Where did it begin? The best guess is among residents of Haskell County, Kansas, and it then spread to military bases in the state.

Flu normally is hardest on the elderly. But the 1918 flu hit healthy, young adults hardest, possibly for two reasons: firstly, they had strong immune systems that overreacted to the virus, and secondly, combatant nations in the Great War had millions of young men crowded together in barracks, trains, troopships, and frontline trenches, enabling infections to spread quickly.

The U.S. military grew from less than 400,000 soldiers in April 1918 to nearly 5 million by the end of the war in November. Many Americans soldiers died on ships carrying them across the ocean before they ever set foot in Europe.

The U.S. government minimized concern about the pandemic to keep the attention of people on the war effort. Newspapers reported flu concerns, and health authorities closed Purdue and other schools for several weeks in the fall of 1918, but gatherings of thousands of people at war bond rallies were still allowed. The secretary of the Indiana State Board of Health was Dr. John Newell Hurty, who had earlier been Purdue's first dean of pharmacy.

On October 11, 1918, the same day it was announced that Purdue would close because of the flu, a Lafayette newspaper, the *Tippecanoe County Democrat*, downplayed what was happening. An article in the newspaper showed the conflicting information people were being given: "State Board of Health bans public gatherings. Health officers have the epidemic nearly stamped out at Camp Purdue. There are no serious cases and only a few of a minor character. City Health Officer Dr. Hillis says the ban does not halt crowds attending games played in the open and that they were to be encouraged. He further states that although funerals could not be permitted in churches there was no ban on holding services at the cemetery. There is no danger if you hold a steady hand and the pandemic is well in hand here now. If you have a fever go to bed. The grippe is nothing to fear. It is the complications that follow. Don't cough, spit or sneeze where there are others unless you do it in a handkerchief."[39]

Purdue and other universities in Indiana were closed from October 12 to November 2, but the military students and others being trained on campus were not sent home. They stayed in their crowded barracks and mess halls.

On October 12, nearly 3,000 military personnel on the University campus marched through Lafayette to Columbian Park for a Columbus Day celebration and war bond rally. The parade included forty Army trucks. Thousands of people lined the streets and went to the park for the program.[40] It was a recipe for disaster. No one knows how many men at Purdue or people in Tippecanoe County became sick from that single event, since the information was censored. The war and displays of patriotism and war bond sales were considered more important than the flu.

It wasn't until the war had ended that reports emerged stating three hundred men at Camp Purdue had contacted the flu in the fall of 1918 and eleven had died. This virus had the ability to kill a strong, healthy eighteen-year-old in a matter of hours.

Seven years after the war ended, Hepburn and Sears reported: "When the epidemic was at its worst the girls (on campus and in the community) rendered excellent service as members of the motor corps. As drivers of the ambulance, they were at all times prepared to answer calls. It was in this emergency, in fact, that the young women of the University and the city attainted the greatest heights of service, though their contributions of socks and sweaters, bandages and dressings to their brothers overseas no doubt contributed to that high morale which tided Americans to victory."[41]

There were many challenges to the academic life of the campus. "Conditions unprecedented in every phase of student life created weighty problems, administrative and academic," Hepburn and Sears wrote. "Careful planning was essential if courses and their students were to dovetail. Tact was indispensable in the confusion of authority between civil and the military. Dual authority was indeed a constant impediment to discipline as well as academic work. Instructors were compelled to lenience because of the embarrassments under which students labored. Grades meant no more than an evaluation of such exercises as the students did attend—a military rating requiring later interpretation in terms of University credit. The engineering schools labored under the greatest difficulties. The School of Science more nearly approximated normal conditions."[42]

VICTORY

The end of the war came surprisingly fast on November 11, 1918. When the news was announced, Purdue students and people from Lafayette and West Lafayette joined in celebration. People marched to Camp Purdue. "It was a sight such as was never before seen in this fair Indiana city and the like of which undoubtedly will never be witnesses again, the *Lafayette Journal* reported. "Thirty thousand people celebrated last night and it was not a peace celebration, but a victory celebration."[43]

Businesses, stores, and factories shut down. People danced in the streets. The Purdue military band and the University military detachments led a parade through Lafayette. Purdue coeds paraded the Victory Bell—the first time women had been given the honor of parading the Bell.

"The city streets were thronged during the early morning but long before the time set for the start of the parade, the streets were impassable," the newspaper said. "The parade stood in line awaiting the soldiers and sailors from Camp Purdue. After a short wait the strains of the Camp Purdue military band's music floated from lower Main Street and the crowd cheered wildly."[44]

Fifteen hundred Purdue soldiers marched behind the band along with Naval Reservists, and twenty Army trucks. The parade was three miles long.

Lieutenant James Manson wrote about Armistice Day in France where he was being treated at a hospital after being gassed. He had recovered enough to have outpatient privileges:

> At breakfast the rumor persisted that the armistice had been signed but we had not received a newspaper and there was no official confirmation. [They went into town and finally learned the Germans had signed the armistice at 6 a.m. and it would go into effect at 11 a.m.]. As we turned away from the bulletin board at the newspaper office we found ourselves surrounded by a group of five French girls and one French soldier. Before we knew what was happening we were half smothered under an avalanche of hugs and kisses. Every girl insisted on kissing each of us and the French soldier, a boy not yet out of his teens, gave each of us a big smile, a snappy salute, and then a kiss on each cheek. The sidewalks and streets were swarming with the happiest mob of people seen in France since the fall of the Bastille. Everyone was simply wild with

> joy, men and women, boys and girls, soldiers, and civilians of all ages and in all kinds of costumes were singing, dancing, laughing, crying, hugging, and kissing not only with one another but with every American in sight. A dozen parades were marching around Place de Jaude at once. One was led by a band, others by singing groups of young people and one by a man playing violin. They would go aimlessly through the park and along the streets picking up new marchers along the way or occasionally breaking up to start two or three new parades. A favorite maneuver was for a group of perhaps eight or ten girls to lock arms and go running thru the street until they saw an American soldier. When they caught one they formed a tight circle about him and the ransom they demanded for his release was a kiss. That wasn't at all hard to take, but after having been surrounded a dozen times in a single block and kissed a hundred times or more we felt as tho we had been in a wrestling match. Before we found a place where we could sit down [in a restaurant] we had to run the same gauntlet of merry makers, but one group was different. We were stopped by a well-dressed family group consisting of a middle aged man, his wife, a grown son, a daughter possible twenty years old and two little girls of about eight or ten. They cried "Vive la Amerique" and they first shook hands. The young man was very solemn as I took his hand and the father, mother and daughter had tears in their eyes as they shook hands and then kissed us on both cheeks.
>
> The celebration went on for more than twelve hours and became even more intense. It ended about nine p.m. with fireworks.[45]

Back at the hospital Manson joined three other patients singing "until 1 a.m. when the ward nurse came in and told us she thought we had better be getting some sleep."[46]

In 1919 the Purdue *Debris* reported nine alumni, students, and faculty had received service cross medals during the war.[47] The issue also reported that "ambulance section 508 which was organized at Purdue in 1917 . . . added to the glory of the school and displayed the valor of the college man in the great campaign on the western front the past year. This section which is largely composed of Purdue men . . . received the rare distinction of having the Croix de Guerre bestowed upon the whole unit, besides having the medal of honor given to some twenty-five individuals."[48]

Serving in the ambulance service was dangerous and stressful. On September 30, 1917, former Purdue professor Lieutenant Maxwell Erwin McDowell wrote about his experience in the French ambulance service:

> I made it to the hospital [from the front] in twenty-five minutes. Two surgeons with their rubber gloves on and a dozen nurses and stretcher bearers were waiting for me as I came into the dimly lit courtyard. Out came the first stretcher. For just a moment the doctor bent over it then straightened up and said quietly 'mort.' The second was still alive and as the doctor said "quick," the bearers started him for the operating table. . . . A nurse, an old priest who speaks English [later] said to me "you have had a bad night of it monsieur." "Yes," I said. "I only brought one of the first load in alive." "And he died on the table," replied the priest. I guess he must have seen my face for he hastened to say, "Oh you mustn't worry about it my son. Nothing could have saved those poor fellows." But I had to get out in the air and walk about a bit.[49]

After the Armistice, military law courses at Purdue were eliminated. "More effective use of supervised study was sought and with the prospect of early demobilization students were urged to make up lost work," Hepburn and Sears wrote. "To this end the semester was prolonged to March 1, 1919, and students who had withdrawn from the University prior to December 21 were permitted to reenter their classes immediately after the holidays with the prospect of semester credit for successful work. The executive committee waived some of the usual requirements of students. Sophomore science men in the SATC or the Naval Reserve were excused from modern language and seniors in agriculture who had been in the military or Naval service were excused in 1919 from any thesis requirement."[50] Extending the first semester to March 1 shortened the second semester in 1919 by one month.

President Stone praised the military students who studied and trained on campus but never got to Europe. "Their consuming desire was to reach the scene of active fighting and when the fortune of war denied them this privilege it was their great disappointment," he said. "Wherever their duty lay it was well done and their response to their country's call will ever be the most glorious event in the University's history. That among so many some should not return was inevitable. Purdue mourns for those as a mother for her sons, comforted by the knowledge that their loss was the price of liberty which will ever be more precious by virtue of its costs."[51]

Sixteen percent of the 4,006 Boilermakers who served in the military during the Great War were sent overseas. Both of President Stone's sons, Richard and David, served and came home. Sixty-seven Purdue men died in military service and are memorialized in the Memorial Union and with a plaque in the Union's

Great Hall. Five died in accidents. No cause of death is listed for eight men. Seventeen died from battle injuries. The remaining thirty-seven died from disease—the flu.[52]

Class of 1915 graduate Robert Earl Symmonds was one of those who died. Perhaps sensing a war was coming, he left Purdue in 1914, entered the U.S. Military Academy, and graduated in 1917. He was shipped to Europe in December. On November 3, 1918, he asked his commanding officer to assign him to a company having contact with the enemy. He led the company in an attack that very night and was wounded. He died from his wounds on November 22, eleven days after the armistice.[53]

Also among the forty-six Purdue men who died in the service during the Great War was Lieutenant George E. Glossop. Handsome, tall, and slender with wavy blond hair and gray eyes, Glossop graduated from Purdue in the spring of 1915 with a degree in electrical engineering. While at Purdue, Glossop was involved in athletics and other extracurricular activities. He was captain of the 1913–14 football team, was an All-Western Conference athlete, and played both center and halfback on offense as well as defense. Glossop was appointed freshman basketball coach at Purdue in November 1914. He also had been on the basketball and track teams and earned varsity letters in all three sports. As a student he was active in the Varsity Club, Canoe Club, American Institute of Electrical Engineers, Jeffersonian Debating, Athletic Association, Student Council, and Student Union Committee. He was a member of the Aeolian Club, which in December 1915 became Lambda Chi Alpha fraternity.[54]

After graduating from high school in 1907 and before enrolling at Purdue, Glossop had enlisted in the Navy. He was a coxswain on the USS Louisiana, steering the ship, and was part of the "Great White Fleet" that sailed around the globe from December 1907 to February 1909 aboard ships that were painted white, making friendly visits to foreign posts and displaying the United States's naval strength. He played football in the Navy and was selected quarterback on the All-Navy team.

Immediately after his commencement ceremony on June 9, 1915, he married Alfrieda Herdrick. They had met several years earlier after a Purdue-Indiana game. They moved to South Dakota, where he coached the South Dakota State School of Mining and Technology basketball team. He also coached high school teams and became football coach and athletic director at Whitman College in Walla Walla, before volunteering for service in the Army in May 1918.

On May 10, 1918, Glossop was selected to represent Purdue at the officers' training school at Camp Zachary Taylor in Kentucky. He served as an instructor in artillery. On December 1918, world-famous playwright, Purdue graduate, and University *Alumnus* editor George Ade wrote about what was happening on campus in October before the war ended: "Further suspension of University classes announced by Dr. Stone. Sad news received—Glossop, football captain in 1913, a fine athlete and popular fellow dies at Camp Taylor of influenza."[55]

He was twenty-nine years old. He left behind his wife Alfrieda and two children, one-year-old George Jr. and Sarah Ellene, who was born just one month before he died. Under his accomplishments the 1915 Purdue *Debris* stated, "It might well be said, 'here is a man.'"[56]

Little was done to help the men who served in the Great War. In those days, "there was no G.I. Bill of Rights for veterans, only a rehabilitation program for those disabled during the war," Purdue historian Knoll wrote. More than one hundred disabled men were enrolled at Purdue after the war. Another two hundred were in the Purdue Federal School operated by the University.[57]

The war had a long effect on those who survived it.

James Byron Manson returned to Indiana after the war to his wife Catharine and strong support from his family. He had tuberculosis and Bell's palsy, unexplained facial muscle weakness or paralysis, possibly related to his gassing. He was awarded the Croix de Guerre and the Silver Star.

Upon his return, needing fresh air and a quiet time to restore his mind and body, he and Catharine drove to Oregon to stay with her brother, who had an apple orchard. He then returned to Crawfordsville to pursue his career in civil engineering.

He and Catharine had a son, James B. Manson Jr. In 1927, they took a trip back to France where he introduced them to Jean, a kind French nurse who had cared for him after he was gassed. He continued a rewarding life and successful career in Indiana and retired to St. Petersburg, Florida in November 1956. He died in January 1957 at 61 years old.

Maxwell Erwin McDowell did not return to teach at Purdue. He taught at Columbia University in New York City and become a recognized authority in taxes. He retired from Standard Oil of New Jersey. He died December 16, 1954, in his Scarsdale, New York home at the age of sixty.

Julius Leopold Born returned from the war and had several different jobs, including sales manager of the Swartz Building Company in Detroit. He moved to

Lafayette in 1936 to care for his critically ill mother. He was a bridge champion and instructor. He died November 2, 1941, from an apparent self-inflicted bullet wound after years of suffering with arthritis. He was fifty years old. In his estate he established a scholarship at Purdue named for his parents.

More than sixty million soldiers fought in the Great War and more than nine million died. The story of the Americans who went "Over There" is the story of boys, really, most of whom had never been far from home. It's the story of them seeing France almost as tourists when they first arrived, before being sent to the front. France was so different from their hometowns, so much older. They drank their first wine, and lived through days of endless, tedious boredom, punctuated by hours of sheer, heart-pounding terror that would mark them for however long—or short—their lives would be.

PROFILE
CHARLES R. BROUSE

CHARLES R. BROUSE GRADUATED FROM PURDUE UNIVERSITY IN JUNE 1917, BUT LEFT CAMPUS before commencement to serve as an artillery officer "Over There" in the Great War that had consumed Europe since 1914. He survived and wrote a one-hundred-page account of his experiences in France. His description of his experiences on battlefields and in the sidewalk cafes of Paris provide an informative narrative of what it was like for a U.S. military officer who, like so many others, had never been out of Midwestern America before in his life.

Brouse saved what he wrote, and no doubt took it out from time to time during his life to remember a time when he was young, drank his first wine with fellow officers and French women, kissed French women, risked death, and saw men die in ways too horrible to ever forget. When he died, his beautiful, descriptive narrative was passed to his heirs, who eventually sent it to the Virginia Kelly Karnes Archives and Special Collections Research Center at Purdue University.

Excerpts from his story, "My Army Experiences in the World War, May 1917 to January 1919":

> [Brouse's ship sailed for England in late March 1918.] At half past three in the afternoon a trembling was felt on the ship . . . Upon peeking out a port-hole and the deck doors the dock was seen to be slowly becoming smaller and smaller and gradually faded into the rest of the blurred, smokey mist. We had left home—our dear old United States—bound for war-worn France with no idea of what we had before us. How fortunate it is for some of us that we are unable to see what the future has in store for us.[1]

* * *

Corporal John L. Byrne, who later got to be a close friend of mine, and who was a fat cheerful Irishman, sang out, "well boys there's one good thing about this trip. We get six good meals a day—three down and three up." This was just enough to make two of my men hit the rail.[2]

* * *

When we passed the famous [Glasgow, Scotland] shipyards we marveled at the hundreds upon hundreds of ships in the process of construction and most of the work being done by women.[3]

* * *

[At Le Havre, France] the officers were allowed outside the camp but the men were not. We noticed a little café just outside the gate and across the street with the sign "Dubonnet" on it and we went in and had our dinner. Thereafter we called the place "Dubonnet's Café." Then we went down into town and saw a number of signs with "Dubonnet" on them and we thot that there must be quite a number of cafes owned by this man Dubonnet. It was not until several days later that we were enlightened to the fact that Dubonnet was the name of a French wine. It was here in Le Havre that I had my first taste of French sour wine, and to my surprise I found I liked it. So did the men. They were not allowed outside the enclosure but the British soldiers were. The last day we were in Le Havre I was surprised at how many of the men requested me to loan them money. They hadn't been paid for two months and thus I didn't think much of it. But I found out the reason later on, early the next morning, when half of the battery were half drunk. They had shined up to the "Tommys" [British] and "Tommy" had bought their wine for them and passed it to them through the fence.[4]

[They next camped at Mailly, France where officers took weekend trips to Paris and] . . . frolicked with the girls at the Follies Bergère. Paris, during the war and especially during the time of the many air raids, was a vastly different Paris from that so well known to the many tourists who visited there before the war. The old time carefree gaiety and laughter were lacking and in their place was a quiet simple determination to win or die in the attempt. Every statue and bit of art was carefully protected by huge piles of sandbags boarded up against them. In contrast to the gay colored costumes of the girls and women were

> the many people in deep mourning. The streets were thronged with military men. . . . At night not a single light showed out of any place. . . . One beautiful warm evening we had walked down thru the little village and past the dirty, homely, smelly stone houses with their red or thatched roofs out onto a peaceful country road. We had hardly reached the open country beyond the old houses when we saw coming around a bend in the road a sight which was most peculiar and interesting and took one back to the middle ages. It was that of a very old shepherd walking in the midst of a flock of nearly three hundred sheep playing the typical story book shepherd's pipe, while running around, apparently everywhere at once, were the small shepherd dogs acting with seemingly human intelligence. We stopped to watch with wonder and delight at this little procession as it passed us on toward the village, feeling just as tho we had stepped out of modern times into an old time fairy story.[5]

Brouse enjoyed the French cuisine and one evening gathered together a group of Beta Theta Pi fraternity brothers from other U.S. universities for a huge dinner. Another evening at a café they ordered wine they didn't like and shared it with Italian soldiers from a machine gun battalion. They loved it.

> I was more or less nervous inside as we approached the front, for I didn't know what was before me. Capt. [Raymond] Linton on the other hand was perfectly calm and I thot that I could at least show calmness even if I was in more or less a panic inside. So very casually I asked, "Captain, can the German lines be seen from here?" His answer was "Oh yes. They're right over the hill there." It took me quite ten minutes to be sufficiently assured that there were no Germans behind each tree we passed or that no shells would be lighting on the road directly ahead of me before I could trust myself to speak again.[6]

* * *

> While watching the crew on No. 2 Gun, we heard the whining sound—eeeeeoooooo-Bang! It was a 77mm shell of the Germans which had come our way but had lighted in the hills about two hundred meters from us. Instantly I was in an internal panic but noticing that the lieutenant and the men were perfectly calm, even joking about it, I thot I could at least ACT as tho I were calm. However, I made sure of the location of the dugout. It was but a moment later I heard that eeeeEEEEOOOOSHSHSHSHSH—Bang!! This I heard from

the inside of the dugout. How I got in I have never remembered. This was my first experience under shellfire. Everybody undergoing his initial experience of shellfire is scared. He may not show it externally but it is human nature to feel so. However, one soon learns to differentiate between those shells which are coming in his direction and those which are not and he soon becomes accustomed to shells screeching overhead and all around and merely drops into the nearest ditch or hole, where there be mud or not, in order to protect himself as far as possible from flying shell fragments. When a shell bursts, the fragments fly up and out and for that reason a shell may burst three feet from a man lying on the ground and not a fragment will touch him. Besides this, conditions of war convert all men into fatalists, As they say, if they get hit they will get hit and it is only when "Fritz gets your name on a shell" that you are hit. There was a story prevalent "over there" that a certain ammunition wagon driver was exceedingly reckless and when admonished by his comrades he said that Fritz hadn't got his number. Not long after he was hit by a flying shell fragment and when taunted about his name at last being on a German shell, he replied, "Naw, he didn't have my name on it. He only had the initials."[7]

* * *

The woods, which at one time were pretty dense, had been terribly thinned and devastated by German shell fire. Whole trees had been shot down and in some places the ground had been terribly chewed up by shells. Every one of [the German shells] went far over us and did no harm, although we were forced to take cover more than once because we thot they were coming our way. One man wrote in a letter that he heard the shells singing the old hymn "Nearer My God to Thee."[8]

* * *

On the night of Wednesday, September 11, we got the word that the big drive would commence the next day with an artillery preparation commencing at one o'clock in the morning and the advance "over the top" at five o'clock. Our regimental chaplain, a big-hearted Irish Catholic, came around and received confessions from the Catholic members of our battery and gave the others much spiritual comfort. All day and night rain continued to fall and the weather grew colder with a driving wind. The night was as dark as a pocket and so nasty that one would much prefer to stay close at home in front of his grate fire. All during the evening the steady tramp, tramp, tramp of troops could be heard slushing and slopping their weary muddy way up towards the front lines. . . . At five minutes to one o'clock in the morning of September 12 . . . there was a flash dimmed by the rain and mist in the sky somewhere two or three miles west of us followed several seconds later by a dull boom of some gun, seeming to be sort of signal to get ready for the great battle to come. . . . At one minute to one o'clock the order to "load" was given and could be heard echoed from the other batteries in the neighborhood. Soon could be heard the cries of the gun commanders, which was repeated by the telephone operators at the guns to the battery commander in his station. . . . At precisely one o'clock it seemed as if all hell were let loose at once. The sky which but a moment before was pitch black was suddenly torn asunder with thousands of flashes and detonation of guns of all sizes. Everywhere in whichever direction one looked could be seen the flickering dancing intangible flashes . . . of hundreds of flaming mouthed devils from Hell pouring forth their destructive screeching and screaming messengers of death. The noise and pounding vibration were terrific and some of the flashes so blinding at times that it seemed impossible to make one's eyes adjust themselves rapidly enough to the ever changing condition of darkness and daylight. The ground literally rocked and shook as the guns of all sizes continued their ceaseless earthquake like explosions. . . . This inferno continued until five o'clock when just as a clear beautiful dawn was breaking in the east it seems as tho the noise and flashing had been doubly increased where before it hardly seemed possible that any more din or uproar could possibly be added to it. . . . Over towards the north hundreds of different colored signals could be seen being sent up by both sides as our men went "over the top." Copper colored lights, red lights, yellow lights, white lights, green lights, umbrella rockets, star shells, aeroplane signals, and almost everything generally used for signals on the front lines seemed to be in the air at one time. Over the field around us moving silently in groups of twenty to thirty were hundreds of infantry reserves making their way in ever winding paths thru the uneven fields and tortuous barbed wired entanglements.[9]

* * *

One night while we were waiting for orders to move, Lieutenant Cahill and I conceived of the idea of inculcating better battery spirit by teaching the men a few catchy songs and getting them to sing. So, Sunday night with some camouflage as the arbor and the full moon shining down on a clear war sky we got together the men who could and liked to sing and we taught them songs. My ukulele . . . was accidentally packed in my bedding roll and I had the use of it that evening.

[To the tune of "Back Home in Indiana"].

Back home again, in Indiana
I had never seen a soldier
Till the war broke out
Anybody would have told yer
I was rather stout
But by now I am so thin
My shape won't fit my skin.

When I was home in Indiana
I was quite another size
I lived on ham and eggs and turkey legs
And griddle cakes and pies.
The sort of folks I used to stay with
Let me thru the pantry roam
When I think about the meals I got away with
Then I long for my Indiana home.[10]

* * *

After eating a cold and rainy breakfast out under a leafless tree I was shown the billet where my bed had been made up, and I laid down and attempted to sleep. But as this was a new place and the billets had recently been occupied by German officers and men, of course, everything left behind by them was regarded by our orderlies as a souvenir. It was said that England was fighting for the supremacy of the seas, France for her country, and the Americans for souvenirs.[11]

* * *

After the shock of the explosion of [a] shell I heard a little buzzing sound coming near me and ducked my head. A piece of shell fragment about the size of my little finger whizzed past my face so close that I felt the breeze of it and spatted into the ground not a foot from my head. When I picked it up it was so hot that I could not hold it. After I realized what a close shave I had had from going to join those who had gone to help "push up the daisies" I felt nervous and shaky for nearly half an hour after.[12]

* * *

Everything had been going along pretty smoothly and regularly, and the rumors of early peace and rapid advances of the Allies had filled the men with great visions of eating Christmas dinner at home. HOME—what wouldn't we have given at that time to have been transported just for one small hour back to our homes and among our loved ones in the States.[13]

* * *

Rumors were circulating that the war would send end with a German surrender when Brouse and some friends spent the night in a deserted chateau.

The next day we met some French girls and sang and danced with them most of the afternoon. After dinner we returned to Angers in a drenching rain, but content with having had such a good time.[14]

* * *

On the 11th of November, perhaps the most famous date the world has ever known since the time of Christ, the armistice took effect. Everything stopped operating and absolutely everybody capable of doing so got out into the crowded streets and in the cafés to join in yelling, singing, cheering, dancing, laughing, crazy and happy mob. France literally went crazy, Champagne flowed like water, and the songs and prayers of thankfulness that went up were almost drowned by the revelry of celebration. Lines of officers and men, both American and French, French civilians, men and women and boys and girls, everybody arm in arm swung down the streets laughing and singing in a most carefree manner. Crowds of girls would surround an American and would not

> let him loose until he had kissed every girl at least once and sometimes more. Of course, that was hard on the poor Americans. Everywhere could be heard the cries by the French people, "Vive la Amerique" answered by just as many Americans soldiers with "Vive le France!" . . . On a sidewalk away from the the crowd were three little peasant women simply crying and unable to talk. This celebration lasted for two days when the people were simply worn out physically from the exertion.[15]

On January 17, 1919, Brouse's ship landed in Hoboken, New Jersey. He was discharged from the military five days later.

> "I was very glad to be a free man again after nearly two years of Army life. But I have gained in experience that for which many men would have given several years of their lives. I had had my ups and downs, had seen another part of the world, and how they live, had been thru some pleasant and some terrible experiences, some of which I wish to forget, and had returned to my home and loved ones better off physically and mentally than I was before I left. I have no regrets that I did this for my country, and I do not regret getting back to start life over again."[16]

He returned to Rockford, Illinois. He lived with his parents and sister and worked as a salesman. He never married. Later in his life, he became a math teacher and superintendent of the Briggsdale, Colorado schools. He died unexpectedly of a heart attack on February 22, 1950 at 57 years old.

U.S. Representative Justin Morrill (later U.S. Senator) from Vermont, sponsor of the Morrill Land Grant Act.

Purdue campus in 1876. Military Hall is the single-story wood-frame building to the far right. Image courtesy of Purdue University Libraries, Archives and Special Collections.

Purdue University professor Harvey Wiley, first captain of the Purdue Corps of Cadets.

Abner Pickering, Purdue professor of mathematics and Commandant of Cadets. Image courtesy of Purdue University Libraries, Archives and Special Collections.

Early photo of Purdue University Military Band. Image courtesy of Purdue University Libraries, Archives and Special Collections.

Newspaper cartoon depicting Uncle Sam chasing Pancho Villa back into Mexico. Clifford Berryman, "I've Had Enough of This," *Washington Evening Star*, March 10, 1916.

Pancho Villa statue in Palomas, Mexico in the area where he crossed the border to raid Columbus, New Mexico in 1916. Photo by author.

Purdue student James Byron Manson served with Purdue Battery B at the Texas-Mexico border. He later also served in World War I. Image courtesy of Purdue University Libraries, Archives and Special Collections.

Purdue alumnus George Glossop. Image courtesy of the Purdue University Elmore Family School of Electrical and Computer Engineering Alumni Wall of Fame, Class of 1915.

Purdue University President Winthrop Stone. Stone's presidency lasted from 1900 to 1921. Image courtesy of Purdue University Libraries, Archives and Special Collections.

James Byron Manson, Purdue alumnus and Great War artillery officer. Image courtesy of the James Byron Manson family.

BORN, JULIUS LEOPOLD, La-Fayette, Ind. "Ike."

B. S. in M. E. A. S. M. E. (1) (2) (3) (4). Athletic Association (1) (2) (3) (4). Y. M. C. A. (4).

Julius is "home grown," so to speak as he resides in the big city just across the river. In his four years attendance at Purdue he has become a levee boat chaser of the worst type, habitually catching the one just behind the one he should have caught. The turning point of his career came when, as a freshman, he was canned from the Purdue Army and assigned to "Doc Bond's Specials" consisting of those unfit for war. Under Doc's able tutelage, "Ike" began to shine among his fellows as a wit, and today stands as the pride of the Senior Class for his sparkling humor.

Julius Leopold Born, Purdue alumnus and Great War artillery officer. As pictured in the 1913 Purdue *Debris*.

Purdue Student Army Training Corps barracks (WWI) with Heavilon Hall in the background. Image courtesy of Purdue University Libraries, Archives and Special Collections.

Charles Brouse, Purdue alumnus and Great War artillery officer. Image courtesy of Purdue University Libraries, Archives and Special Collections.

Purdue Armory, 1918. Image courtesy of Purdue University Libraries, Archives and Special Collections.

PART 2

1918–1945

5

AERONAUTICAL ENGINEERING TAKES OFF AT PURDUE

> *Lieutenant George W. Haskins of Dayton, Ohio, will come [to Gala Week] in a plane. He will arrive Sunday or Monday morning with resolutions of the Dayton Alumni Association drawn up at a meeting of that association Friday at the English Club.*
>
> *PURDUE EXPONENT*, SUNDAY, JUNE 8, 1919

In the spring of 1920, the Purdue University senior class president and the class secretary summed up their thoughts in the student yearbook *Debris* as they prepared to face their futures. They remembered a poem recited at the beginning of every school year, with the freshmen required to sit in the balcony.

Class President Kenneth Huffine and Secretary Dorothy Clark wrote: "Remember that first convocation when we all sat up in the balcony in awed rows and heard for the first time, 'Twinkle, twinkle, little star; we are freshmen so we are?'

"There were 715 of us then," they continued. "Now, 309 of us are leaving. Quite a discrepancy thanks to the war . . . The greatest period in all history has been our own. We went to war in our first April [on campus]. Some of us came back wounded and five [in the class of 1920] gave their lives. Purdue's military life was entirely changed by the war. In the old days we practiced shoulder arms and fought momentous skirmishes in Happy Hollow. The SATC came and went. Now, all is changed to Field Artillery. The development of aeronautics under the engineering college probably will be another result of the war."[1]

Students of the Class of 1920 were men such as Glen Raymond Blackburn—also known as "Blackie"—from West Lafayette. "Sickness and too much war kept Blackie from graduating with his old '16 class," the *Debris* noted. "But he has come back to the erudition factory and proved that a few years of wide world sandwiched between a college career increases a man's capacity for work and for making friends."[2]

Max Francis Becker was captain of the Purdue baseball team in his junior year. "The Mexican fracas and World War took Beck away from varsity baseball and a degree in '17," the 1920 *Debris* said. "He is still known to his classmates as a real man and valuable friend. His mature judgement, practical experience and irrepressible zeal fit him well for the work of a successful engineer."[3]

There were many similar senior profiles in the 1920 yearbook.

PURDUE AERONAUTICAL ENGINEERING

Huffine and Clark were correct about Purdue being changed by the war. The war changed everything. They were also correct about a program in aeronautical engineering coming to Purdue. It would have an enormous impact on research at the University and would expand Purdue's ties to the military and U.S. industry.

The start of aeronautical engineering at Purdue traces its roots to Sunday, June 8, 1919, when Lieutenant George Haskins, Purdue Class of 1916, flew onto the campus from McCook Field in Dayton, where he was based.

Haskins was born in Waterville, Ohio, outside of Toledo, in 1892, before Orville and Wilbur Wright accomplished the first flight at Kitty Hawk, North Carolina, in 1903. Like many young men of his time, Haskins did not start his college studies at the age of eighteen. He was twenty years old when he enrolled at Valparaiso University in northern Indiana. He spent his freshman and sophomore years there and came to Purdue as a junior.[4]

A handsome young man who combed his hair straight back, Haskins's degree was in mechanical engineering. After graduation, he did work using compressed water to pump water out of the ground. Three days after the United States entered the Great War in Europe in April 1917, Haskins enlisted and applied for the Army Air Service. His application was accepted, and he did flight training and also studied at MIT. Upon completion of this work, he was assigned to McCook Field in Dayton and became an assistant to the chief of engineering. McCook was an important training and flight-testing field.[5]

Haskins came to Purdue during Gala Week 1919, which included commencement and alumni reunions. He carried with him a petition he said was from the

Dayton, Ohio Alumni Club, asking the Board of Trustees to establish aeronautical engineering at Purdue.

The *Purdue Exponent* reported on Haskins's upcoming visit in its final edition of the semester on Sunday, June 8, 1919: "Lieutenant George W. Haskins of Dayton, Ohio, will . . . come [to Gala Week] in a plane. He will arrive Sunday or Monday morning with resolutions of the Dayton Alumni Association drawn up at a meeting of that association Friday at the English Club. Haskins will probably be here all week and demonstrate aerial maneuvers with his plane. . . . This proposed means of journeying to an alumni reunion and Gala Week events will mark an epoch in the history of the university—since it will be the first time that an alumnus has returned in an airplane."[6]

The story was picked up by the Lafayette newspapers. The *Lafayette Morning Journal* reported on Monday, June 9, "Lieutenant Haskins has been stationed [in] Dayton and left there at 11:20 [Sunday] morning. Although flying against a strong wind and having to stop twenty miles east of Indianapolis because of lubrication troubles in the engine and again in Indianapolis for gas and oil, he reached here and alighted on Stuart Field at 5:20. Besides attending the commencement exercises and visiting his fraternity brothers at Delta Upsilon house, Lt. Haskins is also here on official business in the matter of securing the cooperation of the university in carrying on research work in aerial navigation and by so doing recognizing the air service as one of the more important branches of military service. Lieutenant Haskins stated that should the university decide to enter upon the research work it would be one of the pioneers among the colleges and universities of the country in the work and would greatly enhance its reputation as a technical institution in doing so."[7]

As the home of Wilbur and Orville Wright, Dayton was the right place for launching a resolution on aeronautical engineering at Purdue. But despite Haskins's claims it didn't come from the Dayton Alumni Club, since there was no official Dayton Alumni Club at that time. If there was an unofficial club, it might have had just one member: Haskins. It's doubtful the story in the *Exponent* was in error because it even included the location where the vote on the resolution was taken—the "English Club." Perhaps Haskins just met with one or two other Purdue alumni in Dayton, and they named themselves the Dayton Club. However it happened, the proposal took hold.[8]

Haskins arrived on campus too late for his resolution to make the Board of Trustees agenda during Gala Week, but he continued to press his case. He wrote about the potential of flight in an article in the *Purdue Engineering Review* 1920.[9]

Purdue did start an aeronautical engineering program in 1921 with four elective courses in the School of Mechanical Engineering. An aerodynamics laboratory with an airplane and several flight engines was opened on campus in Heavilon Hall.

The establishment of aeronautical engineering at Purdue emerged from a military pilot who believed that the Great War had established the important role flight would play in the future of the United States and the world.

After visiting Purdue with his proposal, Haskins became upset that the Army was not developing a strong air service and was instead selling its planes, many of them to "barnstormers" of the day who flew them at community events around the country, demonstrating flight and giving people rides for a fee. In 1922, he left the Army with the rank of captain and went to work in private industry.[10]

PURDUE MEMORIAL STUDENT UNION

Also in the immediate post-Great War period, the University was nearing a decision to honor the sixty-seven alumni who died in the service between 1917 and 1918. Since the beginning of the twentieth century, Purdue students, faculty, administrators, and alumni had had a common goal of creating a space where Boilermakers could gather. Students had begun gathering in a room above Southworth's Bookstore in Purdue Village. Other universities had built or were in the process of building facilities that were named student unions.

In 1912, Purdue began moving toward construction of a student union, but progress was slow. George Hayes, who would graduate in 1912, proposed the idea; the student council endorsed it; and the Class of 1912 made a financial contribution to the project. On April 17, 1912, a union financial campaign committee was formed and graduating seniors pledged to donate $5 per person to the project.[11]

At the close of the Great War, it was decided the new facility would be a Memorial Union, honoring the men who lost their lives while serving in the military, and also those who served. The determination to honor Boilermakers from the Great War ultimately helped the fundraising for the Memorial Union to succeed.

According to the University history of the Union, on November 11, 1920, the second anniversary of Armistice Day, "student leaders called a mass meeting in Fowler Hall to ask for student pledges. It is rumored that in order to ensure participation by all they locked the doors and would not let anyone leave until a pledge had been assigned. All such fundraising drives were completely separate from University programs and were sponsored mostly by students, interested faculty members, and friends of Purdue."[12]

On September 12, 1920, a headline in the *Purdue Exponent* said that students had pledged $326,335. Coupled with $235,000 from alumni, that made a total of $561,335. In an emotional talk, popular professor Thomas Moran said: "We are here today to honor the [men] who died and the [more than] 4,000 who served in the recent war, representing Purdue, and it is for them that we are to erect a great and holy monument. Let us break ground in the spring, lay the corner stone on Memorial Day, and dedicate the building when the 1922 class graduates.... We must erect upon this campus a Union Building which will be an object lesson to future generations. Here is our chance to do something for God, for Country, and for Purdue."[13]

As often happens, the project got started a little later than Moran projected. Groundbreaking was June 13, 1922, and the cornerstone was set in place November 25, 1922.

The Purdue history of the Memorial Union states, "In August of 1923 a crowd watched cranes put the twenty-five-ton sections of milled limestone in place to form arches over the main entrance of the building. Construction continued through the latter part of 1923 when funds were exhausted. The following year the Purdue Union Association formed as a separate financing corporation and secured a loan of $200,000. In order to support payment of the loan each student paid a fee of $4 per semester."[14]

Only partially completed, the Memorial Union opened September 9, 1924, at the beginning of the academic year. About $400,000 was needed for completion. According to the official Purdue history of the Memorial Union, when it opened, "the main floor had temporary pine floors and the walls and ceilings had not yet been plastered. The second floor was not sufficiently finished in order to be available for use. Construction continued as funds became available and the original building was completed in 1929."[15] The names of those who completed their pledges to the Union fund drive dating back to 1920 are inscribed on a bronze display on the first floor of the Memorial Union.

The Memorial Union would continue to be added to and remodeled through the years. The first part of the Union Club hotel was added in 1929. The east wing, including the bowling lanes and the anniversary drawing room, were added in 1936, the same year that the South Ballroom was added.[16]

From the beginning, however, the center of the building was the Great Hall, where the men who lost their lives in the Great War were memorialized. During the years that followed more Boilermakers who lost their lives in other wars were also memorialized. Since 1941, a glass case has held the battle flag that the Purdue Company B took with them to the Texas-Mexico border in 1916. Memorial services are held in the Great Hall every November 11.

ROTC FORMS AT PURDUE

With the Student Army Training Corps (SATC) program in full swing, the student cadet corps at Purdue was suspended from July 1, 1918 to January 1919. It was then reorganized into a Reserve Officer Training Corps (ROTC), according to the terms of the National Defense Act of 1916.

Lieutenant Robert Kirkwood was back with Purdue in the spring of 1919. He led six other officers and eleven non-commissioned officers in military training. The reorganization he led resulted in an artillery unit replacing the previous infantry unit.

In an article headlined "The New ROTC at Purdue," the 1919 *Debris* reported, "Taps was sounded over the old Cadet Corps and the SATC at Purdue on March 1, 1919 and on March 3 the reveille of the Field Artillery Reserve Officers Training Corps [ROTC] was the initiation of a new era in the military life of Purdue. . . . By her record in the war Purdue mapped out her own military future. Her technically trained sons allied themselves in larger number with the field artillery than with any other arm. That indicated her keen interest in field artillery. The fact that an unusually large percentage of those men became officers in their chosen arm clearly showed that Purdue was eminently fitted to train the field artillery officers of the future."[17]

Purdue's was one of twenty-two field artillery units established at universities across the nation, and the Boilermakers considered theirs the biggest and the best. The corps was organized with a headquarters company, five batteries, and the military band. About 850 students were enrolled.

Although the ROTC had been inaugurated under the terms of the National Defense Act of 1916, the war had slowed the ability of universities to commission a large number of officers. By 1920, Army ROTC units at universities had only produced 133 officers. Following the war, the United States adopted a stance of isolationism towards international affairs, resulting in a smaller Army. During those years, university ROTC units nationwide focused on producing officers for the Army Reserve.[18]

With one of the best and biggest university armories in the nation, the Purdue ROTC program continued to grow and excel through the 1920s.

"Purdue University supports and is honored by one of the best ROTC units in the country," the *Debris* wrote in 1929. "Best because it is a specialty branch, that is, it is a completely motorized unit. In this one course for which University credit is given, more opportunity for gain is given to the student than in any other curricular activity. In this course mathematics, history, grammar, directness, conciseness, and the leadership of men as groups and as individuals is properly stressed and thoroughly covered."[19]

GEORGE HASKINS RETURNS

In 1929, Haskins, who had flown into Purdue during Gala Week 1919 with a proposal to create an aeronautic engineering program, was recruited to Purdue to lead the program he had proposed ten years earlier. It was the year before Neil Armstrong was born in Wapakoneta, Ohio.

Haskins had a reputation at Purdue for working very hard. His wife, Dorothy, had died, and he poured himself into his job day and night.

"For eight years of turbulent development, [he] carried a tremendous load," H. B. Knoll wrote in *The Story of Purdue Engineering*. "In his time the Air Corp made substantial donations of equipment, and the Supercharger Laboratory placed in the vanguard of all such laboratories in the country. A wind tunnel of a twelve-inch cross section was constructed for tests on models. In one period, Haskins taught nine different courses, counseled students, prepared laboratory plans, and 'supposedly,' he said, did research."[20] In 1937, Haskins left the University, having transformed aeronautical engineering at Purdue. What had been a small program in mechanical engineering would soon become its own school. He moved to the Civil Aeronautics Administration.

Haskins was recalled to active duty when the United States entered World War II. In addition to several commands, he was sent to MIT to research on superchargers. He also served in the Indochina theater during the war.[21]

A newspaper article written about him during the war stated:

> A few years back the Glenn Martin Aviation Company was sponsoring teams of combat fliers for test purposes. The teams had good planes, some of the best in the air in those days, but they were having difficulty in attaining proper altitude for certain maneuvers.
>
> "Get hold of George Haskins," a company executive said. "If anyone can straighten us out, he can."
>
> "So, George Haskins was ordered to work on the problem, and after only two weeks of intensive study and work, he set an altitude record which still stands for the particular [censored] type of plane: 37,000 feet. Since then, many of the combat planes in use in the U.S. evidence marks of his influence in cowling, arrangement, and method of cooling.[22]

Haskins retired as a full colonel at the end of the war and went back to the Civil Aeronautics Administration. His son, George Haskins Jr. studied at Purdue before entering the Air Force in 1950. He flew F-86 fighter-bomber jets during the Korean War. After leaving the military, he became a pilot for United Airlines.[23]

George W. Haskins Sr. retired in Santa Monica, California. He had spent a lifetime in aviation, going from flying open cockpit biplanes made of wood and muslin to welcoming the jet age. In his retirement, the space age emerged—with a particular connection.

In 1928, when he married Dorothy, his closest friend had served as his best man. The friend was an executive at Standard Oil. Haskins knew him from back in the days when they served in the air service at McCook Field. In those days, flying was everything for these guys. The best man not only stood beside Haskins at the wedding, he also flew the newlyweds on their honeymoon. That best man was Edwin Aldrin. Edwin Aldrin had a son, Edwin Aldrin Jr. Everyone called him "Buzz."

On July 20, 1969, Haskins sat in a chair in his living room and watched the NASA Apollo 11 mission on his television.[24] He was born before the first flight took place at Kitty Hawk. He helped develop early flight techniques and aeronautical engineering design. And that night he watched Neil Armstrong, who had been educated in the aeronautics program that he had proposed and advanced, step down the ladder of a lunar lander and set his boot on the surface of the Moon, saying, "That's one small step for a man, and one giant leap for mankind."

Waterville, Ohio, where Haskins was born, is only seventy miles from Wapakoneta, Ohio, where Armstrong was born and went to high school.

The other man who walked on the Moon that day was the son of Haskins' best friend—Buzz Aldrin. Few people had a closer personal relationship to that incredible accomplishment than Haskins.[25]

It was an incredible day for the entire world. It was a breathtaking day for George Haskins, and it was fitting that a man who did so much to advance aviation and ultimately space exploration should see the completion of a dream that had filled the hearts and minds of people for millennia: man on the Moon.

On August 27, 1969, thirty-eight days after the moon landing, George Haskins died in Los Angeles. He was seventy-seven years old. He had a great life. He had lived to see one of the most incredible moments in the history of the world.

And he was part of it.

6

THE PURDUE UNIVERSITY AIRPORT

A windsock was hung from a dead tree, the stone ring was in place, and the government representatives were notified by wire that the requirements had been met.

H. B. KNOLL, *THE STORY OF PURDUE ENGINEERING*

David Ross had dreams. Big dreams. Throughout his life he never stopped dreaming. And for most of his life, his dreams centered on Purdue University.

A wealthy industrialist who had grown up in Brookston and nearby Lafayette, Ross graduated from Purdue in 1893 with a degree in electrical engineering. He started working on the family farm but in time became an inventor, a manufacturer, a financer, and businessman.

Early in the twentieth century, when automobiles were growing in popularity, he developed a steering gear, patented it, and in 1906 created a company, Ross Gear, to manufacture it. He had eighty-eight patents in his life and he started several other successful companies in Lafayette in addition to Ross Gear.

In 1920, he was recruited to Purdue to help raise funds for the Memorial Union, and on July 1, 1921, he was named to the Purdue Board of Trustees. Six years later he was elected president of the board.

The morning after Ross's election to the Board, he walked into the office of Purdue President Edward Elliott, located in Eliza Fowler Hall. He told Elliott he had resigned. Elliott was stunned, as he thought Ross was resigning from the Purdue board.

He wasn't. He was resigning his executive positions with his companies, and for the rest of his life, he devoted his efforts full time to Purdue. He died June 28, 1943.

The dreams Ross had for Purdue required land for the University. He first looked north of the campus. In conjunction with famed playwright and Purdue alumnus George Ade, Ross acquired the land that became Ross-Ade Stadium.

By 1929, when George Haskins arrived to take over aeronautical engineering, Ross was looking southwest of the agriculture campus. To everyone else looking at the land it was a farm field, just as it had been since the nineteenth century when the area was developed. But he saw something else. Ross saw an airport, and he purchased the farm field for Purdue. His dream would lead Purdue to be the first university in the nation with its own airport.[1]

And that airport would help attract a young aviator named Amelia Earhart to Purdue. Already the first woman to fly solo across the Atlantic Ocean, she became an inspiration for women throughout the world and served as a career counselor to female students at Purdue and an advisor to its aeronautical engineering program. She died in 1937, attempting to fly around the world roughly at the equator: an "adventure," as she called it, which had been financed in large part through Purdue.

As the United States prepared to enter World War II, the airport that Ross had envisioned would become among the first in the nation to train young men needed for the Army Air Corps. It would become an important airport for the military throughout the war. And during the 1950s and in the decades that followed, it would play a key role in attracting students to Purdue who would later become astronauts who explored space, including the first and last men to walk on the moon in the twentieth century.

The original dream Ross had for the land was much more than an airport. He envisioned a huge area that, firstly, would continue the University's research in railroad engine technology on a figure-eight track that created two circles. In the middle of one circle Purdue would work on lighter than air ships—dirigibles. The other circle would be devoted to airplanes.[2]

The year 1929 marked the beginning of the Great Depression, and it forced Ross to scale back his dreams. But in 1930, he made several donations of land he had purchased for $37,000, giving it to the recently created Purdue Research Foundation. On November 1, 1930, Haskins and others met representatives of the U.S. Coast and Geodetic Survey and the U.S. Department of Commerce at the site.

Purdue English Department professor H. B. Knoll wrote in his 1963 book *The Story of Purdue Engineering*: "The site, it was agreed, would be placed on government maps as the Purdue University Airport when a windsock was installed and the landing area [was] marked by a ring of light colored limestone. Before the day ended, the windsock was hung from a dead tree, the stone ring was in place, and the government representatives were notified by wire that the requirements had been met."[3] It was an emergency landing site.

EDWARD ELLIOTT, DAVID ROSS, LAWRENCE "CAP" ARETZ, AND THE PURDUE AIRPORT

The man who had originally placed the dream of an airport in the minds of David Ross and Purdue President Edward C. Elliott was a World War I military veteran named Lawrence Aretz, known to everyone as "Cap"—short for "Captain."

Aretz was a native of Minnesota who served in the Army during the Great War. He never went overseas, and he nearly died during the flu pandemic. After the war, he learned to fly at Chanute Field in Rantoul, Illinois. Upon leaving the military, he barnstormed around the country, doing stunts and selling rides to people who were eager to see the earth from above. He also flew for Standard Oil. Eventually, he came to Lafayette to work for businessman Charles Shambaugh as the pilot manager at the city's first airport.[4]

Charles Shambaugh was described as "one of the mechanical enthusiasts of his time, an early builder and driver of racing cars, a longtime automobile dealer, and a contributor to automobile design."[5] Unsurprisingly, Shambaugh's enthusiasm for all things mechanical turned to flight, and in 1928 he opened an airfield at the southeast corner of Eighteenth Street and Teal Road in Lafayette, which he named for himself. Shambaugh Field was the city's first airport.

Dr. A. C. Arnett, cofounder of the Arnett Clinic in Lafayette, was also a strong advocate for an airfield in the city, and very influential in the community. Arnett was a 1907 graduate of Purdue's short-lived medical school. He had been a part of the medical team at Camp Llano Grande in Texas, where the University's Battery B was stationed in 1916 (see Chapter Three).

Shambaugh Field was a source of pride for Lafayette and set the city on a path toward becoming a center for aviation in Indiana. The eighty-acre field was large enough to seemingly accommodate all airplanes of the time. Shambaugh purchased one hundred lanterns and placed them on fenceposts to mark his field for night landings, and qualified as an emergency landing for air mail carriers. According to Knoll in *The Story of Purdue Engineering*, "in five years the (airport) compiled a virtually faultless record. Its planes carried 15,000 passengers and flew 300,000 miles without accident. On one occasion the [airport] was host to an air circus, staged with the help of the American Legion, that was attended by 10,000 spectators. Seventy pilots were trained there."[6] Among those newly trained pilots were Purdue students, who took streetcars and walked to reach the field for their training.

Two of the passengers who flew out of Shambaugh Field were Purdue's president and chairman of the board, Edward Elliott and David Ross. There, they met pilot manager Lawrence Aretz. Knoll wrote, "Aretz earned a large share of the credit for getting aviation started at Purdue. He was at Shambaugh Airport one blustery winter day when someone who said he was President Elliott phoned to ask if he could be flown to Indianapolis to make a speech. The highways were impassable because of snow and ice. Aretz thought that he was being kidded but said that of course he would make the trip. To his surprise, a car pulled up a few minutes later and out stepped Elliott. The two of them worked together to clear the snow away from the plane, and the flight down and back was a total success. Elliott said afterward that the trip had sold him on aviation." Aretz also took Ross on flights over his farmland, convincing him in turn of the bright future of aviation.[7]

While Shambaugh Field was popular with the community and with air enthusiasts, because of the Great Depression it was not financially successful. In 1933, Shambaugh closed the airport and started farming the land. But before he closed, he suggested that Elliott and Ross take Aretz to manage the new Purdue Airport.

The Purdue Airport wasn't much when it first opened in 1930. As Knoll wrote, "the windsock hung lonely and forlorn over empty farmland. One summer the airport, such as it was, had to be closed because, by pure inadvertence, some of the land was plowed and planted. Those doldrums were ended through relief grants made by the Civil Works Administration and support from Ross. The land was graded and drained, and a rotary beacon, course markers, and a boundary and hazard lighting system were installed. Most importantly, a hangar-laboratory was erected, and on September 4, 1934, the airport was officially opened for business as a going concern."[8]

Perhaps not coincidentally, on September 26–28 of that year, Elliott was in New York City taking part in the fourth annual Women's Conference on Current Problems at the Astoria Hotel. Elliott spoke at the conference, as did Amelia Earhart. Elliott and Earhart became fast friends. He invited her to speak at Purdue that fall, and in 1935 and 1936 she spent several weeks at a time on campus each semester working as an advisor to aeronautics and as a career counselor for female students. One of the things that attracted Earhart to Purdue was the fact that the university had its own airport on the campus.[9]

In 1936, David Ross, J. K. Lilly Sr. of the Eli Lilly Company in Indianapolis, and others provided Earhart with funds through the Purdue Research Foundation that she would use for the most exciting adventure of her adventurous life. She used the money to purchase an Electra 10-E airplane from Lockheed. She soon flew it to the Purdue Airport.[10]

In June 1937, Earhart flew that plane from Miami, beginning what she planned to be a flight around the world, roughly following the equator. On July 2, Earhart and her navigator Fred Noonan disappeared while attempting to find Howland Island in the Pacific Ocean. They were never found.

At the time of Earhart's disappearance, it had been only three years since the Purdue Airport had been officially opened "as a going concern." Nonetheless, it would play a key role in the future of the University and the nation.

7

PREPARING FOR WAR AT PURDUE

"Where are you going to get the pilots?"
GROVE WEBSTER

In 1896, Orville and Wilbur Wright took an active interest in human flight that consumed them for the rest of their lives and led, in 1903, to success at Kitty Hawk, North Carolina.

In 1896, Purdue University was a school of 634 students. The pride of the campus was a brand new Heavilon Hall, built to replace the previous engineering building that had been destroyed by fire only two years earlier. Heavilon Hall included a high bell and clock tower on its front side that served as an exclamation point! It had no other purpose than to proclaim that Purdue Engineering had arrived as one of the elite programs in the world.

Also, in 1896, in New York State, Grove Webster was born. Webster would turn seven years old in 1903, the year the Wright brothers flew at Kitty Hawk. When Webster was born, his parents knew nothing about Purdue University, far away in Indiana. And flight was still considered a dream. But forty-three years later, Webster, flight, and Purdue would come together at the first university airport in the nation and play an important leadership role in preparing the United States for another world war.

Webster was born at a time when many people still felt it was impossible or at least very improbable that people would ever fly in heavier-than-air machines. He was about fourteen years old when he saw his first flying machine. He served in the 163rd U.S. Bombing Squadron during the Great War.[1]

After leaving the Army where he had been trained to fly, he continued working in aviation, and in 1930 established an airport directory that covered most of the United States.[2] That was also the year that Purdue Board of Trustees Chairman David Ross purchased the first of several parcels of land and donated it to the University for use as an airport. It wasn't much at first, and surely people must have wondered what would become of this airfield.

As Webster worked to advance flight in the private sector after the Great War, he watched the United States military fall behind European nations in air power. In 1939 the U.S. Army had 4,502 pilots. 2,007 of them were on active duty, 2,187 were reserve officers, and 308 were in the national guard.[3]

Seeing the need for more pilots as the possibility of the United States entering the war in Europe grew ever greater, in December 1938 President Franklin D. Roosevelt announced a program within the newly created Civil Aeronautics Authority. The experimental program would use universities to train civilian pilots who could become part of the Army Air Force if and when they were needed. It was a similar approach as that being used in some European nations, including Germany and Italy, to increase air power.

For years the U.S. military had used Reserve Officer Training Corps (ROTC) programs at universities to prepare officers in the event of war. Roosevelt and others believed universities could also be used to train young men as pilots. They looked for schools that had airports close to campus—and Purdue was the first university to have an airport on campus. Thirteen universities were selected for the new program including Purdue, which became the first to get its training underway. Purdue was authorized to train fifty students, more than any other university.[4]

Purdue launched its program on February 16, 1939. The next day the Lafayette *Journal and Courier* reported: "Flight training of the first of fifty Purdue University students who are expected to qualify by June 30 for the 'Private Pilot Rating' as evidenced by an 'Airman Certificate' issued by the Civil Aeronautics Authority was launched here yesterday afternoon on the University Airport. . . . The start of the training of the Purdue crop of fifty 'fledglings' selected from some two hundred applicants represents the first step in the program designed to train some 20,000 persons as pilots [nationally] within the next two years."[5]

The Purdue program was led by airport operations manager Lawrence "Cap" Aretz, who hired four assistants to help with the training. The *Journal and Courier* reported, "Captain L. I. Aretz, airport operations manager, who is in direct charge of the flight training has flown over 10,000 hours since 1917 when he started his career in the Army air service. He has successfully trained pilots for years and during the past four years alone has given flight instruction to over two hundred different individuals at the Purdue Airport."[6] Aretz was helped by Joe Halsmer, whom he had taught to fly, and Joe's brothers, John and Francis Halsmer. Their Halsmer Airport, which had opened in 1931 near where I-65 and Indiana 38 East are now located, is significant in the aviation history of Tippecanoe County.

On June 16, the *Journal and Courier* announced the training was complete at Purdue and would have been finished June 1, but for inclement weather. There were no injuries and no damage to the airplanes.

The paper said, "The airport holds the distinction of not only having the largest number of novice pilots assigned to it, but also of having the first students in the air under the program, the first to solo, and the first to receive private ratings."[7]

All fifty Purdue students received their pilot's license. More than three hundred young men were trained nationwide that year.

With the success of the experimental program, Roosevelt signed the Civilian Pilot Training Act on June 27, 1939, with a goal of training eleven thousand pilots during the upcoming academic year.

WALKER "BUD" MAHURIN

In the summer of 1939, twenty-year-old Walker M. "Bud" Mahurin entered the Civilian Pilot Training Program.[8]

Born in Benton Harbor, Michigan, he grew up in Fort Wayne, Indiana, and at the age of twelve had his first flight in an airplane. He loved it but was still unsure he wanted to be a pilot.[9] He graduated from Southside High School in 1937 and wanted to attend Purdue to study engineering, but his family did not have the money to send him. He worked for a year to save money for college and entered Purdue to study engineering in the fall of 1938, according to records in the University Registrar's office.[10]

Working fifty hours a week to pay for tuition, room, and board, Mahurin had little time for study, and consequently, limited academic success. In the summer of 1939, he worked in the Fort Wayne City Light and Power Plant as a secretary-clerk. He also took courses at the Indiana Extension Center in Fort Wayne to make up for courses he had not passed at Purdue. And, crucially, he entered the Civilian Pilot Training Program.[11]

In his autobiography, *Honest John: The Autobiography of Walker M. Mahurin*, he doesn't say where he took the flight training. But the Civilian Pilot Training Program didn't begin in Fort Wayne until December 1941, so it's likely he flew at the Purdue airport and took ground classes there.

Mahurin registered for the draft on October 16, 1940. He was enrolled at Purdue in the 1940–41 school year, but his outside work continued to interfere with his studies. The University recommended he take a year off. He applied to the Army Air Corps, and in September 1941 he was sent to Oklahoma to begin military flight training. It was three months before the Pearl Harbor attack.

He went through extensive training as an Army fighter pilot and shipped out for England on January 6, 1943. In May 1943, on his first B-17 escort mission flying a P-47 Thunderbolt, his plane was damaged by enemy fire and he had to return to base. In July, while on a practice flight over England, he got too close to an American B-24 bomber, with the result that his plane was badly damaged and he had to bail out.[12]

Things got better. He quickly became an "ace," having shot down five enemy planes. In November he became the first U.S. pilot in Europe to shoot down ten enemy planes, making him a "double ace." In March 1944, he had to bail out of his plane and was guided to safety with help from the French Resistance. Because of his knowledge of the Resistance, which could help the Germans if he were captured, he transferred to the Pacific theater and was shot down again. He was credited with 20.75 aerial victories in the war. After the war he returned to Purdue and finished his degree in aeronautical engineering, graduating in 1949. He later served as a pilot in the Korean War and had 3.5 more "kills," was shot down again, and spent sixteen months being tortured as a prisoner of war. He was the only U.S. pilot to shoot down enemy planes in both theaters during World War II and in Korea.[13]

Upon his death at the age of ninety-one on May 11, 2010, Doug Lantry, an historian at the National Museum of the United States Air Force at Wright-Patterson Air Force Base near Dayton, Ohio said, "[His) name is familiar to almost everybody in the Air Force. . . . He was known as a very courageous, skilled, and tenacious fighter pilot."[14]

GROVE WEBSTER, THE CIVILIAN PILOT TRAINING PROGRAM, AND PURDUE

Even before Roosevelt signed the Civilian Pilot Training Act in June 1939, Webster was invited to Washington, D.C. by the new chairman of the Civil

Aeronautics Authority, Edward J. Nobel. Nobel asked Webster to join the Civilian Pilot Training Program as chief of the private flying section. Webster was told to organize the program, and he decided to build on what the military had learned during the Great War.[15]

The Civilian Pilot Training Program had their man. Soon Purdue would also have their man to lead its airport for more than thirty years. His name was Grove Webster.

Webster wrote an article for *Aerospace Historian* magazine in 1979, explaining the origins of the Civilian Pilot Training Program. "The World War I program was set up to send the enlisted cadets to one of the participating colleges or universities for an eight-week ground school and, upon successful completion, to a military flying school for flight instruction," Webster wrote. "[I] . . . suggested we follow a similar pattern. The ground school would be taught in a college or university, and the flight training would be given by a fixed-base operator at an airport convenient to the institution."[16] The program was tailor-made for Purdue.

Although the program gave a big boost to the U.S. preparedness for war, there were mixed views of it. A U.S. Centennial of Flight Commission report said, "The military establishment was initially unenthusiastic about the concept, quite unimpressed by any program initiated and administered by civilians. Also, Congress was split along mostly party lines as to the value of the [program]. Isolationists branded the program as provocative saber-rattling that threatened the nation's neutrality; others slammed it as a New Deal pork barrel waste of tax dollars, while supporters touted the positive impacts on the aviation industry and the defense value of a vastly enlarged base of trained pilots."[17]

Webster visited the universities who were selected for the training and received an especially warm welcome from Purdue President Edward Elliott and Board of Trustees Chairman David Ross—the leading individuals in creating the school's airport. In fact, Elliott told Webster that Purdue would like to have him take a position at the university.

In September of 1939, World War II officially began in Europe with the German invasion of Poland. According to the U.S. Centennial of Flight Commission, "After the invasion of Poland, the military value of the Civilian Pilot Training Program became obvious even to the program's detractors. The United States started to evaluate its ability to fight an air war and the results were appalling. Pilots, instructors, and training aircraft were all in short supply. Acknowledging the shortage of trained pilots, both the U.S.

Army and Navy reluctantly waived certain 'elimination' courses for Civilian Pilot Training Program graduates and allowed them to proceed directly into pilot training."[18]

On May 16, 1940, Roosevelt went to a joint session of Congress. Among his requests, as he feared U.S. involvement in the war was approaching, was $1 billion for national defense, including an Air Corps of fifty thousand planes.

"One obvious question was, 'Where are you going to get the pilots?'" Webster wrote. "The immediate result of this action was a greatly expanded Civilian Pilot Training Program. The budget for fiscal year 1940–1941 was increased from five million to thirty-seven million dollars. The number of participating schools was increased from 400 to over 700."[19]

It eventually grew much larger. Ultimately, the Civilian Pilot Training Program trained 435,165 people and worked with 1,132 colleges and universities and 1,460 flight schools.[20] At Purdue, Lawrence "Cap" Aretz and his staff, who were operating the airport under a contract with the University, trained 639 students in the Civilian Pilot Training Program.[21]

The Civilian Pilot Training Program Act included a provision introduced by then-Representative Everett Dirksen of Illinois, stating that "none of the benefits of training or programs shall be denied on account of race, creed, or color." That opened the program to women and African Americans. African American programs were mostly at historically black colleges and universities such as Tuskegee Institute, in Alabama. Two thousand African American pilots were trained.[22] Four women's colleges had training, but female pilots were also admitted to the program at coed universities. Purdue announced in October of 1939 that it would accept women applicants.[23]

With the expansion of the Civilian Pilot Training Program, Webster saw it becoming more and more under the control of the military. On October 8, 1941, he resigned from the program and started a flight consulting service. In announcing his departure, General Donald H. Connolly, Administration of Civil Aeronautics, said: "It is with deep regret that Mr. Webster's resignation is being accepted. The success of the civilian pilot training program owes a great deal to Mr. Webster's untiring efforts and able direction. He has done a magnificent job in a field that had to be pioneered at every step."[24]

One of his first clients in Webster's consulting business was Purdue. On July 1, 1942, he came to work at the University Airport on a temporary basis that soon became permanent. Among his titles for the next thirty-one years was manager of the airport.

The Purdue Airport had been a civilian facility since its inception as an emergency landing field in 1930. But all that changed after December 7, 1941. Everything changed after December 7, 1941.

JAMES DOOLITTLE JR.

Among the pilot's licenses secured by Purdue's Civilian Pilot Training Program was that of James H. Doolittle Jr.

Born in San Antonio, Texas, in 1920, he was the son of James H. "Jimmy" Doolittle, who was among the most famous pilots of his day. Doolittle Sr. was an aviation pioneer who served in World War I. After the war he had piloted coast-to-coast flights, set speed records, and won flying races. In 1929 he became the first person to take off, fly, and land using only his instruments. He was often featured on radio and movie newsreels that covered his remarkable accomplishments in the exciting field of flight.

In the fall of 1938, the junior Doolittle enrolled at Purdue, according to records in Purdue's Office of the Registrar. Purdue had an airport, and the junior Doolittle had his heart set on following in his father's famous footsteps.[25] He studied mechanical engineering at Purdue. Aeronautical engineering courses were then in the mechanical engineering program, and no doubt Doolittle took as many aeronautical engineering classes as he could. In mid-1941, as the drums of war were beating, Dean of Engineering A. A. Potter created a four-year program in mechanical engineering, leading to a degree in aeronautical engineering.

The senior Doolittle visited his son on campus several times, including in the spring of 1940 when he spoke at the University's first annual aviation banquet. The banquet was sponsored by the Purdue Flying and Glider Club. Doolittle Jr. was a member of the Flying Club, which might explain how Purdue was able to bring the famed pilot to campus for a talk.[26]

Doolittle Jr. was popular at Purdue, especially at the airport. He was on his way to fulfilling his dream, following in his father's footsteps.

The fame of the senior Doolittle, already huge before the U.S. entered World War II, was soon about to grow even greater. He would remain a legend in flight into the twenty-first century.

His son would follow him into the military—and soon, sooner than anyone expected.

War was on the horizon.

8

TWO BOILERMAKERS AND A SUNDAY THAT CHANGED THE WORLD

All hell broke loose and before we knew it, the air was full of Japanese planes. I picked the nearest thing and went after him. It was a funny feeling. I was plenty excited and I know I was mad because they caught us on Sunday morning. We went up and fixed them.

GEORGE WELCH

In the early morning skies over Honolulu, Hawaii on Sunday, December 7, 1941, George Welch gripped the stick of his Curtiss P-40 Warhawk. It was the defining moment in his life.

Anger, fear, determination, and adrenaline fueled his body as his hands finessed the controls of his fighter—roll, pitch, yaw—evading the Japanese pilots tailing him and the attacking enemy planes that swarmed everywhere.

Minutes earlier, he had been asleep after a long Saturday all-nighter of partying and poker, but now he was in a battle for his life while trying to save the lives of thousands of people below scurrying amid burning ships, hangars, and airplanes.

In less than two hours, the Japanese attack on Pearl Harbor resulted in severe damage or destruction to more than 350 United States aircraft and nineteen U.S. ships. 2,403 Americans were killed that morning, and more than one thousand more were wounded.[1]

Welch and his fellow fighter pilot Ken Taylor were two of the few U.S. pilots able to get into the air that morning. They believed they were the best pilots on the island: top guns. And they were right. Welch was credited with shooting down four—some accounts said six—enemy airplanes: 14 percent of the twenty-eight Japanese planes lost that day. Taylor was credited with four other kills. Together they destroyed more Japanese planes than any other individuals during the attack.

Just two years earlier, in the fall of 1939, Welch had started his junior year at Purdue University, switching his major from mechanical engineering to science. But when the sun set on December 7, 1941, he was a national hero amid a national disaster who would soon find himself in the Oval Office at the White House being congratulated by President Franklin D. Roosevelt.

Welch and Taylor received the Distinguished Service Cross medal for "extraordinary heroism in action." A lot of people thought they deserved the Medal of Honor.

Welch was born in Wilmington, Delaware on May 18, 1918, to George and Julia Schwartz. The boy's birth certificate lists his name as George Lewis Schwartz Jr.[2] The couple later had a second son and named him Dehn Schwartz. According to George Welch's 1954 obituary in the Wilmington, Delaware *Morning News*, "Although he was the son of George and Julia Schwartz, he and his brother Dehn used the name Welch from the time they were boys and shortly after the war had their names changed legally."[3] Welch was their mother's maiden name.

The parents were concerned that the name Schwartz sounded German and possibly Jewish at a time when there was prejudice against Germans and Jews. George Schwartz Sr. was a chemist with DuPont in Wilmington and had experienced prejudice due to his name.[4]

The name "George Schwartz" does not appear in Purdue *Debris* yearbooks during the time Welch was at Purdue. The name "George Welch" appears in the 1938 and 1939 issues of the *Debris* with his photo.[5] The 1940 U.S. Federal Census lists him as an Army flying cadet in Glendale, California. It lists his name as "George S. Welch, user correction George L. Schwartz." In 1942, the Wilmington, Delaware *News Journal* stated Welch had been received at the White House by President Franklin Roosevelt, "who was surprised by the aviator's boyish appearance." It stated "Lieutenant Welch changed his name before he joined the air corps . . ."[6]

Welch had a wonderful childhood, filled with accomplishments and mischief. His five-foot-nine slender body wasn't built for football, but sports were not his ambition. He wanted to fly.

When he enrolled at Purdue in the fall of 1937, he had his future mapped out. He needed two years of college to be accepted into Army Air Corps flight training. He ended up completing two and a half years at Purdue and two years of mandatory ROTC before being called into active service. He also learned to fly at the Purdue Airport as part of Grove Webster's Civilian Pilot Training Program.[7]

Welch completed his education in the military. In February 1941, he was assigned to Wheeler Field in Oahu, Hawaii. He loved Hawaii.

"Fighter pilots, especially bachelor fighter pilots, were generally in great demand for the social whirl that the residents of Oahu used to mask their uneasiness at being on the ramparts for stopping further Japanese expansion in the Pacific," Al Blackburn wrote in his book *Aces Wild.* "The recently concluded Battle of Britain had greatly burnished the image of all fighter pilots as a romantic, devil-may-care band of brothers who jousted with death from dawn through sunset. George was certainly not one to jeopardize such a view. He entered into the social activities on the island with an enthusiasm only slightly less energized than his determination to maximize his flying skills."[8]

The day before the Japanese attack, Welch and Taylor were assigned temporarily to Haleiwa Field. It was in a remote area where pilots could simulate combat conditions. But there was no social life there. So, on Saturday evening, December 6, Welch and Taylor drove a car into the city. Their night on the town ended in an all-night poker game at the Wheeler Field officers' club. They had barely gotten to sleep when they were awakened by the attacking planes. Wearing his tuxedo pants from the night before, Taylor called Haleiwa Field and told them to get their airplanes ready. Both men hurried into Taylor's Buick hardtop and drove as fast as they could to the airfield. They took Taylor's car because a commander officer had confiscated Welch's car for speeding.[9]

During the attack, Welch's plane was hit by enemy fire four or five times. One of his three .30-caliber guns jammed, but he kept on going, even stopping at Wheeler Field at one point for more fuel and ammunition.

While visiting the White House and his hometown of Wilmington in May 1942, Welch told reporters, "We were mad when the attack came. For one thing, we'd just gotten to bed when they came over and had to get right up again. And we didn't expect an attack, any more than anyone else."[10]

FREDERICK L. MARTIN

Welch wasn't the only Purdue person at Pearl Harbor that morning.

In his classic book based on interviews with people who were there, *At Dawn We Slept: The Untold Story of Pearl Harbor*, Gordon Prange described the arrival of the new commander of the Hawaiian Air Corps thirteen months earlier: "On Saturday night, November 2, 1940, a tall gentleman walked down the gangplank [of the Army transport Leonard Wood]. He had wavy gray hair and thick brows shadowing pleasant eyes. His thin face with its oblong jaw, big nose, high forehead, and large ears looked more scholarly than military."[11]

The tall gentleman was Frederick L. Martin, Purdue class of 1908. Martin was born in 1882, long before flight, in the small Indiana town of Liberty. He studied mechanical engineering at Purdue and showed a strong interest in the Army. He joined the Army after graduation and was a major during the Great War, serving in the U.S. and in Europe with occupation forces. In 1920, he was assigned to the Army Air Service.[12]

In 1923, Martin was named to lead a U.S. Army team of four airplanes in a flight around the world, stopping every night along the way. After pilots were selected, along with a mechanic for each airplane, Martin led his team in training for the mission, which began in Seattle in April 1924. On April 30, Martin and his mechanic, Sergeant Alva Harvey, were reported missing in a blinding snowstorm in Alaska. They had survived a crash and were forced to walk through snow, fog, and bitter cold until they were found with only slight injuries on May 11.[13]

Unable to wait for the commander of the mission, the three other planes had gone ahead and reached Tokyo, Japan. The Army originally planned to get Martin a new plane and allow him to catch up with the others and lead the mission. But ultimately it was decided that too much time had elapsed, and the three remaining planes continued without him. A second plane was later lost off the coast of Iceland, but a replacement was sent. The two original planes and one replacement completed the first around-the-world flight, returning to Seattle on September 28, 1924.[14]

Martin thought he had lost his moment in history. But he was about to become a central figure in the events of history leading to U.S. entry into World War II.

In addition to military concerns, Martin was placed in a delicate interpersonal situation in Hawaii. Relations between various commanders were strained. Prange wrote: "[Martin's] assignment placed him in an ambiguous position. As commander of the Hawaiian Air Force, he had direct access to Major General H. H. 'Hap' Arnold, chief of the Army Air Corps [who was taught to fly by Purdue graduate Cliff Turpin], but he remained under the command of [Lt. General Walter] Short, a foot soldier to the soles of his boots. The situation could not have been more delicate, and indeed, Martin had received specific instructions from Arnold to end the undeclared civil war which had raged on Oahu between the Army, its Air Corps, and the Navy."[15]

According to Prange, one of Martin's goals was to provide an outlying field for his air forces so all the airplanes would not be positioned on the ground together in one place.[16]

Martin worked very well with Navy Rear Admiral Patrick N. L. Bellinger, and together they came up with a report that was classified until after the Pearl Harbor attack. The report was submitted March 31, 1941, and it predicted the Japanese attack. This "Joint Estimate Covering Joint Army and Navy Air Action in the Event of Sudden Hostile Action against Oahu or Fleet Units in the Hawaiian Area" (also known as the Martin-Bellinger Report), began with this summary:

> (a) Relations between the United States and Orange [code for Japan] are strained, uncertain, and varying.
> (b) In the past Orange has never preceded hostile actions by a declaration of war.
> (c) A successful, sudden raid, against our ships and Naval installations on Oahu might prevent effective offensive action by our forces in the Western Pacific for a long period.
> (d) A strong part of our fleet is now constantly at sea in the operating areas organized to take prompt offensive action against any surface or submarine force which initiates hostile action.
> (e) It appears possible that Orange submarines and/or an Orange fast raiding force might arrive in Hawaiian waters with no prior warning from our intelligence service.

A summary of "Possible Enemy Action" concluded:

> (a) A declaration of war might be preceded by:
>
> 1. A surprise submarine attack on ships in the operating area,
> 2. A surprise attack on Oahu including ships and installations in Pearl Harbor, or
> 3. A combination of these two.
>
> (b) It appears that the most likely and dangerous form of attack on Oahu would be an air attack. It is believed that at present such an attack would

most likely be launched from one or more carriers which would probably approach inside of three hundred miles.

(c) A single attack might or might not indicate the presence of more submarines or more planes awaiting to attack after defending aircraft have been drawn away by the original thrust.

(d) Any single submarine attack might indicate the presence of a considerable undiscovered surface force probably composed of fast ships accompanied by a carrier.

(e) In a dawn air attack there is a high probability that it could be delivered as a complete surprise in spite of any patrols we might be using and that it might find us in a condition of readiness under which pursuit would be slow to start . . .[17]

If the military took the report seriously, nothing was done to implement its recommendations. In fact, planes at Wheeler Airfield were ordered lined up in rows, close together. The stated reasons for this were to guard against sabotage and to avoid alarming the public about a possible attack. It ultimately made the airplanes easy targets for the attacking Japanese.[18]

On the morning of December 7, 1941, Martin was preparing breakfast at his home. He heard the explosions and immediately understood an attack was taking place. He grabbed his telephone and began issuing orders. He hurried to his headquarters and telephoned Bellinger to find out where the Japanese carriers were located. Bellinger had no idea.[19]

Prange said that, according to eyewitnesses, Martin's face was ashen and grim.[20] In addition to the attack, he was suffering from an ulcer that had broken open that morning.[21]

After the attack, Martin was relieved of command in Hawaii. But an investigation cleared him of any errors. In fact, he had predicted what would happen in details eleven months earlier in the Martin-Bellinger report.

Martin continued in military command positions. In June 1942, he took command of the Second District Army Air Forces Technical Training Command in St. Louis, Missouri, although poor health forced his retirement on July 31, 1944.

George Welch went on to become a World War II triple ace and hero. He flew 348 missions and continued to enjoy getting into mischief whenever the opportunity arose. He received the Distinguished Service Cross, the Silver Star, the Distinguished Unit Badge, the Distinguished Flying Cross with two Oak Leaf

Clusters, and the Air Medal with two Oak Leaf Clusters. He was credited with shooting down sixteen enemy planes and he had eight more "probables."

Welch reached the rank of major and retired from the military in 1944. On the recommendation of General "Hap" Arnold, he was hired by North American Aviation as a test pilot. At Muroc Field (later Edwards Air Force Base), he flew test flights on the XP-86 Sabre jet. On November 13, 1947, Welch flew the plane faster than the speed of sound, making him the second person to break the sound barrier. The first, officially, was Chuck Yeager—but to this day, many people claim Welch was first.[22]

On October 12, 1954, Welch flew an F-110A jet past the speed of sound. The plane had a reputation for stability problems and Welch ran into problems controlling it. The plane went out of control. Miraculously, the ejection seat fired, and Welch separated from the plane, but the parachute was torn, and he fell to earth at a high rate of speed. He still had a pulse when crews reached him, but moments later, it was over. He left a wife and two sons behind.

In January 1942, when Welch received the nation's second highest medal, the Distinguished Service Cross, it was pinned on his uniform by another man who had won the same award many years before—Major General Frederick Martin, a fellow Boilermaker.[23]

Martin and Welch died in 1954 and are buried within five hundred yards of one another at Arlington National Cemetery. Welch's grave marker reads "George Schwartz Welch."

9

THEY ALL WANTED IN ON IT

We had just returned from church. . . . When we heard the news it was like someone had died. My mother was sort of crying. Here I was fifteen years old and in no time at all I'd be in it. And I wanted to be in it.

MAURI WILLIAMSON

In the fall of 1940, a group of political leaders and influential private citizens, including famed aviator Charles Lindbergh, formed the America First Committee. Its goal was to keep the nation out of war. But the winds of war were already blowing in the United States. And as the months passed leading up to the December 7, 1941 attack on Pearl Harbor, some people were preparing.

In June 1940, the Purdue Board of Trustees voted "that the University take all possible steps to ensure the most efficient contribution to national defense," as required by the state and federal governments.[1] Moreover, the theme of the opening convocation at Purdue in September of 1940 was being fit to face the demands of the coming year.[2]

Those demands became even more demanding on September 16, 1940, fifteen months before the attack on Pearl Harbor, when U.S. President Franklin D. Roosevelt signed a law creating the nation's first draft during peacetime. Men between the ages of twenty-one and forty-five were required to register.

One month later, a group of Purdue students asked President Edward C. Elliott for his permission to demonstrate against the draft on campus, including the wearing of black armbands. The answer was a firm "no." In response, the students called for an immediate public meeting on campus. The response from Elliott was another firm "no"—no demonstration, no black armbands, no meeting. When Elliott said "no," he meant "no more discussion." And the students obeyed.

By 1941, if some people were still hoping for peace, many young men were anxious to get into the battle raging in Europe. Professor Elmer Bruhn arrived at Purdue in January 1941. He would later become the University's first head of Aeronautical Engineering and Air Transportation. He remembered a June 1941 meeting on campus with students in the Army Air Corps aeronautical engineering program. There were two twelve-week programs with fifty Army air cadets in each one. They came from forty universities; many had mechanical engineering degrees. They trained for flight operations and aircraft maintenance at Purdue and then did further training at Chanute Field in Rantoul, Illinois.

"As I entered one of the larger classrooms in the mechanical engineering building, the group as a whole appeared to be terribly downcast," Bruhn would later write. "When I asked the reason for all the gloom, they replied, 'Professor, the way the Hitler war machine is rolling to victories, we are fearful this war will be over before we finish at Chanute Field and get our commission.'"[3]

In 1941, a popular course in Purdue Physical Education titled PEM 12 included what was called a "torturous 550-yard obstacle run." Soon young men classified 4F and physically unfit for the armed services were taking the course hoping to improve their chances of serving. After completing it, about three hundred were accepted into the military.[4]

The December 7, 1941, Japanese attack on Pearl Harbor was a surprise to the United States and to the world. But the declarations of war that followed were not a surprise to everyone. Many people expected that the U.S. eventually would enter the war, but not so suddenly and not with so great a loss of ships, planes, and people.

ARTHUR SHAK

Sunshine was warming Honolulu, Hawaii by 7:00 a.m. on Sunday, December 7, 1941. The sky was partly filled with white clouds but mostly bright blue. The temperature was in the low 70s. There was a refreshing breeze blowing across the landscape from over the deep blue ocean water. It was another beautiful day in paradise for the 179,000 residents who called the city home.

People were awakening. Some planned to go to religious services. Some planned to go to golf courses or the beach. Some were looking forward to a day away from work, family gatherings, or leisurely meals with friends. The U.S.

national anthem played on loudspeakers in Navy ships docked at Pearl Harbor. It was a quiet, peaceful morning like Sundays had always been before.

In less than an hour the bombs started falling. Explosions destroyed buildings, planes, ships. They shattered lives.

That morning, Arthur "Art" Ten Sing Shak was an eighteen-year-old boy living in a Honolulu boarding house near the University of Hawaii, where he planned to enroll. Born a U.S. citizen in 1923 on the Hawaiian island of Kauai, he had graduated high school in the spring of 1941 and moved to Honolulu to prepare for his future. He worked in the mail room for Contractors Pacific Naval Air Bases at Pearl Harbor. Sunday was a free day for the young man with his entire life before him.

He heard the airplanes. He heard explosions. At first, he thought it was just routine training at the U.S. military base on the island ten miles from where he lived. "We didn't know anything was going on," Shak says. "We thought, hey, this is another nice Sunday morning. Planes flying around, there were planes flying around all the time—until we finally saw the big red sun painted on the planes. We said, 'These are Japanese planes. What are they doing here?' Announcements on the radio said, 'You guys are being bombed by enemy planes.' I thought it can't be. Japan is so far away. What are they doing here? You don't expect war when you've been at peace all this time."[5]

He and a friend later drove to the naval base. They never forgot the sight of ships on fire and sinking.[6].

The attack by 353 Japanese airplanes lasted one hour and fifteen minutes. When it was finished more than 2,400 U.S. personnel were dead. Nineteen U.S. Navy ships were destroyed or damaged. Airplanes and military buildings were in flames. Art Shak's life changed forever in that hour and fifteen minutes. Lives changed that early morning all around the world. Shak had friends in Hawaii of Japanese ancestry. The attack caused painful strain in their relationships.

Shak quickly became focused on joining the United States military in the war that had come to his homeland. The Army was looking for aviation cadets. He signed up and started training in September 1942. By March 1944 he was a navigator on a B-24 nicknamed "Guardian Angel" based near Foggia, Italy, where he flew bombing missions targeting munition supplies, manufacturing facilities, oil refineries, airfields, and railroad yards in Italy, Germany, Austria, and the Balkans. He was assigned to the 49th wing of the 15th Air Force. The ten-man crews lived in tents with the officers and enlisted men living separately. As an officer, Shak flew thirty-seven missions but received double credit for some because they were what he called "tough," bringing his total to fifty-one. His "number one tough mission" was bombing a German oil refinery in Ploesti, Romania.[7]

Shak is one hundred years old and among the few who remain in the twenty-first century to tell this story. His hair is white, and he smiles often. He is an excellent golfer, and played until he was 98. As he talks in the winter of 2024, he can see in his mind the groups of about thirty B-24s flying in formation, with anti-aircraft flack exploding all around them. After one flight there were sixty holes in Shak's airplane. On another they lost two of four engines, a fuel line was severed, and when they made an emergency landing on the tiny island of Vis in the Adriatic Sea they were completely out of fuel. "It's scary," Shak said in a 2020 interview. "I wouldn't say I was nervous, but I wasn't falling asleep. . . . You can see somebody get hit. You can hear things hitting against your plane. When it's not that bad, it's like somebody throwing rocks against your car. But when it's a direct hit like that—boom—it's a loud sound."[8]

They would get several days of rest after a mission. And then they would go back up again.

The war in Europe ended in May 1945 and Shak was sent to the Pacific Theater where he was a navigator on a C-47. Among his final military flights was a mission that began on Tinian Island. Less than twenty-four hours later, the Enola Gay would begin its mission from the same airfield carrying a uranium bomb codenamed "Little Boy." The Emperor of Japan announced surrender on August 15. Shak was there at the beginning and at the end of the war for the United States.[9]

Shak returned from the war with a Distinguished Flying Cross awarded for heroism and extraordinary achievements. He immediately enrolled on the G.I. Bill at Purdue (see Chapter 11) where his brother had considered going when the war first started. Shak lived in Cary Hall, studied civil engineering, and golfed on the university course as often as he could. He graduated in 1949 and received a master's degree in 1951. He was only able to go home about every other summer. But he loved Purdue.

Shak married his high school sweetheart. They had four children and three grandchildren. He worked in civil engineering in the continental U.S. and Hawaii. In 2019, he was awarded a Congressional Gold Medal given to Chinese Americans who served in World War II. The medal and ceremony acknowledged their patriotism and their struggles, including immigration restrictions. One in five Chinese Americans served during the war.

Shak celebrated his one hundredth birthday on October 3, 2023. In December 2023 he was awarded the French Legion of Honor, that nation's highest award. At the award ceremony in Hawaii, he sang the national anthem of France, "La Marseillaise."

He sang it in French—a language he had learned in high school and still remembered a full, long lifetime later.

HARRY MICHAEL: ORIGINS

On the day of the attack, Harry Michael, a 19-year-old student at Purdue, must have wondered what the "demands of the future" held—for himself and for his friends.

Michael was a sophomore. A small-town boy, the second oldest of five children, he was the son of Plomer Michael, a Great War veteran who farmed 150 acres on the banks of Turkey Creek, two and a half miles west of Milford, Indiana, southeast of South Bend. Harry had grown up among eight hundred people in the town of Milford, attending a one-room schoolhouse until he graduated into high school. He was a good student. He played on the football, basketball, and baseball teams. The school yearbook called him "our hard-driving substitute guard" on the basketball team. He was elected to the student council during his freshman, sophomore, and junior years, and was president of his junior class.[10]

He was a young man of strong convictions. When his gym shoes were stolen from his basketball locker, he thought the school should replace them. The school refused. So, he practiced in his socks until the school bought him new shoes.

At Purdue, Harry Michael was studying animal husbandry. He was on the football and track teams and was a member of Alpha Gamma Rho fraternity.

Early in the morning on Sunday, December 7, 1941, he woke up in Cary Residence Hall, went downstairs, and looked at the front page of the student newspaper, the *Purdue Exponent*. There were typical college campus stories: articles about the debate team, the YWCA Coed Capers, and a Christmas party in the Union. But those weren't the stories that caught Michael's attention.

He focused on an article about foreign war correspondent Betty Wason, who was scheduled to speak that afternoon in Purdue's one-year-old, six-thousand-seat Hall of Music. A native of nearby Delphi and a graduate of Purdue, Wason had been arrested and held briefly by German Nazis. She was in West Lafayette to tell her story.

Another front-page article in the *Exponent* that morning announced Erika Mann was scheduled to speak in the Music Hall the following Saturday. Her talk would focus on Nazi education methods. The newspaper said she was a native of Germany who had fled the country and had been doing radio broadcasts from London for the BBC. She was followed by so many people that German Propaganda Minister Joseph Goebbels broadcast counterprogramming that personally attacked Mann.

The war was in the news that morning in Indiana, but the Pearl Harbor attack was not. The morning newspapers had gone to press hours before the attack. With time zone differences, it would be afternoon before Michael heard a radio broadcast detailing what had happened on the Hawaiian Islands so far away.

His life was going to take a whiplash turn. He knew it. And he had one burning emotion coursing through his body.

He wanted to get in on the fight.

PURDUE STUDENTS RESPOND TO ATTACK ON PEARL HARBOR

William Moffat, from Berwyn, Illinois, near Chicago, was a sophomore at Purdue in the fall of 1941. He had a football scholarship that required him to wait tables at Cary Hall three hours a day. He was working in the Cary Hall dining room near the end of the afternoon meal when word of the attack reached him. "The room was almost empty," Moffat remembered in an interview in the mid-1990s. "We turned on the radio and that's when we heard. We said, 'Here we go.'"[11]

He, too, wanted to get in on the fight. By February 1942, he was gone from the Purdue campus and in Navy flight training in Jacksonville, Florida.

Mauri Williamson was in high school in the small Indiana town of Economy on the day Pearl Harbor was attacked. "I remember Pearl Harbor Day," he said in a 1995 interview. "We had just returned from church. . . . When we heard the news it was like someone had died. My mother was sort of crying. Here I was fifteen years old and in no time at all I'd be in it. And I wanted to be in it."

When he did get in it, the job was tough, even stateside: he was helping to care for those who had been injured, both physically and mentally. "I was in the

Navy," Williamson said. "I ended up working in a psychiatric hospital in California.... We saw a lot of massive injuries.... I remember one guy in our ward whose face didn't look like a face. It had been blown away.... We had a lot of Marines.... They came back with one leg, no legs."[12]

Williamson went straight from high school to the war and then enrolled at Purdue in 1946 after the fighting was finished. He later became head of Purdue's Agricultural Alumni Association.

In January 1941, another student, named James H. Doolittle Jr. was in the middle of his junior year studying mechanical engineering at Purdue. As detailed in Chapter 7, his father, James H. Doolittle Sr., was one of the nation's most famous aviators and a World War I ace. So, it was not a surprise when the Lafayette *Journal and Courier* carried a page-one story saying the twenty-year-old Doolittle was seeking an immediate appointment as an Army flying cadet.

The United States wasn't even in the war yet. But Doolittle Jr. wanted in on it.

"Revealing his plans to carry on the Army aviation tradition of his intrepid father, young Doolittle said he would leave his junior studies at Purdue and enlist immediately for the nine-month scholarship course if his appointment is granted," the newspaper reported. "James Jr. already holds a private pilot's license. Said he: 'The thing I want most is to follow in my dad's footsteps. I want to be an Army pilot. I think it is every young man's duty to try for an Army flying cadet scholarship.'"[13]

His father approved the decision, and the application from Doolittle Jr. was accepted. He was awarded his Army pilot wings on October 31, 1941. His father pinned them on his chest. After further training, he was deployed in June 1942 to fly combat missions in the Pacific.

In April 1942, James H. Doolittle Sr. won a Medal of Honor presented by Roosevelt and was promoted to brigadier general for planning and leading an air attack on Japan, four months after the Pearl Harbor attack. It was the first American airstrike on Japan, and a great morale booster for the nation.

After dropping their bombs, the plan was to land in China because they would not have enough fuel to get back to their U.S. aircraft carrier in the Pacific Ocean. There were sixteen crews of five men on the raid. Three crew members died, one while bailing out of his plane and two drowned at sea. Eight men were captured by the Japanese. Three of them were executed and one died from disease. As discussed in chapter 7, the senior Doolittle survived and became an Air Corps icon in American history.

REACTION TO PEARL HARBOR ATTACK AT PURDUE

In December 1941, the *Exponent* didn't publish on Mondays, so the first issue of the newspaper after the Sunday attack on Pearl Harbor was Tuesday, December 9. A huge headline across the front page called for calm: "Administration: Study as Usual."[14]

"The immediate reaction of the University administration was that Americans were in for a long war, perhaps five years or more; that the University is a school for much-needed technicians; and that it consequently would continue to function much as before, was a view frequently expressed," the page-one story said.[15]

Purdue President Elliott, who was in absolute command of the University, did not hesitate to give orders to his students, including calling a special convocation within the week after the Pearl Harbor attack. The speaker at the convocation would be Elliott. "A fateful decision has been made," Elliott wrote in the *Exponent* on December 9, ahead of that meeting. "The nation is at war. Many serious days are ahead for each of us. No one appreciates more than I do your disturbance of mind and spirit. However, during the present hours of national shock and personal confusion, one thing is clear. Now is the time to furnish proof of our unity and loyalty. Until it is known just what your new duties are to be, your exclusive business is to tend strictly to your usual business as students. This means chins up, heads clear, and firm brakes upon tempers and tongues. Youth such as you are going to be needed by the country as never before. You will show good sense by not being too impatient, but by waiting for proper advice as to your next duties."[16]

The student writers at the *Exponent* urged preservation of civil liberties. "It does not follow that because of hostilities we must abolish free opinion," a front-page editorial said. "We must avoid hysteria; now is not the time for the 'witch hunts' so characteristic of the first World War."[17]

The Lafayette *Journal and Courier* took a harsher position. "No Japs Enrolled At Purdue," a front-page headline shouted,[18] assuring readers there were no enemies in the community. But the newspaper urged people to be on the lookout just the same. "Be not overly suspicious," a page-one editorial said. "But keep your eyes and ears open for any suspicion of subversive activity. There are important defense industries in our midst. They must be carefully protected from any sabotage attempts. The possibility of such practices is not at all remote."[19]

When Purdue's President Elliot spoke to students, faculty, and staff at the Music Hall on December 15, he received a thunderous standing ovation—a testament to student respect for him, and to their respect for leadership. His talk was also carried live on the University's WBAA radio station. He again urged students to stay in school, at least until the end of the academic year. He said, "It is MY opinion, as far as can now be forecast, that there is very little chance of any . . . young men between nineteen and twenty-one [who stay enrolled at the University] being called into service before the close of the present [academic] year next June.[20]

"The nation must plan for a prolonged conflict," Elliott said. "This conflict is a contest of the strength of the machines and of the technical knowledge of men who make and operate those machines. The final test of your allegiance to the country's cause is to be found in the quality of your determination to get that training, here available to each of you as one of the fortunate few. Modern warfare requires a complicated organization of men and machines. The effectiveness of this organization is dependent upon the skillful fitting of the right men to the right jobs. They also serve who only stay and study."[21]

He presented a "Bill of Responsibilities" for Purdue students:

1. Apply yourself to your work as students;
2. Reduce to a minimum your recreation and social activities that make demands upon your money, your time, your concentration upon your serious tasks.
3. Avoid waste;
4. You have a responsibility for rigid economy to your personal affairs;
5. Help the University to be economical;
6. Stay informed, make yourself rumor proof;
7. Maintain your health and physical fitness.[22]

Elliott saw Purdue University's job as preparing students for war and doing that as quickly as possible. The University instituted adjustments to enable students to graduate faster than the traditional four years. Since the 1920s, Elliott had believed some university students could graduate in three years. When students were called back to campus early after Christmas break, a headline in the *Exponent* on January 6, 1942, announced "Campus Goes On Full War Time Schedule."

Semesters were immediately shortened. The academic year changed from two to three semesters per year. The 1942 yearbook, *Debris*, boasted that Purdue was the first university in the country to switch to year-round classes. To make the new schedule work, final exams were canceled. So were most vacations. Under the new schedule, students could graduate in two years and eight months, fully educated and ready for military service. Even those who enlisted or were drafted before graduation would have acquired more education than if the traditional four-year program had been continued. Female students took noncredit courses in motor repair, radio code, and pistol-firing.

HARRY MICHAEL: WAITING IN THE RESERVES

Harry Michael took President Elliott's advice and remained in school. He took part in required ROTC activities during his first two years at Purdue and continued to participate as an upperclassman. On August 31, 1942, Michael and several of his friends enlisted in the Army Reserves.

Michael was twenty years old, and he still looked like a boy. He was 5'9" and 160 pounds. His hair was blond, his eyes were blue, and his complexion was light. Although he was in a hurry to reach the battlefield, he believed he had signed up for a reserves program that would allow him to finish his degree before active service.

In the fall of 1942, Michael started dating Marjorie Butz, an eighteen-year-old woman who lived in Lafayette. They met on a blind date. Years later Michael would write to her, "I've just been going over our first meeting, our first date. I'll never forget that as long as I live."[23]

PURDUE ADMINISTRATORS ACCEPT WAR DUTIES

Elliott's advice to students to continue at the University for at least the time being did not apply to himself. In January 1942, he took a position with the federal government and served on the Committee on War-Time Requirements for Specialized Personnel. That same year he was named to head the Division of Professional and Technical Employment and Training of the War Manpower Commission. The commission was charged with balancing the personnel needs of agriculture, industry, and the military. Elliott began traveling back and forth between Washington, D.C. and West Lafayette, on a leave of absence from the campus. During his absences, trustees named four men to share the presidential duties: Controller R. B. Stewart; Dean of Engineering A. A. Potter; Dean of Agriculture H. J. Reed; and Vice President Frank Hockema.

H. B. Knoll, whose 1963 book, *The Story of Purdue Engineering*, is one of the most respected histories of the University, was on campus throughout the Second World War, and edited a book about those years titled *1941–1945: A Record of a University in the War Years.*

Knoll wrote, "In Washington (Elliott) directed the allocation of technical men, including physicians and scientists, and determined how the colleges and universities should function. It was a sign of the stringent times that he could easily find a use for all the professional schools but that he had to have his reservations about liberal arts colleges. . . . What he wanted, in brief, was universal military training and the selection of specific persons for specific jobs. When it was objected at a Congressional hearing that many people were afraid of such a program, regarding it as regimentation, he stated, 'We have got to be prepared to give up a large amount of our individual liberty in order that we may have some national liberty left after the job is done.'"[24]

Dean of Engineering A. A. Potter and Controller R. B. Stewart also spent a lot of time in Washington, D. C. during the war years. Potter was chairman of the Advisory Committee on Engineering, Science, and Management Defense Training. He served as director of the National Patent Planning Commission, which studied if the system was working to stimulate innovations.

Both during and after the war, R. B. Stewart was extensively involved with the federal government, the military, with defense and wartime research, and with veterans. At one point both the Army and Navy offered him a commission, which he declined, saying he could serve everyone better from his university position.[25] His titles included Special Advisor to the Director, Office of Scientific Research and Development (1940–1942); Special Assistant to the Bureau of Naval Personnel (1942–1943), Consultant to the Director of the Army Specialized Training Program (1942–1943), Chairman of the Army-Navy Joint Board for Uniform Contracts (1943), and Chairman of the Administrator of Veteran Affairs Advisory Committee on Vocational Rehabilitation, Education, and Training at the end of the war.

PURDUE WOMEN TAKE NATIONAL LEADERSHIP ROLES

Women in the Purdue administration also quickly went on active duty. Dean of Women Dorothy Stratton took a leave of absence from the University and enlisted in the Navy Women's Reserve, also known as the Women Accepted for Volunteer Emergency Service (WAVES). She was called to active duty on August 28, 1942, with the rank of senior lieutenant.[26]

She was encouraged to join the military by Lillian Gilbreth, a visiting professor in Purdue's School of Engineering. Gilbreth had been one of eight women who served on a Women's Advisory Council to the Navy that helped to create the WAVES earlier that year. President Elliott had brought Gilbreth to campus in 1935, along with famed aviator Amelia Earhart. Her husband, Frank Gilbreth, who died in 1924, had been a visiting lecturer at Purdue.

At Purdue, Gilbreth became the first female engineering professor in the country. She had the full support of Engineering Dean Potter. (Earhart, who lacked a college degree, did not have Potter's support—as discussed in Chapter Six, she ultimately served as an academic advisor.)

Gilbreth also had part-time duties in the Department of Home Economics, reflecting her international fame as an industrial engineer and her authorship of various time and motion studies that influenced modern home design. Her research had a focus on domestic efficiency and home design. She and her engineer husband Frank Gilbreth had twelve children, two of whom wrote the book (and later movie) *Cheaper by the Dozen* about their childhood.

Soon after joining the WAVES as a second lieutenant, Stratton was promoted to lieutenant commander and named to head the Women's Reserve for the U.S. Coast Guard. This was a new organization created by Congress on November 23, 1942. The purpose was to give women in the Coast Guard shore duties, freeing up men for sea duty. She decided to name the organization SPARS, a combination of the Coast Guard's Latin motto, *Semper Paratus*, and its English meaning, "Always Ready."

Her first job was to hire an executive officer, and it was the easiest decision she made in her entire life, which lasted more than one hundred years. She selected Helen Schleman, director of Purdue women's residence Duhme Hall. Stratton had worked with Schleman at Purdue since 1934, and they were close friends. Both women served in the SPARS throughout the war, ultimately attaining the rank of captain.[27]

Although both took a leave of absence from Purdue, they returned to campus from time to time. Early in the war, Stratton spoke at a convocation in the Purdue Hall of Music. She said that in wartime, women should train for the jobs that are most needed, not necessarily where they most wanted to be. "In this war, each one of us faces the most important decisions of life," Stratton said. "Essentially this is a war of ideas—a war whose outcome will determine whether or not the persons in this world will have respect for each other as distinct and separate individuals."[28]

Women in the SPARS signed up to serve for the duration of the war, plus six months. Nationally, more than eleven thousand women volunteered for the SPARS between its creation and 1946.

When Stratton and Schleman began their service, the United States Coast Guard did not accept African American women. The Coast Guard operated under the Navy during times of war, and the Navy at that time resisted integration. The first African American Navy officers were not commissioned until 1944. SPARS' policy was changed in October 1944, and in March 1945, five African American women were accepted.

It was a change that Stratton and Schleman both advocated. In a 1943 speech, Stratton had declared her belief that "A soldier in the U.S. uniform is a soldier, not a man or a woman, a white or a Negro, a Christian or Jew, rich man or poor, but a soldier, and as such is worthy of respect." In 1944 when the Coast Guard began to allow the recruitment of African American women, Stratton said, "The corps will make no distinction on the basis of color. All recruits will qualify on the same basis, train together, live in the same barracks and perform the same types of jobs for the Coast Guard."[29]

At the end of the war, Stratton was awarded the Legion of Merit. She left the Coast Guard in January 1946 and accepted other national leadership roles. The first full time Dean of Women at Purdue, she ultimately retired to West Lafayette and died in 2006 at the age of 107, having lived for the entire twentieth century. A U.S. Coast Guard cutter is named in her honor, as is the Purdue's Veteran and Military Success Center.[30]

When Stratton retired from the military, Schleman was promoted to the rank of Captain and served as the second commanding officer of SPARS from 1946 to 1947. In 1947, she returned to Purdue and became Dean of Women in turn, serving until 1968.

Stratton and Schleman were among a handful of the highest-ranking female officers in the military during their service. The rank of Captain and Colonel, one step beneath Admiral and General, were given to women leading the female military branches, such as SPARS, WAVES, and the Women's Auxiliary Air Corps (WAAC). Women could not be named Admiral or General at that time. The first female general was named in 1970.[31] The first woman to become an admiral was in 1972.[32]

It is estimated that 350,000 women served at home and abroad in the U.S. military during World War II. Nearly two hundred Purdue women served.[33]

BOILERMAKERS LEAVE FOR MILITARY AND DEFENSE INDUSTRIES

When the U.S. entered the war, almost all building on the campus stopped. As the Board of Trustees had mandated in 1940, the focus of every student, department, faculty, and staff member was centered on national defense and the war effort.

Students and faculty did leave to join the war. Some were drafted and some enlisted. By June 1942, ninety-two faculty members had left for the military or defense industries.[34] Before the war ended in 1945, about 17,500 Purdue men and women, including alumni and 450 faculty, served in the military. More than five hundred Boilermakers lost their lives in the war, and their names were placed on a roll of honor in the Great Hall of the Union Building along with those from World War I.

HARRY MICHAEL: TRAINING

On March 18, 1943, Harry Michael was among two hundred Purdue ROTC students formerly inducted into the Army and waiting to being called to active duty. Among those who had enlisted in the reserves with Michael the previous August was Velmar Davis. "We thought that we understood a promise from the commandant of ROTC that if we enlisted, we would complete our college degree," Velmar said. "The part of the promise that we did not understand was **when** we would finish our degrees."[35]

Michael remained at Purdue two more months before reporting to Fort Bragg, in North Carolina. He wanted to join the Army Air Corps because he thought that would help him reach Europe faster. He requested a transfer to the Army Air Corps by early 1944. He was the only member of his ROTC class who requested a transfer rather than waiting for assignment to Officer Candidate School training in field artillery.[36]

In February 1944, Michael reported to Sheppard Field in Texas for flight training in a P-38 Lightning fighter plane. On April 27, 1944, in Orange County, California, Michael was sworn in as a cadet in pilot training.

On August 1, 1944, he wrote to his parents that he had "accepted the Lord Jesus into [his] heart." In one of his letters, he described it as if a weight had been lifted from his shoulders. Raised by his parents, Plomer and Ida Michael, in the First Brethren Church of Milford, he had begun to take classes in Catholicism and converted. Marjorie Butz was a lifelong Catholic and Michael had fallen deeply in love with her. "Every day brings us closer, dear," he wrote her in April 1944. "Someday this thing will break and then we can be together forever and ever. Can you think of anything better?"[37]

PURDUE STUDENTS ON THE BATTLE FRONT AND THE HOME FRONT

Those who left Purdue also included people such as William Moffat, who had waited tables at the Cary Hall dining room at Purdue. In January 1943, at the age of twenty-one, Moffat graduated from Navy flight school and shipped out for the Pacific. He would serve two tours of duty on aircraft carriers, flying 144 missions.

The war was terrifying and deadly. "We got shot at a lot between long intervals of trying to keep our marbles," Moffat said in a 1995 interview.

> I was almost shot down over Okinawa. I got the airplane back to the carrier and landed it. It was so badly damaged they just shook their heads and pushed it over the fantail. . . . We lost some guys on every mission. A typical strike would involve twenty or thirty aircraft. We had a tactic where we'd drop something on the enemy with all twenty or thirty aircraft going in and out in twenty or thirty seconds. We'd have to execute this without flying into each other or shooting each other. The first targets we'd try to hit were the anti-aircraft guns. That was when we'd sustain the greatest losses. Maybe three guys would never recover from the dive and go into the ground. A couple others would parachute out and we'd find out later the enemy had chopped off their heads.[38]

On the Purdue campus, some things went on as always. There were "sock hops" and "blanket hops." The Military Balls, among the biggest social events of the year, were held, and on those evenings coeds were not required back at their residence halls or sororities until 2:00 a.m. Normal hours for women were 10:30 p.m. on weeknights and midnight on weekends. Famous bands played on campus, including Tommy Dorsey, Jimmy Dorsey, Glenn Miller, Stan Kenton, and Les

Brown. The songs included "In the Mood," "We'll Meet Again," "Boobie Woogie Blues," "The White Cliffs of Dover," "I'll Be Seeing You," and many more.

In 1941, there were four Purdue enrolled male students on campus for every female. But as the war years passed, the ratio changed to twelve enrolled Purdue women for every man, excluding military and industrial personnel on campus. Because of the decline of male enrolled students, during the war the "All-American Marching Band" (technically a military unit) started accepting female musicians.

A commencement ceremony was held in May 1942, a month earlier than usual because of the new schedule. "With the military atmosphere of the Purdue Armory—consistent with the time—we assembled for the 1942 senior (commencement) parade," the 1942 *Debris* stated. "We wondered if we would be in the Army, Navy, Marines, or industry—if we would show that the class of 1942 was worth all the money spent to educate it."[39] Following commencement, 143 male graduates were sworn in together on campus as ensigns in the Navy.

On September 24, 1942, movie star Dorothy Lamour was on campus taking part in a rally to sell bonds in support of the war effort. She attracted twenty thousand people from the University and surrounding communities to Ross-Ade Stadium on a cold early fall evening. Of the $508,443 raised through the rally, $80,400 was raised during the rally itself at Ross-Ade, with the rest pledged in advance by companies and organizations. Included in the items auctioned to the audience was Lamour's hankie with a lipstick kiss. It sold for $8,000.

"Hardly a single one of the thousands of nearly frozen fans left their seats sitting through almost two hours of the program before the Hollywood star made her appearance in a dazzling beige convertible," the *Exponent* reported. "Two university fraternities, the Delta Upsilons and the Sigma Chis, each bought $500 worth of bonds with the stipulation that Miss Lamour send them a personally autographed sarong."[40] Lamour was famed for her beauty and the sarongs she wore in movies.

Purdue ROTC and other military men on campus took part in the rally. More than two thousand students annually were enrolled in Army ROTC during most of the war years. The Corps at Purdue for many years was the largest field artillery unit in the country. Nationally, university ROTC programs supplied 12 percent of war officers, and their immediate availability and readiness to serve were essential in the earliest days following December 1941.[41] The 1942 *Debris* reported that for sixteen years the Purdue ROTC had been named "best in the Midwest" at the National Inspection.

CIVILIANS AND MILITARY PERSONNEL ARRIVE ON CAMPUS

Throughout the war, civilians and military personnel were sent to Purdue for training. Between June 1942 and June 1943, 1,265 people from twenty-two states, Canada, and Washington, D.C. took training on campus in civilian defense. Upon completion of their training, they returned to their home communities to organize civilian defense efforts.

In April 1943, President Elliott resigned his position in Washington, D.C., at the request of the trustees, and resumed his duties as president full-time. He continued to lecture and advise his students to make the most of their education in preparation for service.

> This is a solemn and significant hour for all of us.... If we are to escape confusion and discouragement, the clear-headed need to remain clear-headed, and the stout-hearted to retain their courage.... Ranking first is the likelihood of the nation calling you from the classroom and laboratory and sending you to a center of training for some form of military service.... I say to you, continue in the University until you may be called upon to enter active service by the provisions of the law.... "What the hell. Let's go. The Army's coming to get us. What's the use of studying. Let's go!" Thus spoke, within my hearing, a day or two ago, an exuberant, impatient young man. He was, I'm convinced, adventure-foolish rather than service-wise. Modern warfare requires a complicated organization of men and machines. The effectiveness of this organization is dependent upon the skillful fitting of the right man in the right place.[42]

In 1943, Purdue ROTC was the largest in the University's history. As the war months and years progressed Purdue again took on the look of a military camp, as it had in World War I. In August 1943 the Purdue Alumni Association published its first issue of *The Purdue Patrol*, a wartime supplement to the Purdue *Alumnus* magazine. The Patrol reported, "More than 3,000 soldiers, sailors, and marines are at present assigned to the University for various types of training transforming the campus into what might be called a combination Naval base and military camp from the standpoint of uniform appearance."[43]

According to *The Patrol*, as the military and civilian defense contractors sent people to the University, total enrollment, including regular students, military, and defense workers, in the November 1943 term had grown to 6,787. Male and female civilian students totaled 2,746, while those in the military numbered 3,734.[44] Some military personnel came to learn trades and were not enrolled as students. The military and civilian students attended classes together.

In December 1943, *The Purdue Patrol* reported that former Boilermaker student Captain Walker M. Mahurin, had received the Distinguished Service Cross "for extraordinary heroism when on October 4, outnumbered in combat, he shot down three German fighters in one raid over Frankfort.[45]

On the same page, *The Patrol* reported the Navy Flying Cross "for extraordinary heroism" had been awarded to former Purdue student First Lieutenant Raymond Hine, a Navy fighter pilot who had been missing since April.[46]

MILITARY AND DEFENSE INDUSTRY CONTRACTS WITH UNIVERSITIES

The arrival of so many members of the military and civilians who needed to be housed, fed, and trained posed both benefits and problems for Purdue and all universities. The government was drafting men who were enrolled in college, and in addition, many university men enlisted. This shrunk enrollment at the schools and threatened the financial stability of universities. Bringing in military and civilian personnel for training gave the schools needed revenue. But how much would the universities charge for all of this? Where would they house all these people? Further complicating the situation, the Army and Navy wanted their own and different contracts.

According to Ruth Freehafer, the biographer of Purdue Controller and later Vice President and Treasurer R. B. Stewart, "Purdue was one of the first schools approached about military training contracts, not only because of its academic reputation, but also because it had modern residence halls and much empty space with so many male students in the service. The first Naval officer who arrived knew nothing about the entire university plant. His original proposition was to take over the entire University plant, decide on the curricula, eliminate all but technical and military-related subjects, then have the remaining staff and students moved to another location. The arrangements for the academic part of the training were not handled by Stewart, but he told the officer that he would provide the Navy University services and provide room and board at a set price."[47] Stewart would not give the military control of the university. Purdue would mix the military into the campus.

Purdue and the Navy reached an agreement, but there were challenges along the way—such as the Navy wanting steaks four times a week, which cost more than the agreed price for food. A more modest menu was negotiated.

As military programs expanded to universities across the country, similar issues and disagreements cropped up. Stewart suggested to the Navy that military officers and university officials from the campuses meet at Great Lakes Naval Station north of Chicago. The meeting ultimately resulted in the creation of a joint service committee to create a uniform contact. Stewart was named chairman of the committee.[48]

Military personnel continued to pour into the Purdue campus for special training. Everywhere people on campus were busy: the Division of Education and Allied Psychology helped pick and train pilots, and the University medical staff performed thousands of physical examinations on civilian and military students.

TRAINING SCHOOLS

Military training programs at Purdue, in addition to the civilian flight training that started in 1939, began one month after the war started. One hundred Army Air Corps Engineering Officers arrived for a three-month course in airplane maintenance.

For more than three years during the war, the Navy had an Electrical Training School on campus. Its headquarters was the parts of Cary Hall where the men lived. In a Navy ceremony, it was renamed the "U.S.S. Cary Hall."[49] Unlike other military groups on campus who wore civilian clothes, these men wore their Navy white shirts, pants, and caps wherever they went, and they marched in unison from class to class "making the campus look like a port," Knoll said.[50] Sometimes they chanted while they marched. At other times they sang songs such as "Mademoiselle from Armentières." About eight hundred of these men were on campus at any given time. In all, six thousand were trained.

Additionally, Purdue had a Diesel Engine Officer Training School that taught two hundred men over seven months. Purdue also trained civilians in ordinance (ammunition and weapons) inspection.

PURDUE AIRPORT

In his history of the university, Knoll said the Purdue airport immediately became a training center exclusively for the military, "and planes buzzed around it like bees around a hive."[51]

After the attack on Pearl Harbor, the name of the Civilian Pilot Training Program changed to the War Training Service. The program continued until 1944, with sixty airplanes based at the airport and forty civilian instructors. People being trained took college courses and private flight training with an agreement that they would enter the military upon graduation.

The Army and Navy sent personnel to Purdue for training. 28 enlisted reserve Army pilots, 534 Navy V-5 flyers, and 166 flight school instructors were trained at the airport during the war. Purdue was considered the number one school in the nation for flight instructors.[52] In addition, eighty-five pilots from Central and South American countries arrived at Purdue for training toward the end of the war. They were part of a U.S. State Department program to train men in airline and airport operations.

ARMY SPECIALIZED TRAINING PROGRAM

In March 1943, the first men in the Army Specialized Training Program arrived on the Purdue campus. They, too, lived at Cary Hall.

Among the first group of 120 men in the Army Specialized Training Program to arrive in West Lafayette were thirty-three African Americans. Some of them became the first African Americans to live in a Purdue residence hall because they came to Purdue through a contract with the U.S. government.

Small numbers of African American students had attended Purdue since the late 1890s. Many of them studied pharmacy and were admitted to serve their segregated communities throughout Indiana after graduation. There was no written policy stating African Americans could not live in a Purdue residence hall. But if any nonmilitary students applied for a room, the request was denied. A small number of African American men lived in an International House on campus with international students. Other African American men and women lived in a segregated community in Lafayette near Lincoln School and St. Elizabeth Hospital. They took city buses to campus and back every day. Purdue residence halls were not officially racially integrated until January 1947.

Nationwide, the U.S. War Department began admitting African Americans to Army ROTC in 1942.[53]

During the war, 227 universities took part in the Army Specialized Training Program, including Purdue. The Army identified academically qualified enlisted men throughout the nation and sent them to universities for education in fields such as engineering. These men also had the opportunity to become officers. Universities with advanced Army ROTC programs, such as Purdue, were selected. With the Army Special Training Program, advanced ROTC on university campuses was suspended. The first two years of ROTC continued during the war.

Purdue's Army Special Training Program continued for one year. "At its peak it enrolled 1,348 men, most of them selected in the training camps," Knoll said. "They were hearty, noisy, able young men, cooperative and friendly but restless. When they moved through a hallway they were like a football crowd entering a stadium before a crucial game. The main program ended abruptly on March 31, 1944, its cancellation forced by the exigencies of war, but a related reserve program for seventeen-year-olds kept some Army trainees on campus."[54]

The program for seventeen- and eighteen-year-olds was called The Army Specialized Training Reserve Program. The young men were called to active duty at the end of the academic term when they reached the age of eighteen.

NAVY V-12 COLLEGE TRAINING PROGRAM

The V-12 Navy College Training Program began at Purdue in July 1943 with 1,263 students and continued during four terms. The program had the dual purposes of providing trained, educated officers for the Navy and Marines, and providing students for universities where enlistments and the draft had depleted enrollment. The military paid the tuition and expenses for these men. Many were housed in Cary Hall, but there were so many men in training at Purdue that in 1943 the University added housing for them in the Agricultural Engineering Building and the Memorial Union. Space was also requisitioned in twenty-two of the thirty-five fraternity houses where members had left to join the war effort.

More than 2,700 took men took part in the V-12 program at Purdue, many staying multiple years. About two-thirds were sailors and the rest were Marines. Men who qualified for the program were sent to schools across the nation selected by the Navy. Many were called to active duty before finishing their degree, but four hundred graduated with bachelor's degrees from Purdue University.

Among them was Arthur Hansen of Green Bay, Wisconsin. He graduated high school in 1943 as class valedictorian and joined the Marines because he liked the uniform. He was sent to Purdue to study engineering. In 1971, he became the first alumnus named president of Purdue, and served in that role until 1982.

The contract that Purdue Vice President and Treasurer R. B. Stewart drafted for the school's V-12 training was used by the Navy at universities throughout the nation. The V-12 program at Purdue was so successful that after the war the Navy started a Naval ROTC at the university.

PURDUE'S UNDEFEATED 1943 FOOTBALL TEAM

The V-12 program had an added benefit to the Purdue football program. The Army Special Training Program did not allow its men to take part in extracurricular activities. But the Navy V-12 program did.

In 1942, under first-year football coach Elmer Burnham, Purdue won only one game. But everything changed in the summer of 1943 when V-12 Navy and Marine personnel from around the nation arrived in West Lafayette. The Boilermakers had an undefeated, 9-0 season in the fall of 1943, and the team ranks among the greatest in Purdue history.

"A surprising turnout of over one hundred gridiron enthusiasts including a host of marine and sailor huskies in the V-12 training program greeted Coach Elmer Burnham and his staff of assistants as Purdue's first summer-time football practice was launched on Thursday July 15 in preliminary preparation for the strenuous 1943 schedule," *The Purdue Patrol* reported in August, noting that "while the bulk of the squad was composed of men who had no previous collegiate experience, the V-12 contingent was responsible for contributing close to thirty lettermen from various colleges and universities over the country."[55]

Guard Alex Agase and fullback Tony Butkovich came from the University of Illinois. Boris Dimancheff was a halfback from Butler University. Quarterback Sam Vacanti came from the University of Iowa. Dick Barwagen was a member of the 1942 Boilermaker team.

Agase, Dimancheff, Vacanti and Barwagen all went on to pro football careers. Agase eventually returned to Purdue as the head football coach from 1973 to 1976. Also on the 1943 team was Chalmers William "Bump" Elliott, who became head football coach at the University of Michigan from 1959 to 1968, and athletic director at Iowa from 1970 to 1991.

Twelve of the varsity letter winners from the 1943 team, including star players Agase and Butkovich, were V-12 players who were transferred away from Purdue for advanced training after the seventh game of the season against Wisconsin, which the Boilers won.

"The long bus ride back to West Lafayette after the Wisconsin game was emotional," sportswriter Bob Collins wrote in *Boilermakers: The History of Purdue Football.* "And there were wet eyes and choked voices as the young men—many of whom had not even met a few months before—said their final goodbyes. In a short time, they had become a team—one of the greatest in Purdue history. And they had become friends."[56]

The Associated Press ranked Purdue as high as second in the nation. But it dropped to fifth after the loss of V-12 players resulted in narrow, seven-point victories in the last two games of the season.

In 1944, the Cleveland Rams made Tony Butkovich a first-round pick in the NFL draft. After only playing in seven of the nine games in the 1943 Purdue season, he was third in the nation in rushing and fifth in the nation in total offense, which included passing and running.

He never played in the NFL. On April 18, 1945, he was killed in action against the Japanese in Okinawa.

Hank Stram was another football legend who played at Purdue in the war years. He arrived on campus as a freshman in 1941. At that time freshmen were not eligible for the varsity team, but Stram was a member of the 1942 team before joining the Army. He came back after the war and played for Purdue in 1946 and 1947. He was an assistant coach for the Boilermakers from 1948 to 1955 and head baseball coach from 1951 to 1955. Stram coached professional football, winning three AFL championships and, in 1970, leading the Kansas City Chiefs to victory in Super Bowl IV. He was inducted into the Pro Football Hall of Fame in 2003. The Kansas City Chiefs' quarterback in the Super Bowl victory was Len Dawson, who played at Purdue from 1953 to 1956.

FREDERICK C. BRANCH

In 1944 Frederick C. Branch came to Purdue as part of the Navy V-12 program.

On November 10, 1945, he became the first African American commissioned officer in the history of the U.S. Marine Corps. The ceremony took place on the 170th birthday of the Marines.

But the ceremony didn't take place at Purdue. A racist incident at a Lafayette movie theater resulted in his transfer to Camp Montford Point in Jacksonville, North Carolina. During World War II, about twenty thousand African American men trained at the racially segregated base that is now part of Camp Lejeune.

Branch was born in Hamlet, North Carolina, in 1923. He was the middle child of seven sons born to a Methodist minister. A good student, he graduated from high school in Mamaroneck, New York in 1941, where he was living with relatives, and enrolled at historically black Johnson C. Smith University, in Charlotte, North Carolina. For his sophomore year, he transferred to Temple University in Philadelphia.

In May 1943 he was drafted, interrupting both his education and a growing romance with a young woman and fellow Temple student who would later become his wife. He reported to Fort Bragg, in North Carolina. Once there, two Marine sergeants came up to him, looked him over, and one of them ordered, "Come with me. You're going to be a Marine."[57]

In 1941, an executive order signed by President Franklin Roosevelt, who was under pressure from several groups (not to mention his wife Eleanor), had opened the Marine Corps to African Americans for the very first time. There had been no African Americans in the Marines before that time. With opportunities opening for national defense work by U.S. industries, African American leaders had pressured Roosevelt to make sure they had the opportunity to benefit from the jobs that would be created. A mass march on the White House was planned.

On June 25, 1941, Roosevelt signed the executive order that stated, "there shall be no discrimination in the employment of workers in defense industries and in government because of race, creed, color, or national origin." This opened opportunities for African Americans in the military, although it would be 1948 before President Harry S Truman signed an executive order banning segregation in the armed forces. Thus, while Frederick Branch was taken to Camp Lejeune, his duty station was Montford Point, where African Americans trained, segregated from the white Marines.

Training at Montford Point and Camp Lejeune was tough. According to the *Philadelphia Inquirer*, "Young Branch became a Marine, marching with an M-1 rifle and slogging through mud, running in his underwear at night until sweat popped out and greedy mosquitoes dined on the winded draftees. It was also where Branch decided he could be a leader. 'I read all the requirements to be an officer . . . and nowhere in there did it say anything about race.'"[58]

After basic training, Branch, who had completed two years of college, applied for Officer Candidate School. He scored high enough for the placement, but he was denied admission. "They told me to shut that blankety-blank stuff up about being an officer," Branch told the Philadelphia *Inquirer* in a 1995 interview. The Marines told him, "You ain't going to be no officer."[59]

He sent his application to Washington, D.C. It came back denied with a message that enlisted personnel had to have overseas duty to be considered for officer candidate school.

In July 1943, Branch was sent to the Ellice Islands (now Tuvalu), in the South Pacific, where he refueled planes and restocked ships. Supply and service jobs were typical of many African Americans who served during World War II.

After his deployment overseas, Branch applied again for officer candidate school. Again, he was denied. He had to have the approval of his commanding officer, whom he had never met. But with the help of a sympathetic Marine sergeant, Branch was assigned to deliver mail to the commanding officer, a colonel.

The Philadelphia *Inquirer* interviewed Branch in 1997. "The night before he was to resume his new duties," it reported, "Branch broke out his parade khakis, then reached for an iron and bottle of starch. The next morning, when the colonel looked up to get his mail, a young black man who looked as if he had stepped out of a recruiting poster stood at attention. 'I left them wondering who I was,' Branch said."[60]

Eventually, the colonel remembered that Branch had applied to be a commissioned officer but had been rejected because he had not approved the appointment. The colonel said that if Branch kept up the good work, he would see to it that the appointment went through. He was good for his word.

Branch and two other African Americans were assigned to a group of roughly three hundred young men who would take part in the V-12 program on college campuses. Branch was assigned to Purdue, where he lived in Cary Hall with the other Navy officers. According to the Purdue Registrar's Office, he enrolled on November 3, 1944. At Purdue, Branch studied civil engineering along with his military training, and made the dean's list.

One evening, he went to a movie theater in Lafayette and took a seat on the main floor. An usher told him he would have to sit in the balcony, the only place African Americans were allowed to sit.

Branch said he was going to sit where he was.

A few minutes later, the usher came back and said that Branch had a telephone call in the theater office. Branch went to the office and found his commanding officer on the line. The commander officer said, "Branch, your liberty's up. Get back to your dormitory."[61]

The next semester, he was not allowed to return to Purdue. While it's not known exactly when the theater incident occurred, he withdrew from the University on June 23, 1945. He finished his officer training at Quantico, in Virginia. His wife, Camilla, whom he had met at Temple, pinned his second lieutenant bars on his uniform. The ceremony was at Montford Point.

The evening of the commissioning, Branch and his wife went to a movie theater near the base. There were no seats on the main floor, so they sat in the balcony. Word soon spread through the theater that Lieutenant Branch was there—the first African American marine officer.

At the conclusion of the movie, people moved to the front of the theater, looked up at Branch and applauded his accomplishment.

World War II was finished by the time he got his bars. Branch went into the reserves and finished his undergraduate degree in physics at Temple. He might have considered graduate school at Purdue, because registrar records show he enrolled again on June 19, 1947. But he withdrew on August 16, 1947. According to the 1950 U.S. Census, he was living with his in-laws in Philadelphia and working as a clerk, when he was recalled during the Korean War to command a platoon at Camp Pendleton, California. He returned to the reserves when the war ended in 1953. He was promoted to captain but resigned his commission in 1955, disappointed at his limited opportunities.

In 1953, he went to work at Dobbins High School in Philadelphia, where he founded the school's science department. He retired in 1988 after a long career. His wife, Camilla, died in 2000 after fifty-five years of marriage. Branch died in Philadelphia in April 2005, at the age of eighty-two. He and his wife raised one child, a godson, from infancy.

Over time, Branch's achievements gained more acknowledgment. In 1977, the Marines named a building after him at the Marine Officer's Candidate School in Quantico. In November 1995, the U.S. Senate passed a resolution honoring Branch "on the 50th anniversary of his becoming the first African American commissioned officer in the United States Marines." On April 25, 2005, shortly after his death, the U.S. Senate passed a resolution "to commemorate the life, achievements, and contributions of Frederick C. Branch." And in 2006, the Marines created the Frederick C. Branch Leadership Scholarship for African American students at historically black colleges and universities (HBCUs) that have Naval Reserve Officers Training Corps programs.

In his *Washington Post* obituary of Branch, Joe Geeter, vice president of the Montford Point Association, a Black veterans' group, said, "Every African American officer can trace his beginnings back to Fred Branch. Each of these officers owes his success to the courage and dedication he showed while going through Officer Candidate School during World War II."[62]

MILITARY AND CIVILIAN TRAINING FOR WOMEN

Some women workers and military service members also received training on the Purdue West Lafayette campus. Among them were the Curtiss-Wright Cadettes, the Radio Corporation of America (RCA) Cadettes, and women from Wright Field in Dayton, Ohio. In November 1943 there were 265 women from the three groups on campus.[63]

In February 1943 the first one hundred Curtiss-Wright Cadettes arrived on the very cold, very male-military Purdue campus. More arrived in the years ahead. Curtiss-Wright was producing dive-bombers and the company needed help training women to do this work. Seven U.S. universities provided the accelerated engineering programs. Nationwide, more than nine hundred Curtiss-Wright women took the classes. Seven hundred sixty-six graduated.

The work was tough. The first Curtiss-Wright Cadettes trained at Purdue took a forty-four-week course, which ran for forty hours a week with no vacations. Later training periods lasted twenty-four weeks. The women were trained not to replace engineers, but to assist engineers. Tuition, room, and board were paid by Curtiss-Wright, and the women received a $10 weekly allowance. Upon completion of the program, they could make $130 to $150 a week at a Curtiss-Wright plant, although their contracts said they could be terminated at the end of the war.

Engineering Professor Elmer Bruhn noted that the Cadettes were a welcome addition to campus. "The one hundred Cadettes for the first program arrived on the Purdue campus on February 12, 1943. I definitely remember that day as there was over six inches of snow on the ground and still snowing. . . . As this very attractive group of cadettes filled the hallways of the aero building, it appeared the aero school men students were very pleased and readily assisted the girls in getting registered and oriented, so to speak. The aero staff seemed to appear in smiles or quite happy with the sudden turn of events."[64]

Ruth Mecca arrived at Purdue for the Cadette training in October 1944. To be admitted she had to go through two days of written and oral examinations.

The women were housed in several locations, including Cary Hall and vacant fraternities. Mecca was in a former fraternity house, "which was lovely," she said in a 2000 interview. "The boys were gone to war so the girls took over. We ate Navy food. It was nice. I enjoyed it very much. The showers and bathrooms they changed for us because we girls complained. At the frat house there were no doors on the toilets and open showers. It was a men's shower, but we didn't want that. So, within a couple of days, we had doors on the johns. And they separated the showers, just put curtains up." Her scrapbook of photos showed young women studying and enjoying campus life. They attracted sailors and soldiers to their activities.

The Cadettes wrote their own words to popular songs of the day, and the lyrics tell us what their experience was like at Purdue. This one was sung to the tune of "Thanks for the Memories":

Thanks for the memories
Of moment, lift, and drag,
Along with Coke and fag
Of lab reports and drafting sports
And metatarsal sag.
Oh, thank you so much!

Thanks for the memories
Of women's residence halls
Of midnight smoker brawls,
Of fire alarms and girlish charms
And greasy overalls.
Oh, thank you so much!
Many are the times that we've calculated.
And many are the times that we've estimated;
But still we're never dated,
Still we are without any beer.

Oh, thanks for the memories,
Of torsion, torque, and shear,
Of sailors with a leer,
Of walks on Intramural Field
Along with you, my dear
Oh, thank you so much![65]

The RCA Cadettes sent to Purdue also arrived in the spring of 1943. Among the subjects they studied were math, drafting, shop, electric circuit theory, electronics, and radio theory. 137 women in the program were housed in the Women's Residence House and Terry House. Meanwhile, the women from Wright Field took twenty-six-week training courses in aircraft radios.

In 1945, the University also had a course in personnel training for Women's Army Corps (WAC) officers. They lived in Cary Hall and took courses for two and a half weeks. They came in groups of ninety. In all, 818 women were trained. The last group included twenty-six officers from the SPARS.

MILITARY ENROLLMENT AT PURDUE EXCEEDS CIVILIAN ENROLLMENT

As the war progressed, military personnel continued to dominate the campus. In November 1944, the University enrollment was 4,024, including 2,450 military personnel and 1,574 civilians. About half the civilians were women—a ratio that had never before been seen at Purdue. The student body also included seventy-five veterans of the war who had been discharged. *The Patrol* reported, "The number promises to be considerably larger as more veterans come back to campus, especially since passage of the 'G.I.' Bill."[66] (Purdue's history with the G.I. Bill is discussed in more details in chapter 11 of this book.)

The residence halls were crowded. Civilian students who lived in them were at first "doubled-up," and finally moved out once rooms were found for them in Lafayette and West Lafayette homes. Fraternities also housed some of the people being trained on campus. The houses, some of which had been forced to close as members were drafted or enlisted, welcomed the income from the boarders. The approximately 1,200 trainees, who came to campus in groups of one hundred for the ten-day Civilian Protection School, were the only nonmilitary people in Cary Hall.

Esther Conelley Boonstra, who graduated from Purdue in 1945, said she and seventeen other female students were forced out of their residence halls to make room for people coming to campus for special training. They were moved to a large home on Waldron Street. Because so many male students had left to serve in the military, women were offered some classes in the Michael Golden Engineering Laboratories and Shops. "We were taught elementary electrical wiring [and] learned to use metal and wood lathes and soldering techniques," Boonstra said. "I made a brass plate and aluminum plates, some cookie cutters I used for years, and small wooden bowls."[67]

The university's peak war-enrollment year was 1943, when the total number of students and trainees on campus totaled 9,002—including all those in military programs, regular students, and women in special training. Of that number, only 2,975 were regular civilian students. Regular degree-seeking students were outnumbered two to one.

Campus life was not unaltered by these changes. For instance, Purdue had strictly enforced a no-smoking policy on campus for many years. It included faculty, staff, students, visitors, and President Elliott even enforced it on the Board of Trustees. But during the war, so many military people came to campus as smokers that the rule was abandoned.

CIVILIAN TRAINING

In his history of Purdue University, *A Century and Beyond*, Robert Topping said, "Perhaps Purdue's greatest contribution to the World War effort was the statewide program in which the university administered training for skilled industrial workers for the war effort."[68]

In 1940, Purdue Dean of Engineering A. A. Potter was recruited by the U.S. Commissioner of Education to help develop a program to meet the anticipated need for more engineers and technically trained workers in defense industries, should the nation go to war. Plans were presented to Congress. In October 1940, the Engineering Defense Training program was approved, and courses began at 144 institutions. By June 1941, nearly 121,000 people had received the special training. In July 1941, chemistry, physics, and production courses were added to the curriculum, and during the following year, enrollment grew to 450,000 men and women at 196 colleges and universities nationwide.[69]

Following the December 7, 1941, Japanese attack at Pearl Harbor and the U.S. entry into the war, the program was further expanded and renamed the Engineering, Science, and Management War Training Act. Every year about 600,000 people across the nation received training at 215 colleges and universities, including Purdue.

C. W. Beese, professor of trade and industrial engineering and head of the University's general engineering program, was in charge of the effort at Purdue. According to university historian Knoll, "Soon after the war opened, Beese suddenly found himself, so far as numbers of students went, at the head of a large university, much larger than Purdue itself."[70] Beese's work and the training offered was not limited to West Lafayette. It operated in one hundred Indiana communities, and in its peak year of 1942–43 enrolled 21,000 men and women, preparing them for specific jobs in war industries. As many as 165 courses were taught in a single year. Knoll wrote, "Citing an extreme to indicate the outer limits, a course titled 'Principles of Ship Fitting' was offered in Evansville and Jeffersonville when those cities began to build marine craft and float them down the Ohio and Mississippi.... The Program was conducted with a vigor born out of urgency, its staff working almost around the clock."[71]

As men were entering military service and leaving their work in factories and offices, women stepped forward to take their place. They needed training. In its first year, Purdue's Engineering, Science, and Management War Training program enrolled more than 4,500 women. Nationwide, the percent of women in the workforce increased from 27 percent to 37 percent between 1940 and 1945. Across the nation, six million women took wartime jobs.[72]

As these women flowed into the workplace, men in management began to wonder what changes they would need to make to accommodate them. They asked Purdue visiting faculty member Lillian Gilbreth what they should do. Gilbreth was among the first female engineers with a PhD, and the second female member of the National Academy of Engineering.[73]

Her answer was quite simple. "Build separate restrooms," she said. Beyond that, women could move right in and do the jobs once limited to men.[74] But at the close of the war as men returned and industries retooled for a peacetime economy, many women were sent home.

Through the war, Purdue helped train about 60,000 workers for industry under the Engineering, Science, and Management War Training Program. Nationally, 227 colleges and universities participated and trained nearly 1.8 million people. Many of the courses were taught by faculty. It was extra work but, along with other programs, it helped to keep the universities opened and the faculty employed as enrollment dropped during the war.

VICTORY VARIETIES

It wasn't all work at Purdue during the war. Albert P. Stewart was the head of Purdue Musical Organizations before, during, and after the war. His featured group was a male glee club. During the war, he continued that group and added a second male club comprised of V-12 students. But the military restricted the time those in the service could be off campus. So, Stewart created a female club, the Purduettes, to travel off campus.

He also created a Victory Varieties series of programs in the Purdue Music Hall to entertain military personnel, students, faculty, staff, and people from the community. The shows featured a variety of acts with one headliner. The word "Victory" referred to the war effort. After the war, the shows continued on fall Saturdays, with "Victory" now referring to football games.

PURDUE LEADERS SERVE THEIR COUNTRY

Beginning in October 1941—before America's entry into the war—R. B. Stewart served on a national committee formed to study government defense research contracts with universities. The U.S. General Accounting Office wanted to know how research money was being spent and wanted accountability. Stewart was sent to eleven universities that had at least $100,000 in research contracts with the government. He questioned the schools about the cost of doing the research, accountability, and whether the work was leading to patents. His report back to the full committee was given on December 8, 1941, the day after the attack on Pearl Harbor.

Stewart biographer Freehafer wrote: "The report outlined in detail the proper management of the relationship of universities to those arms of the federal government furthering scientific research. It presented a uniform contract which could be used for all government-university research." Stewart himself said, "It was the first means of putting teeth into the need to study the cost of what you did in a university. Up to that time, it was just whether you had the money to pay your bills."[75]

Two other Purdue alumni Knoll believed deserved special attention were Claude Wickard and William Batt. Wickard, who graduated from Purdue in 1915, served as U.S. Secretary of Agriculture from 1940 to 1945, leading food production and conservation and composing inspiring slogans such as "food will win the war and write the peace." Batt, who graduated in 1907, served in several positions in Washington, D.C. including the War Production Board. Knoll cited "his courage and insight in integrating war production, in setting the wheels of industry turning in the right direction and in keeping them turning."[76]

THE WAR COMES TO AN END

May 8, 1945 was VE Day: Victory in Europe. Students were told to go to class and if the end of the war was announced, fire truck sirens would be sounded at 9:00 a.m. They were sounded. The students, faculty, and staff gathered in the Hall of Music for a program at 10:00 a.m.

In Lafayette and West Lafayette, church bells rang and sirens went off. But the response was somewhat subdued because the end of the war was expected. And there was still a war against Japan to be dealt with.

The victory over Japan, VJ Day, was announced on August 14, 1945, "setting off a title wave of joy," the Lafayette *Journal and Courier* said. Twenty to forty thousand people danced and laughed, hugged and cried in downtown Lafayette streets the night before when it became obvious what was happening. Who could count how many were actually there? No one could be sure. They were there to celebrate, not count. Nothing like it had been seen since November 11, 1918. And this was even bigger.

Everything closed for the next two days. On August 15, there was music in Columbia Park played by high school and Purdue bands. Churches held special peace services. The weight of the world fell from the shoulders of Americans everywhere.

At Purdue, the celebration also began the evening of August 14. Food was free at the Sweet Shop. Bells rang. All "hours" when women and military personnel had to be back in their residences were extended. On August 15, all-day dancing took place at the Union. And the celebration continued.

In time, people tried to put what had been accomplished into words.

University historian Knoll wrote that the story of Purdue's contributions to the war would take a lifetime of work:

> One man's story, if told in all its significance, would fill a volume. The stories of the 17,500 [Purdue men and women] have an epic quality beyond comprehension—stories of officers and men serving in all parts of the world in all sorts of capacities—as aviators, infantrymen, battalion commanders, ordnance workers, officers, and men in construction and supply, on submarine duty, aboard aircraft carriers, fighting across France and Belgium and into Germany, fighting through the island-hopping campaign north from Australia and then in the Philippines.

So much is known and yet so little is known. It is not known how many Purdue men, because of devotion to duty, competence, and heroism were awarded decorations. But the pages of the Purdue *Patrol* and the Purdue *Alumnus* list hundreds of names of officers and men who earned citations by which their deeds were recognized. It is not known how many Purdue men were wounded, how many were commissioned, how many served in the various theaters of war, how many were in the Navy and how many in the Army, how many were aviators and how many Marines. What is known is that in the total war so bitterly fought and conclusively won, Purdue men and women, in service throughout the world, sailed, marched, flew, fought, and died in a war contribution beyond measure.[77]

James Doolittle Jr. was one of those from Purdue whose contributions were beyond measure. Beginning in January 1942, Doolittle was a bomber pilot in the Pacific theater and later served in Europe. He was awarded the Distinguished Flying Cross and the Air Medal with five oak leaf clusters. He studied at MIT and the Air Force Institute of Technology after the war.

Doolittle continued his Air Force career through the Korean War and was sent there after the ceasefire. He became a major and commanded the 524th Fighter Bomber Squadron of the 27th Fighter Bomber Wing at Bergstrom Air Force Base in Austin, Texas. On April 9, 1958, he was found dead in his office from a self-inflicted gunshot wound to his head. He was thirty-eight years old.[78] His father, James "Jimmy" Doolittle Sr., died September 27, 1993, at the age of ninety-six.

HARRY MICHAEL: HERO

Perhaps the bravery and determination of all Purdue men and women during the years of World War II can best be told in the life of one man: Harry Michael.

Although he qualified as a pilot, there was such a shortage of infantry officers, because of the D-Day invasion, that Michael's orders were changed. In late June 1944, the Army transferred him to Infantry Officer Candidate School at Fort Benning, Georgia. It was a devastating blow to Michael, who wanted to be a pilot.

Two months later he proposed marriage to his girlfriend Marjorie Butz, and she accepted. At about the same time, he had an argument with his father who knew how anxious his son was to get into battle. As a Great War veteran, he knew how dangerous that could be. "I'd rather have you come home as a coward than a dead hero," the father said. He was expressing his emotions as a father. But Michael insisted he would not come home a coward.[79]

In October, Michael wrote Butz that he "would do all within my power to make this a better world to live in and to make it possible for the average American to live a normal life full of happiness. I want our children to be able to take advantage of the things they were born for."[80]

He passed on an opportunity to become a paratrooper, which would have involved more training in the U.S., and in February 1945, he boarded a ship to England. A second lieutenant, he was assigned to Company L, the 318th Infantry Regiment of the 80th Infantry Division. The 80th Division had landed in France at Utah Beach in August 1944. It played key roles in the war and was called the "workhorse" of General George Patton's Third Army. It took part in the Battle of the Bulge from December 1944 to January 1945. The men were seasoned soldiers when Harry Michael arrived to take command of a platoon.

In his biography of Michael, Andre K. DeKever wrote: "When Michael arrived to take charge of his platoon, he was a green second lieutenant who had never seen combat before. Most of the men under his command, however, were battle-hardened veterans from some of the most desperate fighting of the entire war. While soldiers are required to be obedient to their superiors, respect and loyalty are virtues that leaders must earn from their subordinates."[81]

He quickly earned the respect of his men. They were in the lead in an attack on the Siegfried Line, a strong German defense line that stretched nearly four hundred miles and included eighteen thousand bunkers, machine gun nests and tank traps. Michael continued to write Butz from the front.

"We are a little deeper into Germany at this writing," he told her. "I've sure come to respect fox holes. Boy I've been plenty scared a couple of times, but always got through OK. We are in a German town now. I have my platoon in an abandoned hotel. I have some fine men. Naturally I have the best platoon in the company. You should see these boys in action. I just follow them around."[82]

Before dawn on March 13, 1945, Michael's company began an assault on the Siegfried Line near the German village of Neidezerf. The plan was to move through Neidezerf, as a way to penetrate the Siegfried Line.

"The Siegfried Line was considered by one veteran to be 'the strongest net of fortifications ever constructed by the human race,'" DeKever said. "Hundreds of miles long, the line was a solid phalanx of jagged concrete 'dragons' teeth' past which no tank could ride. Inside the concrete walls were hundreds of field artillery pieces, thousands of machine guns and hundreds of thousands of troops guarding against any allied assault into Nazi Germany. Everything that could obstruct a machine gunner's view had been cleared, giving the enemy perfect fields of vision.

"In many respects, Michael was personally at the point of the spear of a much greater attack," DeKever wrote. "The 318th Infantry was the frontline regiment of the 80th Division's assault. At the regiment's vanguard was the 3rd Battalion whose commander placed Company L in the lead. Finally at the tip of Company L was Lt. Harry Michael's platoon where Michael stood at the front of his men as they made their advance."[83]

Michael was leading his men up a ridge before dawn on March 13, staying low so he couldn't easily be seen. Somehow, in a quiet moment, he was able to hear the click of an enemy machine gun bolt. He used his hands to order his men to stay silent and remain where they were while Michael moved forward. He found two machine gun nests with German soldiers ready to fire at his men.

"Before the Germans could open fire, Michael stood up and charged . . . and the momentum took him to the lip of the gun pit before the Nazis could turn, [where he] took four German soldiers prisoner and slung their captured weapons over his shoulder," DeKever wrote.[84]

He sent one of his men to take the prisoners back from the front line.

Another of Michael's men, Private First Class Pasquale Gilberto, said they next heard voices in the woods. "The lieutenant led us around the flank (side) and we rushed them with hand grenades," Gilberto said. "We captured twenty-five Germans of an elite mountain division and got three cannon and twenty horses."[85] The twenty-five captured German soldiers were part of the Waffen-SS, an armed branch of the German Nazi Party.

Michael's men dug into foxholes while he went on two more solo missions that day. During the first, he killed two Germans, wounded four others, and captured six. On the second, he captured seven German prisoners, by himself. In the afternoon, he led his men in a frontal assault on a line of German pillboxes, where they killed ten enemy soldiers and captured thirty more.

In a matter of hours on March 13, Michael had either single-handedly or with his men captured seventy-two Germans, killed twelve, wounded four, and took possession of two machine guns, two artillery guns, and twenty horses. Seventeen of the Germans had been captured by Michael on solo missions.

March 13 was his twenty-third birthday.

The next morning, the Germans went looking for the man and his company who had inflicted so much damage so quickly the day before. Upon finding them, snipers began firing at the platoon. Michael went out on his own, searching for the snipers and drawing enemy fire at him and away from his men. He shot and killed one of the snipers. But the second got Michael.

Nine days later, Harry Michael's parents were notified that their son had died in action.

On March 2, 1946, in Columbus, Ohio, Major General Robert S. Beightler draped Harry Michael's posthumous Medal of Honor around the neck of his father, while his mother, sister, and his fiancée Marjorie Butz looked on. It is the highest U.S. military decoration awarded for "conspicuous gallantry and intrepidity at the risk of life above and beyond the call of duty."

It is the only Medal of Honor awarded to a Purdue University person.

The marching field inside the Purdue Armory is named for Michael, along with a portion of U.S. Route 231 near the campus.

After the war that stopped so many lives, life went on for others. In time, Marjorie Butz married Larry Fitzgerald, a letter carrier, and they had five children. She lived until July 2020. Her obituary read, "She was a devout, lifelong Catholic who believed serving others was important. . . . Marge taught us to appreciate the time we have with those we love."

In one of his last letters to his fiancée, Michael wrote, "Our life is going to be a wonderful one." In another he wrote, "If you want to get me something for my birthday get something for us and our home and then tell me what it is. Darling I am really in love with you and think about you before dropping off to sleep. I say my prayers and think about you until I fall asleep."[86]

PROFILE

JOHN F. BABBITT

STARK MEMORIES FROM THE DAYS OF A WORLD AT WAR ARE REFLECTED IN HIS BROWN EYES that still see vividly what very few people survive to remember today.

Seated in the large study of his large, beautiful home in Tulsa, Oklahoma, Purdue University graduate John "Jack" Babbitt, a tall man with a steady voice, is straightforward and serene. He is ninety-nine years old at the time of the interview. He would live past his 100th birthday. He describes scenes of terror calmly, quickly, almost detached from the horrors he lived through in the skies over Germany during World War II, when he and his fellow pilots and B-17 crew members returned to their base in England after somehow narrowly escaping death, only to go up in a couple of days to do it all again, and again, and again, and again.

As he speaks, the war is seventy-seven years in his past. It was a lifetime ago. But at the age of ninety-nine, the image of sometimes more than a thousand U.S. B-17 bombers flying in tight formation in the skies of Nazi Germany are intense in his sharp mind and reflected in his bright eyes. They are images that have never left him. They never will.

He was twenty-one years old in the winter and spring of 1944 and 1945, piloting the lead plane in the lead squadron, sometimes with a mission commander seated beside him. They flew their missions in daylight when their Norden bombsights were most effective. It was also when the enemy was most effective at seeing them—and the lead plane was the first target the Germans wanted to kill.

With skill, steely nerves, and determination, Babbitt maintained his plane at a constant speed and altitude while the Norden bombsight and bombardier controlled its direction. He didn't try to avoid the attacks coming at him. He flew ceaselessly, steadily forward, with flak from anti-aircraft guns exploding around him and German fighter planes shooting, slicing, and dicing as they tried to break up the formation.

When the projectiles from guns on the ground exploded in the air, metal fragments capable of piercing aircraft and killing men scattered everywhere. The black smoke from the explosions was so thick Babbitt felt he could get out and walk on it. And all the while German fighter planes were attacking him, head-on, coming at him so fast they became a blur, finally passing by him flying upside down. They flew above him and below him and sometimes so close he could see the enemy pilot.

Babbitt and his crew returned to their base after one mission with two hundred twenty holes from enemy fire in their aircraft. But they made it back.

If he failed, his life and the lives of nine others on his airplane would be lost, along with many more in the B-17s that flew behind, above, and below him, all following his lead. The missions could last six to twelve hours and temperatures could drop to fifty degrees below zero in the unheated planes. The men were protected by electrically heated suits.

Babbitt repeats the question when asked if the bombing missions were stressful. "Stressful?" he says. He was twenty-one. He thought he was invincible. "It was stressful from the standpoint you flew out every morning and someone was trying to kill you," he said. "Then you got home at night and you were in your own bed. But you had to get up the next morning and go out and fly again. And that hit some men pretty badly."[1]

He wasn't terrified when he was on a mission and under attack, Babbitt says. He was too busy to be terrified. "It was later on that you got terrified when you realized what you'd been through."

He remembers some men breaking out in tears when they learned they were going after a particularly tough, well-defended target.

Babbitt was part of the Army's Eighth Air Force, which played a key role in winning the war. But it came at a steep price. The Eighth Air Force took half of the U.S. Army Air Forces' casualties in World War II. "We lost more personnel than the Marines did in every one of the battles they were in all across the Pacific," Babbitt says.

How a young man barely old enough to vote in the 1940s came to command a B-17 with ten men on aboard, including himself, leading planes on bombing runs over Germany is the story of World War II and its impact on lives of millions of men and women.

"Today, I wouldn't even loan my car to a twenty-one-year-old," Babbitt says.

He was born on June 24, 1923, in Louisville, Kentucky, into a family with a long history at Purdue University. He can't remember a time when his plans included anything other than going to Purdue.

His maternal grandfather was Charles Philo Matthews, who came to Purdue as an assistant professor in 1896. Matthews was head of the School of Electrical Engineering at Purdue from 1905 until his sudden death from influenza in 1907. "During his identification with Purdue, Professor Matthews did a great deal of research work and was the author of many books and articles," the Purdue *Exponent* reported when he died. "He was one of the best authorities on electric lighting in the country, having been photometrist for the National Electric Light association for a number of years. . . . No one was more popular with the students for he was always very considerate, had a great love for and a deep interest in his classes at the university. . . . To him is due a great part of the credit for the fact that the Purdue Electrical School has risen to be one of the foremost of the country."[2]

Babbitt's father, John F. Babbitt Sr., came to Purdue and graduated in 1915 with a degree in electrical engineering. While at the university, he met Dorothy Matthews, daughter of Charles Philo Matthews. She was also a student but left school to marry without graduating—not uncommon for women in the nineteenth and even much of the twentieth century. On July 4, 1916, she married John Babbitt Sr., in Louisville while he was on a three day leave from the Ohio National Guard, which at that time was securing the Texas border along with Purdue Battery B and guard units from across the nation. The senior Babbitt also served as an artillery captain in France during World War I.

After the war, in 1924, Babbitt Sr. went to work with his uncle, J. V. Pilcher, who had a button and novelty manufacturing company in Louisville. At Babbitt's initiative, the company began making compact cases for women's cosmetics sold under the names Vashé, Pilcher, and La Chic. Babbitt designed and obtained a number of patents for the cases, which today are worldwide collector's items. Since the cosmetic industry thrived during the 1930s, the Babbitt family did not suffer during the Great Depression. Babbitt became president of the company, which later made shell casings during World War II. The Pilcher Company was sold in 1953.

The younger Babbitt graduated high school in 1941. His father asked him to delay college for one year because he was already paying room, board, and tuition for two daughters at the University of Kentucky. The boy worked on a farm during that year and enjoyed it. He even considered going into agriculture, until he learned how much it would cost to buy a farm.

Everyone alive in the United States on December 7, 1941 remembers that day. It was early morning in Hawaii. It was afternoon in Kentucky.

"It was a Sunday afternoon and I was sitting in a movie theater in the outskirts of Louisville and they shut the theater down and came through with an announcement that the Japanese had bombed Hawaii," Babbitt says. "We all got up and left."

His parents were playing golf that day, and he went straight to the country club to see them. "I talked to a fellow there who had been a Marine," Babbitt says. "He said, 'We'll wipe them out in no time.' He was wrong. I figured I was going to be in it and I wanted to be in it."

He started at Purdue in the fall of 1942, studying general engineering. By December he had decided he wanted to be in the Army Air Corps. He was told he could take part in a program where he would be allowed to finish school and then go into active service, or a program that would activate him quickly. He chose to stay in school, but was drafted almost immediately.

What followed was a long period of training during which he became a lieutenant and a pilot, eventually being assigned to fly the B-17 bomber. Some of his training was at the U.S. Military Academy, where the cadets were given the planes to fly when the weather was good. Babbitt's group also flew them when the weather was bad.

"I remember going out and flying in the snow one night," Babbitt says. "It became a real benefit to us. It taught us to fly by our instruments in bad weather. The weather was always bad when we got to England and you'd see a B-17 or a B-24 spinning down because the pilot had lost control and it was going down with the whole crew."

He shipped overseas in fall 1944. He was there during the Battle of the Bulge, a German offensive in December 1944 and January 1945. His B-17 crew was based in Framlingham, England, a town northeast of London. Their first mission was to destroy a bridge to Kaiserwald, Germany. "I don't think we damaged the bridge much," Babbitt says. "It was routine. We weren't under attack." Raids where they weren't under German attack were called "milk runs" or "dry runs."

"Then it got interesting because we went on to some tough targets," he says. "We went over to Berlin a couple of times. After about five missions I was asked to be the lead pilot. As a lead pilot I had to fly every day and practice bombing. It was interesting. Of course, it puts you under a different stress because the Germans always wanted to take the lead pilot out because it would break up the formation.

"We had one terrible misfortune," he says. "We were going to bomb Durban, Germany, an oil tank area. Before we got to Durban the Luftwaffe [German air force] came up. I had never seen so many German airplanes. . . . I was leading the upper squadron. What happened, the lead plane in the low squadron had an engine problem and they had trouble getting in formation. They never did join us. They were about a mile behind us. They couldn't catch up to us and we couldn't deviate. We had to stay in the formation. Those poor devils got hit by the Germans. There were eight aircraft in that squadron and every one of them was knocked down. It was a terrible day."

When the Germans finished with that squadron they came after Babbitt and his formation. They were rescued in the last minute, when U.S. P-51 Mustangs came and shot down the German planes. Only one more B-17 was shot down that day.

On the day of a mission, the crews were awakened early in the morning before sunrise. They dressed, had breakfast, and went to meetings where the mission was explained. As the lead pilot, Babbitt would take off first and fly in circles around the airfield while other crews flew into formation around him.

"At a certain hour and minute, we'd all head off for the coast," Babbitt says. "You had to be precise in your timing. Everything had to work just right. We flew at 125 miles per hour which wasn't fast, but the B-17 was stable."

It was sunrise before all the planes were into formation and on their way. "When dawn was breaking, you'd see some of the most beautiful sites because the Germans might be shooting rockets, V-2s, and you'd see this beautiful contrail go way up and headed for London," he says. "It was horrible, but it was beautiful."

Missions to Merseburg, Germany were the worst.

"Merseburg had synthetic oil refineries and it was critical to the Germans," Babbitt says. "We hated to do it because that was the toughest target. They defended that with anti-aircraft. I don't know how many guns they had. It looked like you could walk on what they were shooting at you."

When the men at the predawn meetings were told their target was Merseburg, they groaned.

In addition to Merseburg, they bombed many cities including Frankfurt, Dresden, Durban, Rotterdam, and Berlin, mostly hitting military targets such as railroad yards and factories. They also had bombing missions to German-occupied Czechoslovakia.

On March 18 and April 20, 1945, Babbitt flew in raids on Berlin and Oranienburg, a town near Berlin and site of a Nazi concentration camp. They were both termed "maximum effort raids" which meant every plane in the Eighth Air Force that could fly participated. The raids included more than one thousand planes, mostly B-17s, and Babbitt flew the lead.

"We took an awful lot of flak," he says. "We didn't have any losses that day in our group. But it was not a pleasing raid as far I was concerned. We were just to pick out a target of opportunity. We were just trying to soften up Berlin for the Russians who were right on the doorway." The bombs killed civilians.

Babbitt flew twenty-nine combat missions. His last flight was one he remembers more fondly, although it also had a nearly fatal incident.

By the winter of 1944–45, more than four million people in the Netherlands lived under German occupation. Many, especially those in large cities, were starving. An estimated eighteen to twenty-two thousand people died during the famine. Prince Bernhard, the German-born consort to Queen Juliana of the Netherlands, appealed to the U.S. and Great Britain for help. By late April 1945, German military officers agreed not to fire on Allied airplanes carrying food to the starving civilians between April 29 and May 7.

The British began dropping food first in a mission titled Operation Manna, a name taken from the Bible. The U.S. mission was named Operation Chowhound, a name taken from American slang.

Babbitt flew the lead U.S. plane in the operation, with the general in charge of Chowhound seated beside him. On takeoff, Babbitt realized his plane was badly overloaded and in danger of crashing. He finally managed to get it off the ground.

"I got on the radio right away and told them to stop all the other planes and check their weight," he said. "It felt good to drop food instead of bombs, but I almost got killed because we were overloaded." He had to fly in circles for an hour waiting for the other airplanes to lighten their load and join him.

"We dropped the food on a soccer field and covered that field from one end to the other," Babbitt said. "I've never seen that much food in my life. We knew the war was almost over when we started dropping food [instead of bombs]."

Germany's surrender was accepted on May 8, 1945, and Babbitt was soon home after the war in Europe ended. He expected he would be involved in the battle against Japan, but Japan's surrender was announced on August 14. After the war's end, he remained in the military and even considered an Army career.

"I was having a good time in the fall of 1945 when I got a telegram from my father," Babbitt said. "The telegram said, 'I have you enrolled at Purdue. Get your ass out.' So, I got my discharge and returned to Purdue." He left with the rank of captain and several medals, including the Distinguished Flying Cross.

While in England, Babbitt met and fell in love with an American nurse named Helen Harden. He and Helen married on December 24, 1945, in Louisville, and he graduated from Purdue in February 1948 with a degree in chemical engineering. The Babbitts had three children. Helen died in December 1984 and in October 1985 he married Jo Lewis. Together, they are involved in philanthropy.

In 2020, the Davidson School of Chemical Engineering at Purdue recognized Babbitt as an "Outstanding Chemical Engineer." Babbitt, who air-dropped food to starving people at the end of World War II, pioneered the manufacture of ammonia, which is used in fertilizer to feed the world. The citation states, in part, "After graduating from Purdue, he began work on the hydrogen bomb project. Babbitt then joined the newly formed First Mississippi Corporation, becoming president of the company within two years. He later joined Agrico Chemical Company, a subsidiary of The Williams Companies, as president, but left to form Devco International, Devco Overseas Company, and several other personally owned companies which designed, built, and operated facilities to process and market sulfur in the United States, Saudi Arabia, and Australia."

Seated at his desk after talking for two and a half hours about his life, his World War II bombing missions, and a very successful career which is still ongoing at the age of ninety-nine, he's not the least bit tired. He still has the knowledge, skill, and steady hand needed by a man making life-and-death decisions in an airplane under attack over Germany or making major business decisions in the front office of a large international corporation.

Babbitt's service in World War II impacted his life. It changed him. It changed everyone who lived through it. Not all the memories are pleasant for Babbitt. Some are hard. And they are never very far away.

"I think about those days occasionally," he says quietly. "I went into the war as a kid.

"And I came out of it a man."

10

WAR RESEARCH AT PURDUE

Most of the research was done on a do-it-now basis. West Lafayette residents had become accustomed to hearing, as they retired for the night even after midnight, the sound of firing as the professors still labored over their guns. Someone complained about the racket and [Purdue President Edward] Elliott made the standard response—"there was a war on."

PURDUE PROFESSOR AND UNIVERSITY HISTORIAN
H. B. KNOLL

Far from the World War II battlefields, the sound of gunfire was common on the Purdue University campus day and night. From its seven test ranges, Purdue researchers fired one million rounds of ammunition between 1942 and 1945, making significant contributions in small-arms engineering.[1]

So, it's not surprising that nearly eight months before the war in Europe ended and eleven months before Japan surrendered, the U.S military was already honoring Purdue for its ordnance research contributions that were helping to point toward an Allied victory.

On the evening of September 14, 1944, Purdue students, faculty, staff, and administrators gathered in the Hall of Music as Brigadier General A. B. Quinton presented the Ordnance Distinguished Service Award to the University. It was the first Ordnance Distinguished Service Award presented to any university in the nation.

The *Exponent* reported, "Quinton, who represented the Chief of Ordnance, assured the University that the service contributed by certain staff members and students was a significant contribution to the superiority in quality and quantity of American ordnance over that of the foe."[2]

With the war still underway, for security reasons the military could not detail exactly what Purdue had done in ordnance research on weapons and ammunition. However, the award stated: "The Ordnance Distinguished Service Award, presented to Purdue University in recognition of outstanding and meritorious scientific and educational contributions in war and peace to the development, manufacturing, and maintenance of ordnance material."[3]

In February 1956, a university report was declassified by the United States Army showing that Purdue's efforts in ordinance dated back to February 1942, soon after the attack on Pearl Harbor. Titled "Purdue University U.S. Army Ordnance Experiment Station Small Arms Division," the report had been completed in May 1947 and covered the time period from February 1942 to December 1946.[4]

When the war began, H. C. Solberg, head of the mechanical engineering department, put together a statement about what research his school was prepared to do and presented it to the military to see what it needed. The Army Ordnance Department had needs Purdue could meet.

In his book, *The Story of Purdue Engineering*, Knoll wrote that, after meeting with the War Department, it was decided the University should do research on small arms. It began small with two full-time and one quarter-time researchers, but quickly expanded to become one of Purdue's major wartime projects, employing fifty people and "thus becoming a sizable cog in the machinery though which the Ordnance Department developed weapons for World War II," Knoll wrote.[5] 123 different people took part in the research over the years.

"Its researchers were pushed with vigor, the test firings on occasion being conducted late into the night in fair weather and foul and personnel were able to show that they possessed not only necessary engineering ability but the stamina and willingness to handle their assignments throughout sixteen- and eighteen-hour working days," Knoll wrote.[6]

"Most of the research was done on a do-it-now basis," he said. "West Lafayette residents had become accustomed to hearing, as they retired the night, even after midnight, the sound of firing as the professors still labored over their guns. Someone complained about the racket and [Purdue President Edward] Elliott made the standard response—there was a war on."[7]

Mechanical engineering professor Dr. George Hawkins was named director of the U. S. Army Ordnance Research Project at Purdue. He became Dean of Engineering in 1953 and then Vice President for Academic Affairs from 1967 until his retirement in 1971. He was a member of the National Academy of Engineering and was internationally recognized for his leadership in heat transfer research. In December of 1945, the U.S. War Department presented Hawkins with a Certificate of Appreciation for his work.

Much of the ordnance research done by faculty in Purdue mechanical engineering centered on gun mechanisms and the heating and cooling barrels of automatic weapons during long bursts of firing. They tested many experimental weapons at the firing ranges built around campus.

The first of Purdue's firing ranges was an abandoned gravel pit and walnut grove just west of the Purdue Airport. It was hastily constructed, and sandbags were used to hold gun mounts in place. Ammunition was fired into a hole at the gravel pit and the concussion from the guns shook walnuts off the trees, sometimes landing on the gunner. In time, all the walnuts in the vicinity of the guns had fallen. Researchers had to herd nearby cattle and horses off the pastureland—a job that took several hours. And they had to carry equipment to the outdoor range every time it was used, from June 29, 1942, until late October 1942.[8]

In October and November 1942 there was an urgent need for tests, and so the researchers created a range beneath the west side stands at Ross-Ade Stadium. It was located at the end of a corridor leading to the locker rooms. Hawkins wryly noted the range was beneath the "sloping reinforced concrete of the stadium and above were the concrete seats which sell for $3 plus tax for Big Ten football games."[9]

The next range was a structure built behind and partially attached to the Mechanical Engineering Building and near the Heat Transfer Laboratory. It was a frame firing house, with a butt to stop the bullets that was constructed of reinforced concrete, sand, and sandbags. Between the two was open air. It was the best firing range to date, but since it was in the center of campus and directly below classroom windows, researchers could only fire weapons from 4:00 p.m. to 10:00 p.m. In the 1947 confidential report, declassified in 1956, Hawkins noted with no shortage of sarcasm that "authorities could more or less tolerate the thunder of planes as they barely cleared the roof tops after taking off from the Purdue Airport and could look upon the trains which brought coal to the Power Plant as unavoidable noise makers, but they drew the line at the firing of .50 machine guns during normal class hours and the hours when towns people wanted to sleep."[10]

The next range was built on a gully near the university tennis courts along Northwestern Avenue. It was bordered by Northwestern on the east, Ross-Ade Stadium on the west, and the university golf course to the west and south. Because it was essentially open-air, bad weather, such as snowstorms, interfered with the work. The range was eventually abandoned, but the location was used for the next three enclosed firing ranges.

One of those ranges was built in early 1944, right before a huge expansion in the research program. It was a building with an ammunition vault, a firing room, a firing tunnel, and observation rooms, according to Knoll who worked at Purdue during the war years. "It could be operated without regard to weather conditions and the enclosed tunnel permitted permanent installations of testing equipment. The range was built in the remarkably fast time of twenty-two working days."[11]

Two similar additional ranges were built. The seventh and final range at Purdue was the largest enclosed artillery range in the country.[12] Knoll said it was so safe that armor-piercing projectiles from six-inch guns could be fired. The distances between the various firing locations and the butts where the bullets were stopped ranged from 6 feet to 161.5 feet.

When all the construction was completed, three enclosed firing ranges, an ordnance laboratory, and five storage vaults for ammunition stood on a hillside above the men's tennis courts.

Hawkins noted in his 1947 report that, in spite of the hazards of firing experimental guns with live ammunition, no one involved with the research was seriously injured. "It is inconceivable that a project in small-arms research as large as the Purdue project could be conducted at no risk to personnel," he wrote. "It is with some pride and thankfulness to fortune that the safety record over a period of more than three and one half years is remembered. Though many of the guns tested were experimental models and six of these exploded, though at least a dozen gun barrels burst during test firings, though personnel were often fatigued after long hours of work, and though the nature of the experiments created some unusual hazards—yet no man connected with the project suffered any serious or permanent injury and no harm whatsoever was done to outsiders. There were accidents and near-accidents, and a few moments when tragedy could have occurred, but in every instance good fortune or good management or both allowed successful termination of the crisis."[13]

Hawkins credited the safety record to the design of the ranges, the rules for test firing, the alertness of researchers and "a run of good luck."[14]

One incident was particularly frightening, with just an instant making the difference between life and death. The researchers were testing a .50-caliber machine gun, firing hundred-round bursts at two-minute intervals. The distance between the firing point and the berm where the bullets stopped was about 150 feet, so communication between the areas was difficult. But a man in the butt area knew that when firing stopped it would be two and a half minutes before it started again. For additional safety, when the researchers were ready to resume firing, a long whistle was blown, followed by two short blasts that indicated firing would begin.

A worker in the range believed the bullets were not hitting the correct spot in the butt. Believing two and a half minutes was enough time to correct the problem, he entered, and picked up a sandbag to correct the problem.

Hawkins reported: "As the worker approached the butt with the sandbag in his arm, he heard the long blast and realized that the time between him and eternity was one second or less. He dropped the sandbag and somehow got to the doorway just as the projectiles began pouring into the butt. He was unharmed but shaken badly enough to have earned a half hour's recuperation."[15]

To paraphrase Elliott: Little time for rest even when frightened half to death. There was a war on.

The researchers had particular difficulty with the .60-caliber machine guns that were very experimental. During early experiments, the guns were fired by a pull on a lanyard forty feet long. Later, the researchers got closer to the gun but stayed behind a sheet of steel. In one instance, the gun exploded, and fragments were thrown as far as fifty feet. But three men behind the steel shield remained safe.[16]

The barrels of some .30-caliber guns being tested were fired in hundred-round bursts or continuously to test their limit. Before the limit was reached, the barrel would usually glow red with heat. But some went from red to yellow, and even white. Barrel temperatures were measured as high as 1400 degrees, and one was estimated at 1800 degrees. The guns got so hot that bullets were fired without anyone pulling the trigger, creating a huge hazard.[17]

MORE RESEARCH PROJECTS

Purdue Mechanical and Aeronautical Engineering were included in other projects. One with the Army Air Force included "a small mountain of research on the fundamentals associated with aircraft power plants including radiators, supercharger drives, exhaust pipes, manifolds, jet-propulsion devices, vacuum pumps, and axial flow compressors," Knoll said.[18]

At Purdue, a Department of Research Relations with Industry had been created in 1928 to align Purdue's resources with the private sector. In 1930, the Purdue Research Foundation was founded "to promote educational purposes by encouraging, fostering, and conducting scientific investigations and industrial research; by training and developing persons for the conduct of such investigations and research."[19] The two groups played key roles in Purdue research during the war. "During the war when research became a pressing necessity in a nation transforming itself into a war power, the Foundation and Department proved indispensable in bringing to the University the problems and the funds through which a large part of the University's contribution in research was made," Knoll said.[20]

The Foundation and Department determined what research the University could do and where it could be done and contracted with external agencies for funding. "In a report for the fiscal year of 1945–46 the financial history of the Department and the Foundation was summarized," Knoll wrote. "Funds from fifty-one sources had provided almost a million and a half dollars for research projects in chemistry alone. . . . Of this sum, about sixty four percent was pledged during the war years 1943, 1944, 1945. The pledges from civilian and federal sources were approximately equal during the war. About three times the sum reported for chemistry had been pledged by external agencies for Department- and Foundation-sponsored projects throughout the University."[21]

Knoll's report on Purdue's research during the war covered 117 pages in his book, *1941–1945: A Record of a University in the War Years.*

CHEMISTRY

Knoll said researchers in Purdue chemistry worked on synthetic rubber, antimalarial drugs, explosives, refrigerants, insecticide carriers, and the extraction of activated carbon from coal.[22]

The town of Oak Ridge, Tennessee, was created by the U.S. Army in 1942 as a production site for the Manhattan Project to develop an atomic bomb. Faculty, staff, and graduate students "wore a path between West Lafayette and Oak Ridge," Knoll quoted President Elliott as saying. "More than a hundred persons at Purdue worked for the Manhattan Project under a budget of more than $700,000. In one branch of this work, they dealt with the recovery of uranium and in another branch with the preparation of fluorocarbons needed at Oak Ridge. Hallways in the Chemistry Building were turned into office space and the hallowed Locomotive Testing Plant, a half century old, was scrapped to make room for this vital war research."[23]

Fifty-two members of the chemistry department received citations from the U.S. War Department for their research work during the war.[24]

PHYSICS

A group from Purdue's physics department was sent to the Radiation Laboratory of MIT for research into radar. Only MIT contributed more physicists to the Radiation Laboratory than Purdue.[25] Among them was John B. Fenn, a research professor of analytical chemistry. He did not return to Purdue after the war, but in 2002 was awarded a share of the Nobel Prize in Chemistry for work in mass spectrometry.

Another group from physics remained on campus to research atomic energy, according to Knoll, and five of them were later transferred to Los Alamos, New Mexico for work on the atomic bomb.[26]

Some of the most dramatic research at Purdue during the war was accomplished by Professor Karl Lark-Horowitz, head of physics. He worked on the properties of germanium, "finding techniques for large-scale production and purification and learning how germanium could be used in crystals for microwave radar," Knoll said. "Without this research the development of the transistor would not have been possible."[27]

BIOLOGY

Feeding military personnel and civilian populations around the world was a huge issue throughout the war. The Purdue Department of Biology conducted research on stored, dried (powdered or dehydrated) eggs to determine the effects of bacteria. According to Knoll, "data revealed that at the higher storage temperatures the total bacteria counts decreased with time, an indication that bacteria were not present in sufficient numbers to cause spoilage of eggs shipped to tropical countries."[28]

The department also did research using laboratory animals on the physiological impacts of high altitudes, important in aviation. "White mice and other animals were subjected to low oxygen atmospheres produced by decompression, so that factors affecting survival in rarefied air could be determined," according to Knoll. "It was found that temperature was highly significant, that water-starvation increased resistance, and that tolerance increased when the rate of decompression (rate of ascent) was slow."[29]

CIVIL ENGINEERING

The School of Civil Engineering at Purdue took part in the artillery research led by the School of Mechanical Engineering. Knoll said additional research was also conducted in the Civil Engineering Joint Highway Research Department and its Materials Testing Laboratory.

These researchers developed techniques in which they could look at aerial photographs taken from as high as 30,000 feet, to determine if the soils were suitable for construction of airports or highways. Purdue studies led to a national soil map to assist in expanding and building new airports.[30]Civil engineering researchers did work on stabilization of soils on airport runways, surveyed thirty-six airport sites to determine advantages or disadvantages based on soils, investigated "load-carrying capacities of soils" for airports and runways, conducted aerial soil studies in Alaska, and helped determine new highways that needed to be constructed.[31]

In Purdue's Materials Testing Laboratory, researchers did tests on military products, including "ammunition, glass land mines, ammunition boxes, spot-welding, welding workmanship, and canvas for use in aviation."[32]

CHEMICAL AND METALLURGICAL ENGINEERING

Five research projects for the government during the war were conducted by researchers in the School of Chemical and Metallurgical Engineering. In their laboratories, faculty made pure mustard gas for use in tests. Other projects involved substitutes for galvanized pipes, welding, the recovery of fats and feeds from garbage, lead as a substitute for zinc and tin, and making cresol from non-strategic material.[33]

Professor Norris Shreve worked on the Manhattan Project, consulting in the production of uranium for the first reactor pile at the University of Chicago along with the first atom bombs.[34]

ELECTRICAL ENGINEERING

Researchers in electrical engineering investigated precipitation static in airplane radio transmissions caused by rain, snow, hail, dust, and other particles in the atmosphere. Work conducted at Purdue on steel conductors for telephone and power lines was found to have a wartime application when copper and zinc were needed for other purposes. "Thus, a peacetime project was found to have a value in the strengthening of the wartime economy," Knoll said.[35]

Purdue electrical engineers worked with personnel at Wright Field in Dayton, Ohio on spark gaps and magneto testing. They constructed "possibly the largest and most versatile [at that time] drum camera oscillograph." Knoll described the oscillograph as "an electronic instrument that will give a visual picture of what is going on in an electric circuit."[36]

Other projects in electrical engineering included: television as a war instrument to track aircraft for anti-aircraft fire; a standard noise generator needed for tests of radio equipment especially in tanks and airplanes; and improved radio control equipment for target airplanes.[37]

AGRICULTURE

According to Knoll, "agriculture, through the school, the experimental station, and extension, probably more than ever before spread its influence throughout agricultural Indiana. It originated a great diversity of wartime enterprises and backed them with openhearted energy, even holding an emergency conference on Sunday in violation of its deepest traditions."[38]

As the war progressed, demand for food became greater and greater, but Indiana farmers with the help of Purdue "raised production to heights which some authorities had said were impossible," according to Knoll. Purdue developed and led special training courses for people in Indiana agriculture. It worked to keep fertilizers on the market that were best for crops and conserved raw materials that were needed in other war production. It improved the taste and nutrition of dehydrated eggs and vegetables, some of which people had found particularly offensive in the earliest days of the war. It also helped in determining where nearly seventy thousand agricultural workers would be placed.[39]

HOME ECONOMICS

The Purdue School of Home Economics was open to any student. Occasionally, a man enrolled, but the overwhelming majority of students were female, as women were often discouraged from studies in other programs. The school was not involved in any direct war research, but the women in the program contributed to the war effort in many ways.

Faculty taught courses for students and the public in nutrition, and assisted Army officers in hiring dietitians. "About eighty graduates and former students served as dietitians in the Armed Forces, while an uncounted number of others, undoubtedly large, put their training to use in war plants," Knoll said.[40]

Although a nursing program did not begin at Purdue until 1963, the School of Home Economics stepped in during the war and taught a class in home nursing to forty-five women. Those who took the course became qualified to do some of the work normally handled by professional nurses.

Knoll said, "The school could not train the fighters for war or do research on weapons, [but] it could use its knowledge of diets, foods, menus, clothing, and similar matters for the support of the civilian economy and it could train the girls needed for technical services in the war plants and elsewhere. These duties the school handled successfully."[41]

PHARMACY

The Purdue School of Pharmacy produced many pharmacists needed by the military and in civilian life during the war years. Its students were also trained in first aid and were offered a course in X-ray technologies. In its apothecary on campus, Pharmacy prepared nearly eighty thousand prescriptions in a single year. Research was also conducted in Pharmacy on antimalarials.[42]

THE DIVISION OF EDUCATION AND APPLIED PSYCHOLOGY

The Division of Education and Applied Psychology conducted research that helped the military in selection and training of pilots. It also worked with industry in hiring workers who were well-suited for the job they would be doing.

Faculty also did research on vision and found that 20–40 percent of employees lacked the vision ability for the work they were doing.[43]

"THE MEN AND WOMEN OF PURDUE DID WHAT WAS EXPECTED OF THEM"

In addition to research performed at Purdue to support the war effort, university graduates did important research in the private sector. John A. Leighty, who received his PhD in chemistry from Purdue in 1936, worked with a team at Eli Lilly and Company in Indianapolis. Leighty helped Lilly become one of the first companies to mass produce penicillin, which saved thousands of lives during World War II.

In 1947, after looking at everything Purdue and Purdue people had done to help win the war, Knoll was overwhelmed by what was accomplished. "In summation, if a summation were possible, it might be said that turn where one will, he will find that the men and women of Purdue did what was expected of them," Knoll wrote.

> The nation needed factories—Purdue men helped to build them. It needed ordnance plans—the engineers who for years have left the Purdue campus to enter industry were not found wanting in their design, construction, and operation. It needed the supervisor's skill to direct the production by which miracles were achieved—Purdue men contributed. It needed knowledge gained through research—Purdue men and women helped to staff the laboratories. It needed leadership—the record needs no further amplification. Technical war, depending for its outcome not only on the courage and sacrifice of millions, but in getting superior weapons to the world battlefronts in quantity and on time, was not made for these Purdue people any more than it was made for the Purdue men and women in uniform. But it was a war they knew how to support, and support it they did, through contribution of almost endless variety and immeasurable significance.[44]

With the end of the war, Purdue's work with the military and national defense was only just beginning. The twentieth century has been called the greatest period of technological and scientific advancement in world history. Most of that came after the war when veterans poured into universities such as Purdue in numbers no one ever imagined.

Purdue's enrollment of degree-seeking students had dropped to less than 4,000 in 1944. But by 1948, it exceeded 14,000. And those students, who had been in such a hurry to get into the fight in 1941, were now in a big hurry to change the world.

Purdue University aeronautics professor George Haskins with famed pilot Amelia Earhart. Image courtesy of Purdue University Libraries, Archives and Special Collections.

Purdue ROTC students fire cannons in front of Fowler Hall on Memorial Day, 1933. Photograph by J. C. Allen. Image courtesy of Purdue Libraries, Archives and Special Collections.

Purdue ROTC students exercise in the Armory, 1930s. Image courtesy of Purdue University Libraries, Archives and Special Collections.

Lawrence Aretz in his Army uniform from the Great War. Aretz became the first manager of Purdue Airport. Image courtesy of Purdue University Libraries, Archives, and Special Collections.

Walker Mahurin, of the 63rd Fighter Squadron, 56th Fighter Group, in the cockpit of his P-47 Thunderbolt, 1944.

World War II hero James H. Doolittle Jr., who learned to fly at Purdue Airport.

George Welch, who responded heroically during the attack on Pearl Harbor.

Frederick Martin, Purdue alumnus who forecast Japan's attack on Pearl Harbor.

Left to right: Captain Dorothy Stratton, U.S. Coast Guard Reserves; Vice Admiral R. R. Waesche, Commandant of the U.S. Coast Guard; Purdue University President Edward Elliott; Lieutenant Commander (later Captain) Helen Schleman, U.S. Coast Guard Reserves. Taken in Hall of Music, Purdue University, following the commencement exercises on February 27, 1944. Photo by J. C. Allen and Son. Image courtesy of Purdue Libraries, Archives and Special Collections.

Purdue Dean of Engineering A. A. Potter (right) meets with University President Frederick L. Hovde during the late 1940s. Image courtesy of Purdue University Libraries, Archives and Special Collections.

A common WWII sight: Navy personnel on the Purdue campus with female students. Image courtesy of Purdue University Libraries, Archives and Special Collections.

Frederick Branch, the first African American Marine officer, with his wife. He started his officer training at Purdue. Image courtesy of U.S. Marine Corps.

Purdue student and Medal of Honor recipient Harry J. Michael, who died in combat in March 1945. Image courtesy of the Harry J. Michael family.

John "Jack" Babbitt, while serving in the Army Air Corps during World War II. Babbitt was captain of a B-17 and flew massive bombing missions over Germany. Image courtesy of Jack Babbitt.

John "Jack" Babbitt in his Tulsa home in 2022, at the age of 99. Photo by author.

Early in World War II, an outdoor firing range on the Purdue campus was used for testing military weapons. Image courtesy of Purdue University Libraries, Archives and Special Collections.

Permanent firing range buildings later became a feature on campus during World War II. Image courtesy of Purdue University Libraries, Archives and Special Collections.

PART 3

1946–2024

11

THE SERVICEMEN'S READJUSTMENT ACT

The Stewart legend... should have been more definite about Stewart's work in Washington during and after the war. It indicated that R. B. had been there doing something but did not say exactly what. The whole story was... that he put his discerning eye on every rule, regulation, and piece of legislation affecting the expenditure of money from the G.I. Bill.

PURDUE PROFESSOR AND UNIVERSITY HISTORIAN
H. B. KNOLL

Bogdon Mareachen was a man who loved to tell stories, tales filled with long pauses to give his audience time to react with laughter. Born in Hammond, Indiana in 1923, he was the son of uneducated immigrants—his father from Austria and his mother from Russia. His mother spoke little English.

He was drafted into the Army during World War II in 1943 and after training spent two years in active-combat areas, he was assigned to a battalion in the Pacific that went in by ship with an invasion force to rebuild from the rubble and destruction that remained when the battles moved on.

"We were hit by suicide aircraft," he said in a 1995 interview. "I lost 117 buddies with one bomb. I was always on the deck of the ship during an attack.... We had fifty-caliber machine guns strapped onto the deck and we'd go after the planes. I could see those eighteen- or nineteen-year-old [Japanese] pilots in those planes. They were so close I could take off my sunglasses, throw them up, and hit those guys in the head as they flew by. When those planes came in they winked at you. They had guns in the wings. As they came in they fired one after the another and it looked like they were winking at you."[1]

He came home from the war in January 1946. Before the war, he had attended a high school that didn't offer the courses he needed to enter college. He was working in a factory when he was drafted. He was admitted to Purdue with the stipulation that he had to take those courses before arriving on campus.

"I was twenty-three years old when I went back to high school classes to catch up on my deficiencies," Mareachen said. "The principal told me, 'You are a veteran and a male and the girls will take to you. I only ask you one thing, you do nothing with the high school kids, especially the girls.'"[2]

Mareachen took a long pause after making that statement, allowing the listener to consider the situation.

He was one of 2.3 million veterans who went to college in the first seven years after the war, thanks to the Servicemen's Readjustment Act: the "G.I. Bill of Rights" that provided veterans with funds including for education, unemployment insurance, and housing.

The bill, passed unanimously by Congress and signed by President Franklin Roosevelt on June 22, 1944 (sixteen days after D-Day), paid up to $500 for tuition, books, and fees. Unmarried veterans also received an allowance of $50 a month, while the allowance for those who were married was $75. The single person's allowance was raised to $64 in 1945 and then to $75 in 1948. Married veterans received $90 a month in 1945, and in 1948 that was increased to $105, with $120 allotted for veterans with children. It was enough to send a generation to college.

Within seven years, three and a half million veterans attended college, technical school, or vocational school, thanks to the G.I. Bill. Between 1940 and 1950, degrees granted by colleges more than doubled. Within fifty years, people who had bachelor's or advanced degrees increased from 4.6 percent of the population to twenty-five percent.[3]

But everyone did not benefit equally from the G.I. Bill. There were challenges for African Americans, who faced discrimination in bank loans and regarding neighborhoods where they could and could not live. They did not have access to the best homes in the best neighborhoods due to racial "redlining."[4] Some universities continued to exclude African Americans. Unmarried women had difficulties getting loans, fewer women than men were eligible for G.I. benefits, and some colleges limited enrollment of women to make room for the huge postwar increase in male enrollment.

The *Pittsburgh Courier*, an African American newspaper, had started a "Double Victory Campaign" during the war in 1942. It spread among African Americans across the country. The Double V was victory abroad against fascism and victory at home against racial injustice. The fight against racism continued after the victories of World War II.

AN EMPTY PURDUE CAMPUS IS INUNDATED WITH STUDENTS

Professor H. B. Knoll, who was at Purdue before, during, and after the war, wrote: "As World War II was coming to an end the campus had an empty almost forlorn look. Most of the servicemen were gone after their training days at Purdue and hallways, classrooms, and laboratories often were vacant and never really alive with students. The university in the summer of 1945 appeared to be resting after four or five years of intense educational research effort. With respect to students, it operated at about half its capacity. Few people were on campus sidewalks, no new construction was underway, and there was scant automobile and truck traffic. Much of the life was gone and the dismal fantasy was possible that the good old days would not return."[5]

By February 1946, though, the rush of veterans was on, and the average of new students admitted to Purdue was one month under twenty-five years old. Some of the men who came were married and brought their children to campus. Men on the Purdue campus outnumbered women by a ratio of five to one. By 1947, 49 percent of students on U.S. college campuses were veterans.

The G.I. Bill changed Purdue. It changed America. And the Americans who benefited from it changed the world. The twentieth century became the greatest period of development in the history of the world in technology, engineering, health and medicine, and many other fields. And much of that came during the last fifty years of the century, through the work of what came to be called the "Greatest Generation," many of them educated by the G.I. Bill.

At the start of World War II, only two out of every five adults in the United States had completed the eighth grade. By 2021, the U.S. Census Bureau reported that 37.9 percent of people twenty-five and older had a bachelor's degree or higher.

In 1940, Purdue had just under 7,000 students enrolled. The number of degree-seeking students dropped to 3,762 in 1944, although additional military personnel were on campus along with people being trained for industry. By 1948, enrollment had more than doubled prewar numbers, to 14,674 students.

Residence halls were filled beyond capacity with students. Veterans were housed in the attics of campus buildings, in unused factories in Lafayette, and in portable housing brought in from former military bases. People in the community rented bedrooms to students. Students were required to have an address in the area to register. Some of them lived in their cars and used the address where they were parked until they could find a permanent place.

Students were employed to help erect the temporary military barracks that came to campus to help with the large number of students. One of those students was Arthur Hansen, who later became president of Purdue from 1971 to 1982. While they were called temporary, some former military structures remained in use until 2003. In addition to the barracks, round-topped Quonset huts were also brought to campus.

Complaints were few. The veterans were overjoyed to have the opportunity for a college education, made possible by the G.I. Bill.

R. B. STEWART AND THE G.I. BILL

Few people knew that one of the key administrators at Purdue was to a large degree responsible for implementing the G.I. Bill for the entire nation—making decisions that ranged from determining how much money the veterans received for tuition, to implementing a requirement that the allowance for a slide rule had to be spent on a Pickett and Eckel, the least expensive of the models considered sufficient.

The administrator was Purdue's legendary financial man Controller R. B. Stewart, who in 1945 was named Vice President and Treasurer. R. B. (Robert Bruce) Stewart, who became well known in Washington, D.C. during the war for his work in standardizing government research contracts and agreements with the Army and Navy for educating and training personnel.

"The Stewart legend . . . should have been more definite about Stewart's work in Washington during and after the war," Knoll wrote. "It indicated that R. B. had been there doing something but did not say exactly what. The whole story was . . . that he put his discerning eye on every rule, regulation, and piece of legislation affecting the expenditure" of money from the G.I. Bill.[6]

On the Purdue campus, Stewart is sometimes called the "father" of the G.I. Bill. To be "father" of the bill would be to create it. The name "G.I. Bill of Rights" came from the American Legion, and the concept came from the Legion along with other veterans' organizations and members of Congress. President Roosevelt had also requested a study to investigate helping veterans when the war ended.[7]

Stewart was not the father of the G.I. Bill. However, he was the chairman of the advisory board to the Veterans Administration and "had a firm voice in the administration of the G.I. Bill of Rights," according to Knoll.[8]

Ruth Freehafer, who wrote a biography of Stewart, said "he was the guardian of the bill since his committee studied and checked every regulation for its implementation. As chairman of the committee which made the concept work, he was instrumental in its success."[9]

In a 1969 oral history interview for Purdue, Stewart said there were two large problems with the Bill that had to be dealt with immediately.

"One [was], what was the cost to the institution and the other—was the student a bona fide student," Stewart said. "And this applies not just to colleges and universities, but to any level of education or training. So, we had everything from the sons of bank presidents taking jobs to get on-the-job training as a vocation . . . [to] small operators—plenty of filling stations who would make a deal with a G.I. [to] come and work."[10] With this ruse, station owners offered the veterans jobs that paid $40 per month. Then the veteran would apply for the G.I. training benefits—which paid $50 per month—and the owner and veteran would split the extra money. Both profited.

There were many questions: whether veterans were full or part time students; what the actual costs were to the schools; who would pay for equipment needed by students in medical and dentistry schools; and others.

Stewart was asked to become chief of staff at the Veterans Administration to administer the bill. But he'd experienced all the trauma he could take working with the government and military in Washington D.C. during the war. So instead, he was asked to chair the committee that would administer it.

One of his major battles occurred early on under the administration of President Harry S Truman. It involved academic freedom.

"Our fights with the efforts of people in the name of anticommunism in those days were rather hectic," Stewart said. "Truman told the staff that he wanted to see the list of textbooks used by [all the universities] because he was going to see that they weren't having any communist textbooks where we were spending our money to send G.I.s to school. I had to challenge that under the law. He had no right to do this. The law didn't go that far. And, of course, I won my position. And then in another instance where we were shown an order [to be sent] to the schools that any institution deemed by the Attorney General of the United States to be subversive could not enroll veterans. I said, 'Now just where in the law does the Attorney General have the right to decide where the veterans go to school? . . . You're putting us in the position where every institution in America is going to have to defend some radical community institution in California because the law just doesn't give you that right.' Well, they desired not to subsidize the communist groups through their education activities. Obviously, we would say three cheers. But there's a way to do this and there's a way not to do it and that was not the way to do it."[11]

Stewart won the argument. But he then learned that the order on subversive institutions was in the mail room ready to be sent out. Stewart said the order should not go out. He was told they would hold it. His response was to order all the mailings destroyed.

"And that's how close we came to having a dictatorship telling the G.I.s where they could go to school," he said.[12]

Stewart remained chairman of the committee until he stepped down in 1956. He continued to serve on the committee through the 1960s.

Carl R. Gray Jr., was an Army general who served as Administrator of Veterans Affairs from 1948 to 1953. He presented Stewart with a certificate of appreciation before Stewart stepped down as chairman. It stated:

"In recognition of the devoted and unselfish service rendered at great personal inconvenience and sacrifice in the interests of veterans of World War II and the Korean Conflict.

"As chairman of the Administration of Veterans Affairs Advisory Committee on Vocational Rehabilitation, Education, and Training, Doctor Stewart[13] has rendered conspicuous service through unstinting effort, wise counsel, courageous integrity, and forceful leadership in establishing sound principles of conducting training programs provided by the Congress for the benefit of war veterans.

"This certificate is presented in appreciation of a distinguished contribution to the government of the United States, to the cause of free education, and to the benefit of veterans of World War II and the Korean Conflict."

In 1964 he was given a presidential citation. It had been on the desk of President John F. Kennedy awaiting his signature when he was assassinated in November 1963. The citation was subsequently signed by President Lyndon B. Johnson, who had planned to personally present it but was unable to do that. Head of the Veterans Administration James S. Gleason Jr. made the presentation. The citation follows the wording of the early document from Gray and states:

"This certificate is presented to Robert Bruce Stewart in appreciation of twenty years of dedicated and unselfish service to his country and to the education and rehabilitation of those who fought her battles in World War II and the Korean Conflict.

"As a member and first chairman of the administrator of Veterans Affairs Advisory Committee on vocational rehabilitation and education, Dr. Stewart has rendered conspicuous service through unstinting efforts, wise counsel, courageous integrity, and forceful leadership in establishing sound principles for providing education and training for veterans and their orphans."

In making the presentation, Gleason said: "Through twenty years Dr. Stewart has consistently followed the position taken during the critical controversial experiences during the first months back in 1944.... He made it absolutely clear to educators of the nation, to government officials, and to all who were concerned in the program that the committee was to function in a forthright manner serving both the government and the schools without being unduly influenced by pressures from individuals or groups regardless of position."[14]

The same could have been said about him throughout his more than thirty-five-year career at Purdue.

REBUILDING JAPAN

While people in the U.S. worked to rebuild their lives, some Americans were in Japan helping to turn an enemy into a friend.

When Howard Ayres arrived in Japan in February 1946, there was an electric power shortage in the war-torn nation. Electric power was rationed. Assigned to the staff of U.S. General Douglass MacArthur, Ayres led rebuilding of the system.

When he left Japan in 1952, he was known as the Electric Power Czar.

Born in Columbus, Indiana, in 1899, Ayres entered Purdue in the fall of 1917 to study mechanical engineering. He left school to serve in the Army during the Great War, returned to Purdue, and received his bachelor's degree in mechanical engineering in 1925. He later earned a master's degree in mechanical engineering and a bachelor's degree in electrical engineering. After graduation, he worked with the Northern Indiana Gas and Electric Company, later renamed Northern Indiana Public Service Company.

In 1940, he returned to active service in the Army and was initially assigned to bases in the United States. But he wanted to go overseas and was ultimately assigned to MacArthur's staff, where his background in electric utilities led to his work in Japan.

When Ayres's work was completed, George Matsumoto, chairman of the Public Utilities Commission in Japan, said: "The seeds of free enterprise that you have sown have taken firmly to root. Your tactful but firm handling of the reorganization of the electric power industry speaks for itself as an outstanding tribute to your abilities as an administrator was well as a technical expert."[15]

In 1983, the Emperor of Japan awarded him the Order of the Rising Sun for his work reorganizing the country's electrical system after the war.

"I was glad to get it," Ayres said matter-of-factly from his home in Lafayette. When he first arrived in Japan, he remembered there was "a general lack of get-up-and go. They were a defeated nation. They were not doing what could be done to alleviate the power shortage."[16]

He was able to accomplish in weeks what otherwise would have taken many years.

A retired Colonel, Ayres died in Lafayette, Indiana, on April 19, 1986.

12

PURDUE, THE MILITARY, AND SPACE

I received a quality education. Purdue had a fine faculty and a wide variety of extracurricular activities to choose from, [and] there were great intercollegiate sports. I found the only problem was that there wasn't enough time to do everything you wanted to do—particularly study.

NEIL ARMSTRONG

It was the dawn of the twentieth century and to students at Anderson High School, the possibilities that lay before them seemed endless.

It was April 1900. It was spring and nature was blossoming around the Indiana school. There was excitement in the air as the assembled students and teachers prepared to listen to an address from the invited speaker, Purdue Vice President Winthrop Stone.

Stone rose from his seat and took the podium.

He stood ramrod-straight as he looked at his young audience. The president of Purdue, James Smart, had died just three months earlier and the board of trustees would soon name Stone his successor.

Stone was a brilliant man. He was the first person at Purdue named vice president. He had a PhD in chemistry from the University of Gottingen, in Germany, at a time when many University faculty did not have a doctorate.

His dark hair was wavy and would soon turn a distinguished white. He was thirty-seven years old in April 1900, lean, a mountain climber who enjoyed scaling tall peaks in Canada. In twenty-one years, he would fall to his death from a mountain summit.

With the new century standing before him, Stone chose to speak that day about the past. He talked about all the incredible advancements in science, engineering, technology, and medicine that had taken place in the nineteenth century—his century.

The nineteenth century brought about the steam locomotive, the Erie Canal, aluminum, the first electric motor, the telephone, the light bulb and electric light, the automobile, aspirin, advances in anesthesia, and so much more.

But the students in Stone's audience that day weren't interested in looking back. They were looking forward into their century that was just being born. And as great as the nineteenth century's accomplishments had been, the twentieth century would eclipse everything that had come before.

As brilliant as Stone was, as visionary as he was, there was no way that he could look into the future and realize that some of the students in his audience that day would live to see a man walk on the moon. And that man would be a graduate of his university.

In 1900, Orville and Wilbur Wright were still three years away from their short but successful first flight at Kitty Hawk, North Carolina. No one at the beginning of the twentieth century envisioned that less than sixty-nine years after Kitty Hawk, Tranquility Base on the lunar surface would capture the heartbeat of the world. In 1900, flying to the moon was a statement of impossibility. A person could say, "You might as well think you can fly to the moon if you think you can make money selling horseless carriages."

In the late twentieth and early twenty-first centuries, young men and women who would become astronauts came to Purdue. They would not have come to Purdue without its military presence on campus and its strong programs in engineering and science. And the early astronauts who studied at Purdue and became world famous helped to attract those who would follow them into space.

PURDUE, THE MILITARY, AND THE U.S. SPACE PROGRAM

Purdue's role in the exploration of space goes back to the 1940s. Beyond science fiction writers, few people envisioned what was not only possible but coming in the days that immediately followed World War II. But there were people who wanted to fly as fast and as high as science, engineering, and technology could take them. Some of them were at Purdue. And it was the military that would provide them with the opportunity to pursue their dreams.

Virgil Grissom was a small-town boy from the town of Mitchell in southern Indiana. He graduated high school in June 1944, enlisted in the Army and was called to active service in August. He wanted to fly airplanes, which to him sounded a lot better than being a foot soldier. But by the time he finished basic training in Texas, the war was nearing an end and there was a glut of pilots. He never made it to flight school or into battle.

On July 6, 1945, he married his high school sweetheart, Betty. He was released from the Army in 1946 and returned to Mitchell, seemingly for good. Grissom took a job with a company manufacturing school buses like other men in Mitchell. But he was restless. He wanted something more.

The Servicemen's Readjustment Act made it financially possible for him to go to college, so he traveled north and enrolled at Purdue University. At Purdue he picked up two things: a love for mechanical engineering and the nickname "Gus." He hated his first name of Virgil. He graduated in the winter of 1950.

In 1947, the United States Air Force had been created as a separate military service and as Grissom was graduating, it was recruiting on the Purdue campus. Recruiters told him that in the Air Force, he could fly. He enlisted.

He had never lost his passion for flight. It was a passion that would take him far in life—all the way into space. It was a passion that would also lead to his death.

At the same time Grissom was on campus another young man there also had dreams of flight. Iven Kincheloe was from Cassopolis, Michigan. He arrived on campus in the fall of 1945, took part in ROTC training, and graduated in 1949 with a degree in aeronautical engineering. He entered the Air Force as a second lieutenant and went into flight training.

He served in the Korean War and afterward remained in the military as a test pilot. On September 7, 1956, he flew the Bell X-2 faster than 2,000 miles per hour to a height above 126,200 feet. Kincheloe became the first person to fly an airplane above 100,000 feet, and for that he was nicknamed a "Spaceman." He surely would have been named an astronaut, but in July 1958, he was killed in the crash of an F-104A at Edwards Air Force Base.

In 1959, Grissom was the first Purdue graduate to be selected by NASA as an astronaut as part of its first astronaut class: the Mercury Seven.

As of 2024, twenty-seven Purdue graduates have been selected as astronauts by NASA or private companies. Fifteen of those future astronauts were involved in ROTC on campus or came to Purdue on other military scholarship programs. Purdue has graduated more astronauts than any other public, nonmilitary school.

There are five reasons Purdue has so many astronaut alumni:

- World-class colleges of science and engineering that attract people interested in flight and space.
- One of the largest and best ROTC programs in the nation, giving people an entry into flight and space through the military—and scholarships.
- An airport located on campus that attracts people who love to fly.
- A program with the U.S. Air Force that sent about 150 of its graduates to Purdue for master's degrees. Seven of them became astronauts. Another was Chesley "Sully" Sullenberger who became a commercial airline pilot and earned the name "Hero of the Hudson" when he landed a disabled airplane on the New York City river, saving the lives of all 155 people onboard and those of countless more who would have perished if had the plane crashed on populated land.
- Purdue quickly gained and has maintained a reputation as a university to attend if you want to be an astronaut.

World War II ended in 1945. Twenty-four years later Neil Armstrong—a Purdue graduate—stepped on the moon. Between 1950 and 1957, four future astronauts graduated from Purdue: Grissom; Armstrong; Eugene Cernan, the last man to walk on the moon; and Roger Chaffee, who would die with Grissom in the Apollo 1 accident.

They didn't know the future that awaited them. And they studied beside many more students whose names aren't widely known today, but who played important roles in science, engineering, the exploration of space, and research vital for national security.

PURDUE'S FIRST FOUR ASTRONAUTS

NEIL ARMSTRONG

Neil Armstrong came to Purdue in the fall of 1947. He had just turned seventeen years old, but he was studying on campus alongside thousands of World War II veterans.

"There was an enormous number of G.I.s who were returning from the service," Armstrong said in a June 2003 interview. "They were in all my classes—lots and lots of vets around the campus. They knew what they wanted to do. They were driven, so they made good classmates. They'd had a few years in the war to consider what they wanted to do when they got out. They were much more focused than my high school graduate colleagues. It was a good experience being with those fellows. Many of them were married and had children. They were very good to work with." He also admitted to being a "scared freshman" surrounded by so many grown men.[1]

While in high school in Wapakoneta, Ohio, Armstrong had considered enrolling at M.I.T. But after watching a football game in Columbus, Ohio in which the Boilermakers beat Ohio State, he decided to take a closer look at Purdue.

He came to Purdue on a Naval Aviation College Program scholarship, the Holloway Plan. He earned his private pilot's license at the age of sixteen and he loved to fly. But his real goal when he arrived on campus was to design airplanes. "I was fortunate to win an appointment to that program, which was a seven-year program," Armstrong said. "It included two years of college, then three years of active duty in the Navy, of which approximately two would be involved in going through flight training."[2] After completing three years of active duty, he would be placed in the reserves and could return to campus to finish his degree.

But as is often the case, plans changed. He was called to active duty in the middle of his sophomore year in January 1949. He went into flight training and received his wings in August of 1950.

The Korean War had started two months earlier. In the fall of 1950, he was assigned to the aircraft carrier U.S.S. *Essex* and flew missions over Korea until the late spring of 1952. Armstrong flew seventy-eight combat missions. His planned three years of active service ended while he was in a combat zone and were extended until the summer of 1952.

He returned to Purdue in September 1952 and flew in a Navy Reserve squadron in Glenview, Illinois while finishing his degree. He was a member of Phi Delta Theta Fraternity.

Armstrong, who died at the age of eighty-two after heart bypass surgery in August 2012, loved Purdue. "It was a wonderful experience, I enjoyed my time at Purdue immensely—before I went into the service and after I came back," he said in a 2003 interview. "I received a quality education. Purdue had a fine faculty and a wide variety of extracurricular activities to choose from, there were great intercollegiate sports. I found the only problem was that there wasn't enough time to do everything you wanted to do—particularly study."[3]

When he returned to campus, he knew exactly what he wanted to do. "My plan was unaltered," Armstrong said. "I was going to get the aeronautical engineering degree, go into the aeronautical industry, and hopefully enter into the design world."[4]

He graduated in January 1955. But, as earlier in his life, his plans changed.

Armstrong picked up more than a degree from Purdue. He met Janet Shearon on campus and they married in 1956. And he became acquainted with another young man studying engineering. His name was Eugene Cernan.

The two young men met at Purdue, sometime between late 1952 and early 1955. At that time, they gave no thought to space travel.

Years later Armstrong and Cernan would become very close friends, never dreaming while at Purdue what lay in their future. One would become the first man to walk on the moon in July 1969. The other would become known as the last man on the moon, as of December 1972—until someone goes again, more than fifty years after he returned to earth.

EUGENE CERNAN

Cernan, from Bellwood, Illinois, near Chicago, arrived at Purdue as a freshman in the fall of 1952. He had applied for a Naval ROTC scholarship and wanted to study engineering at Purdue.

"I passed [the exam] with a high score and signed up for the NROTC program at Purdue—a full-ride scholarship, plus spending money, three summer cruises, and graduation in four years as an ensign in the regular Navy," Cernan said in his book, *The Last Man on the Moon*. "The Navy, however, said the Purdue slots had already been filled and offered me the same deal at the University of Illinois. My father wouldn't hear of it because he felt Illinois wasn't a top engineering school. The Navy then offered a partial scholarship at Purdue, a program with a pittance of financial help, and a commission in the Naval Reserve. I didn't want it because I knew my entire family would have to work hard to pay for me to attend Purdue as an out-of-state student. But at dad's insistence, I reluctantly agreed, knowing that not only would I get a degree, but that I could still get a commission in the Navy, albeit in the reserves, and maybe somehow could spin that into my dream of flying. That was a big decision. My dad insisted he wouldn't have it any other way.[5]

"He was right," Cernan said. "My goal was to get a good education and get into Navy aviation—that's where I was heading."[6]

Cernan's NROTC scholarship would not begin until his junior year. So, he worked at a residence hall dining room to make some money. He participated in NROTC all four years at Purdue and joined Phi Gamma Delta fraternity. He majored in electrical engineering and his plan was maybe to become a Navy test pilot.

"My life started on the fast track at Purdue," Cernan said. "We had to do a lot of studying. My fraternity voted against having a TV. We thought it would be too much of a distraction. Later on, in my junior or senior year, we did get one—but we restricted its use."[7]

In 1956, he graduated from Purdue and went into flight training as a Naval Reserve officer. He soon was accepted into the active-duty Navy.

ROGER CHAFFEE

Chaffee came to Purdue from Grand Rapids, Michigan. As a high school student, he had applied to the U.S. Naval Academy at Annapolis, Maryland. The Naval Academy wanted him to promise, if accepted, to always remain in the Navy, and Chaffee felt he couldn't do that. His academic record was good enough for a Rhodes Scholarship. But he wanted to study engineering and that wasn't offered. So, he applied for, and received, a Naval ROTC scholarship that sent him to Illinois Institute of Technology in Chicago in the fall of 1953.[8]

He did very well. He made the Dean's List, took part in NROTC on campus, and did eight weeks of training on the battleship *Wisconsin* in the summer.

But in the summer of 1954, he asked the Navy to transfer his scholarship to Purdue where he would study aeronautical engineering. The move was approved.[9]

He took some private flight instruction while a student at Purdue, but money ran short, and he stopped. In the second semester of his senior year in 1957 he received flight training as part of NROTC. The Navy Officer Reserve Training Corps program at Purdue got him started in his flight career.

VIRGIL "GUS" GRISSOM

Grissom took flight training after graduation from Purdue and reenlisting in the military. In 1952 he was sent to the Korean War where he flew one hundred missions in a F-86 Sabre. He requested to fly twenty-five more, but that was denied, and he returned to the United States, ultimately becoming an Air Force test pilot.

In 1959, nine years after Grissom graduated from Purdue, he was selected by the newly formed National Aeronautics and Space Administration (NASA) as one of the original seven astronauts for the Mercury Program that began the U.S. exploration of space. On July 21, 1961, Grissom became the second American to fly in space and the third human. Yuri Gagarin from the Soviet Union had been first, on April 12, 1961. Alan Shepard was the first American and second human to fly in space on May 5, 1961.

On March 23, 1965, Grissom was command pilot on the first Gemini NASA flight with men onboard. He was later moved to the Apollo program to prepare for the moon landings and was named commander of Apollo One, which was scheduled to launch on February 21, 1967. But during testing on January 27, 1967, the space capsule caught fire. Grissom, Chaffee, and fellow astronaut Ed White died.

Chaffee had been picked by NASA for astronaut training in 1963 only six years after receiving his bachelor's degree. Also selected in the 1963 astronaut class was Cernan, who was a Navy pilot.

THE KOREAN WAR

Purdue's first two astronauts, Virgil "Gus" Grissom and Neil Armstrong, served in the Korean War, which lasted from June 1950 to July 1953. Ten Boilermakers died in the war and are memorialized in a plaque in the Great Hall of the Purdue Union.

Among the Boilermakers who served in the war was Richard Freeman, who grew up in West Lafayette. His father was Associate Dean of Agriculture at Purdue University. He graduated from Purdue in June 1950 and was commissioned as a second lieutenant in the Marines that summer. The next day he married his sweetheart, Jane. From late 1951 to early 1953, he served in Korea.

"War is bad, I can't see anything about it that makes sense," he said in a 1995 interview. "Many people were killed in Korea. It was a harsh country. It was good to get home. I hadn't seen my wife the whole year I was in Korea. While I was gone our first child, our daughter Debra, was born. I didn't see her until she was six months old. The first thing she did when she saw me was cry."[10]

NEIL ARMSTRONG AND EUGENE CERNAN

Armstrong was not considered by NASA in 1959 when it named the first seven astronauts, including Grissom, because he was not on active duty with the military. President Dwight Eisenhower wanted only military personnel to fly in space.

While Armstrong had always wanted to go into airplane design, his interest had shifted to flight testing. He took a flight test position with the National Advisory Committee for Aeronautics (NACA), which in 1958 became the National Air and Space Administration (NASA). He started flying in Cleveland, but soon was sent to Edwards Air Force Base in California, where he flew the X-15 along with fellow Purdue graduates Iven Kincheloe and Pete Knight. It was the most advanced airplane of its day.

After flying the X-15, Armstrong was selected for a program titled Dyna-Soar in 1960. This was a space plane that would be placed on top of a rocket. It looked a little like the Space Shuttle that would be developed later. The program was canceled in 1963.

While working on Dyna-Soar, he had his eye on the Project Mercury program.

Armstrong was accepted into the second class of astronauts in 1962. In March 1966 he was commander of the Gemini Eight mission. There were problems during a docking maneuver, and the Gemini capsule started spinning before Armstrong got it under control and returned to Earth.

Cernan was next into space, as the pilot of a Gemini Nine mission in June 1966.

After the fire on Apollo 1 in January 1967 killed Grissom, Chaffee, and White, the U.S. space program was placed on hold for twenty-one months during a lengthy investigation into the cause of the tragedy.

In April, eighteen astronauts were called to a meeting. They were told that when the program restarted, it would begin with Apollo 7. The eighteen men would be assigned to six missions, three men on each. But no one knew which mission would land on the moon. The space program would advance as fast as it could to fulfill President John F. Kennedy's goal of landing a man on the moon and returning to Earth safely before the end of the 1960s.

Cernan was assigned to Apollo 10, which launched in May 1969 and did everything except land men on the moon. The moon landing was left for Apollo 11, commanded by Armstrong.

Later, Cernan was given a chance to walk on the moon as the pilot on Apollo 16. He turned it down to get the position of commander on Apollo 17—even though NASA was concerned there would be no Apollo 17.

In December 1972, Cernan commanded the last Apollo mission to the moon. As he climbed back into the lunar lander for a return to Earth after three days on the moon he said, "As we leave the Moon, we leave as we came, and God willing, as we shall return, with peace and hope for all mankind. As I take these last steps from the surface for some time to come, I'd just like to record that America's challenge of today has forged man's destiny of tomorrow. Godspeed the crew of Apollo 17."

Cernan died on January 16, 2017, at the age of 82, still believing that the U.S. would one day return to the moon, where his footsteps remain just as he left them.

FUTURE PURDUE PRESIDENT WAS AIR FORCE DOCTOR TO ASTRONAUTS

Steven Beering was born in Germany in August 1932 to Alice and Stefan Beering. Steven (then named Klaus) had a younger brother named Hans.

In 1943, their lives became entangled with the world war. That summer, Stefan left his family in Hamburg and traveled to Berlin on business. In July, Hamburg was firebombed by the Allies. It was estimated that forty to fifty thousand civilians were killed.

Alice, Steven, and Hans survived, but were picked up by Nazi authorities and sent to an agricultural work camp because of their Jewish ancestry. As an adult, Alice was a practicing Catholic, but she had been born Jewish to Jewish parents and grandparents. The Beering mother and children were liberated by U.S. troops in 1945, near the end of the war in Europe.

After the war, the family was reunited and they were able to immigrate to Pittsburgh where they lived with Alice's parents, who had escaped Germany years earlier.

Steven had received little formal education in Germany, but he was an excellent student, graduating from high school and then the University of Pittsburgh. He was accepted to medical school at the University of Pittsburgh and graduated in 1958, having joined the Air Force in 1957. He did an internship at Walter Reed Army Medical Center in Washington, D.C., where one of his patients was U.S. President Dwight D. Eisenhower, the Allied Supreme Commander during World War II.

Beering was next assigned to Wilford Hall Medical Center at Lackland Air Force Base in San Antonio, Texas, where he became chief of internal medicine and performed medical examinations on astronauts just as the U.S. space program was getting started. His patients included Grissom, Chaffee, Armstrong, and Cernan. He remained there until 1969 when he retired from the Air Force and became assistant dean and later dean of the Indiana University Medical School, in Indianapolis.

He was named president of Purdue in 1983 and had a close relationship with the University's astronauts and people at NASA. He served as president of Purdue until 2000. President Emeritus Beering died in 2020.

U.S. AIR FORCE ACADEMY MASTER'S DEGREE AT PURDUE

Even before Armstrong landed on the moon, another group of military students began coming to Purdue from the U.S. Air Force Academy. Many of them were headed toward service in the Vietnam War before ultimately becoming test pilots. But they had their eye on what NASA was doing in the race against the Soviet Union to the moon.

In the fall of 1962, General Robert F. McDermott, dean of the Air Force Academy, contacted Purdue about the possibility of sending some of their top graduates to West Lafayette to earn master's degrees in an accelerated program. McDermott had modeled the Academy's curriculum after the Massachusetts Institute of Technology. He believed the Air Force needed leaders who were engineers, according to Academy and ultimately Purdue graduate John Blaha, who knew him very well.[11]

McDermott's plan was to have cadets compete for spots in the master's degree program at Purdue. They would be required to take some master's level courses approved by Purdue while still doing undergraduate work at the Academy.

Purdue approved the proposal for a program that would begin immediately after graduation at the Academy in June, run through the summer, and end in January, at the end of the fall semester at Purdue.[12]

In June 1963 the first Academy graduates arrived on campus. About fifteen were selected for the program annually until 1970, when the number dropped to about six per year. The program eventually became known as the "astronaut program," because seven men who took part flew in space, but it was not created to do this.[13]

It was very competitive. In April 1966, McDermott of the U.S. Air Force Academy wrote to Purdue Dean of Engineering George A. Hawkins. "I am sure you will be as pleased as I am to know of the excellent reputation which the opportunity to do graduate work at Purdue has among our students at the Academy," he wrote. "This year, for example, in a class of four hundred seventy seniors, we had fifty-six students who were in strong competition for the fifteen opportunities to participate in the cooperative program at Purdue. . . . As an example of the high regard our people have for this program, I note that two of our graduates who were awarded National Science Foundation Graduate Fellowships elected to use them in this program."[14]

The program ran from 1963 to 1976. Beginning in 1973, the students were given until May of the spring semester to finish their studies.

The seven men who studied at Purdue after the Academy and became astronauts and the year they received their master's degree are: Roy Bridges Jr. (1966), John Blaha (1966), John Casper (1967), Richard Covey (1968), Loren Shriver (1969), Guy Gardner (1970), and Gary Payton (1972). Academy graduate Chesley "Sully" Sullenberger, the famed commercial pilot who landed his airplane on the Hudson River in January 2009, saving everyone onboard, also completed the program, receiving his Purdue master's in industrial psychology in 1973.

The first three academy graduates to arrive on campus were Bridges, Blaha, and Casper.

ROY BRIDGES JR.

Roy Bridges Jr. was born in 1943 in Atlanta, Georgia, sixteen years after Charles Lindbergh flew solo and nonstop across the Atlantic Ocean.

He'd been fascinated with space since the Soviet Union launched Sputnik in 1957, so when he graduated high school in 1961, he went to the Air Force Academy. 1961 was the year of the first successful U.S. and Soviet human space launches, including Grissom. The first Academy class had graduated and been commissioned just two years earlier.

At that time, cadets took a general engineering curriculum which gave them exposure to a variety of areas such as mechanical, electrical, aeronautical, and astronautical. Bridges was interested in astronautical, so he decided he wanted to take part in the cooperative master's program at Purdue, with its focus on astronautical engineering.

Bridges graduated ninth in a class of 524. He was admitted to the Purdue program, and one week after graduating from the Academy, he was moving into an apartment in West Lafayette with fellow Air Force Academy graduate John Blaha.

The Academy graduates took two summer school courses, immediately followed by an accelerated course that began in August and ended before the fall academic semester started in September. That was followed by five courses in the fall semester, ending in January.

"John and I joined a sailing club at Purdue," Bridges says. "We had our first test. I made 21 percent, which was not the lowest grade. Everyone did poorly. So, the instructor said he'd give us ten pop quizzes through the summer and replace our test grade with what we got on the quizzes. My social life ended right there."[15]

In his book, *An Improbable Astronaut*, Bridges says: "These were difficult courses. I never got closer to having an ulcer than I did near the end of the fall semester as I prepared for final exams." In his fall semester, his grades were four As and one B.[16]

He and Blaha did go to football games. And they went to a Thanksgiving potluck dinner where Bridges met a young woman named Benita. He was so busy studying that he didn't ask her on a date until a graduation ball at the end of the semester in January. She accepted. They married on March 26, 1967, after he completed flight training. In December of 1968, Bridges was sent to Vietnam where he flew 262 combat missions.

He was selected by NASA for astronaut training in 1980, and on July 12, 1985, he was pilot on a Challenger space shuttle mission.

Bridges retired from the Air Force in 1996 at the rank of major general. In 1997, NASA named him director of the Kennedy Space Center, a position he held for more than six years. He was named director of NASA's Langley Research Center in 2003. He retired from NASA in December 2005 and became a director with Northrop Grumman, an aerospace and defense company. He retired from that company in January 2019.

JOHN BLAHA

Blaha graduated from the Air Force Academy in 1965 in the same class as Roy Bridges Jr., and worked hard to take part in the Purdue master's degree program. Even while he was studying at the Academy, Blaha also had his eye on the U.S. space program. He believed the master's degree from Purdue would increase his chances of being selected by NASA, and he went for it. "The buzzword was, if you want to be an astronaut, go to Purdue," Blaha says.[17]

In his senior year there were eighty cadets still in competition for the program that year. Blaha took three master's degree level courses in his last year at the Academy. "Near the end of March, we would learn who was selected and thirteen of us actually came to Purdue including Roy Bridges. I was best man at his wedding." Blaha said Bridges was the perfect example of the importance of having engineers in leadership.[18]

Blaha recalls the classes at Purdue as very difficult, and the professors as great and challenging. He was at Purdue before the moon landing and remembers one of the projects was designing a mission to land astronauts on the lunar surface. He loved Purdue.[19]

Blaha flew 361 combat missions in Vietnam. He became an Air Force test pilot and was selected as an astronaut in June 1980. He was a veteran of five space missions and spent four months on the Russian space station Mir. He retired from the Air Force with the rank of colonel when he was sent to Russia in January 1995 for extensive training for the Mir mission. Blaha then flew 128 days in space with two Russian cosmonauts.

JOHN CASPER

"I wanted to be an astronaut since I was ten years old," says John Casper.[20] He succeeded at his life's goal, and his success was helped by a master's degree in astronautics from Purdue.

He arrived on the West Lafayette campus in June 1966 shortly after graduating from the Air Force Academy with a 3.5 grade point average. "It was very challenging," he says. "It was tough. I was surprised at how tough it was academically. I had to do a lot of studying. Purdue was more in depth than the Academy. They had great instructors who were experts in their field."[21]

He also found Purdue to be large and diverse. It was a school with a leading engineering program. But it also had people studying agriculture, science, and liberal arts. Casper lived with his wife on campus in what was then called the Married Student Courts. The students did not have calculators. They used slide rules, as did the engineers at NASA in the 1960s.

In January 1967, Casper finished his studies at Purdue. It was the same month Edward White and Purdue alumni Gus Grissom and Roger Chaffee were killed during a rehearsal for Apollo 1. Casper had met White when the astronaut visited the academy.

"I was face to face with one of my space heroes, amazed that he was so genuine and humble as he described his spacewalk and future Apollo Moon missions," Casper wrote in his book, *The Sky Above*. "He encouraged me to pursue a flying career and my dream of becoming an astronaut."[22]

After Purdue, Casper went to flight school and on to Vietnam where he flew 229 combat missions. He was on one of those missions when Armstrong stepped onto the moon. He was selected by NASA in 1984 as an astronaut, and flew as pilot and then commander on four space flights. In 1996 he retired from the Air Force with the rank of colonel.

PURDUE ROTC ASTRONAUTS

Don Williams, who graduated in 1964, Jerry Ross, who received his bachelor's degree in 1970 and his master's degree in 1972, Mark Brown, who graduated in 1973, and Mark Polansky, who graduated in 1978, all came to Purdue as freshmen and participated in four years of ROTC. They studied engineering and all became astronauts.

DON WILLIAMS

Don Williams grew up on a small farm not far from Purdue. He remembered hot summer days working out in the field and watching airplanes from the University airport flying in the sky.

"I can remember looking up at the sky and the airplanes from that tractor and thinking, 'That looks like a lot more fun than this.' As it turns out, it was."[23]

In 1960, after graduating from Otterbein High School along with twenty-four other students in his class, he enrolled at Purdue on a Naval ROTC scholarship.

"I think Purdue's ROTC program is part of the reason the University has attracted so many astronauts," he said. "It's a large and really strong program.

"I loved Purdue but it was challenging. Coming from a small high school and not really having a strong academic background, it was quite a step up. It was challenging, but it was worth the work. Purdue gave me a foundation to go forward in the direction I wanted to go, which eventually led to being picked for the space program. At Purdue I learned how to ask questions, where to go to find information, how to do technical analysis."[24]

Williams graduated in 1964. He did four tours of duty in Vietnam, flying 330 combat missions. After serving as a test pilot, he was selected by NASA in 1978 to be an astronaut. He flew on two Space Shuttle missions, in 1985 as the pilot and in 1989 as commander.

Williams died in 2016 at the age of seventy-four.

JERRY ROSS

Purdue's Jerry Ross was the first astronaut in the world to fly on seven space missions. Since he set that record, one other astronaut, Franklin Chang-Diaz, has also flown seven missions as of the spring of 2024.

Ross grew up in rural northern Indiana. A lifelong friend, Jim Gentleman, remembered lying on bales of hay with Ross when they were boys in the mid-1950s, looking up at the stars. "One day people are going to go up there," Ross said. "And I'm going to be one of them."[25]

As astronauts were being selected in the earliest days, Ross saw that they were engineers and four of them had graduated from Purdue. He set his sights on being a Purdue engineer.

In the fall of 1966 when he was registering for classes, the University had just ended its mandatory ROTC training for all freshman and sophomore men. But Purdue did require that freshmen take ROTC or physical education. Physical conditioning was part of ROTC training.

The physical education option was swimming, and Ross didn't like the idea of walking across the campus to reach the pool in what would become cold weather in November through January. Besides, he says, "I swim like a rock."[26]

When he arrived on campus, he wasn't thinking about a military career. But he signed up for Air Force ROTC. He selected the Air Force because it was the branch he felt was most involved in space. He quickly discovered he loved AFROTC and he did well. He received an AFROTC scholarship for his sophomore, junior, and senior years.

"I found it to be interesting in many ways," he says. "It was about leadership and history and management. My parents weren't flush with money and I got that three year scholarship. I was also impressed with my fellow AFROTC students and the staff."[27]

He wanted to be a pilot, but an Air Force doctor told him his eyesight did not qualify. He received a bachelor of science degree and a master's degree in mechanical engineering. He met and married his wife, Karen, while at Purdue. After leaving the university, he graduated first in his class in Air Force flight engineer's school, and he became an Air Force engineer who flew in planes with test pilots.

Ross became an astronaut in 1980. His first mission was in 1985. His seventh and last was in 2002, but he continued to work at NASA until retiring in January 2012. In addition to his seven flights, he had nine spacewalks, which ranked third among astronauts as of 2023.

He retired from the Air Force with the rank of colonel in March 2000.

MARK BROWN

Mark Brown grew up in Valparaiso in northern Indiana.

"I was one of those kids that grew up always wanting to be a pilot, and in particular a fighter pilot," he says. "I had that bug from the day I was born, even though I never flew an airplane or was even in an airplane until right before I went to college."[28]

That was a $10 ride at a local airport.

"I was a kid of the fifties," he says. "The space program began in 1961. And in those days, astronauts were bigger-than-life people. I mean, they were up there on the mountain with Moses and God and none of us thought that we could aspire to such greatness."[29]

As a freshman in high school, Brown confessed his dreams to a school counselor who said he was going to have to go to college and get a degree. Brown said his family didn't have the money to send him to college. The counselor told him he could seek admittance to a military academy or get an ROTC scholarship. He talked to an Air Force officer who inspired him to give it a try, and Brown applied for an Air Force ROTC scholarship and admittance to the Air Force Academy.

During his senior year of high school, he was working at the local IGA store as a butcher's assistant. His mother called and said a letter had arrived. He told her to open it and it said he had won a four-year AFROTC scholarship.

"I was asked 'Where do you want to go?'" he says. "I said 'Who has the best aerospace program? Purdue does. I'll go to Purdue.'"[30]

Shortly after that he was told he had not been admitted to the Academy, but was a runner-up, meaning that he would be headed to Purdue in the fall. That summer, Neil Armstrong became the first person to walk on the moon, and Brown arrived at Purdue excited about his future.

"I had this sense of freedom as a new freshman on campus. It was just intoxicating to me," he says. "There were these things called girls at Purdue that I was discovering for the first time and Saturday football games. And after being immersed in that environment for about two weeks, I got called into my AFROTC commander's office and he said, 'Congratulations. Somebody's already dropped out of the Academy. Would you like to go?' I had a friend from my hometown who did go to the academy. I talked to him, and he was complaining about getting up at 5:55 in the morning, and wearing uniforms, and marching from here to there, sitting at attention, and there were no girls. So, when they made that offer, I said, 'Very honestly, sir, with all due respect, I'm going to stay at Purdue.' I have never looked back on that decision. It was probably the best decision I made at that time of my life."[31]

As a young aeronautical and astronautical engineering student, Brown struggled with his studies, which took all his time.

"It was so time consuming, initially, I kind of steered away from leadership positions in AFROTC," he says. "But of course, that's not what the military and AFROTC is all about. When I was a junior getting ready to go home for the summer, I got called in by the colonel in charge of AFROTC. And he said, 'Congratulations, you're going to be the Commandant of Cadets next semester.'

"I found out later that they thought I had the potential to be a good leader, but they thought that I was kind of staying below the radar and concentrating on academics, and they wanted to make sure I did get the balanced experience at Purdue," Brown says. "It was probably one of the best things they ever did. It threw me out in front, made me stand up on the stage behind the podium, take charge, take on that leadership perspective, to organize, give direction, break up tasks, and farm them out and get the job done. And that experience was worth gold to me because learning how to do that, not only paid off in my military career and NASA career, but twenty years later when I went to industry, I felt that I was just kind of going back to what I already knew how to do."[32]

Brown graduated in 1973. After flight training, he earned a master's degree at the Air Force Institute of Technology and in 1980 got a job with NASA in Houston as an engineer. He was selected as an astronaut in 1984.

Brown's first flight as a mission specialist was in 1989. He flew a second as a mission specialist in 1991. In 1993 he retired from the Air Force and NASA and went to work in the private sector.

MARK POLANSKY

Mark Polansky came to Purdue in 1974 from Edison, New Jersey, located a half hour outside of New York City. He served three years in the University's Air Force ROTC.

He was in Yankee Stadium the evening Neil Armstrong and Edwin "Buzz" Aldrin landed on the moon. The game stopped while the crowd joined in singing "God Bless America."

"I was living in Cary Quad as a freshman when Gene Cernan paid a visit one evening to one of the common areas," Polansky says. "I was up close with an astronaut who walked on the moon, and I was naturally in awe. That was the first time that I even thought about really trying to become an astronaut. I then started to look at all of the current astronaut bios, and just about everyone was a graduate of a military test pilot school. From there, my path was somewhat clear in that I needed to join the military and become a fighter pilot. That meant looking at the Navy, Marine Corps, and Air Force. One of my good friends in the dorm was already in Air Force ROTC. One thing led to another, and I wound up joining Purdue's Air Force ROTC as a sophomore with the dream to obtain a scholarship with a slot to pilot training."[33]

He received a two-year scholarship at the end of his sophomore year. His plans hit a bump when he was unable to get an Air Force pilot slot. He was offered the chance to become a navigator, but he wanted to be a pilot. At the end of his junior year, he received a letter from a Navy recruiter in Indianapolis with an offer to become a Navy pilot. When he told the commander of his ROTC unit that he was planning to leave the Air Force for the Navy in order to fly, he was given an Air Force pilot slot within a week.

In 1978, Polansky received his bachelor's and master's degrees in aeronautical engineering. Three future astronauts graduated in the Class of '78: Polansky, David Wolf, and Greg Harbaugh.

After graduation and further training, he flew the F-15 fighter jet. "That was a great assignment, and I was just enjoying the life," Polansky says. "It was great to have the responsibility to be a flight leader. I remember how cool it was to be twenty-four or twenty-five years old and be in charge of a flight of four $20 million fighters coming back from a successful mission. I just thought, you know, your average twenty-four-year-old doesn't get to do these things."[34]

His next assignment was as an Air Force test pilot at Edwards Air Force Base. In 1992, he went to NASA—not yet as an astronaut, but as an instructor teaching astronauts the landing technique of flying a shuttle. In 1996, he was selected as an astronaut and flew three missions in space. On his final mission in 2009, he flew with his Purdue classmate, David Wolf. Polansky retired from NASA in 2012 and now works in the private aerospace sector.

"ROTC provided me with a great introduction to life in the military, and it also provided some early lessons in leadership and service that I have never forgotten," Polansky says. "I actually had no idea upon graduation if I would enjoy flying, or if I'd be successful. Fortunately, flying soon became a passion, and I had the good fortune of being good at it. I had a fabulous career flying fighter jets, including an overseas assignment, and I was then able to attend and graduate from the United States Air Force Test Pilot School. All of this led to a job at NASA. And it all started at Cary Quad during a chance encounter with Gene Cernan."[35]

MICHAEL MCCULLEY AND SCOTT TINGLE

Two other students came to Purdue from the military and went on to become astronauts. They are Michael McCulley, who graduated in 1970, and Scott Tingle, who received his master's degree in 1988. McCulley is retired from the Navy and Tingle is an active-duty captain.

McCulley became a NASA astronaut and CEO of United Space Alliance. (See Chapter 16 for more on this.) He was succeeded as CEO of United Space Alliance by Richard Covey, who came to Purdue from the Air Force Academy and went on to become an astronaut.

Tingle served in the Navy Reserves before coming to Purdue to earn a master's degree in mechanical engineering in 1998. After Purdue, he worked as an aerospace engineer in California. Tingle loved engineering, but while flying an airplane on his lunch break one day, he realized that what he really wanted to do was fly. He went on active duty with the Navy in 1991 and earned his wings in 1993. He flew 54 combat missions in Afghanistan and Iraq.

Now a Navy captain, Tingle was selected for astronaut training by NASA in 2009. He went to the International Space Station in December 2017 and remained there until June 2018. In the spring of 2024, he was training as the Starliner-1 Commander. It will be the first Boeing Starliner crew mission to the international space station scheduled in 2025 after a test crewed-mission in 2024. He believes in the NASA plan to return people to the moon and beyond.[36]

"There's always the (question) 'Why did you climb the mountain?'" Tingle says. "Because it's there. We all travel down the street and look out the window, we're in the backyard and the moon is out there. We can't miss it. It's beautiful. It's there every day. Why would we not want to go there? We need to go there."[37]

Williams, Ross, Brown, and McCulley have been inducted into Purdue's ROTC Hall of Fame, along with Cernan and Chaffee. Grissom, Armstrong, and Tingle did not take part in ROTC at Purdue. Polansky has been nominated for the Hall of Fame Class of 2026.

The Hall of Fame was established in 1974 to recognize men and women with the attributes of leadership, integrity, moral courage, and self-discipline that ROTC develops. Service to the nation, to the community, and outstanding leadership in the fields of business, government, education, or other professional fields are used as the basis for selection.

Purdue's nonmilitary astronauts and their years of graduation are: Charles Walker (1971), Janice Voss (1975), Greg Harbaugh (1978), David Wolf (1978), Mary Ellen Weber (1984), Andrew Feustel (1989), Beth Moses (1992; 1994), Audrey Powers (1999), Loral O'Hara (2009), and Shirish Bandla (2011).

13

A TEAM LIKE NO OTHER: SIX NATIONAL CHAMPIONSHIPS

The Purdue Drill Team was the crucible that melted and forged us into the military officers we became.

WAYNE HENDERSON

It has the best record of any team in the history of Purdue University.

So, it's not surprising that on April 6, 1961, on a beautiful spring day, members of that team found themselves in the White House Rose Garden in Washington, D.C. at a private reception with President John F. Kennedy. The students made him an honorary member of their team, making Kennedy the only U.S. president to be part of a Purdue student organization.

The student organization was the Purdue Drill Team, and from 1947 to 1970, it compiled a record that will never be beaten. The team was the national collegiate champion in 1955, 1956, 1958, 1959, 1960, and 1962. No other team at Purdue has won as many national championships. It also earned second place finishes in the national championships in 1957, 1961, and 1963.

Put another way, it was first or second in the nation from 1955 to 1963—nine straight years. The team took part in other competitions in addition to the annual national championship meet. In a single year, their winning percentage in competitions was ninety-five percent. The team didn't finish lower than second in any competition until 1960. From 1947 through 1958, the team record was 31–2. Through 1959 it was 41–3. At the end of the 1960 season, it was 45–4.

The Purdue Drill Team members bonded into a family that was still holding and planning reunions on campus in 2023. They held what they called their "last reunion" in an emotional gathering in April 2024.

These Purdue students were incredible. They were amazing. They were recognized from coast to coast as the best. At least once, teams that competed against them admitted before the competition even began that the best they hoped for was second place. In an era when people say you don't have to be perfect, they demanded perfection by each of the twenty-four young men who took part in the competitions, led by the twenty-fifth member—a drill team captain.

They marched, 120 steps a minute, tightly formed as a group, their white-gloved hands moving three inches forward and six inches back in absolute uniformity. The white spats above their shoes were perfectly aligned as they hit the ground and stepped forward. They spun their rifles in perfect unison, tossed them back and forth, and marched down the field in such perfection that the twenty-four students were perceived as one.

Then, they would break ranks, but remain in perfect marching cadence, creating formations that sometimes seemed chaotic, before rejoining as if a magnet had pulled them all back together again. They would march one direction down a field and the next moment completely reverse direction.

There was never anything like it at Purdue before. There has never been anything like it since. It was the greatest drill team in the history of Purdue, and quite likely in the history of the United States.

Between 1948 to 1971, Ed Sullivan had one of the most popular television shows in the nation. It was broadcast from New York City. But one night in 1954, he was at Purdue's Elliott Hall, hosting his "Toast of the Town" TV program. While at the university, Sullivan also wanted to see if the Drill Team could perform on a theater stage and appear on his TV show.

The team performed for him—in the Armory. According to the book *The Purdue Drill Team*, "James 'Bud' Malsbary, the drill captain, recalled the discussion he had with Sullivan after the exhibition. Based on space required for the movements, Sullivan decided that there was inadequate space for the performance to fit on the stage."[1]

History, photos and videos of the team are available online at http://purduedrillteam.org.

The Drill Team was a student extracurricular activity. Although they were associated with ROTC leadership, it wasn't officially part of Purdue ROTC. Some of the men who marched were in ROTC, others were not, but all the men practiced long, long hours. Many served in the military after graduation.

Drill Team uniforms changed from year to year and included white spats that highlighted the marchers' feet stepping in unison—precise unison. The students took part in exhibitions and parades and their national notoriety really took off in 1955 at the first National Cherry Blossom Festival ROTC Drill Team Competition in Washington, D.C. The Purdue Drill Team took first place.

The team would recruit new members each fall and spring. Those accepted were called "plebes" and went through rigorous training before they were eligible to compete for selection to competition and/or exhibition teams.

Twenty-four students marched in the competition along with a drill captain. Since there were more than twenty-five students who were part of the Purdue team, they competed to be part of the marching unit before each competition or exhibition. As a result, the marchers were constantly changing with each event and their position in the unit changed.

The team practiced at 6 o'clock in the morning, and in the evening and on weekends. Some Drill Team members had to take an extra semester or year of studies at Purdue because they had spent so much time practicing.

"We did early morning and evening practices year-round; and additional afternoon and weekend practices during competition season, getting our routines down," said Wayne Henderson, who arrived at Purdue in the fall of 1959 and joined Naval ROTC and the Drill Team. "So, it was a heck of a commitment of time. It was just like being a scholarship basketball player or football player as far as the time expectations that we had of ourselves." Only there were no Drill Team scholarships.[2]

The Drill Team influenced the lives of the young men who marched in it. "The Purdue Drill Team was probably the crucible that really melted and forged us into the officers we became, and what the ROTC programs were intended to do," Henderson said. "It's where we learned everything about leadership—and not just leadership giving commands, not hierarchical leadership, but inspirational leadership rather than simply pulling rank on anybody. It was always 'team above self.'"

He continued: "When I got into the Marine Corps, I brought with me this feeling of valuing everyone for what they did. We all survived together. Everybody brought something to the table so that all of us could accomplish our mission. I believe I was successful in the Marine Corps because of what I experienced on the Purdue Drill Team. It was a life-altering experience in a very positive way."[3]

Henderson studied at Purdue on a Navy ROTC scholarship. "I actually had an appointment to the U.S. Naval Academy," he says. "But my mother in Gary became seriously ill. So, I talked to our Congressman and he basically said, 'Hey, we can get you into Purdue, which will be close to home. And it's the same thing as

Annapolis. It's a full ride. But it'll be a civilian school with some military classes. And you can still go on summer training cruises as an NROTC Midshipman.' That sounded great, so I chose Purdue. And it turned out my mom lived to be almost 101 years old."[4]

He started in mechanical engineering and in his junior year switched to industrial engineering with a double major in industrial management. That required a fifth year of study, which was approved by NROTC, as long as he did an extra year of military commitment after graduation.

When Henderson arrived on campus as a freshman, he saw the Drill Team do an exhibition at a football game. He was blown away and knew he wanted to be part of it.

He soon became drill captain and gave commands to the team members as they marched. But his commanding voice isn't the sound he remembers as being important. "Actually, the sounds of the team stomping on the deck and crisply handling their rifles in perfect unison were the most impressive sounds for the judges and the audience, much more than the sound of my voice," he says.[5]

The teams were notified in advance about the size of the marching field and the exact time allowed for performances. If they went too long or short they were penalized. "We knew exactly how long it took to execute each movement," Henderson says. "It might be twenty-eight seconds, it might be forty-two seconds. We had to know all these things and we charted out exactly where each movement would begin and end. There was a lot of complexity behind each performance."[6]

NROTC and the Drill Team training served him well in military service and in his life afterward. In 1965, one year after he graduated from Purdue, Henderson was sent to the war in Vietnam. He was inducted into the Purdue Hall of Fame in 2022. His induction into the Hall states that he "participated in or led more than forty combat patrols, ambushes, search and destroy operations, long-range reconnaissance missions; trained village chiefs and their militia in military tactics; and flew over twenty aerial observer missions calling in artillery or naval gunfire on enemy targets." He was awarded the Bronze Star Medal with a combat "V" for valor.[7]

In 1968, Henderson left active military duty as a captain. He voluntarily entered the Marine Corps Reserve for three additional years as an infantry company commander, after which he was promoted to the rank of major. Upon retiring from AT&T as Director of Network Operations, he founded Capital Dynamics International, and is an internationally recognized business strategist and high-tech executive consultant.

THE BEGINNING OF THE DRILL TEAM

Some sources say seven Marines on campus started the Purdue Drill Team. But the self-identified founder of the team is Gene Bores. Born in Springfield, Illinois, he grew up in Chicago and enlisted in the Navy in 1944. When World War II ended in 1945, he was discharged and placed in the inactive reserves. He entered Purdue in the fall of 1946 with a plan to graduate, receive a commission, and become a Naval aviator.[8]

He took part in Army ROTC at Purdue in case the Navy commission he wanted didn't come through. He had received training as a drill instructor from the Marine Corps. While drilling freshman at Purdue, he believed they learned quickly and enjoyed marching. He was a member of the Scabbard and Blade Army ROTC honorary society, and in 1947, he proposed that it sponsor a drill team.[9]

The team entered its first competition at the Pershing Rifle Meet at Indiana University in 1948. It took first place. In March 1949, Bores was notified he was eligible for Navy flight school at Pensacola, Florida. He left Purdue immediately. But the drill team continued at the University.[10] It was a Purdue Scabbard and Blade ROTC marching unit at the start. But in 1955, it became independent, and thus it was opened to any male on campus who wished to participate.[11]

AFRICAN AMERICAN LEADERSHIP ON DRILL TEAM

Marcus Clarke arrived on the Purdue campus from Chicago in the fall of 1953. His plan was to study chemical engineering and join a drill team if Purdue had one.

"I had a friend from Chicago who was a year older and he went to Tennessee State and got on the drill team there," Clarke says. "We got to talking, and I said, 'I'll see if Purdue has a drill team.'"[12]

He competed on the team as a freshman. In his sophomore year (1954–1955), he was elected Drill Captain and gave the team orders while marching.

The Drill Captain had a huge job. According to the official history of the team, "the Drill Captain ultimately selected the movements to be practiced for the competition. Each competition had rigid judging factors. One of the most rigid factors [and often the most difficult to meet] was the time constraint. The drill captain selected a sequence of maneuvers and movements to showcase the best of the team's abilities. He had to choreograph these sequences to present the best overall effect, work within the defined drill area, and not draw any penalties for over or under the allotted time."[13]

"When I became captain, being an African American, that was quite an honor," Clarke says. "There wasn't another African American on the team."[14]

Purdue did not keep records of the number of African Americans on campus prior to 1972, but the numbers were few at any given time. The first African American student whose photograph appears in the yearbook *Debris* as part of ROTC was Cornell McCullom Jr. in 1953. He was the only African American member of the ROTC honorary society Scabbard and Blade, and he was also on the Purdue Drill Team. He had attended Roosevelt High School in Gary, Indiana, where he was a member of the National Honor Society and student body president, as well as class salutatorian.

While at Purdue, McCullom's U.S. Congressman, Ray Madden, contacted him and urged him to consider an appointment to the U.S. Military Academy at West Point. He became the first African American from Indiana to receive an appointment to the Academy and one of only two in his class. He graduated in 1957, served in Germany, and later earned bachelor's and master's degrees in meteorology from the University of Utah. He served in Vietnam in 1967–68, and was awarded a Vietnam Service Medal, Republic of Vietnam Campaign Medal, and a Republic of Vietnam Gallantry Cross with Palm Ribbon.[15] He and Clarke married sisters.

McCullom graduated from the Command and General Staff College course at Ft. Leavenworth in 1973. From 1974 to 1978, he returned to West Point as commander of the Stewart Airport Subpost. He received an MBA from Long Island University and retired from active duty as Lieutenant Colonel in 1978.

He worked for Federal Express, ITT, and as vice president of the National Action Council for Minorities in Engineering (NACME) in New York City. According to the West Point Association of Graduates, "He maintained his ties to West Point by attending the West Point Chapel most Sundays. After a two-year battle with cancer, he died on 28 August 1993 and is interred at the West Point Cemetery."[16]

AFRICAN AMERICANS, PURDUE ROTC, AND THE MILITARY

It's not known if African American men participated in the mandatory first two years of ROTC at Purdue in the first half of the twentieth century. The University stated all men had to take the first two years of military training. But University policies were sometimes applied differently for African Americans.

Although it was not an approved written policy, African Americans were not allowed to live in Purdue University residence halls until 1947. Most lived in Lafayette, commuting to campus by bus. West Lafayette was a "sundown" community, meaning African Americans had to leave by nightfall. So, it would have been difficult for them to be involved in ROTC training. They probably were not admitted to the second two years of ROTC, nor commissioned as officers until the 1950s.

This was not unusual for the time. In 1940, the U.S. Army had only five African American officers. The Navy only listed 441 African American sailors as of 1937, and the Marine Corps was for whites only.[17] Some African Americans became Army officers in 1940 and during World War II, but Black soldiers mostly served in segregated units. The Navy commissioned its first African American officers in 1944 but kept them segregated.[18]

In 1948, President Harry S Truman signed an order desegregating the U.S. military. It said in part, "There shall be equality of treatment and opportunity for all persons in the armed services without regard to race, color, religion or national origin." This was accomplished by 1951, during the Korean War. However, only three percent of Army officers, and one percent of Navy, Air Force, and Marine officers were African American.[19]

In his freshman year in 1953, Marcus Clarke roomed in Cary Hall with Lamar Lundy, the first African American scholarship athlete at Purdue, who played football and basketball. They became lifelong friends.

Clarke was a cofounder of the Purdue Black Alumni Organization in 1980.

WASHINGTON, D.C. CHERRY BLOSSOM FESTIVAL

In 1952, 1953, and 1954 the Purdue Invitational drill competition was unofficially considered the national championship. Purdue won in each of those years. In fact, between 1952 and 1964, Purdue won its own invitational thirteen straight times.[20]

In 1955, the first official national championship moved to Washington, D.C., becoming part of the annual spring Cherry Blossom Festival. David Baker, a member of the Purdue Drill Team, played a role in creating the competition.

"I initially contacted a personal friend, Congressman Ralph Harvey, who represented my district in Indiana," Baker recalled in 2009. "I asked him what he thought about the Purdue Drill Team marching in the Cherry Blossom Parade in Washington, D.C. He thought it a good idea. I also checked to see if there were any drill meets in the Washington area during that time period. The answer was no, but I said, 'Why don't we set one up and call it the First National Cherry Blossom Festival Drill Meet?' To make a long story short, this was accomplished due to the hard work of the Cherry Blossom Festival Committee, the Purdue Drill Team military advisors, and Congressman Harvey. To say the teams which accepted the invitation were strong would be putting it mildly, including the likes of the Virginia Military Institute and the Citadel who were sure unhappy when we beat them."[21]

In the 1955 Cherry Blossom meet, under the leadership of Captain James "Bud" Malsbary, the Purdue Drill Team won the national championship. The judges gave the team 945.3 points out of a possible 1,000. Purdue finished 177 points ahead of its nearest rival.

Drill Team member Gordon Shaw, a member of the 1955 squad, remembered a competition at the University of Illinois where the judges stopped grading Purdue and just sat down and enjoyed the show. "The judges for the teams used clipboards to record their scores," he says. "About two-thirds of the way through our drill performance, one of the officers scoring us just threw his clipboard up in the air and we heard it hit the floor of the armory. He sat down and just watched us as did the other officers since we were so far ahead of whoever was in second place that they did not attempt to score us any longer and we won easily. This had never happened before, but we were that good in my modest opinion."[22]

Malsbary moved up in rank and became Commanding Officer of the Drill Team by the fall of 1955. "I didn't really want to give up being Drill Captain, but I was very pleased to have Marcus Clarke take over the job," he said. "Marcus was a leader that could and would take the team to new heights."[23]

He did. Purdue won every competition it entered in the 1955–56 season, including the national championship at the Cherry Blossom Festival.

Clarke was so nervous during the national competition and held his sword so tight that when it was over, he couldn't open his hand.[24]

CLARKE: THE DRILL TEAM LED TO SUCCESS IN HIS LIFE

Clarke said that in the winter leading up to the spring festival in Washington, D.C., the team practiced every weekday morning at 6:00 a.m. and again every weekday afternoon. Clarke ultimately gave up being Drill Captain his junior year to spend more time working on his grades.

It consumed time. But participating on the drill team changed the lives and careers of its members for the better. "It boosted my self-esteem," Clarke says. "It helped to develop leadership. The drill team helped me be successful in life."[25]

Clarke graduated in 1957. He completed four years of Air Force ROTC and was commissioned a Second Lieutenant. He was stationed in Texas and was part of the Strategic Air Command, in charge of a laboratory processing photographs from U-2 high altitude reconnaissance aircraft. He later worked as an engineering department manager, plant manager, and district manager for Union Carbide. He also worked as an engineer for Ford Motor Company in Michigan.

"I always felt very confident, not cocky but confident," Clarke says. "I attribute that to my years at Purdue and being on the Drill Team."[26]

VIETNAM WAR ERA

John Trott enrolled at Purdue in September 1959. The young man from Covington, Indiana planned to study agriculture.

"I had no real concept of the military when I came to Purdue," he says. "We had a requirement to do a minimum of two years in ROTC. But what got me interested in the military was [that] I lived in Cary Hall my freshman and sophomore years. There were two guys in the hall I did not know, but they had served in the miliary before they came to Purdue as undergraduates. They had it together better than the rest of us. They had an aura about them. They knew who they were and what they were there for."[27]

He started thinking about joining the military after graduation. Meanwhile, he took the first two years of ROTC at Purdue, and one of his roommates was on the Drill Team.

"I had seen them practice and was impressed with what they were doing. So, I tried out and made the team," he says. "It was a lot of work and a lot of rewards. I liked the discipline, the teamwork, the camaraderie. I guess to this day my best friends are drill team members and Marines."[28]

Although he did not take the second two years of ROTC at Purdue, after Purdue he went to Officer Candidate School and was commissioned in the Marines. He was sent to the Vietnam War three times.

"On my last tour I was an infantry company commander," he says. "It was physically stressful, emotionally stressful, tactically stressful. I had one man I wrote up and he was awarded the Medal of Honor, there were some Silver Star medals. We saw our share of combat and I lost a dozen men. It's an experience that you think about every day. You never get away from it. My favorite people in the entire world are helicopter pilots and Navy corpsmen."[29]

The Navy corpsmen were the medics who treated wounded men in the field. The helicopter pilots took the wounded to hospitals.

"I'm very proud of my military service," Trott says.[30]

Forty Purdue-affiliated people died during military service in the Vietnam War. They are memorialized on a plaque in the Great Hall of the Union. They were men such as First Lieutenant Walter Jordan, U.S. Army, from Griffin, Indiana. He graduated from Purdue in 1966 with a degree in forestry. His tour in Vietnam began on May 19, 1967, and he died in Vietnam less than two months later, on July 10, 1967. He was a platoon leader on a combat mission that was attacked and pinned down by heavy automatic weapon fire. He made repeated movements among his men, calming and encouraging them, exposing himself to weapon fire. He was mortally wounded and posthumously received the Distinguished Service Cross, the Bronze Star, and a Purple Heart. He was twenty-four years old.[31]

As of 2023, six Purdue people had lost their lives in military actions following Vietnam. One died in Saudi Arabia, four in Iraq, and one in Afghanistan. Their names are included on a plaque in the Purdue Memorial Union Great Hall.

MEETING WITH PRESIDENT JOHN F. KENNEDY

Ron Neubauer arrived as a freshman at Purdue in the fall of 1960. He graduated from Bordentown Military Institute in New Jersey, where he participated in Junior ROTC. He was looking for a top engineering university, and when he heard Purdue had a national champion drill team in addition to engineering and NROTC, he knew where he was headed.

He didn't know then, however, that he would be part of the team that would compete in the 1961 Cherry Blossom Festival and have the opportunity to march for President John F. Kennedy at the White House.

Purdue had the good fortune to be in the U.S. congressional district represented by Charles Halleck, from Rensselaer, Indiana. Halleck, a Republican, served in Congress from 1935 to 1969. He was House Majority Leader from 1947 to 1949 and again from 1953 to 1955. He was Minority Leader from 1959 to 1965 and Leader of the House Republican Conference from 1959 to 1965.

As part of their touring activities in Washington, D.C. before the 1961 drill competition, Halleck had arranged for the Purdue Drill Team to visit the White House. The team had performed at the inner courtyard of the Pentagon the day before, but that day, the students were told to wear a coat and tie, not their military marching uniforms. On the morning of April 6, they boarded a bus to the White House. Neubauer said he didn't know they were going to the White House.

"We were halfway there when someone said we were going to the White House," Neubauer says. "I was young and I thought, what in the world are we going to the White House for?"[32]

After a tour of the White House, they were assembled outside in the Rose Garden. "And out walked President Kennedy," Neubauer says. "You could have knocked me over with a feather. I had been a hardcore conservative my entire life, but I was never so taken by the fact I was about to meet the President. It was inspiring that the president would take time out of his busy schedule to meet college kids from Purdue. He addressed our group and made mention that we were the defending champions."[33]

The details of that day remain vivid in his memory more than sixty years later. There had been no plans for the students to meet Kennedy. It apparently was a spur of the moment decision by the president, who probably wanted to do Halleck a favor in return for possible support for part of his agenda. Kennedy was a Democrat and had been newly sworn in as president less than three months earlier, on January 20. He would need to work with Republican Halleck, and perhaps thought honoring the students would help.

The Associated Press reported that one of Kennedy's aides approached the students and said the president would see them if they waited a few minutes. They would wait. They voted on the spot to make him an honorary member of the team and gave him one of their braided shoulder cords.[34]

Kennedy asked the students to show him their formations. They put on a five-minute demonstration without uniforms or rifles.

"We were awestruck, we really were," Neubauer says. "The world was a lot different then. I was awestruck to be in the presence of the President of the United States of America. It was almost overwhelming, a great honor. One of those moments in life you'll never forget."[35]

It wasn't the last time Neubauer was in the White House with a U.S. president. He became a Marine officer after graduating from Purdue and was an aide in the Richard Nixon White House. While serving there, Neubauer met the woman who became his wife, also a White House employee.

"The drill team was amazing," Neubauer says. "I learned so much, I gained so much from the Purdue Drill Team that carried me through my military career and beyond."

At the end of his military career, Neubauer was a Lieutenant Colonel and served as Director of Law Enforcement and Corrections at U.S. Marine Corps Headquarters in Washington, D.C. After leaving the military, he served as a police chief in Florida for three years and as police chief in St. Peters, Missouri for more than fourteen years. He was also executive director of the Eastern Missouri Police Academy. He served as President of the International Association of Chiefs of Police from 1998 to 1999.

In 2007, he was inducted into the Purdue ROTC Hall of Fame.

WOMEN'S DRILL TEAMS

In the late 1950s, some universities sponsored women's drill teams. Judging, unfortunately, was often based on appearance.

In March 1960, a Drill Team Auxiliary for women was formed at Purdue. At this time, women were not admitted to ROTC programs nationally. The men's Purdue Drill Team was the advisory group for the auxiliary, and it was decided the auxiliary would be founded on ability—in the achievement of precision in military drill and attitude, rather than appearance. The objectives of the women's team were the same as the men's: "To foster, encourage, and develop efficiency in military drill; to promote teamwork and cooperation; to advance the ideals of the military establishment; to provide opportunities for leadership; and to help all branches of the ROTC in any way possible."[36]

The girls' team practiced in the co-rec gym and in the armory. Twenty-three members were activated for the first women's team. Initially sixteen marched in competition, but that was later increased to twenty-four. The marching movements were similar to the men's, but the women did not carry rifles. The women performed in exhibitions and had their first competition at an Ohio State Invitational Meet. They won. In 1963 they were invited to the national competition in Washington, D.C., where they won second place. In 1965, the team won the National Inter-Collegiate Drill Championship.

There were marriages among the men's drill team and the women's auxiliary, including John and Nancy Trott. Nancy joined the women's team in 1961, during her freshman year living in what was then called "Hall X," and later named Virginia C. Meredith Residence Hall.

"The other girls in the hall talked up the drill team so we went to a callout," Trott says. "My roommate and I decided to try it and it just seemed like a good group to get involved with. In my sophomore year I pledged a sorority and my big sister was also in the auxiliary. In a large school, it was a small group where you got to know close friends and you knew you were going to be with these people for a while. It was an organization that kept you involved. In addition to marching there were moneymaking operations. One time we sold chocolate chip cookies from Grave's Bakery at a football game to get money for travel expenses. We didn't have any support through the university. It was all on our own to come up with money for travel."[37]

Bonnie Graham Rabert joined the Drill Team Auxiliary during her freshman year in the fall of 1960. She became training officer for pledges in 1961, executive officer of the drill team in 1962, and drill commander in 1963.

"1963 was our biggest competition year," Rabert says. "That was when we marched in Washington, D.C. and won second place nationally. We were a team of sixteen marchers in a huge building. We enjoyed it. We would have enjoyed it more if we had won first place. It was a wonderful group. There was a feeling of teamwork and precision."[38]

The auxiliary had songs to familiar tunes they sometimes sang as they practiced their marching.

We're the girls from old Purdue
Honey, honey.
We're the girls from old Purdue
Babe, babe.
We've been marching all day long
Now it's time to sing a song,
Honey oh baby, mine.
Go to your left, your right, your left . . .[39]

END OF THE DRILL TEAMS

The women's Drill Team Auxiliary disbanded in the spring of 1969. Many of its members had joined a new Army ROTC drill team called the Grenadaires. The Navy ROTC also started a girls' team called the Anchorettes.

The men's Drill Team officially disbanded in the spring of 1970, when Jim Kuemmel, the commanding officer, sent a letter to Assistant Dean of Men Robert Backhaus requesting that University recognition be ended. There were a number of reasons, including that nationwide resistance to the Vietnam War had caused many students to shun military activity.

"Closer to home, other forces were at work to encourage the demise of the team," Kuemmel said. "The final National Championship was brought home in 1962. The final first place trophy [from any event] was brought home in 1966. Spring of 1969 saw the final drill meet in which the Purdue Drill Team marched. We were only good enough for third."[10]

The ROTC programs on the Purdue campus also created their own marching units which drew students from the drill team.

"We had a really poor showing at our callouts in the fall of 1968 and again a year later," Kuemmel said. "We did raise money for a 1969–1970 marching season. I remember that the final call out in 1970 there wasn't a single person that showed up. It was really hard to believe."[41]

The Drill Team members were invited to join the ROTC marching teams. But it was decided to end the team with the best record of success in the university's history. While the team is gone, the members continue to meet. By 2024 when the self-declared "final" reunion was held, there had been eleven Purdue Drill Team and Drill Team Auxiliary reunions.

One other event had a huge negative impact on the Drill Team—the end of mandatory ROTC for all freshmen and sophomore male students.

14

CHANGE

Purdue is dedicated to a program of excellence and we would expect this to continue in voluntary ROTC as in all other phases of academic work. The University will continue to give the fullest cooperation to the programs of the armed services. We are interested in meeting our share of the demand for outstanding leaders as commissioned officers.

PURDUE UNIVERSITY VICE PRESIDENT DONALD MALLETT

Not at Purdue. In 1960, not yet. But times would change.

In early 1960, some universities in the United States began considering making all four years of ROTC voluntary for male students. The question had been raised at universities in Michigan, Massachusetts, Connecticut, Rhode Island, Florida, Ohio, Wisconsin and California. It had come up at Purdue as early as 1959.

Purdue President Frederick L. Hovde wasted no time making his position clear.

"In connection with current discussion about ROTC programs of armed forces in American colleges and universities, the position and policy of Purdue is quite definite," he said in a statement on February 12, 1960. "Purdue desires to maintain a strong, vigorous, competent program of ROTC for all branches of service, Army, Navy, and Air Force."[1]

But he kept his mind open to possible future developments. His statement continued, "However, if and when it becomes clear that the armed services are not willing to support these programs with competent staffs, equipment, and facilities, and by such lack of support indicate that ROTC programs are not worthwhile and useful, then Purdue will consider placing ROTC on a voluntary basis or abandoning it in its entirety."[2]

The Purdue Board of Trustees had required all freshmen and sophomore men to take ROTC since 1889, with the second two years of participation voluntary.

As an alternative, students could take part in the marching band, which was organized as a military unit.

The Morrill Act that had created Purdue and other land-grant universities required the schools to offer ROTC, but it did not require students to enroll in the programs.

According to a news story in the Lafayette *Journal and Courier*, the U.S. Department of Defense and the Army did not agree on the importance of mandatory ROTC training in 1960.

"The Defense Department is following a hands-off policy [concerning voluntary ROTC] on the theory that military requirements can be met with electives and that national defense, therefore, is not at stake," the newspaper reported. "Wilber M. Brucker [Secretary of the Army] reportedly favors compulsory basic ROTC training for the first two college years as vital to national security. He said the peacetime Army requires 14,000 commissioned officers a year and this could not be met without compulsory training. The U.S. Military Academy produces about seven hundred graduates a year."[3]

The *Journal and Courier* noted Purdue had "one of the nation's most distinguished ROTC programs" and "the University's field artillery branch is considered tops in the nation." Four thousand students were enrolled in Purdue ROTC.[4]

The issue at Purdue was settled for the time being. But it didn't go away. On February 8, 1961, almost exactly a year after Hovde issued his statement in support of the military programs, the student University Senate held a long meeting that featured two hours of debate. Ultimately, they recommended that ROTC be made voluntary at Purdue.

The issue had been discussed and tabled at two previous Senate meetings. This time, it was approved by a vote of sixteen to nine. It was a contentious issue, however, and some said the vote did not represent the opinions of the students.

Bob Veatch, student body president, said the students were in favor of the action.

"We are fooling ourselves if we say we haven't had time to get student feeling on this bill," he said. "The issues are quite clear-cut. I introduced the original ROTC bill two years ago."[5]

Purdue's student newspaper, the *Purdue Exponent*, noted that four of the nine votes against the proposal came from female members of the Senate who were not required, or even allowed, to take ROTC.

"A student should be obligated to take courses only so long as they are consistent with his educational objectives," Veatch said. "Compulsory ROTC definitely violates this freedom to choose."[6]

The *Exponent* reported that all three members of the committee who studied the issue were in favor of the proposal to go all-voluntary. But committee member Betty Bloedel did not agree and apparently abstained from the vote. Student Senate member Sherm Lyon said, "If this bill is passed it would be on the basis of Senate opinions, not facts. I do not think we can pass it and expect the bill to have any effect on administration policy."[7]

The committee that studied the issue listed three strengths and three weaknesses of Purdue ROTC. "Strengths: A school with compulsory program commissions more graduates than do the noncompulsory schools; provides a broad base for selecting future officers; and provides initial contact with the military for a greater number of students than would the voluntary program. Weaknesses: insufficient credit is given for time and work involved; students in some academic areas may not participate without remaining longer than the usual four years required for a first academic degree; not all classes are attuned to the academic; and [the] program gives incomplete military orientation."[8]

The issue moved to a referendum among student voters in the spring of 1961. The vote was 3,344 in favor of voluntary ROTC and 2,078 in favor of continuing the mandatory program. While almost 62 percent of those who voted favored voluntary ROTC, the 5,422 students who voted constituted only 33 percent of the University's 16,543 students. The issue went to Hovde and the Purdue Board of Trustees.

On June 3, 1961, Hovde presented to the Board a resolution adopted by the Reserve Officers Association of the United States, Department of Indiana, concerning ROTC training:

> WHEREAS, the modern military services (Army, Navy and Air Force) require leaders of the highest caliber, which necessitates that one have a sound, and often a highly technical, college education, and
>
> WHEREAS, the Army has a requirement of an annual input of some 14,000 junior officers just to keep the present forces staffed (does not build up any Reserve pool); the Air Force requires some 3,500, and the Navy some 3,000, and
>
> WHEREAS, West Point, Annapolis, and the Air Force Academy can only supply a combined total of about 1600 junior officers annually, and WHEREAS, the primary source of obtaining these junior officers is from the Advanced ROTC, and

WHEREAS, the ROTC training has the mission of developing self-discipline, group living, team cooperation, responsibility, leadership and citizenship potential, and an awareness of the requirement for the community and national defense, and protection which will allow individual growth, and WHEREAS, before our society with its free institutions can flourish in peace, it must make certain that it survives, and

WHEREAS, maximum leadership quality can be obtained in junior officers only if there is a broad base of basic ROTC students from which to choose the advanced ROTC candidates, and

WHEREAS, in the Army [ROTC] there are one hundred sixty-two schools, including most of the land-grant colleges, which have compulsory basic ROTC and only eighty-six that have elective basic ROTC; and in the Air Force there are ninety-two schools that have compulsory basic ROTC and only eighty-three that have elective basic ROTC, and

WHEREAS, experience shows that when an institution changes from compulsory to elective basic ROTC, the enrollment in basic ROTC dwindles at least fifty percent (one example of fifty-seven percent and another of sixty-six percent, and

WHEREAS, experience shows that the attrition in advanced ROTC is only five percent in schools where basic ROTC is compulsory, while it is twenty-six percent at those Schools where Basic ROTC is elective, and

WHEREAS, it is consistent to admit an obligation to country in principle and to deny it in practice on the grounds of interference with academic freedom or competing demands for the student's time,

NOW, THEREFORE, BE IT RESOLVED by the Reserve Officers Association of the United States, Department of Indiana, in Convention assembled, this thirtieth day of April 1961, that:

> 1. The Boards of Trustees, Presidents, and other Officers of Purdue University, Indiana University, and Rose Polytechnic Institute, are hereby urged and requested to continue 'compulsory' basic ROTC at these institutions as being one of the best ways these institutions have of recognizing their responsibility to the nation's defense and survival, and their means of helping develop and supply the best citizenship and leadership possible.

> 2. That copies of this resolution be sent to the Boards of Trustees, through the Presidents of these institutions.
> 3. That copy be sent the Governor of Indiana.[9]

After introducing the resolution, Hovde followed up with a statement similar to the one he had issued in February 1960.

"I believe I can tell you at this time that it is the firm intention of Purdue University to retain its requirement of compulsory ROTC training for all physically fit male freshmen and sophomore students until such time as the Department of Defense and the Armed Forces themselves take a clear and unequivocal position that the ROTC program as it has been organized and maintained during the postwar years is no longer a useful and necessary part of the personnel training for our Armed Forces," he said.[10]

After Hovde spoke, Executive Dean Donald Mallet, who oversaw ROTC at Purdue, reported that some students and faculty at the University wanted the first two years to be voluntary. He said the issue is a "problem" and that some universities had eliminated mandatory training and others had retained it. Finally, he said he did not sense a strong feeling about the issue among Purdue students.[11]

Mallet told the board there would be another referendum on the issue in which only male students would vote. He said a faculty committee had been appointed to study the issue and make recommendations. Mallet said he believed the committee would not recommend changes unless they came from the Department of Defense and the armed services, which were studying the program which "may be headed for drastic changes since the needs of the services have changed in terms of numbers and training of their men."[12]

The Board voted to receive the reports as information. The members voted to agree with Hovde's statement. ROTC would not change at Purdue.[13]

Not yet. But times would change. The military would change. And Purdue would change as well.

FREDERICK L. HOVDE

While not a military veteran, Hovde had strong support for the armed services and the Department of Defense. He played a leadership role in defense research during World War II. He supported close collaboration between science, industry, and the military, and believed universities played a major role in this.

He became president of Purdue in January 1946, arriving with the first wave of students on the G.I. Bill. At thirty-seven, he was only twelve to fifteen years older than many of the veteran students. He served as president for the next twenty-five years, the longest term of any Purdue chief executive. He died March 3, 1983.

Born in Erie, Pennsylvania in 1908, he grew up in Devils Lake, North Dakota. Hovde received his bachelor's degree in chemical engineering in 1929 from the University of Minnesota where he was a star athlete, playing on the football, basketball, and track teams. He was Minnesota's star quarterback and was named quarterback of the 1928 All-Big Ten Team. Elected to a Rhodes Scholarship, he spent three years at Oxford University in England where he received two degrees in chemistry and excelled in rugby. He became the third American to win an "Oxford Blue" for performance at the highest level in the annual Oxford-Cambridge rugby match.

Returning to the United States in 1932, he soon accepted a position as assistant director of the newly created General College at the University of Minnesota. In 1936 he became assistant to the president at the University of Rochester, in New York. He was also a chemistry lecturer at the school.

In December 1940, a full year before the Japanese attack on Pearl Harbor, he was summoned to Washington, D.C. and asked to join the newly created National Defense Research Committee. The committee had been created on June 27, 1940, by President Franklin D. Roosevelt "to coordinate, supervise, and conduct scientific research on the problems underlying the development, production, and use of mechanisms and devices of warfare" in the United States. The idea for the committee was presented to Roosevelt by Vannevar Bush, one of the preeminent researchers of his time. Bush founded the company that became Raytheon. He had served as vice president of Massachusetts Institute of Technology and dean of its School of Engineering. In 1939 he was named president of the Carnegie Institution of Washington, which was established to fund and perform scientific research. He would play a key role in the development of the atomic bomb.

In February 1941, only about a month after being named to the National Defense Research Committee, Hovde was one of three men sent to London, England to launch an office based in the U.S. Embassy. The other two men were James B. Conant, president of Harvard University, and Carroll L. Wilson, executive assistant to Bush.

The plan was for Conant and Wilson to stay in London for about a month and return home. Hovde would stay for six months to a year as secretary of the office. While the United States was officially neutral at that time, the British had been at war with Nazi Germany since 1939. In 1941, the Germans were bombing London where Hovde, Conant, and Wilson were based. Hovde was charged with coordinating research in Great Britain and the United States.

As the three men sailed for England, the White House issued a statement that said the "first-hand observation of recent English scientific research and experience is important for the prosecution of America's program of research on problems of mutual defense."[14] German propaganda noted Hovde was a chemical engineer and Conant was a chemist and charged they were going to London to help the British start gas warfare.[15]

Bush's National Defense Research committee included research on radar and a Uranium Committee that studied the potential of creating a nuclear bomb, prior to the Manhattan Project. In 1941, the British were ahead of the U.S. in research leading to a nuclear weapon. One year earlier, the British had created a MAUD Committee to study the feasibility of building an atomic bomb. (MAUD was not an acronym; it was just a word they picked.) British scientists had been working on the question of a nuclear bomb, believing the Germans were also interested in developing it. In March 1941, the MAUD Committee drafted a statement averring that building an atomic bomb was feasible and the explosion would be enormous.

In the early spring of 1941, Charles C. Lauritsen, a Danish-born American physics professor at California Institute of Technology, was in London as part of the National Defense Research Committee working with British scientists on fuse research. One evening he entered Hovde's office at 11:00 p.m. and found him still working, alone. He pulled papers from his pocket. He said the document was so valuable they had to duplicate it immediately and send it to Washington, D.C.

The document was marked "British Top Secret." Hovde told Lauritsen it was against their agreement with the British to copy the classified document. Lauritsen said he had received it from British researchers and that they wanted the U.S. to have it. Hovde and Lauritsen duplicated the document and placed it in the next day's diplomatic mail pouch to Washington, D.C., and Lauritsen returned the original document to the physicist who gave it to him.[16]

Hovde did not say if the document was related to the MAUD Committee. But the timing makes it possible. In his 1980 biography of Hovde, Robert Topping wrote: "The contents of the paper were important enough to cause some skipped heartbeats. It was a British scientific paper which gave proof that the fission reaction produced neutrons with a coefficient greater than one; that is, for each fission that took place in an atomic reaction, more than one neutron would be released. This meant that the chain reaction would go—that an atomic explosion of great and unknown force was possible."[17]

An August 1939 letter to Roosevelt from physicist Albert Einstein had said such an atomic explosion was "possible." The British research proved it would happen, but there was still a huge amount of research to be done. In Hovde's 1983 obituary, the *New York Times* said, "British scientists told the American officials it might be feasible to construct atomic weapons in time for use in the war."[18]

On October 3, 1941, the MAUD Report reached the U.S. through official channels and nine days later Vannevar Bush brought it to Roosevelt who asked how much it would cost and what would be needed to construct it.[19] Earlier that year, Hovde had been sent home to the United States on leave for rest and to be with his family. Before returning to London in October 1941, Hovde was summoned to Bush's office in Washington. Bush told Hovde he had a letter from Roosevelt that he was to deliver to British Prime Minister Winston Churchill. Topping wrote, "FDR had agreed on the part of the United States with Great Britain to take full responsibility for development of the atomic bomb." Hovde carried the letter to Churchill in a waist belt under his clothing.[20]

Hovde returned permanently to the U.S. in May 1942, where Conant named him his executive assistant. In 1943, Hovde was named Chief of Rocket Ordnance Research for the National Defense Research Committee. After becoming president of Purdue in January 1946, he was named chair of the Guided Missile Committee for the Research Development Board in the Office of the Secretary of Defense. He served in the position from 1947 to 1949.

In announcing his appointment as president at Purdue in September 1945, *Time* magazine named him "Purdue's Rocket Man."[21] *Time* called him "the nation's expert of experts on rocket bombs" and reported that "when the Nazis buzzed over their V-1 and V2, Hovde was drafted to devise countermeasures. He has since supervised the entire U.S. rocket-development program."[22]

There were different types of rockets. The bazooka anti-tank gun was among the first U.S. rocket weapons used in combat. Five-inch aircraft rockets were loaded on U.S. P-47 airplanes and one hundred of these were fired against German tanks in the weeks after D-Day.[23]

In 1943, Roosevelt expanded Vannevar Bush's work by naming him director of the Office of Scientific Research and Development. Purdue's controller R. B. Stewart also worked for this office, and the National Defense Research Committee under the leadership of Conant, and including Hovde, reported to it. Research into the feasibility of an atomic bomb became the Manhattan Project, headed by J. Robert Oppenheimer, and involving scientists and engineers across the United States, including many from Purdue.

Under Hovde's leadership of the Rocket Ordnance Research division, a large group of researchers worked to develop different types of fuses for rockets. According to Hovde, "about a year before the war ended, progress on the atomic bomb had reached the stage where they needed help with their fusing problem. Arrangements were made for about one half of our fuse group to work on atomic bomb fuses." Hovde and one of his assistants made occasional trips to Los Alamos, New Mexico to visit with Oppenheimer and check on problems with fusing problems.[24]

On August 6, 1945, he and Lauritsen were in Los Alamos and had an appointment to meet with Oppenheimer at 9:00 a.m. to plan the work for the fuse team during the next six months. "We had just got started talking about what was to be done and the telephone rang," Hovde said in a 1972 interview. "Oppenheimer picked up the telephone and listened and his first words we could hear were, 'And so they chose Hiroshima.' And that was Oppenheimer receiving the news that the atomic bomb had been dropped and was successful in Hiroshima. Needless to say, we never finished our conversation. The news was transferred to everyone at Los Alamos and everything was stopped. There was a celebration. And I happened to be there."[25]

Hovde believed that without the bomb, millions of Allied troops and Japanese would have been killed in an invasion. He called the bomb "a terrible, terrible weapon . . . that man could destroy himself with. He also called it ultimately, "the greatest force for peace," since its use again was so unthinkable.[26]

In recognition of his service during the war, Hovde was awarded the President's Medal for Merit and, from the British, the King's Medal for Service in the Cause of Freedom. While serving as president of Purdue, he was a member of the Board of Visitors to the United States Naval Academy, the Board of Visitors to the Air University, the Air Training Command Advisory Board, the Board of Consultants to the National War College, and the Board of Visitors to the United States Air Force Academy. From 1952 to 1960, Hovde was also a member of the Army Scientific Advisory Panel, and chaired the panel from 1956 to 1958. In 1960, he was on a National Academy of Sciences committee reviewing ship building and modernization of the U.S. Navy.[27]

In 1957 he became a Fellow of the American Association for the Advancement of Science. He was a recipient of the Department of the Air Force Exceptional Civilian Service Award in 1961, and in 1963 received both the Distinguished

Public Service Award from the Department of the Navy and the Distinguished Service Award from the Association of the United States Army. He received the Distinguished Public Service Medal from the Department of Defense in 1970.

VOLUNTARY ROTC

In October 1964, Congress passed the Reserve Officers Training Corps Vitalization Act. President Lyndon B. Johnson signed it and issued a statement on October 14, 1964.

"The ROTC has become familiar to all and has trained many, many thousands of our young men in the leadership so necessary in the three major conflicts in which we have been engaged during this century," Johnson said. "Today, this vital program constitutes the largest single source of trained officers not just for the Reserves, but for the Regular forces as well. I am convinced that the bill I have approved today will bring about a marked improvement in the ROTC programs being conducted in our colleges and universities, and I congratulate the Congress for the changes it has made to this end."[28]

The bill was approved to make ROTC more attractive to college students. Among other measures, it increased scholarship aid and allowed two-year programs in addition to the traditional four years of participation leading to a commission.

By 1965, attitudes toward the military had changed remarkably on many university campuses as a result of the Vietnam War. When President John F. Kennedy was assassinated in 1963, more than 16,000 U.S. military personnel were in Vietnam. By the end of 1965 under Johnson, 184,000 troops were stationed there, and that number would grow.

Students received a deferment from the draft while they continued their studies. But by 1965 with the increased U.S. involvement in Vietnam, many campuses saw demonstrations against the war.

On March 15, 1965, the Purdue faculty recommended ROTC training for freshmen and sophomore students be placed on a voluntary basis beginning in the next academic year. The proposal to Hovde and the Board of Trustees was approved by the University Senate. The proposal had been under study since 1961 when it first came before the Board of Trustees. The Lafayette *Journal and Courier* reported "although under study for several years, the proposed change here results primarily from the provision of the ROTC

Vitalization Act of 1964 . . . adopted by Congress to modernize ROTC programs and make them more attractive and productive of commissioned officers for the nation's active and reserve forces."[29] Similar actions were underway across the nation; Indiana University moved to a voluntary ROTC program at the same time as Purdue.

Vice President Donald Mallett said, "Purdue is dedicated to a program of excellence and we would expect this to continue in voluntary ROTC as in all other phases of academic work. The University will continue to give the fullest cooperation to the programs of the armed services. We are interested in meeting our share of the demand for outstanding leaders as commissioned officers."[30]

The *Journal and Courier* newspaper noted that "for many years, Purdue produced more artillery officers than West Point."[31]

The recommendation approved by the University Senate came from a faculty committee. It was seconded by Colonel T. R. Bruce, professor of military science and chairman of the University's military affairs committee.

"The nation's new ROTC Vitalization Act gives new students entering Purdue next fall greater incentive to consider ROTC training and military careers," Bruce said. "There will be no change in the quality of instruction offered under the proposed voluntary ROTC program. We will maintain the high academic standards which prevail in all courses offered at Purdue."[32]

Colonel Merrill A. Kempton, professor of aerospace studies, said that while Air Force ROTC at Purdue would see a drop in freshmen and sophomore students under the voluntary system, in time the number of commissioned officers would increase. "The quality of the cadet corps probably will be higher due to better screening," he said. "We can see no change in the Air Force's pleasant relationship with Purdue."[33]

Since the Navy ROTC program already followed the provisions of the ROTC Vitalization Act, its leadership did not expect any change in quality or number of students enrolled.

In March 1965, Purdue enrolled 2,180 students in Air Force ROTC, 1,524 students in the Army program, and 284 in the Navy's ROTC program.[34]

The Purdue Board of Trustees approved the change on May 5, 1965. In June, Mallett reported more than 60 percent of male students entering Purdue in the fall of 1965 had indicated they would enroll in ROTC or its traditional alternative, the "All-American" Marching Band.[35]

HOVDE HONORS AND RETIREMENT

Hovde was recognized for his contributions to national defense throughout his years at Purdue.

In 1967, he received the prestigious Washington Award "for his vision and leadership in coordinating the engineering and scientific resources of the nation with the national defense and for continuing contributions to engineering education." The award was jointly presented by the Western Society of Engineers, the American Institute of Mining, Metallurgical and Petroleum Engineers, American Society of Civil Engineers, American Society of Mechanical Engineers, Institute of Electrical and Electronic Engineers, National Society of Professional Engineers, and the American Nuclear Society.[36]

Previous recipients of the Washington Award included Herbert Hoover, Orville Wright, Henry Ford, and Vannevar Bush. Several individuals connected with Purdue had received the award as well. In 1943, it was presented to then Purdue Dean of Engineering A. A. Potter, and in 1954, Lillian Gilbreth, who taught at Purdue and who had served on the Women's Advisory Council to the Navy that helped to create the WAVES also received the award. Purdue graduate Neil Armstrong would later be an honoree, as well.[37]

As the 1960s progressed, student unrest concerning the war in Vietnam continued to grow across the nation. Students protested against the war, against the military draft, and against classified military research. Compared to many other universities, the Purdue campus was relatively quiet—but not entirely free from disruption.

The spring of 1969 would be the most trying in Hovde's twenty-five-year career as Purdue's president. That spring, students marched on the administration building and held a "live-in" at the Memorial Union, protesting a tuition hike. They also asked for an end to ROTC on campus, an end to classified military research, and a statement from the University opposing the Vietnam War. The demands were rejected. The 1862 law that created land-grant universities still required the teaching of military tactics.

On May 1, 1969, students and nonstudents interrupted an ROTC awards ceremony. They sat in the middle of the floor and took over the microphone. They were asked to leave and refused. Special Assistant to the Purdue President John Hicks told police to intervene, which they did, and in the ensuing struggle, four students were injured.[38]

The following December, Hovde announced his retirement, effective June 30, 1971. He said his decision had nothing to do with student unrest. But some people believed that it did.

On May 15, 1970, during an ROTC award ceremony in the Purdue Armory, Hovde was surprised with a Defense Department Distinguished Public Service Medal. The award recognized Hovde's "outstanding and distinguished civilian service to the Department of Defense from September 1947 through May 1969."[39] It was the highest award given to a civilian by the Department of Defense and was signed by U.S. Secretary of Defense Melvin Laird. It marked the first time the award had been presented to a university president.

The citation continued, "During this period Dr. Hovde diligently devoted an enormous amount of his personal interest, time, and effort to each military service as well as to each of their respective ROTC programs. He made significant contributions as chairman of the Committee on Guided Missiles, the Army Scientific Advisory Panel, and as a member of the boards of visitors to the three military service academies. The outstanding and truly exceptional meritorious civilian service rendered by Dr. Hovde has contributed immeasurably to the status, prestige, and overall accomplishments of the Department of Defense."[40]

President Richard Nixon spoke at Hovde's retirement dinner in Indianapolis, on June 24, 1971. Nixon talked about Hovde's accomplishments, including "his service in World War II in the most secret projects against the Nazis, service that perhaps could not even now be talked of in declassified terms because it was of such a highly important nature, and service that only a man with his background was able to perform. Only a very few were chosen, and because of what they did, the war was made shorter and victory came sooner, and he was one who helped."[41]

If ROTC was changing for male students at Purdue and elsewhere in the 1960s, it would soon provide new opportunities for another group that had been denied the opportunity to participate from the earliest days of the program.

That group? Women.

15

WOMEN GET THEIR OPPORTUNITY IN THE MILITARY

My senior year at Purdue, I finished student teaching at West Lafayette High School. The head of education job placement called me into his office. He said, 'Why haven't you signed up to be interviewed for a teaching job?' And I said, 'Because I'm going to join the Navy.' I thought the man was going to have a heart attack. He was really just about ricocheting off the walls.

SALLY WATLINGTON, PURDUE CLASS OF 1960

She is a trailblazer, although she's hesitant to say that. Throughout her life she's been more focused on results than labels.

In 1976, Purdue graduate Sally Watlington became the first Navy woman in the nation to be named executive officer at a major university Navy ROTC program. The program was at Purdue.

It was a great accomplishment. During her years studying at Purdue, women were not allowed to participate in ROTC, or take advantage of the program's unique learning opportunities and military scholarships.

From its formation at Purdue as a corps of cadets in 1876, the military education which was required to be offered at all land-grant universities was available exclusively to men. It was that way at all universities in the nation. And that did not end at Purdue until the fall of 1970, when two women were accepted to Air Force ROTC.

Up until that time, women were only allowed to participate in ROTC auxiliary organizations such as the Air Force Angel Flight, the Army Grenadaires, and the Navy Anchorettes. These did not lead to opportunities to become a commissioned officer. Many activities of the auxiliaries were focused on support for the men in ROTC. Many of the women who participated in the auxiliaries were dating young men in ROTC.

Watlington remembers the late 1950s as a time when women could not wear slacks on campus, when they did not have intercollegiate athletic teams, and when faculty discouraged women from studying engineering, believing they would never have a career in the field. She came to Purdue as a student in 1956 from Rockford, Illinois, unsure of what career she would enter after graduation. Ultimately, she thought she would become a teacher, a common career choice for female students at that time. She quickly became close to people who worked in the Office of the Dean of Women. Some of those friendships became lifelong.

She didn't start thinking seriously about a military career until the second semester of her senior year in 1960 when she heard her mentor, Dean of Women Helen Schleman, talk about her service in the SPARS (the women's branch of the United States Coast Guard Reserve), during World War II. Watlington also knew Beverley Stone, who would succeed Schleman as Dean of Women and would later be named Dean of Students. Stone had served in the WAVES—the women's branch of the United States Naval Reserve. (As discussed in Chapter Nine, Purdue visiting professor of engineering Lillian Gilbreth served on a women's advisory council that helped created the WAVES during World War II.)

In Watlington's senior year, Schleman invited women from Mortar Board, including Watlington, to her home for tea, crumpets, and conversation. Schleman had been second in command to Purdue's Dorothy Stratton in the Coast Guard SPARS during World War II and became SPARS commander after the war.

"That's when I found out more about her experiences in the service," Watlington says. "And that turned my lights on."[1]

She had completed student teacher training at West Lafayette High School and was headed for a job in education when she decided what she really wanted to do was join the Navy.

Watlington remembers the man in charge of arranging teaching job interviews for graduating seniors being stunned when she told him she wasn't going to go into the traditional women's job of teaching. She instead applied for Officer Candidate School in the Navy.

"I thought he was going to have a heart attack," she says.[2]

Watlington went through a lot of screening for Officer Candidate School. She had interviews in Indianapolis and Chicago. "They required women candidates to be interviewed by women," she says.[3]

Watlington was accepted and went to Newport, Rhode Island for training. The women's class was small—just thirty-two candidates.

She began her career in Washington, D.C. and enjoyed her work, but was especially pleased in 1976 to be sent to Purdue, where she had many close friends.

The first woman accepted in Naval ROTC at Purdue graduated in 1976. The military required a female officer in every ROTC program that enrolled women. Lieutenant Commander Linda Lee preceded Watlington as the first female officer at Purdue, in 1972. But Watlington came to Purdue four years later as the first female executive officer (second in command) at a major university.

She was accepted and respected by the male students as well as the females, as she was throughout her time in the Navy. "There were not a lot of women around me during my Navy career," Watlington says. She was never hassled or harassed. "The guys are fine. You just do your job, do what you are trained to do. The men I worked with never had any hang-ups."[4] She said there were some older men higher up who had trouble accepting women.

She moved through the Navy ranks ahead of other women. While she was still at Purdue, she was promoted to the rank of captain, and then in 1979, transferred to San Diego, California, where she served as commanding officer of the Navy Manpower and Material Analysis Center. The next step after captain is the rank of rear admiral.

In 1982, she returned to Washington, D.C. While there, a person on the admiral selection committee told her that she should have been selected. Since she wasn't, she decided to retire at the end of 1983. She returned to the Greater Lafayette area, and the Navy's loss became the community's gain. She has been a very active leader in the community ever since.

"I had a great experience in the Navy," Watlington says. But there were a lot of assignments that were not available to women during her time. "I worked to get those opportunities for younger women," she says. "It's a step-by-step process, it's a slow process, but it was moving forward all the time. It's an open book for women now." She said women in the Navy have equal opportunities with men.[5]

WOMEN IN THE MILITARY

Women served unofficial roles in the U.S. military going back to the American Revolution. During the Civil War, about 3,000 women served as nurses for the Union Army. In World War I, the Navy and Army enlisted women to serve in noncommissioned officer, noncombat roles such as clerical and medical work. In World War II, the Army, Navy, Marines, and Coast Guard created women's units to do noncombatant work. About 350,000 women served in uniform during World War II. About 57,000 women served in the Army Nurse Corps, and 11,000 were Navy nurses.[6]

In 1948, President Harry S Truman signed the Women's Armed Services Integration Act. It allowed women to serve as full members of the military branches, but there were restrictions. Only 2 percent of the people in each branch could be women. Only a limited number of women could become officers and they were unable to command men. They could not serve in combat, and had to leave the service if they became pregnant. They could not serve on combat ships at sea. Women with dependent children were not accepted.[7] Women could not fly military airplanes.[8]

These rules were changed in the decades that followed, and more women began to take the opportunity to serve their country. About 120,000 women served during the Korean War. About 11,000 women were stationed in Vietnam during that war. But they did not serve in combat roles.

Gradually opportunities emerged for women as commanding officers and even fighter pilots. After several years of study and debate, in December 2015 Secretary of Defense Ashton B. Carter opened all combat roles to women in all U.S. services, beginning in 2016.[9]

WOMEN AND ROTC AT PURDUE

ROTC programs on campuses across the United States began admitting women in the early 1970s. Purdue Air Force opened its four-year ROTC unit to women at the start of the 1970–71 academic year. A special two-year Air Force ROTC program would open to women at the start of the 1971–72 academic year. On June 27, 1970, the Lafayette *Journal and Courier* reported, "Dr. Donald R. Mallett, vice president for student services, announced Purdue's acceptance of the program which the Air Force has been operating on a limited trial basis at four other universities during the last year." Those schools were Ohio State, Drake, Auburn, and East Carolina.[10]

Women who completed the program would receive commissions as Air Force officers. The *Journal and Courier* said that two members of Purdue's coed rifle team had enrolled in an Army ROTC class that fall, but noted that "However, this will not involve them in the Army's officer program."[11]

The women of 1970 were trailblazers, but at least one woman had taken part in Purdue's Air Force ROTC in 1964. "A freshman coed created a small stir six years ago by taking an AFROTC course along with the men," the newspaper said. "However, she was not assigned to drill and the Air Force at that time had no provision for her to participate in the full program all the way to commissioning."[12]

By September 1970, four Purdue women had signed up for the Air Force ROTC four-year coursework, and two women were signed up for Army military science courses as electives. Women interested in taking ROTC had come largely from the auxiliary services.[13]

In June 1971, two women took part in ROTC commissioning ceremonies for the first time. They were Second Lieutenant Mary E. Brost, of Boswell, Indiana and Second Lieutenant Nancy Young, of Oakland City, Indiana. They were not ROTC students but took senior-level classes. Brost entered the Women's Army Corps (WAC) program and Young entered the Army's Medical Service Corps.[14]

In 1972, Title IX of the federal Education Amendments Act prohibited sex discrimination in programs that received federal funding. The law applied to practically everything on college campuses, including ROTC programs. Title IX's impact took place over several years, as universities sorted out all the programs that needed to be changed. In addition to opening previously all-male programs to women, it mandated opening all-women programs to men.

The Navy ROTC at Purdue began enrolling women in 1972. Seven women enrolled in the first class.

Purdue was one of four universities in the nation to admit women to the Navy program that year. The others were Jacksonville University in Jacksonville, Florida; the University of Washington in Seattle, Washington; and Southern University and A&M College, a historically Black land-grant school in Baton Rouge, Louisiana.[15]

In a Lafayette *Journal and Courier* story in January 1973, the female Navy students said when they started there had been some teasing from the men. They also said the men were sometimes solicitous to them, such as offering them seats in a full classroom. Some of the women liked that. Others didn't and just wanted to be treated the same as the men.[16]

Purdue's Army ROTC began admitting women in the fall of 1973. The women were free to enter any program other than artillery, infantry, or tank corps. Four women were enrolled. The Air Force was set to commission its first two women on campus in the spring of 1974.[17]

A military draft that had been in effect since 1940 was ended in 1973, and the military went all-volunteer. There was a slight reduction in the number of students signing up for ROTC, but the *Journal and Courier* reported "a definite increase in interest and motivation in those who do enroll."[18]

In 1975, five women were enrolled in their junior year of Navy ROTC at Purdue. Four of the seven who started in their freshman year were still part of NROTC. A fifth had enrolled in her sophomore year.

One of them, Lucy Young, said, "My experiences here have been better than I expected. You've got to have a basically competitive personality to get into the program and you automatically do your best. I find myself enjoying it, especially when I'm directing the drill. It's really increased my self-confidence."[19] Another, Debi Wilson, said she enjoyed the discipline. "It's important, too, to have goals," she said. "Like wanting to fly an airplane. That's what I'm looking forward to next."[20]

Although the military was opening its doors to women in the 1970s, there were still restrictions. Very few were given the opportunity for flight training. But in 1974, six women became the first of their gender to receive Navy wings. One of them was a Purdue graduate. And more were "in the wings" awaiting their opportunity.

CAPTAIN (RET.) ROSEMARY BRYANT MARINER

In the early 1970s, while Rosemary Bryant Mariner was at Purdue studying to become a professional pilot, she met with a visiting airline executive who assured her that women would never fly military or commercial airplanes.[21]

This didn't discourage Mariner. It challenged her. She soon became one of the first women to prove him wrong. Mariner was born April 2, 1953 in Harlingen, Texas. Her father, Cecil James Bryant, was an Air Force pilot and Korean War veteran. Her mother, Constance Estelle Boylan, was a Navy nurse. The family was soon transferred to San Diego, California, where Mariner's father died in a 1956 airplane crash. Deciding at a young age that she wanted to be a pilot, Mariner washed airplanes to make money for flight lessons. She earned her private pilot's license on her seventeenth birthday.

Looking for a college to attend, she came across Purdue, read about famed aviator Amelia Earhart's association with the university and its sponsorship of her final, fatal flight, and also learned that the school had its own airline doing charter flights.[22] In the mid-1960s, Purdue had also become the first university in the nation to offer a four-year bachelor of science degree to students studying to become professional pilots. It became known as the Professional Flight Program in the School of Aviation and Transportation Technology, in what is now the University's Polytechnic Institute.

Rosemary Bryant Merims enrolled at Purdue in the fall term of 1970.[23] In an interview for the book, *A Passion for Excellence: The History of Aviation Education at Purdue*, she said she didn't even know where Purdue was located when she applied, but she knew that was the place for her. When she first saw the campus, she said, "it was the flattest place I had ever seen." She was told as an out-of-state student she could not enroll in the pilot program. She would have to enroll at Purdue, move to campus, and then transfer into the program after she arrived. So, she enrolled in geophysics.[24]

She transferred into the general flight program in technology in the spring semester of 1971 and then enrolled in the professional flight program. She graduated early on December 20, 1972, at the age of nineteen, and enlisted in the Navy. She was the first woman to graduate from Purdue's professional pilot program.

Her decision to graduate in 1972 was motivated by Navy Admiral Elmo Zumwalt Jr., who that year had called for training women to fly Navy aircraft.[25]

The Navy at Purdue had only just started to enroll women in NROTC in the fall of 1972, so Mariner did not have an opportunity to enter the military through that program. She instead was sent to Officer Candidate School in Newport, Rhode Island, where she graduated and was part of the first class of eight women accepted into Navy flight training at Pensacola, Florida. At five feet, four inches, she barely made the minimum height requirement.[26]

In 1974, she was one of the first six female aviators to earn their wings and then became one of the first Navy jet pilots.

That started her on a career of firsts. She was the first woman to qualify to fly a tactical jet aircraft, the A-4 Skyhawk. In 1976, she was the first woman to fly the A-7E Corsair II. She was the first female pilot assigned to an aircraft carrier, the first to land on a carrier, and the first female pilot to qualify as a surface warfare officer. She was the first woman to command a Navy aviation squadron. She commanded a Tactical Electronic Warfare Squadron during Operation Desert Storm in 1991. And in 1993, when Navy restrictions against women flying combat missions were ended, Mariner became one of the first female aviators promoted to captain.

In spite of all her accomplishments, *The Wall Street Journal* said, "For much of her career she was treated as an oddity. An Associated Press story in 1974 called her a 'girl flyer.' Air-traffic controllers were sometimes puzzled when they heard a feminine voice from the cockpit. 'Once in Texas,' she said, 'the flight controller asked me if I had a cold or something.' Mariner was often asked if she was a feminist. 'I'm not a women's libber in a radical sense,' she told United Press International in 1976. In her view letting women fly military planes was a matter of practicality not ideology. Why, she wondered, should recruiters overlook half of all potential flying aces?"[27]

She retired with the rank of captain in 1997, having logged seventeen aircraft carrier landings and with 3,500 hours of flying in fifteen different planes.

In her interview for the book *A Passion for Excellence: The History of Aviation Education at Purdue,* Mariner said,

> I am a very strong believer that we have souls and that those souls are not gendered. You should live your life to the best of your ability in whatever field you go into, trying to do the right thing in front of your fellow humans and in front of God or however you look at how the universe is done. I think in the end that is much more important than being ruthlessly ambitious. I think you will be a happier person. That includes family and all the personal things that we have to do in this world taking care of one another. I encourage men and women to follow that model, including what they call the servant leadership model, because you will be in a leadership position eventually. That's the most important thing you can do in life. It doesn't matter how many fancy medallions or plaques you have hanging on the wall.[28]

Mariner died from ovarian cancer at the age of 65, on January 24, 2019, shortly after that interview. Her husband, fellow Navy aviator Tommy Mariner, was quoted many times explaining how his wife felt about women pilots serving in combat: "An aircraft gun is a great equalizer." She believed that for women pilots to be fully accepted in the Navy they needed to take the same combat risks as men.[29]

In 2022, the U.S. Congress named the Department of Veteran Affairs Community-Based Outpatient Clinic in Ventura, California, after Mariner. Ventura is where she became the first woman to command an operational air squadron.

At her burial service in Maynardville, Tennessee, Navy planes flew the "missing man formation" above the cemetery. But there was one change. For the first time, the formation was flown by all female pilots. It was a "missing woman formation."[30]

CAPTAIN (RET.) VIVIAN LEONARD TURNBULL

Being one of the first four universities in the nation to open Navy ROTC to women brought outstanding female students to Purdue in 1972 and 1973. So, it's no surprise that many of them went on to outstanding careers.

Vivian Leonard Turnbull grew up in Jacksonville, Florida. Her father was a Navy contractor and he suggested she apply for a four-year Navy scholarship. She got it.

She wanted to major in Russian language, and since Purdue offered that in addition to ROTC, coming to West Lafayette in 1973 was an easy decision for her.

"I wanted to go to school out of state. I didn't know a lot about Purdue, but I loved it there," Turnbull says. "I didn't know a soul when I flew from Chicago into the Purdue Airport. I didn't think much about being accepted in the Navy as a woman. I was more nervous about being out on my own for the first time. My parents always raised me to go to college with the expectation I could do what I put my mind to do."[31]

While she started as a Russian major, she later switched to mathematics with minors in Russian and German.

NROTC became her home on campus. "It's such a large university, it has a big student body and it's easy to get lost if you don't have a group to belong to," Turnbull says. "NROTC was that to me. My friends and activities were in NROTC."

In 1975, Turnbull was awarded the national-level Legion of Valor Bronze Cross for Outstanding Achievement in the Reserve Officer Training Corps. The award was presented by then Secretary of the Navy J. William Middendorf II.

She married a fellow NROTC student in June 1976, between her junior and senior years. Her husband Thomas graduated from Purdue and was commissioned in 1975 and was assigned to a frigate out of Norfolk. By December 1976, Turnbull had acquired enough credits to graduate so she could join him in Norfolk.

"Then, of course, he then deployed in February," Turnbull says.[32]

He was gone for six to eight months. He remained on active duty for five years and then entered the reserves. That enabled him to move around with his wife as her career developed. He got a master's degree, taught high school, and worked for a supercomputer research organization. Like Turnbull, he had majored in mathematics at Purdue. He retired from the Naval Reserves after twenty years of service.

The summer before Turnbull graduated from Purdue, she received training in intelligence in Norfolk, Virginia. She loved it, and two years after being commissioned, she began work in Naval intelligence, where she remained for much of her career. She can't talk about what she did working in Naval intelligence. "In generic terms, you try to understand your adversary and provide information on what you believe they're going to do that will help inform decision making," Turnbull says. "I absolutely loved the Navy. When I joined it was 'Join the Navy and see the world.' I had a chance to do that; great people, great missions. I really loved it. It was a wonderful career."[33]

She was a senior executive at the Defense Intelligence Agency after retiring from the Navy in December 2004 with the rank of captain. She and her husband have one son who is a submarine officer and another son who works for the Defense Intelligence Agency—carrying on a family legacy.

When Turnbull was first commissioned, women could not have dependents. If they did, they had to leave the Navy. That changed: one of the many changes and newly opened doors of opportunity she was happy to see during her years of service.

She is a member of the Purdue ROTC Hall of Fame.

CAPTAIN (RET.) LUCY YOUNG

Interviewed in 1975 for a newspaper article during her junior year at Purdue, Lucy Young said she had a competitive personality which was helping her in NROTC at Purdue. It helped her throughout a career in which she became among the first female Navy pilots. Rosemary Bryant Mariner was number six; Lucy Young was number fourteen.

Young's father had served in the Navy during World War II and continued in the reserves after that. Her older brother went to Yale University, took part in NROTC, and became a Navy pilot who served in Vietnam. Growing up in

Connecticut, she wanted to be in the Navy. But she saw no opportunity to become a Navy officer other than completing her bachelor's degree, going to a Navy recruiting office, and trying to get into Officer Candidate School. And at that that time, women were not admitted to Navy flight school.

"There were zero role models" for young girls who wanted to be pilots, Young says. "There was zero scholarship money, zero encouragement, zero anything. There wasn't even a book about a woman Navy pilot."[34]

In her senior year of high school, she saw a news story about the Navy opening ROTC to women at four U.S. campuses. Her life changed. She competed for a four-year scholarship and received one. There was no question where she wanted to go: Purdue.

In the fall of 1972, she was among the first seventeen women in the nation to enroll in NROTC. Her scholarship paid for tuition, fees, books, and a $100 monthly allowance. Purdue had the largest number of female midshipmen. 1972 was the year Title IX was passed by Congress, opening opportunities for women at universities.

Lieutenant Commander Linda Lee was the first female officer on the Purdue campus in 1972 and she helped these trailblazing students integrate into ROTC and campus life. There were a few challenges. "They had to order uniforms for us," Young says. "They had many uniforms for the men, but they didn't have anything on the racks for women."[35]

Sally Watlington arrived later, and Young enjoyed working with her and has maintained a friendship through the years.

"I loved military training," she says. "And every year I won some kind of award."[36]

During the summer of 1975, before her senior year, she was visiting her brother at Naval Air Station Oceana in Virginia Beach, Virginia. While there she met Rosemary Mariner. "I knew she had graduated from Purdue," Young says. "I was so excited to meet her. She was beautiful and articulate and she was flying jets. She convinced me that naval aviation was the perfect goal for me and I started flying that fall."[37]

Young finally had a role model.

At Purdue, Young also played on the women's basketball team, which was a club organization until her senior year when it became a varsity sport. In its first game, the women's varsity team defeated the University of Illinois in overtime on December 2, 1975, 78–74. Title IX resulted in women's intercollegiate basketball at Purdue and around the nation.

During her senior year the Navy paid for flight training for male students who qualified. They would not pay for the women, but they did offer Young a ground school flight program. She financed private flight lessons with her own money, and three days after graduating from Purdue in the spring of 1976, she received her private pilot's license.

By this time the Navy was training female pilots, so Young applied for flight school. Men who qualified went right in, but she had to go before a national selection board. Despite this hurdle, she was selected for admission, began flight school in the fall of 1976, and received her Navy wings in October 1977. Although she had trained in propeller airplanes, she wanted to transition to flying jets. She succeeded and was one of the first six women to fly a Navy jet.

"I went from a cabin class turbo prop where you could sip your coffee to a tactical jet wearing a G-suit, an oxygen mask, a helmet," Young says. "It was a big change but I managed to hang in there. I really liked it."[38]

She next went to Hawaii and did fleet support. She and other female pilots were shore-based: despite transitioning to flying jets, they were not allowed to land on aircraft carriers. In Hawaii they could only fly over them.

"It was a big point of contention," Young says. "We were systematically excluded from going near ships if our point was to land on them."[39] In 1982, Young did become carrier-qualified on the USS *Lexington.*

In Hawaii, Young accumulated more than a thousand hours flying support missions for Pacific fleet units and multinational exercises. On her second tour, she was the first female instructor in the Navy Strike pipeline, flying TA-4J Skyhawks at Naval Air Station in Kingsville, Texas.

She is a veteran of Operation Desert Shield/Storm, and flew missions to Saudi Arabia, Egypt, Greece, and Israel during the conflict. She flew the Navy DC-9.

She left active duty in July 1983 and accepted a position in the Navy reserves in Atlanta, Georgia, where she flew the C-9 Skytrain and became the first female Federal Aviation Administration Test Pilot. She retired at the rank of captain in August 1998.

In May 1986, Young began training as a Boeing 727 Flight Engineer with Piedmont Airlines in Winston-Salem, North Carolina. In October 1987, she upgraded to First Officer on the Boeing 737, flying out of Charlotte. She flew domestic and international commercial flights for US Airways and American Airlines. She retired from commercial flights in September 2019 having logged more than 20,000 hours of pilot time in more than forty different aircraft.

CAPTAIN (RET.) COLLEEN NEVIUS

When she was sixteen years old, Colleen Nevius read an article in *Parade* magazine about the nation's first female Navy aviators, including Rosemary Bryant Mariner. It caught her imagination. She knew what she wanted to do.

The daughter of a career Navy pilot who had served in the Korean War, she was born in Corpus Christi, Texas and "raised at Naval air stations everywhere," as the family moved every one to three years.[40]

As a young woman, she set her sights on becoming what had been impossible until that time: a female Navy pilot. She wanted a college education. She wanted to be part of Naval ROTC. And then she wanted to go to Navy flight school.

Not only did she achieve these things, but she won a Navy scholarship.

She applied to Purdue in 1973, because the year before it had been one of the first four universities in the nation to accept women in NROTC. She accepted their offer of admission. When she got on an airplane and arrived in West Lafayette for registration, it was her first time on campus. "I didn't even know where Purdue was," she says.[41]

Nevius says Admiral Zumwalt played a key role in opening opportunities for women in the Navy. She says he felt the Navy needed to reflect society, which in the 1970s was seeing a massive social change, with more women entering the workforce and finding professional careers. "The '70s was an interesting time period," Nevius says.[42]

At Purdue, she majored in management, and NROTC was a big part of her college life.

"Purdue was a good experience for me," Nevius says. "They did things so well." Sally Watlington was her executive officer while she was in NROTC. "She was a spectacular leader," Nevius says. "She was more politically attuned than we were. We were ready to bang down doors. She said, 'That's not how we do things.' She was right. The men and women I went through ROTC with have stayed in touch, a bunch of us are lifelong friends. That's been special."[43]

She was treated well by male students, and some seemed just oblivious to how new this was. "Purdue is a tough school," Nevius says. People were focused on their studies.

She wanted to be a pilot but had never piloted an aircraft. She described her first experience with a fixed-wing aircraft as "less than exciting. But I was very excited to get in a helicopter. It was love at first sight."[44] That was in Corpus Christi, Texas, the summer after her junior year at Purdue. The helicopter lifted off the ground, it went backward, and then it zoomed around through the air. It was amazing.

She became a Navy helicopter pilot, receiving her wings in 1979. Women were not allowed to be on combat ships at that time, so her opportunities were limited.

"People ask me if it was hard because I was a girl," Nevius says. "I've never been anything but a girl, so I didn't really know. There were times people said things that were really stupid, but I feel like the guys got that too. And that could be dealt with through an eye roll or good grace and humor."[45]

In 1983, she became the first woman pilot to graduate from Navy Test Pilot School and the first woman member of the Society of Experimental Test Pilots. She will never forget her first interview with the commanding officer at the test pilot school.

> He sat down and he looked me in the eye and said, "I don't think you're going to graduate." I thought to myself, "Are they setting me up to fail? Are they going to bring me in and then say 'See, girls can't do it.'" And that was a little paranoia, maybe, of being on the leading edge of changes that were going on.
>
> My second interview was with the executive officer. He looked at me and he said, "You know you're the first woman pilot here. I expect you to work hard. If you can make it you will make it." I found out later that he had talked to my classmates and also pointed out that they had the first woman pilot in their class and that he expected them to treat me as a classmate, no more, no less and that we would graduate as a class. That taught me a lot about leadership, the effect of leadership on attitudes and opinions. My classmates could not have been more supportive. It was a very proud moment to have my name called with the other thirty members of my class and to not get special mention, to just be a member of the class of 1983.[46]

Nevius retired from the Navy in May 2003 with the rank of captain. She is married to retired Navy captain and NASA astronaut Bill Readdy. They have three children, one of whom is a Navy helicopter pilot.

Nevius is in the Purdue ROTC Hall of Fame.

VICE ADMIRAL (RET.) CAROL POTTENGER

Carol Pottenger had a Navy career that began at Purdue in the second class of women accepted in NROTC, along with Colleen Nevius and Vivian Leonard

Turnbull. They remain lifelong friends. Pottenger retired from the Navy as a vice admiral, with a list of accomplishments that helped open the doors of opportunity to many women who followed in her footsteps.

She was among the first women in the Navy assigned to sea duty in 1978. She was the first woman admiral to command a combat strike group. She was the first female admiral to lead a combatant force-type command. She was in charge of manning, training, and equipping more than forty thousand sailors in preparation for deployment to Iraq and Afghanistan and to other global security assistance operations.

She ended her career as deputy chief of staff for capability development at NATO Supreme Allied Commander Transformation in Norfolk, Virginia. She was the first woman to hold that position.

"I had a wonderful career," Pottenger says. "I'm a glass half-full person. You might talk to women who had bad experiences." And she had a few. "But that's not what I remember," she says. "What I remember is people who mentored me and gave me opportunity. I never worked for a woman. All my mentors were men. I had male bosses my whole career. But I've learned how important it is for younger women to look and see success in someone who looks like them."[47]

Pottenger was born in Oak Park, Illinois. Her family moved first to Pittsburgh, Pennsylvania, and then in her senior year of high school they relocated to St. Petersburg, Florida, where an interest in the Navy sparked within her. Women still didn't have a lot of opportunities in the military at that time, but she thought she would be a Navy nurse.[48]

She decided to attend Purdue because it was a prestigious university and because it had started admitting women to NROTC in 1972. She had a great experience at Purdue, where she majored in history, and in ROTC, where she learned that a lot of Navy opportunities for women were opening. She received a Navy scholarship for her last three years of college.

During her junior year in 1976, she was selected Navy ROTC Midshipman of the Year. She was the first woman to receive the honor—only four years after women were first admitted to the program.

Protocol called for the person who received the award to receive a Navy sword. But protocol was behind the changing times: the Navy did not allow women to wear a sword. They considered giving her a chronometer. She told them she wanted a sword. She got it, and as Navy regulations changed, she wore it during several ceremonies during her career.

When Pottenger was commissioned in 1977, women were not allowed to go to sea on ships. She was based in Hawaii as a communications watch officer. Rules changed, and Pottenger was in the second group of women assigned to sea duty in 1978–79. They were assigned to tenders (small boats that repaired and supported ships), which was not an assignment that would have been given to a male officer advancing in his career.

She did a Mediterranean cruise and was later assigned to the staff of a two-star admiral. "He wouldn't take me on deployment," Pottenger says. "He said it wasn't appropriate. I just put that stuff out of my mind. You grit your teeth, keep your head down and do your job."[49]

She had learned a lot from her executive officer Sally Watlington while she was at Purdue. "We all revered her as an excellent leader and role model," Pottenger says.[50]

She had many more wonderful opportunities to serve, and advanced to rear admiral.

She takes the phrase "equal opportunity" and turns it around a bit. "It's not equal opportunity," she says. "It's the opportunity to be equal. You are given opportunity, but it's up to you to make something of it. You have to work and be passionate about what you're doing and invest effort and time to be good at it. And then you should be rewarded. You are given opportunity, and it's up to you to make something of it."[51]

She is a member of the Purdue ROTC Hall of Fame.

MAJOR GENERAL (RET.) ERIKA COVINGTON STEUTERMAN

At one point in her career Erika Covington Steuterman was the highest-ranking female officer in the U.S. Air Force. She retired with the rank of major general in 2011 from a military career that started with Air Force ROTC at Purdue in 1972.

"I loved my military career," Steuterman says. "It's the best job a person could ever have and the best job for a woman at that time. I worked for the National Security Agency, I worked with the CIA on deployments. I did a lot of things most women don't have the opportunity to do—not just job-wise, but experience-wise."[52]

She once went to a demilitarized zone on a helicopter and there wasn't enough space to land. So, the pilot balanced the helicopter above ground and she and an aide jumped out.

"I told a girlfriend about that later and she said, 'Why would you want to do that?' I said, 'Why wouldn't I want to do that?' I did everything atypical for a woman."[53]

Steuterman was born in Lafayette and grew up in Indianapolis. Her father served in the Army during World War II and the Korean War. She applied to three colleges, including Purdue and an honors program at Indiana University during her junior year of high school and was accepted. Her mother had graduated from Purdue in 1950 and her father in 1951.

"My parents said 'You can go to any school you want, but we're only paying for Purdue,'" Steuterman says. "That narrowed my choices. I thought the smart thing would be to go to Purdue. It's a great school. I decided women who went to college ended up doing one of three things. They became a teacher, a nurse, or a secretary. Those are noble professions, but they're not for me. I wanted equal opportunity for promotion, for responsibility, and for equal pay. The military was the only place I could do that and that's why I enrolled in ROTC."[54]

The Vietnam War was still underway, and her parents were the only members of her extended family that supported her decision.

"I figured out if I went in the Air Force, I could be in operations by being an intelligence officer, and that was the closest a female in those days could get to operations where I could get promotions and increased responsibility and equal pay."[55] Military operations are coordinated responses to a developing situation.

Steuterman was also part of the Big Ten flag team with the Purdue All-American Marching Band. But most of her free time was spent with AFROTC.

"I found my niche," she says. "I had no idea it would fit me so well. Going into the military has to be in your DNA. I was organized, disciplined, I was an overachiever. But they did not know what to do with me."[56]

The AFROTC had only started admitting women two years earlier. Steuterman says that in 1972, the men were still getting accustomed to it. An enlisted man fitting her for her uniform was uncomfortable placing a measuring tape on her arms and shoulders. "They were concerned about offending me," she says. "They were very careful."[57]

The women wanted to be treated exactly like the men.

On campus, the ROTC students wore their uniforms one day a week. Steuterman says she received no negative reactions, although the unpopular Vietnam War continued. But she got a lot of stares, probably because people weren't used to seeing a woman in uniform.

She majored in French and German language and spent two semesters abroad in her junior year (1974–75) studying in Strasbourg, France, where both languages are spoken. During the summer before her junior year, she became the first woman to win the Commandant Award at her ROTC training.

She graduated in the spring of 1976, and the military academies began accepting women in the fall of that year. The Air Force offered Steuterman an opportunity to become part of the first class of women and to earn a second bachelor's degree. She turned them down.

"Why would I want to start all over again?" she says. "The academy wasn't an option available to me in 1972. Purdue is a great university. So, no, I'm not going to start all over again just to be in the first class to help mentor women who were four years younger than me."[58]

But since she had spent a year studying abroad, she had to do another year of ROTC. She enrolled for a master's degree in Purdue's Krannert School of Management and was able to finish the two years of work in eighteen months. At Krannert, she met fellow student Ron Steuterman, who received his bachelor's degree in 1975 and his master's degree in finance in 1978.

The couple married in August 1978. "I asked him to marry me in February 1978," Erika Steuterman says. She had Air Force training ahead of her after receiving her master's degree. "I knew when I got done with tech training, if I did well, I could have a choice of where to be stationed. And if I wasn't going to be married, I was going to go overseas and just start traveling the world. It took him a couple minutes, but he said, 'Yes, okay, we'll get married.' And so, then I had to think about, okay, where is my potential spouse going to be able to get a job?"[59]

She did well when she chose to be stationed with intelligence service in Fort Worth, Texas. Her new husband soon found work in Dallas with Texas Instruments, and their married life and careers began.

Steuterman was assigned to a bomber wing. Part of her work was arming nuclear weapons and the personnel who did that had to be armed when they did the work. "The Air Force did not have a whole lot of holsters small enough for me for my side arm because they'd never had a woman do this before," she says. "So, the guys would just laugh at me. I'd strap the thing on it would hang down to my knees. They got a laugh out of it, but they let me do my job."[60]

In 1982 they had their first child, Erin, who was born with intellectual development disabilities. "At that point I could not move around every three to four years with the Air Force and find new doctors, new therapists," Steuterman says. "So, I went into the active reserves—an Individual Mobilization Augmentee. It's one person assigned to an active-duty unit. For the most part I could plan when I went on active duty based on the needs of my children."

The couple had another daughter, Jessica. They lived in Texas for eighteen years and from time to time, Erika traveled to Germany, Washington, D.C., and other bases in Texas as her husband worked in the oil industry.

She also served in Desert Storm in response to the Iraq invasion of Kuwait. "I worked on a team that tried to find all the Scud missiles," she says. "The Air Force had learned that women did not do well going into Saudi Arabia and working with Saudi military. They wouldn't talk to women. You had to talk to a man who would then talk to the Saudi intelligence officer. So, they sent me to Omaha, Nebraska, and I worked that war there."[61]

She also served in the Iraqi Freedom and Enduring Freedom operations to create a stable, democratic Iraq, and in the Horn of Africa.

In 1996 the couple moved to Lafayette, Indiana, where Steuterman continued working for the Air Force and her husband took a position with Purdue. In 2006 she was promoted to major general. It was just two years before the couple's youngest daughter, Jessica, was in an automobile accident that left her with physical, as well as intellectual, disabilities. These challenges in private life came in conjunction with the duties and responsibilities of her new rank.

Women have more opportunities in the Air Force today than ever before, Steuterman says. "We've come a long way. I educate the women in ROTC today about how challenging it was to make it through the ranks in those days. When I went to Fort Worth, I was a new second lieutenant and my boss was a major. He told me women didn't belong in the military. I knew that was going to be a difficult assignment, but I also knew I could outlast him. I knew I had to perform better because I had a lot of eyes on me. He was retired as a major. I retired as a major general."[62]

At one point in her career when she was giving an intelligence report to the commander of the eighth Air Force, she was required to speak from a small booth. The officer told her to come out so he could have a look at her. She did.

"Would he have done that to a man?" she says. "I was mortified. I was so angry I could hardly speak. But he was a three-star general and I was a lowly major."[63] She reported the incident and received a formal apology.

She remembers one wing commander who had an office she learned to walk past very quickly. Every time he saw her go by, he came out and tried to kiss her.

"I was a brand-new second lieutenant and this guy had control of my destiny, my future," she says. "You had to walk very carefully in those days. I'm glad to see our women doing so well today. Every time I go to an Air Force ROTC event at Purdue today it reminds me of what good hands our country is in. These young people are extraordinary."[64]

She is a member of the Purdue ROTC Hall of Fame.

PROFILE

MAJOR (RET.) HEATHER PENNEY

HEATHER PENNEY SAYS HER MISSION FLYING AN AIR FORCE F-16 COMBAT JET OVER WASHington, D.C. and Pennsylvania on the morning of September 11, 2001 was a failure.

Other people would describe it with different words: heroism, bravery, patriotism.

On the morning of 9/11, which started like any other day in America and ended like no other, Purdue graduate and Air National Guard Lieutenant Penney answered the call to duty and took off from Andrews Air Force Base in Washington on a one-way suicide mission.

She and her lead pilot Marc Sasseville (flying another F-16) were looking for United Airlines Flight 93. It had been hijacked by terrorists and was believed to be heading back from Pennsylvania to Washington to crash into the U.S. Capitol, or maybe the White House. The World Trade Center towers in New York City and the Pentagon in Washington had already been attacked, and air traffic controllers had heard radio transmissions of terrorists hijacking Flight 93.

Without time to load missiles onto their planes, Penney and Sasseville were not given direct orders about what to do that morning. The U.S. military doesn't send its people on suicide missions.

But Penney and Sasseville knew what they had to do.

Sasseville planned to crash his F-16 into the cockpit of Flight 93, and Penney would ram her plane into the tail, taking it down before it could reach its target in the nation's capital, killing even more people and damaging or even destroying buildings critical to U.S. national security.

There were forty-four passengers and crew on the United flight from Newark Airport that morning heading for San Francisco. It was a remote possibility, but one of the people on Flight 93 might have been Penney's father, United Airlines pilot and Vietnam War veteran John Penney, who sometimes flew planes departing from the East Coast. But that possibility didn't cross her mind as she searched for the hijacked commercial airplane.

"What we needed to do was so immediate and so urgent that it never crossed my mind that my dad could have been the captain on that flight," Penney says. It was later that she realized what might have happened. On that morning of 9/11 she was just totally focused. "We had a job to do," she says.[1]

Her voice is clear and calm as she recalls that beautiful, blue-sky morning when she left her home, patted her dog goodbye, and headed to work at Joint Base Andrews in Maryland where she was based. She wasn't even scheduled to fly that day. The possibility that she might never return home was the farthest thing from her mind.

As a member of the Air National Guard, Penney was doing what she loved. All her life she wanted to fly. And that wasn't easy for a woman born in 1974, the year Purdue graduate Rosemary Bryant Mariner was one of the first six women in the United States to earn her Navy wings. In the early 1970s, women were for the first time allowed to enroll in ROTC at Purdue and in other units around the nation. Many of those women had dreams of becoming pilots. But while Mariner and others won the opportunity to fly, it would be almost twenty years before they were permitted to fly in combat.

Penney was born in Tucson, Arizona, where her father was stationed at Davis-Monthan Air Force Base. She grew up listening to her dad talk to other combat pilots about their missions in Vietnam. She had a twin sister, and they had a stay-at-home mother, Stephanie.

According to her mother, Penney first announced she wanted to be a pilot when she was four years old. By the time she was in fourth grade, she had added that she wanted to be a combat pilot. Her mother let her have her dreams, even if they seemed impossible at that time. "Go for it," Stephanie said.[2]

When the time came for college, Penney picked Purdue. She and her father visited the campus before she enrolled.

"I ended up at Purdue because it was a great engineering school," she says. "It had an ROTC detachment, and there was something about Purdue that just felt right."[3]

She planned to enroll in ROTC and become a fighter pilot like her dad. But when she arrived on campus in the fall of 1992, she discovered that women could not serve in military combat. Penney decided against enrolling in ROTC. She also discovered something else: she didn't like the major she had chosen.

"I enrolled in general engineering. I thought that I wanted to be an aeronautical engineer because of aviation," she says. "But it turned out I was a rotten engineer. So, I went with Plan B, which actually wasn't ever really a plan. But I ended up in the College of Liberal Arts majoring in English, which I'd enjoyed in high school. I just kind of floated over there."[4]

The summer after her freshman year, she earned a private pilot's license in Denver, Colorado. In 1994, at the end of her sophomore year, she began to follow in her father's footsteps and compete in air races. Penney teamed with fellow Purdue student Krystal Lewis, a junior in aviation technology, to become the first collegiate team ever to compete in the national Air Race Classic, a flying competition for women. Amelia Earhart, the first woman to fly solo across the Atlantic Ocean, had competed in a predecessor of the Air Race Classic.

The Air Race Classic touched down in several Midwest states, starting in St. Louis, Missouri and ending in Columbus, Ohio after flying 2,427 miles. Penney and Lewis finished ninth out of forty-two teams that competed and received a standing ovation at the awards ceremony.

"Our success in the air race gave me a lot of self-confidence in competing," Penney told a Purdue *Exponent* reporter in June 1995. "It's nice to know you can rise to the occasion."[5]

That self-confidence would help build her future, as she rose to the occasion many times.

She completed her bachelor's degree in three years by taking as many as twenty-four credit hours in a semester. Her sister was attending college at another university, and Penney finished early to ease the financial burden on her parents. She also washed dishes at Earhart Hall and worked as a waitress at a restaurant near campus to earn extra money.

Her rush to graduate left her unsure about the future. "I was twenty years old when I graduated," Penney says. "I had some excellent professors who were very good mentors to me, Bob Lamb and Dick Thompson. And they said, 'Heather, you really should consider going to graduate school.' And they encouraged me to take the GRE. So, I did. I applied to Purdue as well as some other universities. But I really wanted to stay at Purdue. I was part of the very first class for the new, at the time, American Studies graduate program. So, I earned my master's in American Studies there."[6]

While a graduate student, she learned that in 1993, the U.S. had actually opened the opportunity to women to participate in combat. She immediately refocused her goals on the military. She entered the National Guard, because that seemed her best chance to fly fighter jets.

"While I was in grad school, I applied to every single National Guard unit that had fighters in the United States because I just wanted to fly fighters," she says. "And at the time a couple things were going on which my dad helped me sort out at the time. I didn't know enough to really be able to connect all the dots. But because the nation was downsizing, following the end of the Cold War and the peace dividend, the nation literally cut the Air Force in half."[7]

People who wanted to be Air Force pilots were being sent to nonflying jobs for three to five years. And even then, it wasn't guaranteed they would become combat pilots. A lot of people looked beyond the Air Force. The National Guard offered Penney the best chance of becoming a pilot if she was admitted.

"There were forms and transcripts and letters, recommendations and letters of intent, and all of that," Penney says. "It was very much like applying for college or applying for a job. It's very competitive to get into these fighter units. For every three hundred applications, they selected ten people to interview and then hired one or maybe two. I was fortunate enough that I got the interview, and I was the backup selectee for the District of Colombia. But they ended up receiving two pilot training slots. So, I was able to go. They said, 'Hey, you might be our second choice, but we got two slots, so you're good to go.' And that was how I ended up at DC."[8]

She was notified of her acceptance in the fall of 1996. But since her enrollment was not immediate, she extended her graduate work at Purdue and received her master's degree in December 1997. She then went through officer training and received her commission in May 1998, which was followed by flight training. She became among the first U.S. women to fly the F-16 and the first woman in the 121st Fighter Squadron of the Air National Guard.

She is known by her call sign, which is created by fellow pilots when a person is qualified for combat.

Penney's call sign is "Lucky," as in "lucky penny."

She likes the name.

She was in a morning meeting at Andrews when the first World Trade Center tower was hit. The people at the meeting didn't see it on television, but they were notified and thought it was probably a private airplane accident.

"It wasn't until the second tower was hit that we realized our nation was under attack," Penney says. "I'm a young lieutenant, a rookie fighter pilot in my squadron in Washington, D.C. But we weren't an Air Defense Alert Squadron. We didn't have live weapons or missiles loaded on our jets, and we couldn't get real missiles in time. We had to get airborne to protect. I was so eager, impatient, but frustrated and angry because we couldn't get authorization to launch. Waiting, just waiting."[9]

According to protocol, on the morning of September 11, 2001, only five fighter units in the United States were armed with live weapons and ready to defend the nation. The 121st Fighter Squadron of the Air National Guard at Washington, D.C. was not one of them.[10]

The 121st Squadron tried to get some missiles for their planes, but there wasn't time. They tried to get an order to fly and protect the federal government, but none came immediately.

On the day of the attacks, President George Bush was attending an event at the Emma E. Booker Elementary School in Sarasota, Florida. He quickly returned to Air Force One and was airborne for his safety. Vice President Dick Cheney was in a bunker beneath the White House. After the two hits on the World Trade Center and a plane had been crashed into the Pentagon, Cheney was told a fourth commercial plane had been hijacked. It had been flying over Pennsylvania, heading west. But it had turned and was on a course for Washington, D.C.

Cheney gave the order to shoot it down.

That was the command they were waiting for at the 121st Squadron at Andrews. Sasseville ordered two pilots to wait and get their planes armed. He told Penney to follow him. He and Penney went to their F-16s and were quickly in the air.

"You have to remember, I was a brand-new lieutenant at the time," Penney says. "I had just earned my combat mission qualification. My priorities as a young woman were simple and clear: Fly good formations, stay visual, and make sure there was plenty of hot coffee, cold beer, and fresh popcorn in the bar."[11]

They headed toward Pennsylvania and flew all around the countryside. They never saw anything. In fact, passengers on Flight 93 had engaged the hijackers and crashed the airplane before Penney and Sasseville were even able to take off. But Penney and Sasseville didn't know that.

Penney's father was not on Flight 93. But John Penney had worked with Flight 93 captain Jason Dahl and knew him well. Dahl and everyone on board Flight 93 died when it crashed in Pennsylvania.

Later that day, Penney helped escort Air Force One and President Bush back into Washington, D.C. She also worked in the days and weeks after 9/11 flying missions to protect the airspace above the capital.

"We had a job to do," she says. "We immediately went to flying 24/7 combat air patrols over D.C. I flew the midnight to 4:00 a.m. shift because I was single. I had no family. And that allowed the other guys in the squadron to have a more normal schedule with their families."[12]

There wasn't much time for her to deal with any emotions following September 11, 2001. She was too busy.

"To the extent that it affected me, I was angry that we didn't get there in time, not in terms of a survivor's guilt or anything like that. I was angry that the system failed us. The organizations failed us, the intelligence failed us. I was angry about that. But I didn't spend any time dwelling on it. I didn't spend any time ruminating on it or feeling sorry for myself or feeling traumatized. We had a job to do, and so we had to keep on keeping on and do our jobs."[13]

Her service continued in the years after 9/11 as the National Guard was used in overseas military missions. In 2003, she flew more than a dozen missions in the early days of Operation Iraqi Freedom. Her experience with night flying using night vision goggles prepared her well for nighttime "scud hunting."

She had daughters born in 2004 and 2006. As a then part-time member of the Air National Guard in Washington, D.C., she also took a full-time job with Lockheed Martin from 2006 to 2018. Her portfolio included the F-22, F-35, F-16, and the T-50 in the Air Force's competition for their new advanced jet trainer.

"I left the National Guard fighter squadron in 2009 because by then I was a single mom and I just could not keep up with the combat deployments," Penney says. "So, I moved over to our sister squadron, the 201st airlift squadron, and flew the C-38 for them, and became an instructor pilot there."[14]

The 201st provided short notice transportation for government officials and high-ranking U.S. and foreign dignitaries. In 2015, when the 201st divested the C-38, she transitioned to the Air Force Reserves, working in the Pentagon. She retired from the military with the rank of major in 2020.

In 2023, she was a senior fellow at the Mitchell Institute for Aerospace Studies, and worked on defense policy, research, and analysis. She has continued to fly, owns antique airplanes, and takes part in jet airplane races.

Penney received the Emerging Voice Award from the Purdue College of Liberal Arts and the Purdue Alumni Association in 2012. In 2022 she received Purdue's College of Liberal Arts Distinguished Alumni Award. She received the Outstanding Aviator Award from the Wings Club Foundation and the International Aviation Women's Association.[15]

She and Sasseville started doing interviews and public speaking about their experience on 9/11 about ten years after the terrorist attacks. In her speeches about that day, she talks about courage and fear. She talks about bringing the nation together again for a common purpose, as it was after 9/11.

Penney's talks are not just about the drama and trauma of the day. She wants the people who hear her story to "connect to a greater meaning—the meaning of what it means to be an American, of honoring the heroes of that day, the first responders. And how can we honor their legacy? By being our better selves," she says.[16]

"Sass and I were mission failures that day," Penney says in one of her talks. "The passengers on Flight 93 [and all 9/11 first responders] are the true heroes. I've come to realize that heroism isn't something unique or possessed by only a chosen few. The key is acknowledging the fear, but don't obsess on it. Don't think about it."[17]

When the passengers boarded Flight 93 on the morning of September 11, they were just going on a business trip, coming home from vacation, going to see Grandma, she says.

"They were just like you and me," Penney says. And they became heroes. "We all have that totally ordinary, everyday hero inside of us. So why wait for a national crisis to bring that hero out. Don't we need everyday heroes? . . . . Bravery isn't the absence of fear. It's acting in the face of fear, doing the right thing, even though it might terrify us. We must overcome our fears to do our duty. And that duty is service. . . . What do I mean by service? It is acting with the recognition that there are things in this world more important than us or our self-interests.[18]

Penney says she's often thought of the passengers on Flight 93, their fear of the hijackers, their fear of dying, their fear of leaving their loved ones forever.

"You may remember Todd Beamer," she says in a talk. "He was a software account manager, a devoted father who taught Sunday school with his wife, an avid sports fan, and a passenger on Flight 93. As they were getting ready to charge the terrorists, Todd's last words to the group were, 'Let's roll.' They chose to overcome their fears in order to serve and protect our nation. They did it for us. They weren't just courageous, they were heroic. You see, heroism isn't just big courage. Heroism is about belonging. This is the essential piece of heroism, belonging. And we do that by choosing connection, finding common ground. It creates trust, shared purpose, community. On 9/11 and the days that followed, we came together as a nation. It didn't matter what race or tax bracket or sexuality or political party you were, what mattered was that we were all Americans.

"When I raised my right hand and took my oath of service, I didn't swear to protect and defend only those that looked like me, acted like me, voted like me, lived like me." Penney says. "No, I and every other service member are bound by oath to protect and defend our nation and our Constitution. And that means everyone. Imagine a world where we all are brave, we all serve. We live in a world that needs more heroes. So don't wait for your moment. You must be ready. And the truth is, we can't wait. We need you now.

"So, let's roll."[19]

R. B. Stewart was first controller, and then vice president and treasurer of Purdue University. After World War II, he was the long-time chairman of the committee that oversaw the administration of benefits of the G.I. Bill. Image courtesy of Purdue University.

Purdue astronauts and Navy pilots Neil Armstrong (left) and Eugene Cernan (right) at the dedication of Purdue University's Neil Armstrong Hall. Image courtesy of Purdue University.

Future moon walker Neil Armstrong in Navy uniform. Image courtesy of NASA and Purdue University Libraries, Archives, and Special Collections.

Purdue's first astronaut, Virgil "Gus" Grissom, who graduated in 1950 after serving in the Army during World War II. He joined the Air Force after receiving his Purdue degree. Image courtesy of NASA.

Astronaut Roger Chaffee came to Purdue on a Navy scholarship. Image courtesy of NASA.

Purdue's national championship drill team meets with President John F. Kennedy in the White House Rose Garden in April 1961. Photograph by White House photographer Cecil Stoughton. John F. Kennedy Presidential Library and Museum, Boston.

In 1971, President Richard Nixon spoke at the retirement dinner in Indianapolis for Purdue University President Frederick L. Hovde. Before, during, and after World War II, Hovde worked in national defense technology research. Image courtesy of Purdue University.

Purdue graduate Sally Watlington became the first Navy woman in the nation to be named executive officer at a major university Navy ROTC program. The program was at Purdue. She is holding a photo of her friend and mentor Dorothy Stratton and the U.S. Coast Guard ship named for Stratton, in honor of her role as the founder of the Coast Guard Women's Reserve. Image courtesy of Purdue University.

Purdue alumna Rosemary Bryant Mariner was among the first six women to earn their Navy pilot wings. Image courtesy of Smithsonian Institution.

Purdue graduates Lucy Young (right) and Rosemary Bryant Mariner (left). In 1972, Young was among the first seventeen women in the nation to enroll in NROTC and became one of the first six women in the nation to fly a Navy jet. Photograph courtesy of Lucy Young.

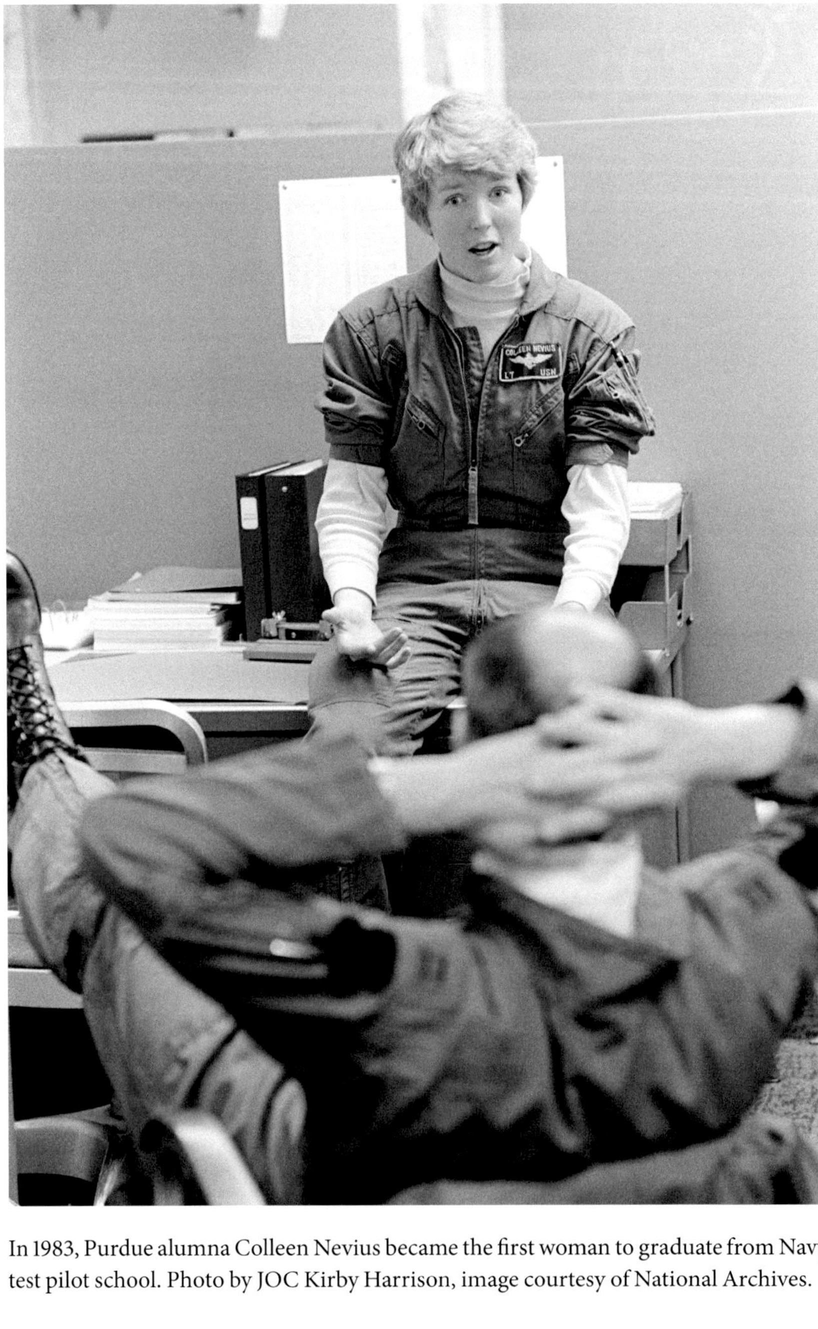

In 1983, Purdue alumna Colleen Nevius became the first woman to graduate from Navy test pilot school. Photo by JOC Kirby Harrison, image courtesy of National Archives.

In 1978, Purdue alumna Carol Pottenger was among the first women in the Navy assigned to sea duty. She retired from the Navy as a Vice Admiral. Image courtesy of the U.S. Navy.

Vivian Turnbull was among the first women to enroll in Purdue NROTC. She arrived at Purdue in 1973 on a Navy scholarship and graduated in December 1976. Turnbull spent much of her career in Naval intelligence. After retiring from the Navy, she became a senior executive in the Defense Intelligence Agency. Image courtesy of the U.S. Navy.

At one point in her career, Purdue graduate Erika Steuterman was the highest-ranking female officer in the U.S. Air Force. Her career started in 1972 in Purdue's Air Force ROTC. She retired as a Major General. Image courtesy of the U.S. Air Force.

On September 11, 2001, Purdue graduate and Air National Guard F-16 pilot Heather Penney flew a potential suicide mission to down a commercial airplane that had been hijacked by terrorists over Pennsylvania. Photo by Tim Engle. Image courtesy of Heather Penney.

16

NAVY ENLISTED SCIENTIFIC EDUCATION PROGRAM AND PURDUE

In essence, the Navy Enlisted Scientific Education Program is an investment program. The Navy, by putting the candidate through college, invests in his potential for service as a commissioned officer. . . . If you make it into the program, which as you'll see is no easy matter, you will receive an uninterrupted education.

U.S. NAVY BROCHURE, 1967

John McCain was a United States Senator from Arizona from 1987 until his death in 2018. He was the unsuccessful Republican Party nominee for President of the United States in 2008. Earlier in his life as a Navy pilot on a bombing mission over North Vietnam, he was shot down and captured by the North Vietnamese Army on October 26, 1967, and then beaten and tortured until his release on March 14, 1973.

Among the men he most admired in captivity was Captain Michael Christian, a fellow Navy pilot who was also shot down in 1967, captured, and imprisoned by the North Vietnamese. In 2001, when Christian, who graduated from Purdue in 1964 as part of the Navy Enlisted Scientific Education Program, was inducted into the University's ROTC Hall of Fame, McCain sent a letter.

"His patriotism and resilience helped us keep alive our hope and our pride in difficult circumstances. I think of Mike often," McCain wrote.[1]

Christian's story has never been forgotten, not at Purdue and not by the men who served with him. It was a vivid memory for Medal of Honor recipient Air Force Colonel (Ret.) Leo Thorness, who died in 2017.

"You've probably seen the bumper sticker somewhere along the road," Thorness said in a speech. "It depicts an American flag, accompanied by the words

'These colors don't run.' I'm always glad to see this, because it reminds me of an incident from my confinement in North Vietnam at the Hỏa Lò POW Camp, or the 'Hanoi Hilton,' as it became known."[2] Among the men he was imprisoned with were Christian and McCain.

In nominating Christian for the Purdue ROTC Hall of Fame, classmate and friend Clint D. Sadler, who retired as a Navy commander, remembered that it was three years before Christian's wife, Charlotte, received word that he was alive and had been captured.

"It was then [that] our thoughts shifted to how he was being treated," Sadler wrote in his nominating letter. "We all cared a great deal for Mike; but part of his charm, and perhaps at times his Achilles heel, was his stubborn hardheadedness. We all knew he would be an SOB if he was caged. Unfortunately, our worst fears were realized as Mike became one of the most severely beaten prisoners over the longest period of time in the history of the United States military."[3]

Christian's story has been told many times, by many people, in many ways. But it's always the same.

During their last years of confinement, the men were often allowed outside to bathe by drawing water with a bucket from a concrete tank. One day Christian found a handkerchief rag and he sneaked it into his cell. At night, when guards weren't watching, he cleaned the rag. He made red and blue colors from ground-up roof tiles and painted stripes on the rag. Using a bamboo needle and thread from his blanket he sewed on stars and created an American flag. He sewed the flag on the inside of his shirt and every day the prisoners of war would hang the shirt on a cell wall and recite the Pledge of Allegiance.

About once a week, the Vietnamese guards would strip the men, send them outside, and go through the prisoners' clothing. They found the shirt and the flag. That night they pulled him out of the cell. "We could hear the beginning of the torture before they even had him in the torture cell," Thorness said. "About daylight they pushed what was left of him back through the cell door. He was badly broken. Even his voice was gone."[4]

In the days that followed, Christian slowly recovered. And in time he found another piece of cloth. With his eyes still almost swollen shut from the beating he had received, he began to fashion it with red and blue paint and hand-sewn stars into another U.S. flag. And the beatings continued.

McCain said, "One of my fondest recollections is stirred every time I hear our Pledge of Allegiance. For it was with Mike, standing before a tiny flag he had covertly made for us to pledge our allegiance to our country from a distant prison cell, that our love for America's blessings was so vividly reaffirmed."[5]

Mike Christian was liberated from the prisoner-of-war camp on March 4, 1973. His second Silver Star Medal citation says: "For conspicuous gallantry and intrepidity while interned as a Prisoner of War in North Vietnam on 20 June 1969. His captors, completely ignoring international agreements, subjected him to extreme mental and physical cruelties in an attempt to obtain military information and false confessions for propaganda purposes. Through his resistance to those brutalities, he contributed significantly toward the eventual abandonment of harsh treatment by the North Vietnamese, which was attracting international attention. By his determination, courage, resourcefulness, and devotion to duty, he reflected great credit upon himself and upheld the highest traditions of the Naval Service and the United States Armed Forces."[6]

But what the men who served with him remember most are his American flags.

Tragically, after all he had been through, Christian died in a fire in Alabama on September 4, 1983. Funds were raised for a scholarship in his name to be awarded to Purdue Navy ROTC students.

NAVY ENLISTED SCIENTIFIC EDUCATION PROGRAM

Christian came to Purdue on a program titled the Navy Enlisted Scientific Education Program (NESEP). This national program, launched at Purdue, brought hundreds of men and women to the University for an undergraduate degree. A December 1967 Navy career publication, *All Hands*, noted that "In 1956 the Navy sent a group of fifty-four enlisted men to Lafayette, Indiana, to study electrical engineering at Purdue University. This was the birth of the Navy Enlisted Scientific Education Program, a two-pronged educational plan for studious, career-minded enlisted men and women."[7]

After the initial success at Purdue, the program was expanded to twenty-one other universities. At the height of the program, Purdue, with about 220 Navy Enlisted Scientific Education Program personnel on campus every year, was the most popular training site in the nation. Between the program's official beginning in 1958 and 2006, about nine hundred Navy men and women participated in the program at Purdue, most of them between 1958 and 1980.[8]

While the program was open to women, they ran into some obstacles. Edelene White, a NESEP Purdue graduate in 1974, was among the first women to attend the program at Purdue. She remembered that some University administrators tried to discourage her from attending. They failed. And when she graduated in chemistry and went on to Officer Candidate School, it was recommended she train with Navy nurses. She said "no" and trained with men.[9]

The NESEP students took part in campus activities. Jim Cech, who graduated in 1975, was part of the Student Council committee that brought the rock band Jefferson Airplane to campus. "I met them at the Purdue Airport and the first thing [singer] Grace Slick said was 'What are you doing in the middle of a cornfield?'"[10]

Purdue's Elmore Family School of Electrical and Computer Engineering lists the names of all the NESEP students on its website and states: "This page is dedicated to the men and women of the Navy Enlisted Scientific Education Program who were assigned as students to Purdue University beginning in 1958. The program selected sailors and marines serving in our fleet and assigned them to Purdue to obtain a four-year engineering degree. Most of these men and women studied electrical engineering, were commissioned as Naval officers, served their county, and following their service led U.S. industry to the forefront in the fields of electronics and computing."[11] In addition to these engineering alumni, some of the Navy personnel listed on the website graduated from the School of Science.

It was a strict, tough program. Only one in three who applied were accepted. In exchange for the Navy paying for their education, the enlisted personnel had to serve about nine months in the service for every six months they spent in college. The Navy paid their full salary while they studied. For many, the program changed their lives.

"In essence, the NESEP is an investment program," the Navy said. "The Navy, by putting the candidate through college invests in his potential for service as a commissioned officer. . . . If you make it into the program, which as you'll see is no easy matter, you will receive an uninterrupted education. The maximum is four years of college, including summer sessions. Staying in school once you're there is a full-time job. The Navy enforces its academic standards. Unacceptable conduct or evidence of 'just getting by' could mean disenrollment from NESEP and return to the fleet."[12]

MICHAEL MCCULLEY

The NESEP students at Purdue were outstanding. Among them was Michael McCulley, who became a NASA astronaut and the CEO of United Space Alliance. United Space Alliance (USA) was jointly owned by The Boeing Company and Lockheed Martin Corporation. It was created in 1996 and brought into one company more than thirty contracts to support the Space Shuttles. It was dissolved in 2019. The shuttle program had ended in 2011.[13]

McCulley's life got off to a hard start. Born in 1943, his father was killed by a drunk driver when he was nine years old. His mother took the family, including McCulley and his sister, from where they were living in San Diego, California to a small town in Tennessee where she had family. They struggled financially. McCulley finished high school in the spring of 1961.

"I did okay in high school," McCulley says. "I graduated on a Friday night and on Monday morning I was at Great Lakes Naval Station north of Chicago starting basic training."[14]

There was no money in the family to continue his education, so he decided to join the Navy to "see the world" as its recruitment advertising promised. But in addition to seeing the world, he wanted practical training that would lead to a career. His plan was to fulfill his minimum obligation to the Navy, leave, and take his training into the private sector. He became a missile electronics technician and was assigned to submarines.

"Then I started really liking the Navy and decided I was going go to stay in for awhile," he says. "And if I was going to stay in, I thought about being an officer."[15]

He was smart. He applied to the Naval Academy Prep School. The mission of the school is to prepare midshipmen for the Academy at Annapolis, Maryland. He worked hard and McCulley did well at the school and received a congressional appointment to the Academy.

But there was a problem. His mother had been supported by benefits she received to support her children. But those ended when McCulley and his sister turned eighteen years old. "I found out Mama was destitute," McCulley says. "I was sending her $200 a month from my Navy pay. And that was her total income."[16]

If he went to the Naval Academy, he would only be paid about $55 a month, and that was not enough to support his mother. He was forced to turn down his appointment to the Academy and prepared to be returned to the fleet for sea duty. But people in the Navy supported advancing his career.

"I had a strong recommendation and my record in submarines was really good, so instead of going back to sea, I was sent to San Diego for prep school for NESEP," he remembered.[17] As a student in NESEP, he would receive his full Navy pay and receive a full college tuition scholarship, which meant that he would be able to get an education and support his mother.

When the time came to select a school, he planned to go to Vanderbilt University. It was only a two-hour drive from where his mother lived. He would be able to take care of her while he attended classes. But the Navy officer he reported to had other ideas. The officer said, "You're going to Purdue." McCulley obeyed orders and said, "Yes sir."

In the fall of 1965, he found himself on a university campus he had never visited and knew nothing about. He had never even been in the state of Indiana before. But obeying orders was the best decision of his life.

"To tell you the truth I was scared for the first year and a half," McCulley says. "I came out of this little town in Tennessee and I had okay grades. But when I got up to Purdue I was overwhelmed. I had grown up in the Navy. I had no idea what a campus like Purdue was going to be like. I was running scared. I just studied all the time. My grade point was about a 3.8 [and I needed a 2.8 average GPA to continue in the program]. I finally realized I could do this and stopped worrying about graduating and started concentrating on learning."[18]

When a Purdue graduate student with a grant disappeared from campus, the Navy and Purdue granted McCulley a fifth year to complete that research. With that, he was able to receive a master's degree at the same time he received his bachelor's degree. Since the graduate degree was presented in the morning and the undergraduate degree in the afternoon, he might be the only Purdue alumnus to receive his master's before his bachelor's.

"Purdue sent me on my way to the rest of my life," McCulley says. "I had no idea until I got there and graduated how highly Purdue engineers were valued. If you had a degree from Purdue, you were ahead of everyone else. My time at Purdue was fun. It was absolutely some of the best times of my life."[19]

The Navy NESEP scholarship also changed his life.

McCulley became a jet pilot, taking off and landing on air crafter carriers. In 1984, his application to become an astronaut was accepted by NASA. In October 1989, he was the pilot aboard NASA Space Shuttle STS-34 which launched the Galileo spacecraft that explored Jupiter. He spent 119 hours and 41 minutes in space.

In 1990, he left NASA and the Navy and became launch director for Lockheed Martin at the Kennedy Space Center. From 2003 to 2007, he was CEO of United Space Alliance.

Years after his space flight, he was on a commercial air flight when the woman sitting next to him told him about her career and asked him what he did for a living. He had a *USA Today* newspaper on his lap, and the lead story was about Galileo discovering water on one of Jupiter's moons. He pointed to the article with pride.

"I did that," he said.[20]

HENRY DAVIS

Autaugaville is a town on Alabama State Route 14 about halfway between Selma and Montgomery, Alabama. When Henry (Hank) Davis was born there in 1938, about 450 people lived in the town, although Autauga County had a population of about 20,000. It was a tough place and a tough time for African Americans like Davis to live in and grow up.

"I promised myself I would never go back," Davis says. "It was very close to slavery at that time. I [lived] with my grandmother and we picked cotton and chopped cotton [removing weeds with a hoe]. The pay was $2 a day to chop and $2 for picking one hundred pounds of cotton which I never did in a day."[21]

"The schools were segregated," Davis notes, as was the rest of the town. "I had to walk past the white school to get to the black school that was a mile away. The white school had a gym. We didn't. We played basketball on dirt."[22]

From that start in life, with help from the U.S. Navy, the Navy Enlisted Scientific Education Program, and Purdue University, Davis earned a degree in electrical engineering, retired from the military with the rank of lieutenant commander, and went on to a successful management career in industry with Corning, Michelin, and NASA. He also established a lifelong friendship with fellow Purdue NESEP graduate Michael McCulley.

After graduating from high school in 1956, Davis received a one-year scholarship to Alabama A&M College, today known as Alabama A&M University. A historically black land-grant college, it was not yet accredited by the Southern Association of Colleges and Schools when Davis arrived.

At the end of the one-year scholarship, he decided he wasn't on the right track. A teacher asked him what he wanted to do with his life. He said he wanted to be a physician, but he didn't have any money for education. She told him to apply for a scholarship and go after his dreams.

He did, and in 1957 sent an application to Michigan State University. He was accepted, but since he did not receive a scholarship, he turned down the offer and went to live with his mother in Detroit. He had hoped to find a job there but relocated when he was unsuccessful. "My father lived in Cleveland," Davis says. "I went there and found a job working in a department store for $1 an hour. I did that for six months and got a job as an orderly at Cleveland City Hospital."[23]

He was in the field of medicine, but not in the way he had hoped. Living conditions for African Americans in Cleveland in the 1950s were better than in Alabama, but still not great. "They didn't have white and black water fountains," Davis says. "But where I lived was sort of a ghetto. The black people moving north from the south ended up in the ghetto."[24]

So, he made one of the best decisions of his life. On January 15, 1958, two months before Elvis Presley was sworn into the Army, Davis joined the Navy.

In 1948, President Harry S Truman had signed an executive order desegregating the U.S. military. Real equality would come slowly, but in 1958 Davis's boot camp was fully integrated. Throughout his Navy career, all the bases were fully integrated, but sometimes that ended when they left the base and went into town.

He qualified for jobs in electronics and was interested in aviation electronics, so he received training in that field. His basic training was in San Diego, California. He got further training at a base near Memphis, Tennessee, and was stationed at Norfolk, Virginia, where he was selected to actually fly on planes as an aviation electronics technician and radio operator.

In Norfolk, he was arrested for running a stop light. He was also charged with operating a car without a license, although he did have one. For traffic violations, a judge sentenced him to five days at a penal farm. He was worried about how that would impact his Navy career but was told "everyone understands what happened."[25]

His plan was to stay in the Navy for six years and then to attend college and medical school on the G.I. Bill benefits. Life changed his plans. He married in 1961, had a son, and decided to stay in the Navy and get further training.

A friend suggested he apply for NESEP. "They won't take guys like me," Davis said, but he applied anyway and was selected for the very competitive program.[26] He went to San Diego for a six-week program to improve his math skills and was admitted to Purdue, the University of New Mexico, and the University of Colorado. He picked Purdue because a man from the university came out and interviewed him in person. The others didn't.

In the fall of 1964, he arrived on campus at Purdue and enrolled in electrical engineering. He studied hard, struggled in calculus, and found a tutor who turned his grades around.

"Purdue was a good experience," Davis says. "I got a good education. That scholarship was a turning point for me."[27]

When McCulley arrived in 1965, they became quick friends and have remained close ever since.

In January 1969, Davis graduated from Purdue and was commissioned as a Navy officer. Although he was too old to go into pilot training, he flew in airplanes as a bombardier and navigator. He remained in the Navy until 1979, often being deployed on six- and seven-month cruises on aircraft carriers. But he had a wife and four children and decided he needed to spend more time with them.

"The Navy was good to me," Davis says. "I had a great time. I never thought a kid from Autaugaville would get to fly in a jet airplane. I was ready for my next promotion when I decided to retire."[28] He went to work for Corning as an engineer but was quickly moved into management. He left for one year to work at Michelin before returning to Corning.

In 1994, McCulley convinced him to talk to a person at NASA. He was subsequently hired to head the NASA Technology Transfer Program in Houston. The program works to take innovations from the space program and use them in other projects to benefit people and the nation.

Davis retired from NASA in 2002 and now lives south of Lexington, Kentucky.

One result of the NASA Technology Transfer Program was a collaboration between NASA, Dr. Michael DeBakey, and other physicians on a life-saving heart pump for people awaiting heart transplants.

At the end of his career, Davis finally got to work in the medical field.

17

ROTC AT PURDUE

ROTC helped teach me the importance of discipline in one's life. ROTC helped remind me to complete each assigned task to the best of my abilities. ROTC gave me leadership opportunities. ROTC helped show me the importance of teams and in delegating tasks to various team members in order to achieve superior results. ROTC surrounded me with instructors and midshipmen of high ethical and moral qualities—which kept me on the "straight and narrow."

JOSEPH ALFORD, PURDUE CLASS OF '66

In Air Assault training in the summer after her sophomore year at Purdue University, Army ROTC student Angela Lange got to rappel out of a helicopter hovering at seventy to ninety feet above the ground.

"Air Assault is a ten-day course and it's the ten hardest days in the Army," Lange says. "In the final phase we learned how to tie hip-rappel seats and how to rappel. And if you're lucky and the weather lines up, you get to rappel out of a helicopter. When you're up there it's kind of scary as the helicopter moves up and you're sitting on the edge, the door's wide open, you're looking down, you're like, 'Wow, this is pretty real.'

"And then you hook yourself up and you've just got to rely on your equipment, your skills, and the person below who's making sure you're good. And you don't really have much of an option. Once you're hanging out that door, you're going down one way or another. It's so exciting."[1]

Today's Purdue ROTC students have many occasions for excitement as they anticipate jumping out of helicopters, flying jet airplanes, and taking on leadership in infantry units or aboard ships at sea during military careers that offer amazing opportunities. And among those opportunities is serving their country.

Twenty-first-century Purdue ROTC is far removed from the experiences of the university's corps of cadets in 1876, camping out along the Wabash River and placing a dead rooster beneath their commander's pillow. ROTC today is physically tough and mentally challenging. It is a home away from home for students in college where they find an identity, make lifelong friends, and prepare for leadership in careers many have dreamed about for a lifetime.

About five hundred students on the West Lafayette campus enroll at Purdue Army, Navy, and Air Force ROTC each year. Students in the Navy program can also become Marine officers, and Air Force students can choose a Space Force career.

An ROTC program is also active on the Purdue University Fort Wayne (Ind.) campus. Purdue Fort Wayne Army ROTC is an extension campus that falls under the Ball State Army ROTC program in Muncie, Indiana. "While we have our own full-time staff and act, for the most part, independently, we conduct major events like dining out, staff ride, FTXs [Field Training Exercises], and extra club events with Ball State," says Mac Hathaway, Fort Wayne Army ROTC Recruiting Operations Officer.[2]

Purdue University Northwest Army ROTC, in Hammond and Westville, Indiana, is an extension of the University of Illinois Chicago ROTC program, according to Erik Namestnik, U.S. Army Captain and assistant professor of military science at the university.[3]

Indiana University, Purdue University Indianapolis [IUPUI] has been under reorganization and will open for the fall 2024 semester as separate campuses. "In the reorganization, Purdue will not offer ROTC in Indianapolis," says Prof. Mathias Sutton, head of the Division of Military Science and Technology (MST) in Purdue's Polytechnic Institute. "Rather, IU-Bloomington (Air Force) or IU-Indianapolis (Army) will provide ROTC commissioning for PU-Indianapolis ROTC students via what are called 'cross-town' agreements. PU-Indianapolis ROTC cadets will train in Indianapolis with students from other Indianapolis-based colleges/universities." This is similar to what had been happening at IUPUI.[4]

The ROTC programs at all the campuses provide important experiential and learning opportunities for the students.

"It is just so unique," says Angela Lange, who trained in Purdue West Lafayette Army ROTC. "The experiences you gain here, you can't really gain anywhere else. You learn so many things about peer-to-peer leadership, which I think is one of the hardest leaderships to do—where you're equals, but you're trying to get each other to do things. You learn time management, that's a huge thing. You really learn how to hone into that, be able to do your schoolwork and ROTC work and also have the social life that everyone wants in college."[5]

Academically, Purdue's ROTC programs are part of the university's Polytechnic Institute. But it hasn't always been that way.

In 2014, Purdue's Polytechnic Institute was called the College of Technology and its dean was Gary Bertoline. At that time, Purdue ROTC reported academically to the College of Liberal Arts and administratively to Student Services.

The then commanders at Purdue ROTC—Colonel Seth Bretscher, Air Force; Lieutenant Colonel Jerry Hubbard, Army; and Captain Troy Mong, Navy—met with Bertoline and asked to become part of his college.

"There was a huge disconnect because we reported to two different organizations," Bretscher says. "It just made sense to try to move underneath one entity. And it made perfect sense because the whole idea behind the College of Technology, and now the Polytechnic Institute, is it's really experiential learning. It's not theoretical the way engineering is. It's not designed the way engineering is. The Polytechnic Institute is really, really cool because they actually do nuts-and-bolts things. It's hands on. It's taking, not designing, but it's taking what already exists and how do you do this well, and then how do you manage and lead in those areas? And that's exactly what the ROTC programs do. It's not theoretical, it's experiential leadership training for college kids."[6]

The Polytechnic Institute enrolls the second largest number of ROTC students at Purdue, after Engineering. The military branches accept students from all colleges on campus. But by 2014 they had a stronger emphasis on STEM fields—science, technology, engineering, and math.

Bertoline agreed with the move and talked to leaders in Liberal Arts and Student Services who were okay with the change. The new Division of Military Science and Technology (MST) in what was later named the Polytechnic Institute was created in the summer of 2014 with Mathias Sutton as head. Sutton is also associate head of the School of Engineering Technology in the Polytechnic Institute. The MST Division is a liaison between the ROTC branch leaders and the greater university community.

Sutton is the perfect man for the job. He received his bachelor's degree from Purdue in 1983 and his master's degree in 1986. He did not enroll in ROTC. But after receiving degrees from Purdue, he went to Officer Training School and was commissioned an officer in the Air Force. He served eight years of active duty and another twenty-two years in the Air Force Reserve. He received his PhD from Purdue in 1998 and joined the faculty. As head of the MST Division, he also chairs the university's Military Programs Committee, which provides feedback and suggestions to the ROTC programs. Sutton says the committee also reviews the ROTC military faculty nominations from the respective services when vacancies occur.

Sutton enjoys his role and is a huge supporter of ROTC. "These programs are tremendous opportunities for students," he says. "Many cadets and midshipmen receive scholarships, which help offset tuition or room and board expenses. ROTC scholarships bring about $5 million to the university every year. The students come here as eighteen-year-olds and they learn a lot. They learn about leadership and time management. There's discipline in the military. On certain days of the week, they start exercising at 5:30 or 6 in the morning and they have to be there. And if you're going to be there at that time, you have to go to bed at night. And these are not things that all college kids do very well.

"There are people who came to this university who go on to have incredible careers. Many came here because of Purdue's ROTC programs," he says. "They liked Purdue, but they came because of ROTC. So, ROTC is good for the students and it's good for the university."[7]

Purdue grants the commanders of the ROTC programs adjunct faculty status with the titles of professor of aerospace science, professor of military science and leadership, and professor of naval science. Students wanting to be commissioned in the military have to take four years of ROTC. But students who want to try it out can enroll during their first two years and then leave. Also, any student at Purdue can enroll in an ROTC class for credit if they desire, Sutton says.

ARMY ROTC

In 2023, Lieutenant Colonel Kevin White was a professor of military science and led the Purdue AROTC. Army ROTC is the oldest branch on campus with direct links back to the original corps of cadets in 1876.

White graduated from Clemson University in 2003. He enrolled at Clemson from his home in Pennsylvania because of a two-year ROTC scholarship.

"It was going to cover the bills for me and so I said 'Sure I'll do that for two years,' and I wouldn't have to make a commitment to the Army," he says. "And then I got down there and really enjoyed it. I did well and thought I'd give it a try. I ended up getting a three-year scholarship."[8]

He flew Kiowa helicopters, which are used for observation, utility, and fire support. He served tours in Afghanistan, Kuwait, Iraq, and Syria.

He loves serving at Purdue and will probably retire from the position at the end of his career. He has ten to twelve instructors working with him, plus three or four support staff. While the total number of students in Army ROTC varies from year to year, normally from about 150 to 170, the goal is to commission twenty-three students each year. It usually exceeds the goal. The Purdue AROTC program is diverse and includes about thirty-five percent female students.

"We have anywhere from ten to fifteen national scholarship board winners," White says. "The students coming in here [have scored] 1220 or higher on the SATs, with 3.7 GPAs. They're involved in multiple sports. They're incredible."[9]

After their junior year, all the AROTC students in the country go to camp and are graded according to their abilities. They make a list of what they would like to do in the Army, and the better they are rated at camp, the greater chance they have of getting their top choices. Ninety-two percent of the Purdue students get one of their top five picks. Eighty-two percent get their first choice.

ANGELA LANGE, SOCIOLOGY, LAW AND SOCIETY, '23

Growing up in Naperville, Illinois, outside Chicago, Angela Lange knew nothing about ROTC until her junior year of high school when she began considering her college choices.

"Someone my sister had played softball with was at Purdue in the Army ROTC program," she says. "So, I reached out to her and talked about what it was all about, what you do, what you learn. It sounded very interesting. ROTC was kind of on my radar. I was already interested in Purdue at that point. So, that lined up nicely. And from that one conversation, ROTC seemed like something that would be a good opportunity for me, something I'd be interested in, and I went for it."[10]

She applied for a national four-year ROTC scholarship and didn't get it. But she received a three-year ROTC scholarship at Purdue.

Lange entered Purdue in the fall of 2019, had a wonderful semester, and slammed right into the COVID pandemic in March 2020. The students were sent home to continue the semester remotely. But they returned for in-person classes in the fall of 2020 when some other universities remained closed.

During the spring 2023 semester, she was a battalion commander with tremendous responsibilities working with the students and the Army officers. She loved rappelling from the helicopter in Air Assault training. Running a twelve-mile obstacle course wearing Army boots and carrying a thirty-five- to forty-five-pound rucksack was a bit harder. She had to finish the course in less than three hours—and she made it.

In the summer of 2023, after graduation and commissioning, she will report to Fort Benning, Georgia for Basic Officer Leader Course.

"At first, infantry was kind of high on my list," Lange says. "It's very, very physically demanding, taxing. I was confident I could do it, but I wasn't sure if that's what I truly wanted to do. Armor kind of goes hand in hand with infantry. You're doing a lot of the same things. You are in combat vehicles so you're not walking around everywhere. You're driving around, it's a little easier on the body, better for the long term. It seemed like something very different, unique. I gravitated right towards it."[11]

ROTC, she says, is about learning to work with people from many different backgrounds. "You learn how to work together as one cohesive team, being able to lead them through and come together at the end of the day to achieve one common goal that is way bigger than yourself," she says. "That's one of the coolest things is that we're all doing this for reasons bigger than ourselves, the whole program, the whole Army. It's everyone having different backgrounds but having one common goal for an end. It's pretty unique. It's great."[12]

CODY CRAWFORD, RUSSIAN LANGUAGE AND POLITICAL SCIENCE, '24

In 2023 Cody Crawford was a Purdue senior majoring in Russian language and political science. He was in Army ROTC.

His hopes and dreams to eventually work in military intelligence got a huge boost in the summer after his junior year when he spent eight weeks in Stuttgart, Germany. "They actually put in my top-secret clearance paperwork, which is pretty unusual for a cadet to get," Crawford says. "I got to go to Special Operations Command Europe and work with them. And I actually worked in the intelligence directorate."[13]

Crawford came to Purdue from Union City, Indiana, because it was close to home and it had a great program in Russian language. "And also, Purdue has one of the best Army ROTC programs in the country," he says. His family has a military history and he's always wanted to continue that heritage.

In his senior year, he served as battalion executive officer in a program that places much of the responsibilities on cadet leadership.

"ROTC teaches a lot of peer leadership and just kind of getting yourself out of that shell," Crawford says. "When I first came into the program, I was a pretty shy kid just coming out of high school. But stepping into my positions in ROTC has really helped me get out of that shell."[14]

Crawford says that at many ROTC programs around the country, the military officers in charge do a lot of the planning and work and the cadets are given less responsibility. "Here at Purdue, they give us responsibility," he says. "Here at Purdue, it's almost entirely cadet-led. Purdue does an outstanding job in preparing officers to go into their first duty station."[15]

Crawford is married. His wife is also a Purdue graduate who received an Army commission through ROTC. The Army Joint Married Couples program will work to get them stationed together. His wife, Anna, is a cyber officer.

He will start out in the Army in Stryker infantry. "I'll spend four years going through that," he says. "And once I am promoted to captain, I will go to something we call a captain's career course, which is just additional training you need to take command as a captain. But instead of going to the infantry side, I will transition to military intelligence."

Purdue Army ROTC has positioned him for success.

"I probably spend about forty-plus hours a week working on just battalion things," Crawford says. "It's more or less my full-time job. But I'm still a full-time Purdue student. I take eighteen credit hours and I have other commitments as well. I still have to work out, I still have extracurriculars and homework. With all of that, ROTC really forces you to learn how to do time management. I know that's a kind of big issue for a lot of college kids. And ROTC is a great way, especially here at Purdue, of teaching you how to really do that effectively."[16]

KAREN GIBSON, INDUSTRIAL ENGINEERING, DECEMBER '86

Karen Gibson arrived at Purdue from Bozeman, Montana in 1982 without a clear idea of what she wanted to do with her life.

She enjoyed science and math, so engineering seemed like a good major. At Purdue, she would have to pay out-of-state tuition, so when the Army offered her a four-year ROTC scholarship, she thought that was a smart choice. But she didn't know what she would do when she completed her degree and four-year military obligation after graduation.

Her path forward became crystal clear shortly after commissioning. When she retired from the military in 2020, she was one of only two female three-star generals in the Army, having served as Director of Intelligence for the United States Central Command and in other high positions. In 2021, she was selected to be Sergeant of Arms of the United States Senate, where she leads a force of nine hundred people as the chief law enforcement and protocol officer for the upper house of Congress.

If she didn't know where she was going when she enrolled at Purdue, she found a career that was perfect for her—thanks, in part, to Purdue ROTC and her engineering education.

Gibson was born in Lafayette, but her family moved to Bozeman when she was four years old. She was a third-generation Boilermaker, so despite the family's move west, she always believed she would one day study at Purdue.

"My Montana upbringing deeply influenced me and who I am," Gibson says. "But I knew I wanted to go to Purdue, and I wanted to be an engineer. Purdue was known for its Women in Engineering program. I loved math and science, and we had an excellent engineering school in Bozeman—Montana State University. But I was eager to get out of town and attend school somewhere else. When I was accepted to Purdue, my father, who was a Purdue engineer himself, said, 'Congratulations. How are you going to pay that out-of-state tuition?'"[17]

Easy. She was offered a four-year Army ROTC scholarship, which required four years of service in return for four years of tuition. But at eighteen years old, she had no intention of making the Army her career.

Her mother's father had been in Army ROTC at Purdue, as had her father, who served during the Vietnam War era, so the Army seemed a good choice. Army ROTC also offered greater flexibility regarding majors than the other services.

It took a while for the program to ignite a fire in her life, and nothing about it really sparked her interest until she attended Northern Warfare School at Fort Greely, Alaska the summer after her sophomore year.

"I absolutely loved it," Gibson says. "We learned technical mountaineering and conducted small boat operations on a river. We spent a week on a glacier with crampons and ice picks and all roped in together as we leaped across cracks in the ice. Also, although I didn't expect to, I really did enjoy summer camp. So, I think it was less the academic setting of ROTC in the classroom, at least initially, and more those real-world, real-life military experiences in the summer that I found to be challenging and exciting and had me looking forward to becoming a military officer."[18]

When she graduated and received her commission, she was sent back to Alaska for her first assignment.

"I'd been in Alaska for about four months when they sent me to the winter phase of Northern Warfare School, which was snowshoeing and skiing and building and sleeping in snow caves," Gibson says. "Our culminating event was a ten-kilometer biathlon competition, which we did with a twenty-five-pound ruck, our M-16s, helmets, full combat gear, and Army boots. These were actually big military-issue mountaineering boots and we used long, heavy, wooden skis with metal edges. What I didn't tell anyone was that growing up in Montana, I had skied competitively in high school."[19]

She was the only woman in the course and finished second in the race.

"That was when I learned that once you demonstrate exceptional competence, people will stop worrying about which bathroom you have to use," she says. "And I found that doing well at Northern Warfare School meant I became accepted in that organization. I stayed in Alaska in the 6th Infantry Division for five years and developed a reputation for competence. Now, until you develop a reputation across the entire Army, you may find that you have to prove yourself again in every assignment. But once I demonstrated competence, real leaders wanted me on their team. Good leaders just want the best. They don't care about race or ethnicity or gender, they just want the best performers. And I found that the more serious the mission, the more important that was. I learned that if I sought the most demanding assignments and performed the toughest jobs well, good leaders would want me on their team."[20]

It was in Alaska that she realized she wanted a career in the Army.

"In Alaska, I fell in love with being a soldier," Gibson says. "I loved the way it challenged me in every dimension, every facet of my being—mentally, physically, emotionally, intellectually, spiritually. And each time I accomplished something, they would give me a job that was a little bit harder. I thrived on that challenge. I also found that I really enjoy leading and building teams. It was deeply satisfying to work with other men and women who were similarly committed to a cause in defense of the nation. And that was very motivating for me, quite frankly."[21]

Alaska was not a luxury assignment. Her unit spent weeks in the field in temperatures fifty degrees below zero—real temperature, not windchill. They slept on the ground without even a stove for warmth, but she loved it.

She also fell in love with a fellow Army officer, Kim Chapman, an infantryman and a graduate of Penn State University. They married and had their first child in Alaska.

To stay together, she followed him to Hawaii for her next duty station. At first, she was not enthusiastic about her assignment to a strategic intelligence unit, housed in the mountains of Oahu, in a tunnel beneath a pineapple field. But as she began providing intelligence support to real-world missions, she also fell in love with being an intelligence officer.

"I was part of a team that was intercepting and exploiting communications signals in the Pacific," Gibson says. "Then China started lobbing missiles into the Taiwan Straits, and suddenly we're releasing products that have 'White House' on the distribution list. Now, it was several years before I found out that doesn't mean the president actually reads what you've written, but it was enough to inspire and motivate me as a young officer. I loved knowing that we were producing useful information that would be used by policymakers, national and military decision-makers, and I found that very exciting."[22]

During her Army career, she led the Intelligence Operations Center for ground forces in Korea. She led the Intelligence Operations Center at the four-star headquarters of General Joseph Dunford Jr. in Kabul, Afghanistan. Dunford was Commander, International Security Assistance Force and United States Forces-Afghanistan from February 2013 to August 2014. He later became Commandant of the Marine Corps and Chairman of the Joint Chiefs of Staff.

She deployed to East Africa as Director of Intelligence for a combined joint task force in the Horn of Africa and served as Director of Intelligence at the U.S. Central Command. "I was responsible for all intelligence support to military operations from Egypt to Pakistan, and Yemen to Kazakhstan. That includes Afghanistan, Iraq, Syria, Lebanon, the Persian Gulf—all the tough problems," she says. "That was a very thrilling job. But probably my best experience was being the Director of Intelligence for the multinational coalition to defeat ISIS in Iraq and Syria. That was the most meaningful assignment of my entire career."[23]

After retiring in 2020, she taught at Georgetown University and did some consulting. Appalled by the attack on the U.S. Capitol on January 6, 2021, she volunteered to join a team that was assessing security issues at the House of Representatives. Two weeks into that project, the Senate Majority Leader Chuck Schumer selected her to be Sergeant at Arms for the Senate. She is the forty-second person to hold the position since 1789 and the second woman. With a female deputy and female chief of staff, she leads the first all-female team to occupy the Senate's top three security posts.

She has responsibility for physical security, personal security, cybersecurity, and more, both in Washington, D.C., and in Senate offices across the country, continuing a career in public service that she's found deeply rewarding. Her excitement for her career is apparent in her enthusiasm and smile when she talks about it.

"When I graduated, I knew I would go into the Army for four years, and I thought I'd figure out what I would do with myself then," Gibson says. "I didn't think about the Army as a potential career path. But what I did in the Army is what I always imagined I would do with my life. I sought adventure. I wanted something exciting and challenging. I wanted to see the world. I wanted a meaningful career where I could make important contributions to my community, the nation, and society. It was often hard, but I relished that. I enjoyed the challenges that came with military service."

She has been inducted into both the National and Purdue ROTC Halls of Fame and has earned master's degrees from the National War College and from the National Intelligence University.

"I'm grateful for the education I received at Purdue," Gibson says. "And I am grateful for the foundations of leadership and discipline I received from ROTC. Purdue has such a great reputation, even internationally. When I served in Korea in particular and told my Korean counterparts I was a Purdue grad, their eyebrows went up and their eyes got big.

"I'm very proud of my association with Purdue."[24]

NAVY ROTC

Captain Christopher Nelson, commanding officer of the Purdue NROTC unit, knew he was destined for a military career as far back as middle school.

"I grew up in rural Oregon. It's kind of like Indiana. It was a pretty quiet, small town. I read a lot of books about military history. World War II history interested me. So, I think I kind of skewed that way early in middle school thinking the military was a good place for the way I was wired. And then when I went to high school, my parents moved to Virginia and that school had junior ROTC. I joined that as a sophomore. I did three years in that and really enjoyed it; I liked the good mentors. A few of my classmates—we all seemed very simpatico. We were very much on the same wavelength in terms of how we thought about things and the things that we cared about."[25]

He joined the Navy in his junior year of high school on a Delayed Entry Program after his senior year. But he applied for and received a three-year Navy scholarship and decided to go to the University of Colorado at Boulder instead. "[The Navy's] scholarships are very, very powerful in terms of what they offer," he says. "I was an out-of-state student at Boulder the whole time and the Navy didn't complain at all about my out-of-state college bill."[26]

As an undergraduate, Nelson majored in international relations, transferring from his initial major of engineering. But he later went back to Colorado to get an engineering degree. Nelson received his undergraduate degree in 1994 and was promptly commissioned in the Navy.

The Navy was the perfect fit for him. "I think it was the shipboard lifestyle that attracted me, the romantic side of going out to sea and sailing over the horizon," he says. "That very much interested me. And when I did my first cruise, I definitely enjoyed my time at sea quite a bit."[27]

Nelson served at sea in the U.S., Europe and the Middle East. In Bahrain, "he commanded all Riverine Forces permanently stationed in the 5th Fleet operating area—providing maritime security to military sealift and prepositioning ships assigned to Naval Forces Central Command," according to his official military biography. After his tour in Bahrain, Nelson served at NORAD, and the U.S. Northern Command as Chief of Current Operations, before arriving at Purdue in December 2021.[28]

In recent years, there have been about 100–120 midshipmen in Purdue NROTC at any given time, and about thirty percent of those students are female. The program was started on campus after the success of the Navy V-12 program at Purdue during World War II. (See chapter 9 for more information about this program.)

NROTC has a number of summer programs for the midshipmen.

"The Navy side is doing something every summer they're on scholarship," Nelson says. First they go to Great Lakes Naval Station, north of Chicago, for two weeks of indoctrination before they come to the college. The next summer they do a week on a ship, a week on a submarine, a week with the aviation community, and a week with the Marine Corps. And then the next summer is a fleet cruise. They go somewhere and do something operational, fly with jets, get in a helicopter squadron, or spend a couple weeks on a ship. And then the last one is their senior cruise—their first class crew where they're basically a junior officer in training."[29]

He enjoys watching the students "maturing in a place where there is discipline and some strict guidance and oversight," he says.

About seventy-five percent of the Navy students are on scholarship. Purdue NROTC commissions twenty to twenty-five students every year.

Nelson loves working at Purdue and says the campus and community are very supportive of the military.

"All my peers were a little jealous when I told them I was going to Purdue," he says. "They said, 'You're going to go live on campus?' I said, 'Yeah, I'm going to live on a university campus in a small town in Indiana and get paid very well to do it.' So, I can't complain. Can't complain at all."[30]

MYERS HOGAN, INDUSTRIAL ENGINEERING, DECEMBER '23

Twenty-two-year-old Myers Hogan has had one ambition his entire life. "Ever since I could walk, I've wanted to fly," he says.[31]

Navy ROTC at Purdue is giving him a chance to get his feet off the ground.

He came to Purdue from Biloxi, Mississippi and was attracted to the university because of its excellent school of industrial engineering and the reputation of its Navy ROTC program.

"I come from a pretty blue-collar town in the South," Hogan says. "Southerners, they really appreciate family, they appreciate hard work, tough people. And I think I was attracted to the Midwest for very similar reasons. Midwestern values and Southern values are a lot more similar than I think people realize. Also, I came to Purdue because Navy ROTC here is one of the finest units in the country. And the industrial engineering program here is also one of the finest in the country. So those three things kind of really added up in my mind and then made it one of the better choices for me."[32]

He's studying at Purdue on a Navy scholarship and describes NROTC as the biggest part of his campus experience.

"I have made some of the finest friends I could ever possibly ask for through this program," Hogan says. "But I think the key to this program is, you have to buy into it. Early mornings suck, right? You look at all your friends and they're all doing whatever, whenever they want to. They can stay up to all hours, they can be unproductive, they can really do whatever they want. But in ROTC, you have to be disciplined about your time. You have to be disciplined about the things you do. You have to take care of your body, you have to take care of your mind, and you have to want to succeed. I think for a human being to really look at his situation and be content, you have to totally buy into it. And that's what I did when I came here. I wanted to do as much as I could. I wanted to learn as much as I could and I wanted to put myself in a position where when I graduate I will get the most out of my educational experience."[33]

He graduated in December 2023 and is already a licensed private pilot.

"I don't know yet what I'm going to do next, but I do want to fly," Hogan says. "Obviously any job I get, I'm going to be happy with it. I want to be in the Navy, I want to lead sailors. I want to do cool stuff. I want to be in a position to make a big impact. I want to be the best officer I possibly can be. So, I'm not saying I'm not going to be happy with any job because I absolutely will be. But the dream is aviation."[34]

DOMINIC GIACOMIN, SUPPLY CHAIN MANAGEMENT, '23

Dominic Giacomin came to Purdue from Columbus, Ohio, in the late summer of 2019. At that time, he had really wanted to go to the U.S. Naval Academy in Annapolis, but that didn't work out.

His mother and brother had graduated from Purdue, so he decided it would be a good school for him and enrolled in Navy ROTC. His father had participated in Navy ROTC at the University of Notre Dame.

It finally worked out well for him. In the spring of his freshman year, he received a three-year Navy scholarship through Purdue. However, he had also reapplied to the Naval Academy and this time, he was accepted.

He chose to stay at Purdue.

"It was probably the hardest decision of my life, but one I'm very much glad I made because the leadership experience that I've gotten here I think is unmatched, even if I went to the Academy. I mean, I've been privileged to hold a lot of positions in our battalion, including now our battalion commander.

"I found that I really thrived at Purdue," he says. "I thought I was developing more, getting a balance of that college life and real world, being able to make decisions and having personal responsibility as a student. And also, I had that military training and the rigorous environment that our midshipmen undergo."

"Doing class projects, we feel that we often are required to take charge of group projects," Giacomin says. "We get taught how to do it. It's not something that comes naturally, which speaks along the lines of 'leaders aren't born; they're made [and] they're developed.' And without the unit here to help us develop that leadership, I would not have the people skills that I have today. I would not have the confidence that I do have in group settings to take charge, doing public speaking, and creating a vision to unite around and to act upon."[35]

Giacomin has had incredible experiences in the summer programs as well as campus ROTC.

"I think what I've gotten most out of it is leadership abilities and developing my leadership philosophy, and also understanding the value of people and how important it is to take charge, but also work well with one another and build a team mentality around what you're doing, whatever it may be."[36]

He's working now to reconnect alumni with the Purdue NROTC program.

"Doing that brings into perspective how much opportunity comes with commissioning from this unit and graduating from Purdue, because there is a wide range of really cool jobs that we've seen some of our alumni have," he says. "It really sets into perspective what someone in my class may go on to achieve in their lifetime and what interesting things are yet to come from the people here, because we're really just in our development stages. It's really an honor to be here at this unit. And especially coming from someone who chose this unit over the Naval Academy, I don't regret it."[37]

JOSEPH ALFORD, CHEMICAL ENGINEERING, '66

In 1961, Joseph Alford visited Purdue for a prospective students' day on campus.

"Purdue went all out to make me feel welcome, tailored my visit to my individual interests, and accommodated every request. The campus tour included an inside look at the engineering buildings and laboratories I was likely to have classes in. Student ambassadors showed me around, including dormitory and food service options and intramural recreational facilities, and provided great insight on what campus life was like. I was very impressed. Purdue seemed to be a good fit for me. It was good chemistry. I just felt like I belonged there," Alford says.[38]

More than sixty years later, the University is still a perfect fit for Dr. Alford, who launched his military service through Purdue Navy ROTC, and served in the Vietnam War, before beginning a career with Eli Lilly and Company. There, he became a leader in bioprocess automation, batch process control, computer system validation, online data analysis, alarm management, process analytical technologies, and applications of artificial intelligence—all of which involved use of computer systems.

Alford and his team's creative use of computer systems resulted in him receiving the company's top three corporate technology awards, which are for engineering excellence, product/process development, and information technology.

He has received national automation technology awards from both the American Institute of Chemical Engineers (AIChE) and the International Society of Automation (ISA) and is an elected Fellow of both organizations. He has received Purdue's Davidson School of Chemical Engineering Outstanding Chemical Engineer Award, the Purdue College of Engineering Distinguished Engineering Alumni Award, and the University of Cincinnati College of Engineering's Distinguished Alumnus Award. He has been inducted into the Process Automation Hall of Fame, and also the Purdue ROTC Hall of Fame.

Born in Boston, Alford grew up in Cincinnati. His father was the chief jet engine designer for General Electric. In high school, Alford might not have been able to accurately define what an engineer did, but everyone advising him said that if one was proficient and passionate about math and science which he was, then an engineering degree should be his next goal. Purdue seemed a perfect fit to mold his future. He took general freshman science and calculus courses, and then applied and was accepted into the chemical engineering major.

In 1961 when Alford arrived on campus, ROTC was mandatory for all freshman and sophomore male students. It involved extra work, but in hindsight he knows it was worth it.

"ROTC was a very positive factor in my development as a person and as a professional," Alford says. "For example, every Thursday afternoon on campus, the Navy ROTC battalion went out to the fields behind the co-rec building for two hours of drill and we had to be in spick-and-span shape. We had to be clean-shaven, have ironed our uniform, polished our belts and shoes, and be carrying a clean rifle. We were inspected, marched in most weather conditions, and said 'Yes, sir' a lot. It was good for me. It helped develop discipline and character, although it wasn't necessarily enjoyable at the time."[39]

At the end of his sophomore year, he decided to continue in NROTC for his junior and senior years, and to graduate with a commission as an officer.

"After two years at Purdue [in the early 1960s], I had a tough decision to make," he says. "I could drop NROTC and take my chances at being drafted into the Army after graduation, a perceived fifty-fifty proposition. Or, I could continue NROTC for two additional years, graduate with a commission in the Navy, and serve my country for two years of active duty plus six more in the reserve—mostly on my own terms. I chose the latter. I was very happy to commit to serving my country, but I wanted some control over what kind of service it would be."[40]

ROTC was an important influence on his life.

"ROTC provided some direction for the first part of my adult life, serving two full years of active duty in the Navy," Alford says. "ROTC helped remind me to complete each assigned task to the best of my abilities. ROTC gave me leadership opportunities. ROTC helped show me the importance of teams and in delegating tasks to various team members in order to achieve superior results. ROTC surrounded me with instructors and midshipmen of high ethical and moral qualities—which kept me on the 'straight and narrow.'"[41]

Alford met his future wife, Marti, at a Purdue dance in 1964. It was the first computer match dance ever held in the Midwest and it was covered by the Purdue Exponent, as well as by ABC and CBS regional television.

Alford explained details of the dance.

> Two Purdue electrical engineering professors were enlisted to write a computer program to run in Purdue's IBM System/360 mainframe computer to match up men and women students who signed up to attend the dance. The computer program accomplished this by considering attendees' answers to twenty multiple-choice questions that were answered when attendees registered for the event a few weeks before the dance with answers to the questions punched into IBM punch cards. The IBM punch cards were the way data and programs were often fed into a large computer back in the 1960s. An interesting aspect of the dance, given the theme of the dance, is that only as many men could be accepted to attend as the number of women who signed up. This was an issue as the ratio of men to women at Purdue at the time was about 6:1. So lots of hopeful men students could not be accommodated since not enough women signed up. I was one of the fortunate ones who signed up early. Still, the total number of student attendees was over 1,200. All the attendees were given numbers. Then, at the beginning of the evening's event, all the men were put in one large room and lined up, with the women in another room. An announcer read out the numbers of each matched couple, who then came out of their staging areas and met in front of the network cameras. Of course there were lots of mismatches—as how much can you really know about a person based on twenty questions? I ended up spending the entire evening and the rest of my life with my match, as we soon got lavaliered, then pinned, then the wait while I completed Naval active-duty service, then engagement, then marriage in 1968. We have been told (informally) that we were one of two couples, from more than six hundred who met that evening, who ended up getting married. We only met thanks to the dance. We probably would not have otherwise met, as I was a senior in chemical engineering at the time (there was only one female student in my class) and my future wife was a freshman with a food and

> nutrition-related major. It was ironic that a computer was involved in matching us up, as I then spent most of my professional career working with computers in automating manufacturing processes.[42]

As of 2023, they had been married fifty-five years, had three grown sons and several grandchildren.

He graduated in January 1966, using an extra semester of study because of the demands of the chemical engineering curriculum and four years of NROTC classes. After receiving his commission, he spent three months in Navy schools and then reported to the USS Coral Sea, CVA-43, an attack aircraft carrier with a home port in Alameda, California. The ship spent seven months of each year deployed in the Vietnam War, and five months back in Alameda getting ready for the next deployment.

Alford was initially assigned to the ship's weapons department. But he wanted to be in engineering and put in a request for a transfer, although he didn't think it would be approved.

The request went to the captain of the ship, who then talked to the chief engineer.

"The chief engineer said, 'I have twelve junior officers in my department. Their college degrees are mostly in history, philosophy, psychology, and the like. None of them have engineering degrees and most dislike being in the engineering department. It's hot and humid down there. If you have a junior officer with an engineering degree that actually wants to be in the engineering department, please give him to me.'"[43]

And so, the transfer was approved.

During his first deployment, he was the Assistant Boiler Division Officer—a good position for a Purdue Boilermaker. The department had 212 enlisted men who were responsible for operating and maintaining the ship's twelve boilers, which provided steam to the ship's engines, flight deck catapults, generators, and ship services needing hot water.

During his ship's second deployment, he was the Electrical Division Officer, overseeing 120 enlisted men responsible for operating the ship's electric generators and maintaining all the ship's thousands of electrical circuits. "For at least four hours per day, I stood watches in the ship's engineering 'main control' room—which was where all engineering operations were monitored and/or controlled, including, for example: boiler operation, main propulsion, electrical generation, freshwater generation, and communications throughout the engineering plant and to the ship's bridge," Alford says. "Initially I was an assistant watch officer, but soon learned the ship's engineering plant in detail, passed all required written and oral examinations, and was named as a watch officer, in charge of all engineering operations on the ship when on watch. I was told that I was the most junior officer in the history of the ship to have qualified as an Engineering Watch Officer."

Alford also had other collateral engineering duties, such as being in charge of one of the ship's stations when refueling at sea from an oiler supply ship. He was also in charge of a major section of the ship for damage control purposes during "General Quarters."

The ship normally cruised up and down the coast of South Vietnam, about fifty miles offshore, launching and recovering aircraft in direct support of ground troops. During his second deployment, the ship was ordered to North Vietnam, where pilots were assigned to destroy the supply bridges and routes in and around heavily defended Hanoi. Some of the ship's planes were shot down by surface-to-air missiles and anti-aircraft fire during these missions.

"One of the most impressive aspects of serving on the USS Coral Sea was to see and be part of a highly cooperative and complex organization of over three thousand sailors—all highly coordinated and working together in a 'can do' positive spirit to accomplish the ship's mission," he says.

At the end of two years of active duty, Alford continued his military obligation in the reserves. His contributions there included improving war gaming capability in both the Cincinnati and Indianapolis Naval Reserve Centers. He enjoyed reserve duty enough that he ultimately extended his total time in the Navy reserves to twelve years. He left as a lieutenant commander, serving at the time as the executive officer of the Indianapolis Naval Reserve Center.

Alford credits his Navy service for showing and teaching him the "practical side of engineering," which complemented the "theoretical side" he had acquired in getting his Purdue degree. In fact, it was experiencing the practical side of engineering that really ignited his passion for engineering and motivated him to seek additional engineering degrees. So, when he left active duty in 1968, he enrolled at the University of Cincinnati where he used G.I. Bill benefits to support his studies, earning first a master's degree and then a PhD in chemical engineering.

Alford then started a thirty-five-year career at Eli Lilly and Company, headquartered in Indianapolis, in 1972. His accomplishments and those of the teams he led or was a member of were many.

"Most of my career was spent in automating the company's bioprocesses that were used to make medicines," he says. "There was almost no automation of bioprocesses in the pharmaceutical industry when my career started. Today they are highly automated, making significant use of state-of-the-art technologies. I ended my Lilly career in 'corporate engineering' as an 'Engineering Advisor,' the top engineering title at the time."[44]

For one project, he led the team that automated the world's first manufacturing process in which microorganisms' DNA was modified in order to make a commercial product—in this case human insulin. This led to the eventual elimination of society's dependence on animal pancreas glands as a source of insulin for diabetics.

"We were widely recognized as an industry leader in implementing new technologies and advancing the state of the art in automating manufacturing bioprocesses," Alford says. "Some of the awards that I received were the result of pushing the frontiers of science forward regarding computer control of manufacturing bioprocesses, working with great people, and having solid support from management."[45] For example, his teams were using artificial intelligence in manufacturing applications in the 1990s, over twenty years before the technology gained wider notoriety and acceptance in industry.

In retirement, Alford has continued to give guest lectures at Purdue, participate in industry-academia consortiums, serve on the Selection Committee of the Purdue ROTC Hall of Fame, help in other ways with Purdue's Department of Chemical Engineering, serve on several technical journal advisory boards, author articles for several technical journals, serve on College of Engineering accreditation teams, and volunteer in his community. He has also been a long-time friend of Purdue's NROTC unit, including, for example, presenting the keynote address at their Spring 2002 banquet, sometimes known as their "Dining In, Mess Evening."

"I've always been fascinated with medicine," Alford says. "And the pharmaceutical industry allowed me to combine several of my passions—for example, to work in chemical engineering, including use of computers for process control, but in a way in which I was contributing to the field of medicine by manufacturing medicines for people. I loved combining those multiple interests and passions.[46]

"Those interests and passions have included a lifelong love and respect for the U.S. Navy and appreciation for Purdue's role in preparing me for Navy service."[47]

AIR FORCE ROTC

Purdue students interested in flight and military careers have a role model in Colonel Ken Callahan, commander of the university's Air Force ROTC unit and its professor of aerospace studies.

He is a command pilot with more than three thousand hours in the C-141, C-5, T-37 and MQ-1B aircraft. From 2009 to 2010, he commanded the 46th Expeditionary Reconnaissance Squadron at Joint Base Balad, Iraq, overseeing all Air Force remotely piloted launch, recovery, and base defense activities. He also served as the Director for Remotely Piloted Aircraft Capabilities, Headquarters Air Staff, the Pentagon, Washington D.C., where he advised the Deputy Chief of Staff for Intelligence, Surveillance and Reconnaissance on current and future remotely piloted aircraft capabilities and policies.

He received a PhD at Purdue while serving in the Air Force as part of the Purdue Military Research Institute. (See chapter 21 for more details on this organization.)

Callahan started his career at Southern Illinois University where he enrolled in ROTC. After his freshman year, he was accepted to the Air Force Academy where he graduated with distinction in 1992. He has a Doctor of Management degree and a PhD in history, specializing in American history and the history of technology.

"At Purdue I teach five sections of the senior-level course, which in the fall is national security strategy and global hotspots," Callahan says. "We look at what's going on around the world. And then in the spring, I teach leadership, how to counsel airmen or younger guardians that they may be leading in the future. And we go through the military code of justice counseling techniques, how to account for people from different backgrounds, diversity inclusion issues. And then the last month and a half is teaching them how to come on active duty, which is harder than it sounds, but how do you end process, how to get your ID card, what does your pay scale look like, what's your retirement plan? We actually go through all that."[48]

Typically, Purdue Air Force ROTC enrolls about two hundred cadets every year. Purdue AFROTC is among the largest programs in the nation.

The highest ranking for an Air Force ROTC unit is to be among the top ten percent of units nationally, and Purdue's unit consistently achieves that. The Air Force unit at Purdue commissions about forty students each year.

The United States Space Force ROTC was established in December 2019 as part of the Air Force. Purdue Air Force ROTC gives select students the opportunity to commission into the Space Force and pursue military careers in space operations, cyber warfare operations, intelligence, developmental engineering, and acquisitions management. The Purdue Space Force ROTC was among the first in the nation. In addition, Purdue has established a partnership with the U.S. Space Force to utilize university research, innovation, and talent development as a member of the Space Force's University Partnership Program. In 2023, Callahan says about thirty-seven Purdue Air Force ROTC cadets are interested in the Space Force program.

Air Force is the third oldest ROTC unit on the Purdue campus, established in 1949 after the Air Force was founded in 1947.

ADRIAN FLORES, AERONAUTICAL ENGINEERING, '23

Adrian Flores wants to fly. More than just flying, he wants to be a test pilot.

And that's why he came from Miami, Florida, to Purdue to study aeronautical engineering and to enroll in Air Force ROTC.

Before enrolling at Purdue, he was considering a community college in Florida, but he started looking at aeronautical engineering.

"There was just something that I really liked about Purdue," he says. "When I was in high school, I didn't really know anything about it. I was actually more into architecture at the time. But I was kind of losing interest in architecture. I did an internship, so I just applied to this school for aeronautical engineering and I got in."[49]

He applied to Purdue because he learned it was among the top aeronautical engineering programs in the nation, but he wasn't immediately accepted. He studied for a year at Purdue and was accepted into the major in his sophomore year.

"It was a last-minute decision; I chose to come to Purdue and join Air Force ROTC at the very last minute," Flores says. "And it was actually after I watched a rocket launch at Cape Canaveral, which is about four hours away from my house. I watched a Falcon Heavy launch from SpaceX and I did the whole museum tour in Cape Canaveral. It's a great museum. It inspired me to come and try this."[50]

In the spring of 2023, Flores was a senior. He graduated and was commissioned in December. The Air Force allows him extra time to finish his engineering degree.

At the time of this writing, Flores is waiting to hear if he will be accepted into flight training. He already has his private pilot license and forty hours of flight time.

He is the wing commander at Purdue Air Force ROTC.

"ROTC has definitely been a transformative experience for me," he says. "I came here not from a military background. My parents are lawyers. I didn't really know a lot about the military. My grandparents served in World War II, but they never talked about it with me. So, I didn't have any idea of what was going on here when I showed up. And it took me a semester to acclimate. I'm still acclimating, honestly. I'm still growing and learning. But what I've gotten out of this is character development, confidence, and leadership skills. The whole point of this is leadership."[51]

And a dream to be a test pilot.

NATHAN GANTI, MECHANICAL ENGINEERING, '24

Nathan Ganti is the student leader focused on developing Purdue cadets who want to go into the Space Force.

"I've been spearheading that program here this semester," Ganti said in February 2023, his junior year. "We're one of the leaders in developing officers for the Space Force right now."[52]

He grew up near Philadelphia and was attracted to Purdue by its reputation in his major (mechanical engineering), and ROTC. He came to Purdue on an ROTC scholarship and also received a scholarship from Purdue.

"I've always liked science and math and the Space Force is going to be a lot more of a technical and STEM-oriented branch of the military," Ganti says. "And then, beyond that, they're bringing a lot of newer ideas, modernizing the way that we structure things, like longer assignments. I thought it would be really cool to be on the cutting edge of what our military is doing, both on the technical side in space, in that kind of final frontier [and] also on the cutting edge of how we run our organizations and manage our teams. So, I wanted to be on the leading edge."[53]

He has clear short-term and long-term career ambitions.

"My hope is to join the Space Force as an operator, doing a couple things there, hopefully tasking satellites," he says. "I know there are lots of highly classified missions that those operators do, related to missile tracking and things like that. So, I was hoping to do that. Beyond that, Space Force is very technically oriented, so actually the majority of officers there have a master's degree of some sort. So, it is my ambition to eventually get a master's in mechanical engineering and/or get an MBA. I'm aiming to go for twenty years in the Space Force right now."[54]

The military was well aware of Purdue's history in space when it launched the Space Force on the campus.

"We got the jump early because of all the astronauts who have come through Purdue. We knew that we had a reputation here and being such a strongly technical school, we knew that we'd be one of those places that the Space Force would really like to get their hands into. So, we started stepping up our program here and it's definitely developed to be one of the biggest in the country."[55]

One of the biggest. And one of the best.

THERESA CARTER, INDUSTRIAL ENGINEERING, '85

At the end of four years in Purdue University AFROTC with a degree in industrial engineering, Theresa Carter listed her top career choices in the Air Force.

Her first choice was human factors engineering. She listed behavioral science second. She wasn't sure what to list third, so she talked to her noncommissioned officer-in-charge, a technical sergeant, and he told her to list civil engineering.

When the assignments arrived, she got civil engineering. Unhappy with the results, she went to her commandant of cadets, Major Bruce Johnston. She trusted him. He had been encouraging and helpful to her. He was a person who brought out the best in people. She told Johnston she was considering an education delay from the Air Force to study for a master's degree at Purdue and perhaps get a better assignment when she finished.

"No," Johnston said. "You need to do civil engineering. You can do well at it. There aren't many who can do good at it, but you're one of them. So, get out of my office. That's what you're going to do."[56]

When she retired from the Air Force thirty-one years later, she had been the first female civil engineer promoted to brigadier general and then to a two-star major general. And she had also been the first woman to serve as the Air Force Civil Engineer—the career field's highest-ranking officer responsible for "organizing, training, and equipping the 60,000-person civil engineering force and for planning, development, construction, maintenance, utilities and the environmental quality of Air Force bases worldwide valued at more than $251 billion," according to her military biography.[57]

As the Purdue AFROTC commandant of cadets, on July 17, 1985, Johnston pinned Carter's Second Lieutenant single gold bar on her uniform. On August 13, 2013, Carter asked him to also pin on her major general second star.

A military career that started with a four-year scholarship to Purdue ended at the top echelon of the Air Force, where from beginning to end, she wanted to be known as an officer who happened to be female. She served at bases throughout the nation, in Germany, and in the Middle East as part of Operation Desert Shield.

In 2011, she was named to the Purdue ROTC Hall of Fame.

Carter was raised in Albuquerque and had never been east of New Mexico before enrolling at Purdue in 1981. Her parents had offered to pay for in-state college tuition, but if she wanted to go out of state, she would need a scholarship. She wanted to go out of state.

Her brother had done AFROTC, and he encouraged her to do the same, saying that's where she would have the most opportunities. She competed for and won an AFROTC four-year scholarship. Her father had been injured while serving in the Navy during World War II and she also received a Disabled American Veterans Organization scholarship.

Carter came to Purdue University to study computer science. The department had been created in 1962 as the first degree-awarding program in the nation.

"I arrived at Purdue in August of 1981," Carter says. "I had no idea how bad the humidity was in the Midwest. It was summertime and I lived on the eighth floor of Earhart Hall with no air conditioning."[58]

West Lafayette was hot and humid in the summer and cold and damp in the winter, she said. But she persevered. Within half a semester she realized computer science wasn't for her, and she transferred to industrial engineering, where she had a particular interest in human factors engineering.

In her freshman year there were ten women in Purdue AFROTC. Two received commissions after their senior year. The remaining eight left the program during the first two years.

The cadets all had jobs to perform. In the first semester of her junior year, she had a staff position, and she requested it again for her second semester. Johnston called her into his office.

"What's this, I hear you want to do a staff job?" Johnston asked. Carter told him engineering was hard. She was trying to balance her time. "Okay, that's interesting," he said. "But you're going to be a flight commander."[59]

She didn't see herself in that leadership role. "I didn't have the image," she says. "I wasn't the prototypical cadet, a fighter-pilot-type-looking person. I didn't have a commanding voice like a drill sergeant. I said, 'Sir, I don't think I can do that.'"[60]

"It doesn't matter. That's what you're going to do," Johnston said. "You're going to figure it out."[61]

"I was scared to death half the time," Carter says. "Am I doing things correctly? Am I presenting the right example for the freshmen and sophomores? But he was right. That experience was good for me. Major Johnston was a fantastic mentor. He would never solve a problem for you. He would just ask you questions to help you solve it on your own, which I greatly appreciated."[62]

For the fall semester of her senior year, she was named cadet commander.

Carter was a distinguished AFROTC graduate in the spring of 1985. Her first assignment was Tinker Air Force Base in Oklahoma City. She had an opportunity to do a master's degree in industrial engineering at the University of Oklahoma and graduated in 1988. She also received a distinguished graduate Master of Science degree in resource strategy from the Industrial College of the Armed Forces in 2003.

In January 1989, she was at Shaw Air Force Base near Sumter, South Carolina. While there, she was deployed in support of Operation Desert Shield.

"For the Gulf War, we were deployed to an air base in the United Arab Emirates and they had some of their military working with us," Carter says. "At one point I was trying to contact our commander on a radio and I said, 'I'll come to where you are.' He said, 'No, I'll contact you when I'm ready.' It turned out he didn't want to have me in front of UAE enlisted members who were supporting us in setting up the tent city. Their view of women is a lot different than ours. I told him afterward, please let me make that call. I have to figure out how to handle situations like that, but don't make that decision for me."[63]

She also was based in Saudi Arabia, where if women left the base they had to wear the traditional clothing required of all women. "It was pretty constricting," she says. "But in the wake of the Khobar Towers bombing we pretty much didn't leave the base anyway."[64]

Her Air Force biography says that one-third of her career was spent in command positions of a civil engineering squadron, mission support groups, two air base wings, and a center.

She commanded Joint Base San Antonio (JBSA) and the 502nd Air Base Wing in Texas with responsibility to support more than 250,000 military personnel, military dependents, and retirees.

"In San Antonio, we had a rash of training instructors being charged with sexual harassment and assault, and I was the court martial authority, which is the individual responsible for evaluating whether to charge airmen with serious crimes," Carter says. "Those responsibilities coupled with serving as the JBSA commander made it a very stressful job."[65]

Her career culminated in leading a major Air Force reorganization, consolidating installation support work at ten intermediate commands. She created the Air Force Installation and Mission Support Center and served as its first commander from February 2014 to July 2016.

There were special pressures to being a high-ranking female officer. People would tell her they believed she would be the first female civil engineer promoted to brigadier general. That was an added weight on her shoulders, she says. She didn't want to let them down.

"People who are cheering for you don't know how much of a lightning strike it is to be promoted to general, because there are so many people who are qualified," she says.

Carter received the School of Industrial Engineering's Outstanding Industrial Engineering Award in 2010. She was named a Purdue Distinguished Engineering Alumna in 2013 and in 2020 was appointed to the Purdue Board of Trustees.

After retiring from the Air Force, she received a Doctorate in Business Administration from Drexel University and is continuing her research on leadership in complex "team of teams" settings. She is an independent consultant working with the Department of Defense and private corporations. In May 2023, the University of Oklahoma awarded her an Honorary Doctor of Humane Letters.

"The Air Force is an absolutely great career choice for women," Carter says. "What kept me engaged and excited was the people I worked with, the opportunity to lead people and feel like you're making a difference. The thing I miss the most in retirement is the people."[66]

PROFILE

LIEUTENANT GENERAL (RET.) CHRISTOPHER P. WEGGEMAN

CHRIS WEGGEMAN CAME TO PURDUE FROM CONNECTICUT IN 1983 WITH A PLAN TO BECOME a physician. He enrolled in biology in the College of Science. He knew nothing about ROTC, but he saw fellow students walking around campus in uniform. He discovered that the Armory was a "beehive" of activity. He was intrigued.

"I stopped in at the Armory and talked to Air Force Captain Chuck Weaver. I asked him about ROTC and what it would entail and could I join ROTC with the intent of being a doctor," Weggeman says. "I learned a doctor was called a flight surgeon in the Air Force and I learned about the path to serving as a physician in the United States Air Force."[1]

Thirty-eight short years later he retired from the Air Force, not as a flight surgeon, but as a three star general who flew F-16 airplanes before taking multiple commands that led him to become the Deputy Commander of Air Combat Command, headquartered at Joint Base Langley-Eustis in Virginia. The command operates more than 1,300 aircraft, 34 wings, and 19 bases, and has more than 70 operating locations worldwide with 98,000 active and civilian personnel. When mobilized, the Air National Guard and Air Force Reserve contribute more than 700 aircraft and 53,000 people to the Air Combat Command.

Weggeman's career journey started with Purdue ROTC.

"ROTC taught me confidence," Weggeman says. "It taught me self-control. It taught me the power of personal discipline. It taught me the power of fitness, of teamwork, and how to lead teams. It gave me a competitive spirit and tenacity, which is important. As someone who flew for twenty-five years in a fighter [jet], that's important if you want to survive and thrive in the fighter aviation community. Our professor of aerospace studies, Colonel Jerry Sherrill, a Vietnam-era fighter pilot and test pilot, also taught me the power of your team and people.

It's not just all about the mission, although the mission is very, very important. But without the power of the people, you're never going to get to the targets and bring everyone home safe. You're never going to get to the objectives you need. He wanted us to compete as individuals to the absolute maximum. But at the end he always said, 'Listen, when you go to war, you go to war as a team.'"[2]

Weggeman's older brother Peter graduated from Purdue with a degree in nuclear engineering. He had visited his brother on campus and liked the university. But when the time came to find a college for himself, he initially started looking at East Coast schools. However, his dad, who had four children, looked at tuition and thought Weggeman could get a better deal as a Boilermaker while also graduating from a prestigious university.

Weggeman began his studies in genetics but switched into physiology in his sophomore year. He also moved into ROTC in his sophomore year, intending to pursue a career in the Air Force.

What attracted him to the Air Force? "Beyond a calling to serve my country, I think it was the technology and the power of planes and imagery and aviation," he says. "It really wasn't a calling to aviation specifically initially." But aviation did eventually call him, and he answered.[3]

He loved his time as a student at Purdue.

"Purdue teaches you how to learn," he says. "I had a great memorization kind of brain, a visual learner, photographic memory. But that only gets you so far. I learned that Purdue was great at testing you for synthesis. Do you understand the concepts, and can you apply them in different contexts outside of what the textbook says? And when I figured that out, it really was a light bulb moment for me where I was like, 'Wow, okay.' I had a physiology teacher who taught us all the theories about respiratory systems, circulatory systems, and all that. And then the exam was one question: 'Design the perfect frog.' What a great question! If it could be the perfect frog, what would it look like and why?"[4]

Neil Armstrong, an earlier Purdue Navy pilot, had similar thoughts about a Purdue education when a professor assigned him to criticize Bernoulli's Law. "It was right then that I realized they weren't teaching us facts and information," Armstrong said. "They were teaching us how to think. And that turned out to be extremely important in many of the situations I encountered through my life."[5] It took him to the moon and back.

In Weggeman's senior year, he was the Air Force ROTC Cadet Wing Commander. During his sophomore year, he went through medical tests at Grissom Air Force Base. "I went through that whole thing, poked and prodded, blood test, eye test, ear test, all that stuff," he says. "And I was sitting in my gown, the backless gown on the crunchy paper on the table in the doctor's office. And the doctor came in really quick at the end and he just said, 'Yeah, cadet, everything looks good. You're Cat One-certified, best of luck.' And he puts my manila folder in another folder on the back of the door and he started to walk out. I said, 'Hey, sir. I have no idea what you just said. What does that mean?' He said, 'Oh, you're Cat One-qualified. You can fly if you want to.'" And that was when he learned he was going to be a pilot.[6]

He graduated from Euro-NATO Joint Jet (ENJJPT) pilot training at the top of his class and went on to training in the F-16. During a Zoom internet interview, a large photo of an F-16 in flight is right behind him, looking like it will roar right over his head.

In thirty-four years, he went from a second lieutenant to a three-star general. He earned two master's degrees in Military Arts and Sciences from the Army Command and General Staff College and the Air War College. He also graduated from and later served as an F-16 instructor pilot at the prestigious USAF Fighter Weapons School at Nellis AFB Nevada, known as "The Home of the Fighter Pilot." He also flew combat missions in Desert Storm.

Operation Desert Storm began January 17, 1991, after Iraqi forces invaded Kuwait and refused to withdraw. It opened with a bombing campaign against Iraq, and ended with the coalition, American-led liberation of Kuwait on February 28, 1991.

In Desert Storm, Weggeman's squadron commander was Mark Welsh, who later became Air Force Chief of Staff—a four-star general. Weggeman's last flight assignment was commanding the 52nd Fighter Wing at Spangdahlem Air Base, Germany, as a one-star brigadier general in July 2012.

"And then ironically, Mark Welsh was the Chief of Staff at that time," Weggeman says. "And he said, 'Hey, I need a leader, a combat-proven air domain leader that can operationalize cyberspace as a war fighting domain for the Air Force. I pick you.' And so, the last nine and a half years of my career as a general officer, I spent operationalizing cyberspace for the Air Force over a series of assignments culminating in [serving as] the Commander of Air Forces Cyber Command—the entire cyber enterprise for the Air Force. We built our thirty-nine Air Force Cyber Mission Force teams for the U.S. cyber command. In 2018, we brought cyberspace into Air Combat Command during my tenure, and my job was then to integrate cyber operations into the Command and lead the stand-up of DoD's first Information Warfare organization, [the] 16th Air Force."[7]

After retiring in September 2021, he went to work with Deloitte in their cyberspace and strategic risk offering portfolio. He is the executive advisor to the Department of the Air Force Account and lives outside of Nashville, Tennessee with his wife Ann (Clawson). They met at Purdue on the Armory drill floor in the summer of 1985. Their son Sam also went to Purdue.

As both an alumnus and a professional, Weggeman is getting more and more involved with Purdue. "I want to get more involved in the cybersecurity and other things that Purdue is doing so well, obviously the hypersonic stuff," he says. "I think that Purdue's brand is rising rapidly, which is impressive."[8]

SPECIAL FORCES AIR SUPPORT

Chris Weggeman has only told this story once before. It should be told again and again.

It was only expected to be a four and a half hour scouting mission, intercepting Iraqi armor and artillery prior to the Desert Storm ground invasion. But Chris Weggeman and his F-16 flight leader, then Lieutenant Colonel Andy 'Fish' Perona, found themselves on a mission providing close air support to a Special Forces unit on the ground inside Iraq. From take-off to landing, the total mission lasted more than nine hours. Weggeman and Perona spent more than ten hours strapped into the seats of their jets.

Helicopters from the 160th Special Operations Aviation Regiment (known as the "Night Stalkers"), flying at night only feet above the sand, had dropped an eight-man reconnaissance unit at a "hide-site" deep in Iraq, at what they thought would be a deserted agricultural area. It was not. It was being actively farmed, and Iraqi Army and military equipment were present.

Within a few hours, three children, a boy about five years old and two girls about seven years old, spotted the Special Operators while walking with a man believed to be their father. The children "walked right up to their hide-site, stood on their toes and looked right into their observation portal and saw the heavily armed warriors staring back at them," Weggeman says. With their weapons ready, the Special Operators asked their lead, Chief Warrant Officer Chad Ballwanz, what they should do. "We did not come here to shoot the children of our enemy," Ballwanz said. The children ran to tell the nearby man what they had seen and the four hurried off to tell Iraqi soldiers. The Special Operators knew they were going to face a fight for their lives against overwhelming odds. They were correct. They radioed for help as they watched about 150 Iraqi Republican Guard forces in armored personnel carriers advancing toward them.[9]

Weggeman and Perona were alerted to the problem by radio from their base (the Airborne Battlefield Command and Control Center—ABCCC). They were notified of the need for Emergency Close Air Support for Operational Detachment Alpha-525 when Perona checked in with ABCCC while they were enroute to their originally planned target area.

"We have an Army Special Forces unit pinned down requesting immediate close air support," was the message.

"Our adventure began," Weggeman says.

"I'll never forget the first time I heard his voice. 'We need immediate close air support on the approaching armored personnel carriers and two-ton vehicles.' There was a loud, urgent, and existential tone in his voice."[10]

The weather and flying conditions were very poor above 3,000 feet. The visibility was terrible, with blowing sand and smoke from the oil fires started by Iraq forces. "For us aviators, that's a 3,000-foot ceiling with three miles visibility," Weggeman says.[11]

Fortunately, Weggeman and Perona had already accomplished airborne refueling. Perona was carrying two 2,000 lb bombs, Weggeman had four cans of cluster bombs, and they both had 510 rounds of 20 mm high-explosive incendiary in their cannons.

Perona dropped a 2,000 lb bomb ahead of the lead vehicle.

"I saw the bomb release as he [Perona] pulled hard up and to the left," Weggeman says. "I followed the bomb to impact, and it went into the sand a few meters in front of the lead vehicle—poof, a puff of sand, but no explosion. Because of the low ceiling and tight pass, the bomb did not have sufficient time to arm. It needed 4.8 seconds time of fall and only had about 4 seconds."[12]

Since they were flying too low to use the big bombs, Weggeman dropped two cans of cluster bombs. With a flight ceiling of less than 3,000 feet, Weggeman had to adjust techniques to attack from the very low altitude. The two cans functioned perfectly, halting the Republican Guard advance.

During the next seven hours, F-16s took turns providing continuous close air support. "We dropped every bomb we had and shot every round of 20 mm ammunition on the advancing Iraqi enemy," Weggeman says. Blackhawk helicopters from the 160th Special Operations Aviation Regiment picked up the eight-man team and took them safely to advancing U.S. Army Forces, escorted by the F-16s. After the war, Special Forces Chief Ballwanz said, "Having F-16s for close air support is like your big brother—I mean, *really* big—showing up in a street fight."[13]

"Because of the bold and audacious power of American warriors, trained and ready to employ countless forms of state-of-the-art technology in combat, eight special forces went home to hug their loved ones—moms, dads, wives, sisters, and brothers," Weggeman says.[14]

In a talk to military personnel in February 2023, Weggeman noted that it takes more than technology to succeed. "The most critical element in cyberspace operations is NOT copper, or silicon, or lithium. It's *carbon*, it's you—the bold and audacious cyber warrior," he said. "And when you are properly trained and inspired, there is absolutely nothing you cannot accomplish.

"I know what some of the world's most advanced multidomain technologies can do. I know what coming home from combat feels like. And I know the most powerful weapon system on the planet . . . is you!

"Lead on!" he concluded.[15]

For their acts of heroism and extraordinary achievement that day, Weggeman and the other F-16 pilots were awarded the Distinguished Flying Cross with Valor Device.

18

SUPPORT FOR MILITARY SERVICE MEMBERS AND FAMILIES

In my experience working with campus partners, when I have a military-connected student having an issue, they've always been readily available to walk us through the process of how we can rectify a situation.

MORGAN TORRES, DIRECTOR,
DOROTHY STRATTON VETERAN AND MILITARY
SUCCESS CENTER, PURDUE UNIVERSITY

In 2015, during her junior year of high school, Morgan Torres signed up for the U.S. Army Reserves. She spent that summer in basic training learning how to become a soldier.

Upon graduating from high school, she applied to Purdue University, was accepted, and spent that summer in Army training. Prior to starting college, she reflected on being ill-prepared to navigate higher education coming straight from her service training during the summer.

When Torres received her cell phone back after completing her service training, she received a great deal of communication from the University and one text message from the Purdue Veterans Success Center. That one text made all the difference in getting her situated and supported when making her way to campus.

It took a lot of hours, but people at the Center understood her problems, got her registered, helped communicate and advocate her situation to the offices of Housing, Advising, and others, figured out her military education benefits to help pay her expenses, and straightened out many more issues in time for the start of classes.

By the fall of 2022 Purdue graduate Torres herself was director of the Center helping about 2,100 veteran students, as well as active military, their dependents and spouses on the West Lafayette campus and at Purdue's Polytechnic program in nine Indiana communities. In the fall of 2023, the Purdue Board of Trustees renamed the center the Dorothy Stratton Veteran and Military Success Center. Stratton was a Dean of Women at Purdue and founding director of the U.S. Coast Guard SPARS. (See chapter 9 for more information on Stratton.)

DOROTHY STRATTON VETERAN AND MILITARY SUCCESS CENTER

The Dorothy Stratton Veteran and Military Success Center serves as a wraparound suite of services available to military-connected students. As these students come to Purdue, the center connects them to peers on campus who are also military-connected and who serve as mentors for them. From there, the staff of Certifying Officials walk these students through their service-connected education benefits.

"These benefits can overlap and be incredibly complex," Torres says. "With the right team however, the student can truly explore all the financial assistance that is available to them. From there, the student can engage in the many social events, service events, and leadership opportunities provided by the Center."[1]

Some of those opportunities include celebrating the Month of the Military Child; attending Purdue's Tri-Service Veterans' Day Tailgate and Military Appreciation Football Game; taking part in the annual Veterans' Week celebration; and participating in end-of-year senior send-off events, graduation events, military-specific career fairs, and a variety of other career-focused workshops that benefit these students. Moreover, pending their usage of the G.I. Bill, the student may also qualify to work within the Center as a work-study student providing assistance to the office and their fellow colleagues.

Lastly, the Center acts as a true safe area of transition assistance when a student is leaving a structured military lifestyle and becoming someone who can truly flourish within civilian society. The center's Education to Occupation program affords students several opportunities to plan ahead for their post-education careers.

Events such as the Military-Specific Career Fair are held each semester and hosted by the Center. During this event, on-the-spot offers are given to students who are seriously interested in the opportunities employers present. There are several skill-sharpening workshops as well, such as a workshop on how to use LinkedIn, resume critique services, chances to have free professional headshots, and a walk-through at the Center for Career Opportunities Closet, where students can acquire professional business clothes and other mentorship opportunities.

The center also advocates on these students' behalf by providing Purdue staff with awareness training that highlights the areas of unique challenges that military-connected students may face. This "Green Zone Training Workshop" is held each semester and is always well attended—speaking to Purdue staff's openness and desire to learn more about their military-connected population.

Some active-duty service members come to Purdue through the Purdue Military Research Institute (PMRI) program to pursue a higher degree. (See chapter 21 for more information about PMRI.) Since these students are on active duty, they have a strict timeline for completion of their program. If they have difficulty enrolling in required classes, that could cause them to return to military service without the degree.

"There's a massive amount of pressure," Torres says. "What happens if they don't get into a class because they did not receive priority registration, for example."[2]

Unlike their classmates, military students can also be called into training during the fall or spring academic semesters. Their training may extend into the traditional Monday through Friday school schedule, creating scheduling conflicts for the soldier-student.

"They have to attend [training]," Torres says. "That obviously runs into their academic schedule with their classes. Fortunately, we have a military absence leave policy that helps with this. This policy was also written to help and support the additional training required of National Guardsmen and Reservists, commonly known as 'Annual Training.' This is a prolonged, likely fourteen-day-plus training that is scheduled throughout the year. It can become extremely problematic for the student when this mandatory training is scheduled at the same time as their final exams week or syllabus week. As a soldier-student, you might find yourself always putting out scheduling fires and making up exams and quizzes."[3]

In addition to practical concerns, such as establishing a permanent residence, military-connected students are also coping with profound lifestyle changes when they come to campus.

"I would say the number one issue that our service members, our military-connected students, face is a loss of camaraderie, a loss of identity," Torres says.

"If you can imagine, you go from active duty to a place like Purdue. You go from a situation where your day is set for you—what you wear and what you will eat, and when you will brush your teeth. This is a very structured lifestyle, and they go from this to a very free opportunity on campus. You get to pick your schedule, pick what you wear, pick where you eat, what you eat, and on and on. They understand structure and they value structure. They value showing up for each other, being accountable to each other, responsible for parts of each other's lives, which is very much the military essence. And they go to a place within society where there's just not that structure."[4]

SOME OF THE BEST STUDENTS COME FROM THE MILITARY

While there are unique background challenges for military-connected students transitioning into civilian society, individuals with a military background are extremely capable and incredible students.

"On average the graduation rate, the GPA rate, the overall grade reports are higher than that of a traditional eighteen-year-old student who is just out of high school," Torres says. "There's a degree of discipline. There's a respect for professors who are above you, someone you report to. I think having a military background, you immediately seek a chain of command and you immediately ask, 'If you're in charge of me, what are your expectations of me? I need to know the parameters.' And I see that so often with our students."[5]

Torres says faculty, staff, and students at Purdue are friendly toward the military-connected students and in her experience, always willing to learn more about their unique experiences.

"Everyone is very cordial and very understanding of the different challenges that can arise with this particular demographic of students," she says. "In my experience working with campus partners, when I have a military-connected student having an issue, they're always readily available to walk us through the process of how we can rectify a situation. That is absolutely my experience."[6]

As she talks, Torres exudes excitement for the Center and the work it's doing every day to help military-connected students navigate their transition to higher education. In many ways, this role has been a natural progression for her. As a Purdue student, Torres served as the first female president of Purdue's Student Veteran Organization. After graduation, she found herself serving as the assistant director of the Center. She stepped into the lead role in 2022, when founding director Jamie Richards, who had hired her, moved to a position in the College of Veterinary Medicine. Like Torres, who draws upon her own experiences in the military and as a Purdue student to lead the center, Jamie Richards' role in the creation of the Center came out of his own experience as a Purdue military-connected student.

THE START OF THE VETERANS SUCCESS CENTER

Richards started at Purdue as a full-time employee and student in 1999, graduating in 2005. He was also a Navy Reservist. At that time, military benefits were handled through the Office of the Registrar. In 2003, he was deployed in the Iraq War.

"At the time I was a full-time employee at Purdue, working third shift," Richards says. "And I was also a full-time student at spring midterms—in fact, I had already completed the midterm for three of the four classes. I received a phone call from the Reserve Center on a Thursday night and I was told, 'Report to the Reserve Center Tuesday—you're leaving.' They ended up moving the report date to the following Thursday in order to secure flights for us to get to our predeployment location in Mississippi. In a week, I had to figure out how to pause being an employee and a student.[7]

"I worked with my supervisor, and with the help of HR, we figured out what I needed to do as an employee," he says. "Then I went to the registrar's office and said, 'Here's my orders. I leave next week.' Amy Kingma was Purdue's School Certifying Official, and she said, 'I'll take care of everything.' I had no idea what the outcomes for the classes would be and honestly, my focus was on the fact that I was going to Iraq. I just was not aware of the policies or any rights or responsibilities around a mobilization. For every class in which I completed the midterm, I received a grade and partial credit, and it was considered completed for curriculum purposes. I ended up only having to take one course over, so it was not a lost semester."[8]

After graduating in 2005, Richards accepted a position as the assistant to the Chancellor at Ivy Tech Community College in Lafayette. In 2008 he was deployed again, and this time he went to Iraq, where he served as an individual augmentee in a Navy construction battalion from June 2008 to April 2009. When he returned, he was asked to become the certifying official at Ivy Tech, which would mean working with military students and veterans on benefits such as the G.I. Bill and tuition assistance. But he wanted to do much more.

"I learned to become the school certifying official and processed the G.I. Bill," Richards says. "But while there, I also believed that we needed to do more than just process benefits. We needed to have a space for student veterans to connect and there had to be programming to support them, to help them transition, to help with their career, all those things. So, we started what was a small Veterans Center at Ivy Tech on the Lafayette campus."[9]

At the same time, Purdue was moving to improve its support for military families, including active military, veterans, and family members. In 2011, Purdue Vice Provost for Undergraduate Academic Affairs Dale Whittaker asked J. Eric Dietz and David Hankins, retired Army and Air Force officers in the University's Homeland Security Institute, to lead the production of a white paper on how to make Purdue a more veteran-friendly university. At the time, veterans were receiving support through a program for nontraditional students. Assistance for military-connected people came from the Registrar's Office, the Dean of Students' Office, and the Provost's Office.

"We received a grant from the Purdue Military Family Research Institute to assist in growing support for Purdue student veterans," Hankins says. "The Veterans Success Center was one of the ideas we presented in the white paper that was requested by Dale Whittaker. I drafted the paper and shared it with Eric Dietz. Then we presented the paper to all of the Purdue stakeholders."[10]

The plan was to create at Purdue a model program, making it a best-in-class institution for assisting the military population. It included a Veterans Success Center that would bring all the services into one office.

"I thought it was a good idea," Whittaker says. "What I was focused on was getting graduation rates up and serving different groups of people according to their needs."[11]

"The reason we needed a Veterans Success Center was almost immediately apparent, due to the growing number of undergrad student veterans and because there was no single place where they could go and get assistance," Hankins says. "As we started, we got all of the stakeholders across Purdue together. That was a chore in itself, and we found out quickly that the left hand didn't always know what the right hand was doing. When we got approval to hire a Veteran Coordinator, several of us had Jamie Richards in mind because Purdue veterans worked closely with the Ivy Tech student vets where Jamie was employed. Jamie applied for the position and we lobbied for his hire, and in fact, he was then hired."[12] He was hired by Dan Carpenter, a retired military officer who became Purdue's Executive Director for Student Success Programs.

Bob Mindrum, then director of the Purdue Memorial Union, believed the Union was the perfect place for a Veterans Center. The Union had opened as a memorial to Purdue people who lost their lives in World War I. The Great Hall in the Union specifically honors all Purdue people who lost their lives in the nation's wars.

Creation of the center was approved by the University, and Richards received support for moving the people who took care of G.I. Bill certifications out of the Office of the Registrar and into the new Veterans Success Center. In addition to funding from the Office of the Provost, a $20,000 grant was received from Home Depot Foundation and Student Veterans of America to help fund the center's creation.

In late spring 2013, renovations began to outfit an office on the second floor of the Purdue Memorial Union. The space was dedicated on September 11, 2013 as the Veterans Success Center. The dedication ceremony was attended by local elected officials and campus dignitaries. A flag flown over a base in Afghanistan was donated by a deployed student and Richards, and Ryan Keen, then president of Purdue's Student Veterans Organization, built the handmade flag display case. The center's services have expanded to continue to support the growing military-connected population, but it is still housed in its original space in the Union.

Carpenter says Richards was the major force in accomplishing all this.

"I hired him and he reported to me," Carpenter says. "But it was Jamie's tenacity and drive that really got us from just picking a couple of people and giving them a space and really started making some things happen on behalf of student veterans. Jamie has a significant legacy in this.

"It's been a tremendously successful center because it's been for student veterans and really all military-connected students [including their families], because there's a lot of students who use benefits who aren't veterans," Carpenter says. "There are a lot of active-duty military who are studying here. There are reservists, and Guard soldiers and so forth, and the center certainly serves as the one-stop shop to process their benefits and do all of the business side of that. But it also is their place: their geographical place and their organizational place. And a lot of veterans will affiliate quickly with it because it's an immediate connection to their previous experience. So, in that way, it's been very successful at creating a place where lots of them have a connection."[13]

MORE HELP FOR MILITARY PEOPLE: THE PURDUE MILITARY FAMILY RESEARCH INSTITUTE

Every summer, a group of women student veterans and service members from around the United States arrive on Purdue's campus to take part in the Focus Forward Fellowship, a national mentoring program to help them enhance academic and career skills and build a community of support for success.

It's just one of many research and outreach projects that the Military Family Research Institute engages in to help the men and women of the armed services and their families. Founded in 1999, the institute conducts research and outreach for communities and professionals who serve military and veteran families. It is one of the longest-established military initiatives at Purdue and one of the top such institutes in the country.

It has five strategic goals: "Support the military communities that serve military and veteran families; strengthen the motivation and capacity of civilian communities to provide support; generate important new knowledge; influence policies, programs and practices that affect families; and create and sustain vibrant learning organizations."[14]

The founding codirector and now director of the Institute is Dr. Shelley MacDermid Wadsworth, a distinguished professor in Purdue's Department of Human Development and Family Science.

Military families perform an enormous service to the nation, and they face many challenges. "They work long hours," MacDermid Wadsworth says. "They don't have a lot of control over their schedules. They give up quite a few rights when they join the military. They relocate more than civilians do, and that means changing schools and doctors and finding new housing. It's logistically challenging and makes it difficult for military spouses to maintain employment and grow careers. And so, they tend to be significantly underemployed, and earn less than their civilian counterparts. At the same time, they tend to be very adaptable and resilient, which makes it possible to learn lessons from them that can benefit all families."[15]

ISSUES FACING MILITARY FAMILIES

There are many other issues facing military families.

"Women are a minority in the Department of Defense and the Department of Veterans Affairs, so it can be hard for them to get healthcare that is well suited to their unique needs," MacDermid Wadsworth says. "They face challenges because in many cases, the equipment or the tools that they need to do their jobs are not well designed for women. And that puts them at increased risk for injuries. Women in the military also are much more likely than men to experience sexual assault."[16]

At the same time, military people are selected for their ability to deal with the challenges they face. "It's important to point out that many people who would like to serve in the military are denied admission because they lack some of the characteristics that are needed, or they have things in their background that make them ineligible.[17]

"The military is selective and people are selected to be resilient, and then they're trained and supported in growing their resilience skills," she says. "In general, the storyline that comes through when you look at all of the data about military families is that there's a tremendous amount of resilience, but they also are families who experience challenges. Military members and their families experience frequent periods of family separation. They may be deployed to dangerous places, whether that's for natural disasters or peacekeeping or combat. They face a lot of transitions."[18]

Military families interact with a complicated array of systems, MacDermid Wadsworth says. These include the Department of Defense and the Department of Veterans Affairs, as well as education and healthcare systems for themselves and their families, and much more.

"We like to think about ways to try to make these systems work better around families," she says. "How do you get the Department of Defense and the higher education system to function well together? And how do we link community systems together so that they can coordinate their work better on behalf of military and veteran families?"[19]

MILITARY FAMILY RESEARCH INSTITUTE PRIORITIES

In its research, the institute pays a lot of attention to the lived experiences of families. The institute also focuses on families who might not normally get a lot of attention.

"We talk about families on the fringe," MacDermid Wadsworth says. "For example, families who are not the typical kind of military or veteran family. And we try to learn about their experiences. We're collecting data now for a large study of children who are adolescents today, but who early in their lives experienced a lengthy parental separation due to the wars.[20]

"I call these young people the OIF/OEF generation, for Operation Iraqi Freedom and Operation Enduring Freedom—the Iraq and Afghanistan wars," MacDermid Wadsworth says.

"We're doing check-in on what I call the OIF/OEF generation of kids to see how they're doing, to see if that early challenge provided them with extra resilience or if it disrupted their development in any way."[21]

In 2014, the Purdue Military Family Research Institute was invited by the Indiana National Guard to colead an effort called Joining Community Forces Indiana.

"With the Indiana State Department of Veterans Affairs, the Indiana National Guard, and us representing the land grant university, we work together to lead efforts to coordinate work in communities across the state that supports military and veteran families. We also pay attention to state policies or state programs that might need to be changed to do a better job of providing that support," MacDermid Wadsworth says.[22] Thus, this effort addresses the systems in cities and towns that affect military and veteran families.

The institute's largest program is Star Behavioral Health Providers. With a Department of Defense partner, it trains community-based behavioral health providers in communities across the country to be better prepared to serve military and veteran families. And they make it possible for military and veteran families to find those providers, thereby helping to strengthen systems for addressing mental health problems.

The program is receiving funding from the National Guard Bureau. It is operating in more than forty states and is on the way to becoming a national program offered by the National Guard.

"It's always very important for communities to support the military members and their families who live there," MacDermid Wadsworth says. "Every city, town, and rural area in the country has military-connected people in it, whether it's parents of service members, or service members themselves, veterans, or other relatives. And military service is always placing demands on families. So, they always have needs. And veterans, of course, have needs that are evolving as they get older. We have more than two million veterans now of the OIF/OEF conflicts, a substantial percentage of whom have service-connected injuries or disabilities that may affect them for the rest of their lives. So, they always have needs. And it's very helpful when community organizations can be mindful about what might be unique or special about military connected people because there might be resources that they can offer or suggest to those families that might be helpful to them. There might be special attention that they need because of their experiences. A community organization is going to be better able to serve those people and to establish a connection with them if they have a little bit of understanding and knowledge about that population."[23]

The institute's Reaching Rural Veterans program works to strengthen resources and services for at-risk military and veteran families who live in rural areas. "Like other MFRI initiatives, this effort tries to help existing systems work more effectively to serve military and veteran families," MacDermid Wadsworth says. "In partnership with Cooperative Extension, Reaching Rural Veterans brings together food pantries, faith communities, and community organizations to engage with at-risk veterans and their families. The program has been implemented in four midwestern states and has demonstrated that it can successfully engage with large numbers of veterans and increase their connections to programs and services they need.[24]

"Many people are surprised to find a Military Family Research Institute at Purdue," MacDermid Wadsworth says. "I'm very glad that it's here, not just personally, but professionally. I think it's very important that we're here. First of all, our Purdue department, Human Development and Family Science, has a strong interest in studying families in context and understanding the challenges that they face. And this is one of the biggest challenges. So, it's important that we pay attention to it. Any organization that is trying to do a good job for the military needs to pay attention to military families because service members cannot do their jobs without significant support from family members. And I think Purdue would be doing the military a disservice, honestly, if they weren't paying attention to that."[25]

REACHING OUT TO FARMER VETERANS WITH DISABILITIES

In 1978, Bill Field, a new member of the Purdue Agricultural and Biological Engineering Department faculty, began working with a farmer who had experienced a spinal cord injury as the result of a motor vehicle crash. With technical assistance from the Braun Corporation of Winamac, Indiana, a salvaged school bus wheelchair lift was mounted on the side of a large four-wheel drive John Deere tractor that enabled the farmer to transfer from his wheelchair to the operator's seat of the tractor. With a few modifications to the tractor foot controls, the farmer was able to continue, largely independently, working his fields. An article about the tractor modifications was published in the *Indiana Prairie Farmer* magazine and a short video clip of the farmer successfully accessing and operating the tractor was shown during halftime of the televised Peach Bowl football game in which Purdue competed that year. This media attention began a flood of tens of thousands of inquiries from all over the U.S., Canada, and numerous other countries seeking solutions for accommodating farmers with disabilities in agriculture-related occupations.

Initially named the Breaking New Ground Resource Center after a farmer suggested the name, the Purdue program has been a leader in breaking down barriers for farmers, ranchers, agricultural workers, and their families to achieve greater independence in their chosen career path, despite physical limitations. Working through the Cooperative Extension Service located at all land grant institutions, resources began to reach persons not only disabled by physical conditions, but by their rural, often isolated locations.

Since the very beginning, veterans with disabilities have been an important part of the clientele that this program serves. This included veterans from World War II, the Korean and Vietnam conflicts, and more recently the War on Terror. One World War II veteran received technical assistance on managing his New York blueberry farm by using an all-terrain utility vehicle and mechanized mulch applicator. A Vietnam veteran from North Carolina who lost both legs and an arm due to a land mine was able to modify a large John Deere tractor to allow him to custom-bale 10,000–15,000 large round hay bales annually for his neighboring farmers.

In 1990, with support from then Senators Tom Harkin (Iowa) and Patrick Leahy (Vermont), along with then U.S. Representatives Jamie Whitten (Mississippi), and John Myers (Indiana), and many others, a provision was added to the 1990 Farm Bill authorizing the U.S. Department of Agriculture to establish what became known as the AgrAbility Program. Funding was initially provided to establish eight state and regional projects and the National AgrAbility Project at Purdue. The program has grown to projects in twenty-one states with collaborators that have included Easter Seals, Goodwill International, Arthritis Foundation, and the Farmer Veteran Coalition.

With support from the CHS Foundation, a large agricultural cooperation, a full-time Veteran Outreach Coordinator was hired to facilitate and expand outreach to veterans with disabilities returning to civilian life, to help them transition back more readily into agricultural careers. Colonel Cindy Chastain (Ret.) filled this role from 2014 to 2021 and was replaced after her "second" retirement by Colonel Joseph Ricker (Ret.) in 2021. Both colonel-coordinators have continued to farm, with Colonel Ricker being recognized as one of Indiana's outstanding farmers in 2023, at the Indiana State Fair.

Specific outreach activities provided as AgrAbility services have included:

- On-farm technical assistance by rehabilitation specialists
- Assistance for new and beginning farmers
- Access to over 150 webinars on a wide array of agricultural-related topics
- Support group events such as farm tours and carry-in meals
- Mental health first aid training
- National and regional workshops in more than thirty states
- Documentation of approximately 2000 adaptive aids with application to agricultural worksites
- Paid career exploration opportunities through a USDA grant to veterans in agriculture

To date, thousands of veterans have participated in these activities with incredibly positive results. One veteran testified before a Congressional hearing that "if it weren't for the AgrAbility connections, I wouldn't be here today."

AgrAbility Projects work closely with the Farmer Veteran Coalition to reach out to as many veterans as possible, offering both technical and financial assistance. They also promote programs such as "Homegrown by Heroes," which encourages consumption of food produced by veterans.

As of 2023, approximately twenty percent of AgrAbility clientele are veterans with disabilities resulting from military service, workplace injuries, and diseases such as arthritis. This has led to an increase in the number of educational events that specifically target veterans such as mental health first aid for veterans, beekeeping for vets (the "Heroes to Hives" program), and ongoing support group initiatives.

Efforts by the AgrAbility Team have led to recognition from the U.S. Departments of Agriculture, Labor, and Education; the President's Committee on Employment of the Handicapped; the National Black Farmers Association; the National Safety Council; and the American Society of Agricultural and Biological Engineering.

19

PURDUE GLOBAL, PURDUE UNIVERSITY ONLINE, AND THE MILITARY

This world class education through Purdue Global is something that really should make us proud. We should go into the world knowing that we truly can make things better, and we can make our workplaces better as a result of the grit, determination, and persistence that we all share as Boilermakers.

KELVIN GUMBS, PURDUE GLOBAL, '21

As a chief warrant officer, Kelvin Gumbs had a very successful career in the United States Navy. He enlisted after graduating high school in Stillwater, Oklahoma. His twenty-two years of service took him around the world, including multiple aircraft carrier deployments in support of operations Iraqi Freedom, Enduring Freedom, and Inherent Resolve. He was deployed on the U.S.S. Abraham Lincoln twice and the U.S.S. Nimitz, both nuclear-powered aircraft carriers. During his career, he held responsibilities that included leading and managing hundreds of people and supporting various support functions.

But he believed there was something missing in his life: a college degree.

In 2018, while stationed at the Naval Air Station Lemoore, in California, Gumbs did something about that. He enrolled in Purdue Global and in 2020 received an associate degree in small group management. It went so well that in 2021 he earned a bachelor's degree in professional studies.

In October 2022, he was invited to speak at a Purdue Global commencement held on the West Lafayette campus in the Edward C. Elliott Hall of Music. There he observed a tradition at Purdue Global commencements: graduates with military connections were asked to stand. A huge number of black-robed students stood to thunderous applause.

In his commencement talk, Gumbs talked about the balancing act of adult education, especially for people in the military.

"When you are dealing with the things that adult learners, especially military adult learners, deal with—your military duties, your families, your civic and community service duties—when you put all those things together, it's really, really hard to be an adult learner as a military service member.[1]

"We're Boilermakers," he told them. "This world-class education through Purdue Global is something that really should make us proud. We should go into the world knowing that we truly can make things better, and we can make our workplaces better as a result of the grit, determination, and persistence that we all share as Boilermakers."[2]

He credits that commencement speech and his visit to campus as the catalyst for affording him the opportunity to interview for a new role at Purdue for Life Foundation. On January 1, 2023, he retired from the U.S. Navy and began work as an executive director of military educational partnerships in the Office of Industry Partnership, generating opportunities where Purdue can extend its reach of service to the military-affiliated community.

Purdue Global, as well as a separate program, Purdue University Online, have both been a huge benefit to U.S. military personnel serving around the world.

NEARLY ONE-THIRD OF PURDUE GLOBAL STUDENTS HAVE A MILITARY CONNECTION

Purdue Global, an online degree course that is part of the Purdue University system, launched in 2018. Six years later, it had about 36,000 students. Of that number, about 10,000 were affiliated with the military, either as active-duty service members, veterans, or military family members who are also entitled to special benefits in the Purdue Global program. About sixty percent of the military-connected people taking classes at Purdue Global are active-duty military. Twenty-five percent are veterans, and fifteen percent are military family members.

Purdue University Global, formerly Kaplan University, was purchased by the Purdue system from Graham Holdings Company in 2018 for $1 and a thirty-year service agreement for back-office support. The online school has 350 faculty, along with 1,550 adjunct instructors, and focuses on career-oriented fields for students that lead to certificates, associate's, bachelor's, master's, and doctoral degrees.

Dr. Frank Dooley has been the chancellor of Purdue Global since May 2020. His voice is filled with excitement for the program that advances Purdue's 1862 land-grant mission to take education out to the people.

"We're growing," Dooley says. "We want to see more students walking across the stage with a degree at commencements. Student success is a very high priority for us."[3]

That emphasis on student success is creating all kinds of opportunities for people in the military to earn degrees from wherever they are stationed. Purdue Global operates on four quarters rather than two semesters a year to increase starting-point opportunities for students. Classes are held all year-round, including during summers.

Military-connected students' successes are particularly recognized at the conclusion of their time as students. In addition to asking military-connected people to stand at Purdue Global commencements held around the nation, military personnel have their rank and branch posted on video screens as they walk across the stage. Beginning in October 2022 and continuing at every commencement moving forward, Purdue Global has partnered with the Purdue for Life Foundation to host a military appreciation banquet the evening before graduation. Created in March 2020, the Foundation deepens the Purdue alumni family's ties to the University, drives and coordinates all alumni-related activities, and works to garner support for the University.

MILITARY BENEFITS THROUGH PURDUE GLOBAL

Military people have many benefits available to them through the G.I. Bill, and other programs such as tuition assistance to help pay the costs. Purdue Global also offers special benefits to military-connected students. For example, credit toward degrees may be granted for military training that has been assessed for its educational content.

"Let's say you're in the Army at Fort Bliss in Texas and you are going to be a military police officer," Dooley says. "When you go into the Army, you get training in that. What our criminal justice faculty did is they looked at the training you received in the Army and then they looked at the curriculum and they said, 'Oh, well that's a concept we teach in Criminal Justice 102. And that's a concept in 104.' At the end of the day, they're able to give the students about one year's worth of college credit for the Army training they received."[4]

Military personnel are able to earn degrees faster based on training they have already received.

"The Army has levels of specialization and with each one of them, to get a promotion from a specialist one to specialist two, you have to show mastery of concepts," Dooley says. "And that's what we've tied our learning to. We're trying to make the training they're getting in the Army, which is really robust, the equivalent of transfer credit. In some cases, our faculty is going to say to the Army, 'What you're doing here is important, but that's not worth a credit. But if you could add this, we could do a credit.' And in some cases, the Army has relooked at their training as well."[5]

Alex Giberson, an Air Force veteran, is vice president of Student Success and Military Affairs. He works for Kaplan and helps Purdue Global Students.

"I think of us as a managed service provider," he says. "We provide all of the backend support. We do the admissions, we do the financial aid, we help the students through all of their registrations, enrollment and then sustained processes. But we do that in support of Purdue University Global."[6]

THE MILITARY SUPPORT CENTER

Purdue Global has a program called the Military Student Support Center that helps military-connected students navigate their enrollment and educational experience.

"We consider active duty to include reservists, National Guard and those on active duty," Giberson says. "So basically, if you put on the uniform, you are entitled to our best—be it discounts, be it support, everything.

"We have steep discounts," he says. "There are two types of funding that are going to be involved with these groups. The active duty is going to be using primarily tuition assistance. That is a specific amount of money that each service branch sets up that their servicemen and women can utilize towards their education each year. Most of them will use that first. The veterans will traditionally gravitate to VA funding and there are multiple types of VA funding where we are set up to assist them through everything. But most importantly, we have teams. We have a team of eighty folks that is dedicated to serving military service members, veterans, their spouses, and dependents. That's all they work with, are those folks. So, they're very well trained in all things military. Most of them were veterans themselves or spouses."[7]

Jeff Smith, a graduate of the United States Military Academy, is the director of military student success.

"There's a great level of pride, personal pride that we're helping folks that are helping us," he says. "I have eight teams that report to me. We've broken it down so that we can better serve our students and so that we have it at school level. They develop expertise around programs. For example, we have the Business team, so those folks only work with military students that want to go into the School of Business, or we have Health Science. There's quite a bit of support.

"If you express interest and you come to me and I was a student success manager, you're going to be with me from that first conversation until you graduate. And we're going to do everything in between. We have support functions that have elevated expertise. So, for example, when you really get down into the nitty-gritty, if you're using Title IV funding through the Department of Education to supplement either your tuition assistance or G.I. benefits, then we're available as a resource. We have student success centers. We work closely or in concert with the deans and their people to make sure we're providing the correct, best information and getting students set up for success."[8]

If an active-duty military person gets deployed immediately, they have policies for a leave of absence.

"This is the right thing to do," Giberson says. "That's it. It's the right thing to do. Take care of the people who take care of us. People don't understand the sacrifice, the real sacrifice, not just by the service member, but by the spouses as well. Believe me, they're out there serving as much as their spouses are, men and women. It is very difficult to go through a deployment and have your spouse all of a sudden pick up and manage and do all the things. Think about any age group within that. You've got soccer moms that now have to juggle all of the appointments for the family, pick up the groceries, pay the medical bills, get everything done. So, your help goes on and on with them every step of the way."[9]

There are also benefits to nonmilitary students.

"We recognize corporate training programs as well," Dooley says. "So, we will sit down with a company, and tell them 'Show us the training and development work that you've done in your firm.' And the other thing, let's say we have a whole bunch of students studying cybersecurity. There are all kinds of courses you can sign up for. We administer tests. If you score high enough on that test, we'll say, 'You know what? You don't need to take Cyber 101. You're at a 201 level. So, let's jump you into 201."

Eighty-five percent of the students in Purdue Global are older than twenty-four. On the West Lafayette campus, about ninety-seven percent are younger than twenty-four. The younger students in Purdue Global are largely in the military.

"Purdue has this deep, deep history with the military," Dooley says. "When I was in the Provost's Office, the Veterans Success Center reported up to me. I know the Military Family Research Institute. I know the Purdue Military Research Institute [PMRI]. I've worked with the ROTC commanders for a long time. So, it really didn't surprise me to see this strong military connection with Purdue Global. But I think when you put it all in a room together and you see the energy of all these programs playing off of one another it's inspiring. This does matter. We're doing what we should be doing."[10]

"This was part of the original land-grant mission—military tactics," he says. "And I think now that we're this twenty-first century land-grant, that the fundamentals haven't changed. And I think maybe that's what kind of defines Purdue in many respects. You find something strong and basic, and you keep after it. You keep after it, you keep after it. That's really what we're doing. But with Purdue Global, we're able to do it at such a great scale."[11]

As the executive director of educational partnerships, Kelvin Gumbs says he is working with programs throughout the Purdue system as well as Purdue Global.

"My focus is online education, be it Purdue Global, Purdue University Online, Purdue Polytechnic," he says. "And then I'm also exploring some other ideas to support folks like the team over at Purdue Military Research Institute [PMRI, chapter 21] or even the [Dorothy Stratton Veteran and Military] Success Center. But I work across the system to represent our online offerings and it's been really exciting. There's no shortage of opportunity for Purdue in the online space.

"I think the sky is the limit for Purdue Global," he says. "Purdue Global has the ability to serve the military community at a huge scale [without] sacrificing the academic rigor that is Purdue. I'm finding in this job that every time I get to engage with someone from the Department of Defense and we talk about Purdue's ability to provide online offerings to the tune of more than two hundred offerings, it's very surprising to them. And it opens their eyes to the fact that wow, a world-class Purdue system is really within their fingertips. It's really exciting to be able to communicate the strength of Purdue. I think the sky's the limit."[12]

PURDUE UNIVERSITY ONLINE

Purdue University Online is a program completely separate from Purdue Global. Purdue Global is the Purdue system's online university, primarily serving working adults with life experience and often some college credits but no degree. It has its own faculty.

However, Purdue University also offers a number of the same graduate degrees and certificates that are available on campus in a fully online format, including a Professional Doctorate in Technology degree. These programs—Purdue University Online—serve students who want to learn directly from Purdue's faculty without having to come to campus.

In 2022, Purdue University Online was ranked as the eighth best program for veterans by College Consensus. More than twelve percent of all fully online students who accepted their offer of enrollment in 2022 were either active-duty military or veterans.[13]

More than one thousand military-connected people were taking classes through Purdue University Online during the 2022–23 academic year. Overall, in the fall of 2022, there were a total of 4,056 students in fully online programs and an additional 248 who were in hybrid programs.[14]

In the fall of 2023, a Purdue University Online Learning 2.0 Military Advisory Board was created with a goal of doubling the number of military-affiliated learners in both the Purdue Global and Purdue University Online programs by 2026.[15]

Purdue University Online is part of the University's distant-learning programming that reaches back more than one hundred years and is part of its land-grant mission to bring education to people. "Purdue University Online serves as a professional support organization to deliver programs that are owned by the colleges," says Christopher Martin, Executive Director, Operations and Student Experience for Purdue University Online. "We are focused on the graduate level. Our programs are graduate-level or noncredit programs, so we serve a different audience than Purdue Global."[16]

Purdue University Online does not offer undergraduate degrees, but it does offer undergraduate courses for residential students. Many of the courses offered on Purdue University Online originated with the university's colleges and schools.

"But, we also through a central Purdue University online perspective, scan the broader market to understand what businesses are looking for or what Purdue alumni are looking for, what is needed in the market," Martin says. "And we may take ideas to a college and see where we can find what does the market need and how does that align with content that we have or programs that we're offering."[17]

ETHAN MICHAEL SNEIDER

In the summer of 2021, Air Force Captain Ethan Michael Sneider received a Doctor of Technology degree from the Purdue Polytechnic Institute. He saw and toured the West Lafayette campus for the first time in his life in March 2023.

Purdue University Online has changed his life, he says.

Sneider grew up in Concord, Massachusetts, outside of Boston. He had dreamed about being in the military ever since he was a boy and received a G.I. Joe toy. But far more important, he wanted to be like his dad, Richard, and earn a doctorate at Purdue.

He accomplished both. Sneider was serving in the Air Force, based in Hawaii, in the fall of 2019, when he enrolled in Purdue University Online and began to study remotely for his doctorate. It would not have been possible without Purdue University Online.

"What's great about Purdue is that I was looking for something that was one hundred percent online and was asynchronous," Sneider says. "When we were looking at universities, I knew what I wanted. First, I wanted to be online and second, it had to be a tier-one school. And my dad actually got his PhD in industrial engineering and computer science from Purdue in 1980. That was everything I was looking for. I wanted to continue in his footsteps and get a doctorate from Purdue as well."[18]

In 2014, Sneider had earned a bachelor's degree in business administration from the University of Massachusetts Amherst. His plan was to enter the military, but he knew he would have a better opportunity being placed in work he wanted to do if he received a master's degree first. So, he went to Haifa University in Israel and earned a master's degree in national security in 2016. He was subsequently admitted to Officer Training School with the Air Force and graduated in the fall of 2017.

"The Air Force seemed like it was the best fit because it was more technology focused," Sneider says. "I felt like it would align with where I'd like to take my career, whether it's inside or outside the military. And the Air Force allowed me to have some ability to select what type of career field I would enter."[19]

The Air Force was a perfect fit. And so was Purdue University Online.

"I was able to communicate with all my professors about my situation," he says. "I was in Hawaii at the time and so I would have my full duty day. And then after the duty day and on the weekends, that's when I would do all of my coursework. The time difference didn't impact my ability to complete my work. And I ended up defending my dissertation while in Qatar. I had a lot of support, which was great."[20] G.I. Bill benefits paid about half the cost of his degree program.

A trip to campus in March 2023 was especially fun for Sneider, now officially a Purdue alumnus. He had an opportunity to meet faculty in person, as well as to see the World's Biggest Drum.

Sneider says that his degree has already paid dividends with career opportunities. "Personally, I feel like the degree has given me credibility in my career field in Air Force cyberspace operations."[21] Recently, he was selected to spend six-and-a-half months in the Air Force MIT Artificial Intelligence Accelerator.

"My Purdue degree has allowed me to get some of these opportunities where I can contribute," he says. "I am extremely thankful for this opportunity that the degree has given me. The support from the university has been invaluable. It's been a great part of my career to have studied at Purdue."[22]

20

GRADUATE DEGREES FOR U.S. COAST GUARD AND ROYAL AUSTRALIAN AIR FORCE MEMBERS

I am writing to formally thank you for the sustained contribution in post-graduate training you have made over the past twenty-five years to the Royal Australian Air Force.

2010 LETTER TO PURDUE PROFESSOR ALTEN F. "SKIP" GRANDT JR. FROM D. E. TINDAL, AIR COMMODORE, DIRECTORATE GENERAL TECHNICAL AIRWORTHINESS–AUSTRALIAN DEFENCE FORCE

It was the most frightening time of his life.

In August 2017, Coast Guard Lieutenant Commander J. R. Carrillo rallied the crew of his MH-65D Dolphin helicopter.

They were stranded in a corrugated World War II hangar south of Houston, near the coast, and the entire area was being battered by Hurricane Harvey, a Category 4 hurricane that would kill more than one hundred people and do $125 million worth of damage.

"This is what we get paid to do," Carrillo told his crew. "All of us are going to fly this aircraft together. This is what we're going to tell our grandkids about."[1]

They were the only helicopter crew in the area, and people were calling for help. So, at 4:00 a.m., flying by instruments because he was unable to see, Carrillo got his helicopter in the air and went to save lives.

A news story reported that Carrillo and his crew "performed Urban Search and Rescue, a dangerous mission area that's almost impossible to practice. Dodging light poles on interstates, weaving between buildings and performing hoists from altitudes as high as 150 feet to avoid power lines coursing through flooded neighborhoods, Carrillo led his crew into neighborhoods to identify and rescue the most critical victims. When the aircraft was full, Carrillo would return to Ellington Field in Houston to drop off survivors, refuel and launch again."[2]

For his bravery and his skill and "extraordinary heroism," Carrillo was awarded the Distinguished Flying Cross for the rescue of seven people. It was a medal that had been awarded to Purdue astronauts such as Guy Gardner, Eugene Cernan, and Gus Grissom.

Before receiving the honor, Carrillo had to inform Dr. Tyler Tallman, a Purdue assistant professor in Aeronautical and Astronautical Engineering, that he would be missing his class for the event. At the time, Carrillo was at Purdue studying for a master's degree in structures and materials engineering.

He was excused from class that day.

Carrillo is one of a large group of Coast Guard officers over the years who came to Purdue to study for an advanced degree. Dr. Alten F. "Skip" Grandt Jr., distinguished professor emeritus and head of the School of Aeronautics and Astronautics from 1985 to 1992, said the Coast Guard program with Purdue engineering had started before he arrived on campus in 1979.

"The U.S. Coast Guard began a regular schedule of assigning active-duty officers to Purdue Aeronautical and Astronautical Engineering [AAE] for graduate study," Grandt says. "All were experienced Coast Guard pilots with the mission of earning an MS degree from AAE. Most pursued the nonthesis option and performed some sort of independent study on an advanced topic, while at least two did complete a formal research thesis. One of those, Norman V. Scurria Jr., retired with the rank of Admiral."[3]

By the time he retired in 2016, Grandt had been the graduate advisor for many of the fifty Coast Guard students.

In addition to U.S. military students, Purdue Aeronautics and Astronautics have provided graduate education for military personnel from Israel, South Korea, the Republic of China (Taiwan), and the Royal Australian Air Force.

ROYAL AUSTRALIAN AIR FORCE

The largest group of international military graduate students has come from Australia. This program has changed the lives of the officers who studied at Purdue, and it has benefited both the Royal Australian Air Force (RAAF) and the West Lafayette university.

"It's just one of those things," says Adrian Morrison, the first RAAF officer to earn a master's degree at Purdue. "I look back at my career and just know how lucky I am in terms of what's popped up. Because there could have very easily been someone else who was chosen and I would've ended up with a very different path through my own career."[4]

The program was started by Grandt in 1984. Grandt had met RAAF Wing Commander Rod Locket at a short course he taught at Georgetown University, in Washington, D.C. Locket was based then at the Australian Embassy in Washington.

For many years the RAAF had sent military engineers to the Cranfield Institute of Technology in England. They studied aircraft design, received a master's degree, and returned to their home country. The program worked well. But there was a need for the RAAF to have a better understanding of technology, especially associated with fatigue and fracture mechanics in modern aircraft.

Grandt has technical interests in the general area of damage-tolerant structural analysis. He received his bachelor's and master's degrees and PhD from the University of Illinois. After his studies at Illinois, he took a position with the United States Air Force, working in the Materials Laboratory at Wright-Patterson Air Force Base. While there he picked up an interest in aeronautics, and the fatigue and fracture of aircraft structures.

In March 1984, RAAF Air Commodore and Director General of Engineering E. J. Whitehead wrote to Grandt introducing Morrison and asking that he be enrolled at Purdue for a master's degree specializing in aircraft fatigue and technology. At the time Grandt was chairman of the graduate student selection board for the School of Aeronautics and Astronautics.

Whitehead wrote:

> The requirement within the RAAF for officers with a detailed knowledge of structural fatigue is increasing. Our F-111 fleet already has a problem fatigue area which requires periodic inspections to ensure structural integrity. As you may be aware, Australia will shortly begin to bring F/A-18 aircraft into service and the RAAF is determined to be prepared for any possible fatigue problems which may arise with these aircraft.
>
> Current postgraduate courses undertaken by RAAF aeronautical engineers provide excellent all-around coverage of basic aircraft design. The degree of coverage is, of course, given at the expense of depth in many areas; one of the areas receiving [in our view] inadequate coverage for our future needs is that of fatigue technology. . . .

> The Purdue Graduate School has been chosen by RAAF after our Washington-based staff carried out an exhaustive evaluation of all the graduate programmes in fatigue technology offered in the U.S. I am sure you are aware of the work done by Wing Commander Rod Locket in this evaluation. RAAF specialist engineering staff are impressed by the level of technology covered in the Purdue course and look forward to a continuing association with Purdue in the future."[5]

The plan was for Morrison to finish his degree in eighteen months and then undergo one year of training with the U.S. Air Force at Warner Robins Air Logistics Center Fatigue Laboratory, in Georgia.

"This was a neat part of the program," Grandt says. "They came here and got the theoretical work and then went to Warner Robins applying it."[6]

The program has continued well into the twenty-first century, although the Warner Robins portion was discontinued. Thirty RAAF officers had graduated by 2023. Grandt supervised fifteen of the Australian officers before his 2016 retirement. When Grandt retired, oversight of the program went to Purdue professor Michael Sangid, Reilly Professor of Aeronautics and Astronautics.

"All these guys are wonderfully qualified," Grandt says. I was graduate chairman at the time we started, but that had nothing to do with it. They wanted to study fatigue with me. It was one at a time. So, it was not an official program. It's never been an official program. But it's unofficial and it's lasted."[7]

In July 2010, Grandt received a letter of appreciation from D. E. Tindal, air commodore with the Directorate General Technical Airworthiness—Australian Defence Force:

> I am writing to formally thank you for the sustained contribution in postgraduate training you have made over the past twenty-five years to the Royal Australian Air Force and in particular to the Directorate General Technical Airworthiness [DGTA].
>
> The strong relationship the RAAF has developed with Purdue University has been possible through your hard work and dedication to world-class education and research in fatigue and fracture. These personal traits have made Purdue graduates very valuable since you have instilled in them a fundamental understanding of fracture mechanics principles. As structural integrity managers within DGTA they have achieved over the years exceptional

outcomes in solving fatigue-related problems on numerous Australian Defence Force Aircraft.

The education and training you have provided all RAAF Purdue graduates represent a distinguished and enduring legacy. On behalf of all the staff you have worked with in the DGTA over the last two decades, and all the aircraft programs you have assisted throughout the Australian Defence Force, I thank you for your efforts."[8]

ADRIAN MORRISON

The first person in the RAAF/Purdue program was Adrian Morrison, who grew up in Brisbane and joined the Air Force as an engineering cadet straight out of high school.

"Around six weeks after I finished high school, I was on a plane in Melbourne to go to what we called the Engineer Cadet Squadron to start aeronautical engineering study at the Royal Melbourne Institute of Technology (RMIT)."[9]

The RAAF paid his way through four years of college and upon graduation commissioned him as a second lieutenant in the engineering branch. He says he was lucky to be selected for the program. But actually he was a very good engineer.

"The Australian Air Force goes through its process of selecting people for various jobs and I popped up primarily because I had very good results in my engineering degree," he says. "So that sort of showed up as putting me up there as a candidate for the job. Somehow I managed to fall into the right place at the right time."[10]

He loved studying at Purdue.

"It was a big adventure, a huge adventure for someone who'd only ever been overseas once and that was on a one-week ski trip to New Zealand with my brother," he says. "So going and doing this was certainly a big adventure and quite exciting. Then I went down to Warner Robins for twelve months and worked with the U.S. Air Force. That was a pretty exciting time. And then back into Australia working in the fatigue part of our engineering empire. This has been a good program for Australia. And a good program for the U.S., too."[11]

When he returned to Australia, he spent six years working in aircraft fatigue, including drafting the RAAF's aircraft fatigue management policy. He also worked on managing two sets of major fatigue tests for the Hornet combat aircraft and for the PS-PC-9 trainer.

He's worked with the F-111, a supersonic combat airplane; the C-17 Globe Master, a huge cargo plane; and the KC-30 tanker that does in-air refueling.

In 2009, he transferred to the Australian Air Force Reserve, and in 2023 was nearing retirement with the rank of group captain colonel.

"It's great to see that the Purdue program continues on and that that relationship is maintained," Morrison says. "It was a great time at Purdue. I really learned a lot. It was a fantastic grounding in the technology. When I went to Warner Robins, I found myself placed in a position where a lot was expected of me and I was the guy straight out of the master's degree [program], and I was able to really apply it to the U.S. Air Force straight away. And that was magnificent."[12]

KEVIN WALKER

Like Adrian Morrison, Kevin Walker started his career at RMIT in Melbourne while also taking military training with the RAAF.

"There was an Air Force base and we actually lived on the base and traveled into Melbourne for our studies during the day, and then back to the base," he says.[13]

Morrison was a couple years ahead of Walker, so when he graduated and received his commission, the Purdue program was already up and running.

"The Australian Air Force recognized that equipment was becoming more complex and more engineering input was required to support and sustain aircraft fleets going forward," Walker says. "We did realize pretty early on that for aircraft, structural fatigue was a concern and was something that we needed to be vigilant about."[14]

The RAAF was flying the F-111 supersonic combat jet and they needed to maintain them.

"It's really an amazing aircraft," he says. "I absolutely love it. We realized to manage that aircraft, we really need to know about fracture mechanics and about crack growth and fracture. The old fatigue methods weren't going to get us there. So that's really where it got applied in a major way for the first time there, or the first significant time, definitely, in a military context."[15]

In the mid-1990s, Grandt headed a Purdue team of materials scientists, structural engineers, and statisticians that conducted a four-year research project studying issues associated with aging aircraft. The project was funded with a $3.3 million grant from the U.S. Air Force Office of Scientific Research.

Walker graduated from Purdue in 1987 and then spent a year at Warner Robins Air Logistics Center Fatigue Laboratory. He returned to Australia and worked on the French fighter jet, the Mirage.

"We had been operating the French Mirage fighter and there'd been some fatigue problems," Walker says. "In some cases, there were actual cracks that they were monitoring. And they said, 'Okay, we want to slow those cracks down. We're going to limit the flight envelope of the aircraft to slow those cracks down.' Sounds like a good idea. Well, it turns out, not necessarily. What we discovered was that actually, the occasional very high load actually slows the crack down. In the case of the Mirage, they had told the pilots, 'Hey guys, no going over five-G.' But in reality, the occasional six-G or even seven-G maneuver probably would've been beneficial. And no one really even would've thought that because it's counterintuitive, it's not what you would have thought. That was really hard for us to get our heads around."[16]

Grandt says the research was helpful to everyone.

"Kevin's experiments were some of the first to really prove that eliminating the big loads wasn't necessarily good," Grandt says. "Theoretically we knew that. But Kevin did some very careful experiments that showed that."[17]

Walker's work also showed that repairing aircraft cracks with rivets was not beneficial.

The benefits of the program have flowed both ways: from Australia to Purdue, to the United States and back to Australia. "It brought us together as a team," Walker says. "And we still do [work together] today."

He says the RAAF/Purdue program has had a major impact. "Having engineers in the Air Force system that have been through the Purdue experience really is critical and important," Walker says.[18]

21

PURDUE MILITARY RESEARCH INSTITUTE (PMRI) GRADUATE DEGREES FOR ACTIVE MILITARY OFFICERS

These are outstanding men and women. They are very disciplined, self-driven people. We admire their service to our country and we're glad to be part of the educational processes to support that. PMRI is a win-win-win. Everybody wins. The individuals win, the military wins, and the university wins. Absolutely this program will continue to grow.

PURDUE UNIVERSITY PRESIDENT MUNG CHIANG

U.S. Air Force Major Glenn R. Peterson grew up north of Chicago, always aware of Purdue University and its great reputation. His godmother, an aunt from Valparaiso, Indiana, graduated from Purdue and so did her son and daughter.

What he didn't know then is that as a thirty-two-year-old officer in the Air Force, a husband, and a father of three young children, he would have the opportunity to study at Purdue for a PhD in materials engineering.

And he'd be paid to do it. And he wouldn't have to pay tuition and fees. And he'd have a housing allowance from the Air Force.

"Being able to go to Purdue and put that on my resume is something spectacular to me," Peterson says. "Years ago, this opportunity seemed out of reach. I'm so very grateful. I'm hoping a Purdue PhD takes me where I want to go. Without the Purdue Military Research Institute (PMRI), I wouldn't be here."[1]

PMRI GROWS RAPIDLY

The Purdue Military Research Institute was officially launched in 2014. In the fall of 2023, the program admitted student number 197—all of them active-duty military officers—to the West Lafayette campus to study for advanced degrees. The officers receive their military pay, along with a housing allowance, and the tuition and fees are covered through a university fellowship.

The PMRI graduate school fellowship program has very rapidly grown into a huge success. It now supports more active-duty officers than any graduate school in the nation, other than the Air Force Institute of Technology and the Naval Postgraduate School.

The focus of the program is on active-duty military officer PhD candidates in science, technology, applied math, and engineering, but other fields are considered. Master's degree candidates are also considered. About thirty to forty percent of the people in the program are PhD candidates, and the rest work on master's degrees. The PhD program must be completed in three years and the master's allows up to two years for completion. That's fast, but the PMRI on-time success rate for finishing on time is an outstanding ninety-five percent-plus.

The program focuses on collaboration with the military, providing the chance for military-connected students to study with Purdue University faculty conducting world-class research. Much of this work is in areas of great importance to the Department of Defense and to national security, such as hypersonics, energetic materials and systems, cybersecurity, and secure microelectronics (chapter 22). PMRI students are matched with Purdue faculty working on national security and Department of Defense-funded projects. Other research projects that parallel Department of Defense interests are possible as well.

PMRI also offers a summer program for cadets and midshipmen from military academies, Purdue's ROTC detachments, and for undergraduates participating in other related programs, such as Veterans to Energy Careers. The summer program introduces them to research. It also recruits them for Purdue's graduate school.

PMRI partners with the Army, Navy, Marines, Coast Guard, Air Force, and Space Force. As an educational outreach program, it is in step with the University's founding land-grant mission to open the doors of education to people, and to serve the state and nation.

It has the full support of Dr. Mung Chiang, who became president of Purdue University in January 2023. Chiang is very familiar with PMRI. He's been at the University since 2017, when he came to West Lafayette from Princeton University as the Roscoe H. George Distinguished Professor in the Elmore Family School of Electrical and Computer Engineering. From July 2017 to June 2022, he served as the John A. Edwardson Dean of Purdue Engineering. And from April 2021 to December 2022, he was the executive vice president for strategic initiatives at Purdue, with a focus on expanding Department of Defense and national security partnerships and research.

"In the past two years, we have tripled the number of students coming into PMRI per year," Chiang says. "These are outstanding men and women. They are very disciplined, self-driven people. We admire their service to our country and we're glad to be part of the educational processes to support that. PMRI is a win-win-win. Everybody wins. The individuals win, the military wins, and the university wins. Absolutely, this program will continue to grow."[2]

There is a fourth winner in PMRI: the United States of America that gains from the research led by these military officers educated at Purdue.

Mitchell E. Daniels, Jr. was president of Purdue when PMRI began, and he gave it strong support throughout his tenure in the office. He became president emeritus in January 2023.

"I'm proud of what we're doing, and I think that frankly, any public university ought to see this [serving the military] as a high priority and a responsibility," Daniels says. "Many obviously don't, which I think is disappointing, even disgraceful. But clearly Purdue feels more than obligated. We feel proud to assist in all these ways. This is another example of the ways in which we try to do our duty as citizens."[3]

PURDUE COLLEGE OF ENGINEERING

PMRI is part of the University's College of Engineering. In 2023 *U.S. News and World Report* ranked Purdue's engineering program tied for fourth best in the nation, with an undergraduate student enrollment larger than the first three ranked universities, combined.[4]

Purdue's John A. Edwardson Dean of Engineering Arvind Raman says PMRI was built and expanded on previous programs that brought military officers to

Purdue for advanced degrees. Engineering, he says, was the best college in which to place PMRI.

"If you look historically at officers from the military who came here to get degrees, there are some disciplines where they would all go," he says. "For example, if you're a Navy officer, you're probably going to go to nuclear engineering or electrical engineering at Purdue. There's a history of that. And, of course, some would go to Purdue Polytechnic Institute as well."[5]

The program started with a collaboration between two people at Purdue, Dr. Joseph Pekny, a professor of chemical engineering, and Dr. J. Eric Dietz, director of the Purdue Homeland Security Institute and a professor in the Department of Computer and Information Technology at Purdue Polytechnic Institute.

Pekny came to Purdue in 1990 after receiving his PhD from Carnegie Mellon University in Pittsburgh. He was a founding director of Purdue's Discovery Park. Discovery Park is an interdisciplinary research area launched in 2001 during the administration (2000–2007) of then Purdue President Martin Jischke.

An Indiana native, Dietz graduated in 1984 from Rose-Hulman Institute of Technology after earning a Bachelor of Science in chemical engineering. He earned a Master of Science from Rose-Hulman in 1986 and a PhD in chemical engineering in 1994 from Purdue, where he met Pekny. He took part in ROTC at Rose-Hulman and retired from the Army with the rank of lieutenant colonel in 2004 after twenty-two years of service. He led Army acquisition and research programs including power systems, chemical sensors, and command and control systems.

He came to Purdue in May 2004 as managing director of the University's Homeland Security Institute in Discovery Park. He also became associate director of the e-Enterprise Center at Discovery Park.

Pekny and Dietz looked at the possibility of bringing more active-duty military officers to Purdue for advanced degrees.

"Joe Pekny and Eric Dietz got the sense that this was an untapped opportunity," Raman says. "They asked, 'Why don't we do more of this?' It's a total win-win-win situation. Not only do we bring the talent here, but after these officers graduate from Purdue and go back to the military, they will rise to higher positions. They're going to be in places where they can influence decisions regarding where research funding goes."[6]

FIRST STUDENTS

Dietz and Pekny began by recruiting two Army majors, Victor Nakano and Reid Vander Schaaf, to Purdue in 2005 to pursue civil engineering PhDs in the three-year time period allowed by the military. They were part of the Uniformed Army Scientist and Engineer (UAS&E) PhD program seeking to bridge the gap between Army and academic labs. Dietz had been part of this program before coming to Purdue.

Some Purdue faculty questioned whether it was possible for them to complete a PhD in three years. Pekny, Dietz and others said—"Let them try and see if they can." They finished in a little less than three years, graduating in 2008.[7]

Their experience was a trial run for what became PMRI.

Nakano and Vander Schaaf studied under Purdue civil engineering professor Dulcy Abraham. "Both these men were very, very motivated students and I worked very closely with them to ensure that they followed a timeline which was acceptable to their employer, which was the U.S. Army," Abraham says. "Both Eric and Joe worked very closely with me, and they ensured that I was doing things the right way."[8]

The program was good for the Army officers. It was also good for other Purdue students and the faculty.

"The program was an excellent avenue for interaction," Abraham says. "I had outstanding Army officers in research and learning opportunities at Purdue while I was engaging with scientists and researchers from Army labs. What I felt most excited about was the commitment of the students to excellence, because both these students also served as mentors to my younger, junior graduate students. And they had a high level of expectation. They would tell me things such as, 'That person will not fit well in our group because they're not committed to excellence.' If a younger student was interested in something, they would work very well with them. They were motivated; they worked very well with the younger students to move them up. What I appreciated from my interactions with the Army students was their commitment to excellence, discipline, and timely delivery. These are all things that they do in the military."[9]

In March 2005, Dietz took a leave of absence from Purdue when then Indiana Governor Daniels named him the first executive director of the state's Department of Homeland Security.

His initial two-year appointment was expanded to three. He returned to Purdue having established a relationship with Daniels, who was confident in his abilities.

In 2013, Daniels's second four-year term as governor ended and he was named president of Purdue by the University's Board of Trustees. Daniels and Dietz were working together again.

DISCOVERY PARK WAS CATALYST

In the first years of the twenty-first century, Discovery Park became a catalyst for many research enterprises taking place at Purdue. PMRI originated out of a Discovery Park center.

"Discovery Park was founded in 2001 under President Martin Jischke to catalyze growth of the research enterprise and ultimately all aspects of the university engagement education," Pekny says. "There were four original centers: the e-Enterprise Center, the Burton D. Morgan Center for Entrepreneurship, our Bindley Bioscience Center, and the Birck Nanotechnology Center. Next, a second generation of centers started including the Energy Center. And then in the third wave, when Mitch Daniels came, he wanted to put an emphasis on innovation and entrepreneurship and company formation. So, I became director of the Burton D. Morgan Center for Entrepreneurship after doing several roles in Discovery Park. And one of the programs that we founded was to invite faculty to submit innovative ideas that would help Purdue grow in innovation and entrepreneurship.[10]

"Eric was one of ten faculty who submitted an idea that he had prototyped earlier with the two Army majors," Pekny says.[11]

All ten proposals received funding, including the graduate degree program for military officers. The Office of the Vice President for Research issued a challenge for the PMRI program. Dietz and Pekny were asked if they could recruit ten officers to campus each year.

"To challenge us, they set a number that they thought would be bigger than we could get," Pekny says.[12]

Dietz was offered initial funding for the ten scholarships a year, each lasting three years. When he had no trouble filling them, they next looked at growing the program. PMRI began including military officers who were sent to campus for an advanced degree on a scholarship provided by the military. Also, some Purdue ROTC graduates had to wait for their military assignment after being commissioned. So, they began working with PMRI to earn master's degrees while they waited.

The PMRI class enrolled more than thirty members in the fall of 2022 and again in 2023, and the ninety-five percent success rate is more than enough proof that military officers can complete the PhD program in three years.

MILITARY STUDENTS ARE FOCUSED

"Military people getting done in three years is not necessarily an anomaly," Dietz says. "When they start, they already know where they're going. We can't say that with everybody who's here studying for a degree. I think anybody who knows where they're going to work when they're done will be able to get finished faster. And the officers have a minimal amount of risk because our track record shows that we work out a lot of the details to make sure the faculty/student coupling works. They're going to graduate on time. We're not going to damage anybody's career."[13]

The faculty is very supportive of PMRI and the military graduate students.

"Purdue is a conservative campus," Pekny says. "Purdue has always had a tradition of supporting military activity. And it's patriotic. The military's research is intense, and it dovetails with our mission. Our competitors are very much less military-friendly. This is an area where we can compete without any of our traditional competitors being much competition."[14]

Dietz says one military officer in the program told him he prefers not to wear his uniform on campus.

"And it's not anything negative," Dietz says. "It's because they get to their meetings late because people stop them and ask them why they're here and thank them for their service. Really, it causes them to take more time to go from point A to point B because this campus is so very friendly."[15]

Dietz says the officers in PMRI are often at mid-career, meaning that they're in their thirties.

"We're getting a much more mature population that's been seasoned by as much as ten years or more of military service," he says. "So, they've got organizational skills, communication skills, budgeting skills that would rival some of our faculty."[16]

PMRI LEADERSHIP

Pekny says the program has benefited from having military people such as Dietz and Dave Hankins in charge. Hankins is PMRI's senior project manager, and he's been with the program from the beginning.

"In addition to Eric being the founding director of PRMI, we've been very fortunate to have Dave Hankins as the managing director," Pekny says. "He's a retired Air Force colonel. And when he was in the Air Force, he served in the Air Force Personnel Center. So, he knows how officers are placed in their roles, and he knows exactly how officers will be placed here. He developed a close relationship with the Air Force and then ultimately with the other services using his knowledge of the Personnel Center and the fact he was a retired colonel and, like Eric, he's been tireless in recruiting all these officers."[17]

Hankins retired from the Air Force in 2002 at the rank of colonel after serving almost thirty years. His previous assignments included serving as commander of Purdue's Air Force Reserve Officer Training Corps. He has worked for Purdue since retirement from the Air Force.

SUPPORT FROM ADMINISTRATION

Hankins says PMRI receives tremendous support from the university administration, including Presidents Daniels and Chiang, and Deans of the Graduate School, including Mark Smith, who was Dean when the program began.

"President Daniels would always tell us that we're doing this because we owe our nation's warfighters the very best tools possible, be it through the education of their officers or via our technical research," Hankins says. "They're protecting our very way of life and so we want to partner with them using the research power of the two thousand faculty who are here and ready to assist them in achieving that goal."[18]

"It's important to point out that from the personnel point of view, being selected to come to a university like Purdue to get a graduate degree through the military is a big deal," Dietz says. "Only maybe one in more than twenty is even going to get a chance during their careers to do this. So, it's a unique thing, but it's also one of those things that you've bet your career on getting it done on time. And that's what Dave and I have been doing with the military officers who get selected and sent here. We've made sure that it's a pretty safe bet for them.

When people say this is a good deal for everybody, I just want to reinforce that it certainly is for the officers. During my time in the Army when I got my PhD, a third to half of the officers who studied for graduate degrees went back to the military without a diploma. Since we've started, we've only had three who have not finished on time."[19]

There are many potential opportunities in the program—such as giving military personnel from different branches experience working together.

COLLABORATIVE WORK

"What we're hoping to do is to get these people to work more collaboratively," Pekny says. "If that happens, that actually is another spark that we can create for the military by having the various services working together—the Army, the Navy, the Air Force, Marines, Coast Guard, and Space Force—having officers all work on areas of common interest. There's a great benefit to have these officers go back to their service and work in those areas, knowing collaborators from the other services, knowing techniques and concerns from those in other services, and to have an appreciation for going back and forth. And so, we think that's another kind of key tangible that PMRI offers."[20]

As Purdue is rapidly expanding its research in national security and with the Department of Defense, PMRI has the opportunity to match PhD candidates with areas of research importance to the military.

"PMRI used to be just about getting a degree, getting done in time, and supporting the officer," Pekny says. "Now, we have these research concentration areas and if we get officers involved, we can actually help decide what their PhD is, so that it's what the officer wants to do, and it also has a maximum impact in the military when they go back. That's another evolution of PMRI that's just starting to come."[21]

Dietz says the approach of PMRI is to strengthen the military, and not just by writing a research paper. "We want the officers to go back to the military to implement the research that they've learned about here at Purdue with partners from industry alumni and friends," he says.[22]

The program is still new and evolving.

"It's still a work in progress," Pekny says. "We continue to innovate, and the idea is to continue maneuvering PMRI to have maximum benefit to the military, maximum benefit to how fast the military innovates, and how fast we can continue to innovate beyond our peers—our near-peers and our peers internationally. This is still very young and we're still just scratching the surface as to what can be done."[23]

PMRI MAKES A DIFFERENCE

"The reason I continue to work here is that PMRI is making a difference for the officers, the military, Purdue, and the nation," Hankins says. "It's worth us spending the time to try to find the right faculty/student match where the student has the greatest opportunity to be all that they can be to achieve great things. The reason I continue to work with PMRI is that it is making a difference."[24]

Dr. Shreyas Sundaram is the Marie Gordon Professor in the Elmore Family School of Electrical and Computer Engineering. His wife, Dr. Neera Jain, is an associate professor in Purdue's Department of Mechanical Engineering. She had worked with PMRI students and invited Sundaram to join her at the annual Christmas banquet that honored the students.

"At a banquet I saw all these amazing students celebrating being here at Purdue and celebrating their accomplishments," Sundaram says. "And I said, 'Wow, this looks amazing. I'd like to get involved with this.'"[25]

Hankins connected him with PMRI graduate students.

"The students have been amazing," he says. "I've been very, very pleased and privileged to work with these students because they come in with a sense of maturity, a sense of responsibility. That comes from their military background. They take their job seriously. They're ready to do the hard work because research is not like classes. You have to be stubborn, and you have to be willing to deal with things that don't work out the way they're supposed to. And these students come in from day one understanding this."[26]

The administration and faculty are very excited about PMRI. And so are current and former students.

CHARLES E. ANKLAM III

Dr. Charles E. Anklam has always believed in the power of education. His love for learning led him to become the first military officer to earn a scholarship and a PhD at Purdue through PMRI.

"Growing up I knew that education was the path to success, but didn't have the opportunities, so I had to create my own," Anklam says. "I enlisted in the Marine Corps in 1994 right out of high school. I met my soon-to-be wife Angela early on and together we quickly identified that the path to success was to be achieved through education. We were married in 1996, and together we embarked on what became a journey as lifelong learners."[27]

As a Marine sergeant stationed in Maine, he earned an associate degree in 1999 from New Hampshire College (now Southern New Hampshire University) by taking night classes from a satellite campus on the Brunswick Naval Air Station (now closed). His wife also studied, commuting daily to Portland, where she attended the University of Southern Maine.

The associate degree enabled him to compete and be selected for the Marine Enlisted Commissioning Education Program (MECEP). MECEP allows Marines to obtain their bachelor's degree and commission. Anklam's studies were not funded, but Marines in the program remain on active duty and are issued orders assigning them to a university. He attended the University of Florida, participated in NROTC, and graduated and received his commission in 2002.

"I was the first person in my family to complete a four-year college degree," he says. "My wife obtained her Bachelor of Science degree the semester before me. I was hooked. I had a passion for education that stuck with me, and I continued to pursue educational opportunities at every opportunity."[28]

Following his initial Fleet Marine Force tour as an infantry officer, which included two Iraq deployments, he completed a master's degree by attending night school, and his wife completed her master's degree, becoming a speech language pathologist.

His next Fleet Marine Force tour included two Afghanistan deployments. At the conclusion of that tour in 2012, he was selected to serve as the Marine Officer Instructor at Purdue Naval ROTC. It was there that he met Dietz and learned about the PMRI program that Dietz was trying to get up and running. While working at Purdue, Anklam thought about enrolling in a PhD program.

He initially was accepted into Purdue's political science PhD program, but quickly learned his interests were better aligned with the College of Technology (now Purdue Polytechnic Institute). Midway through his first fall semester, he transferred. During his second year, PMRI came online and Anklam considered enrolling.

"I only had three years to accomplish the program and at first didn't know if it would be possible," he says. "After speaking with Eric and Dennis Depew, who at the time was the dean of the college of technology, I realized that it would technically be possible, but would be very difficult to complete within the timeframe I had available. At first, I was apprehensive because I had just returned from two back-to-back Afghanistan deployments where I served as an infantry company commander. I had spent the majority of the past two years away, and we had three children now, with my youngest not yet three years old. I knew that undertaking this degree path would take up an incredibly large amount of my family time, since I still had to work my primary job teaching Marine ROTC. After some deliberation, my wife and I decided that it would absolutely be worth it, so I applied and was accepted in the initial PMRI cohort. What sold it for me was the incredible support Eric showed from the beginning. It was apparent he, and the entire PMRI program, were committed to see me succeed."[29]

It was hard work.

"For three years I balanced my family, work, and pursued my PhD," Anklam says. "And in 2015 I became the first PhD graduate from the program. Eric's support was invaluable, and throughout my studies he served as an academic advisor, as well as mentoring and supporting me. Today he remains a trusted friend and mentor and we still talk regularly."[30]

His Purdue PhD has opened many professional opportunities for him.

"As an active-duty Marine, I am currently one of only a handful in the Marine Corps with a PhD," he says. "Following Purdue, I was selected to attend the Army's Command and General Staff College at Fort Leavenworth, Kansas. After my next operational tour, I was selected to serve on the staff of the Commandant of the Marine Corps. From there, I was selected to serve on a newly created billet by then Chairman of the Joint Chiefs of Staff, Marine Corps General Joseph Dunford."[31]

It was then called the Joint Force Development Team on the Joint Staff J-7, at the Pentagon. Four members from each branch of the service were chosen to work closely with academia, industry, and the Department of Defense to streamline the development and acquisitions process helping to overcome the erosion of technology needed for national defense objectives.

"As part of this job, and because of my academic background, I was selected to work at the Defense Advanced Research Projects Agency (DARPA) within the Adaptive Capabilities Office," Anklam says. "From there I was selected to attend the Strategic Studies Program at Massachusetts Institute of Technology. I have found that pairing my academic skills obtained at Purdue with my understanding of broader strategic goals of my service and the Department of Defense enabled me to bridge the gap and create better synergy between academia, industry, and the military in some of our most challenging areas."[32]

As he always believed, education has been a key to his success.

"Throughout my entire adult life, I have continuously pursued educational opportunities, finding that each step and accomplishment opened yet another opportunity," Anklam says. "I enlisted in the Marine Corps with a high school degree and today have risen to become a Lieutenant Colonel with a PhD, having commanded up to the battalion level. As parents, the example of continuous pursuit of education also instilled in our children a love of learning. We currently have one daughter in nursing school, another daughter who will enter Purdue University this fall and enroll in Air Force ROTC, and our son has plans to attend Purdue for engineering."[33]

GLENN PETERSON

The determination of Purdue University president Mitch Daniels to keep the University open through the COVID-19 pandemic helped Glenn Peterson convince the Air Force to place him in PMRI.

Peterson was sold on PMRI before the pandemic hit in the winter of 2020. Purdue closed briefly, after spring break in March 2020 until the end of the semester, on May 9—about six weeks. Students took classes online during that time.

But while some universities were planning to continue virtual learning, Daniels announced Purdue would be open for most in-person classes in August 2020. It was an all-campus project through the summer to accomplish that.

In June 2020 Daniels testified before the U.S. Senate Committee on Health, Education, Labor, and Pensions on Purdue's plans to open in the fall.

"I was stationed in Washington, D.C. at the time," Peterson says. "That was news where I was. And it helped solidify the argument that I was making to the Air Force to let me go to Purdue. I said, 'Look, the university president is speaking to Congress. They're going to open in the fall, which is not the case for other institutions where you're sending officers to study.' So, it actually helped persuade the Air Force to let me come to Purdue. It was a better business decision than sending people for PhD programs at other schools that were virtual."[34]

He got the assignment, but finding housing was difficult. His family had to do virtual walk-throughs of homes they were considering buying in West Lafayette.

They lost out on several homes. They did find a place in a welcoming neighborhood and arrived on campus in August 2020.

Peterson grew up in Lake Villa, Illinois, north of Chicago.

"Growing up in the Chicagoland area, if you were interested in engineering, you went to Purdue or the University of Illinois," he says.

He received a four-year Air Force scholarship, and financially it made more sense for him to enroll at the University of Illinois where he would get in-state tuition. He took part in ROTC all four years at Illinois.

The 9/11 attacks had taken place while he was a child, and this affected him. He was attracted to the military at a young age, and part of that was patriotism. His family holds strong patriotic views, with his father having served as an officer in the U.S. Naval Reserves. Both his grandfathers served in WWII and Korea, and numerous uncles, cousins, and brothers served as well. The call to serve was installed in him at a young age.

"I think another aspect for me, as an engineer, [is that] there are certain programs and technologies that you might be exposed to as a junior military officer that you would otherwise not be exposed to as a civilian until much further on and senior in your career," he says.[35]

He is colorblind, and neither the Army nor the Navy would give him a scholarship because of his eyesight. So, he chose the Air Force, and is happy he did.

Peterson graduated from the University of Illinois in 2013 with a bachelor's degree in nuclear engineering. He next earned a master's degree in nuclear engineering from the Air Force Institute of Technology.

He applied for an Air Force fellowship to earn a PhD. Three officers were selected. Peterson was one of three alternates and was told if he could find funding, the Air Force would convert his alternate slot to a primary. So, at that point, he started calling different schools that he knew had some kind of military affinity.

"I talked to a professor at Purdue who was very receptive, and he said, 'Have you checked out PMRI?'" Peterson says. "I reached out to Dave Hankins. And then from there, the rest is history, as they say. But I will say one of the things that was incredibly attractive about Purdue was the receptiveness of the faculty to working with a military student. Every professor was positive, and every professor considered everything possible."[36]

"I had called a few other schools that might have a more prestigious name," he says. "And sometimes their first response was, 'I will not be told how to do business with the military.' And okay, I get it. This obviously will not work for us.

Thank you for letting me know up front. And there were other schools where the professors I talked to were very willing to engage with military students, but the problem was that there was really no infrastructure at those schools to keep the odds of graduating high. There is a saying in the military, 'Collaborate to graduate,' and being one military officer in the sea of thirty-thousand-plus other students seemed daunting."[37]

Purdue had the infrastructure, though. It wanted to work with the military. Its program was up and running and successful. He enrolled at Purdue and PMRI.

"The typical student would really struggle, probably, to do it in three years," he says. "I think this is really the appeal for what the military students are bringing. We're used to being given a task and we just have to get it done—find a way. Other students might not tolerate that as well. But I think it's just a different mindset that we're bringing to the equation."[38]

The military students' experiences instill them with an attitude where failure is not acceptable and not an option.

Peterson came to West Lafayette as a captain. While at Purdue, he was promoted to the rank of major. He plans a career in the Air Force and will go into project management when he graduates.

"My hope is that I'm going to take this PhD and all the knowledge I've learned, and I'll use it to manage other smart people in programs and projects that are generally very technically challenging. I'll be able to draw on skills and really a network that I've obtained while I've been here at Purdue to solve those problems. And better yet, I'll have the credentials to back it up."[39]

Peterson graduated on time in August 2023, with a PhD in materials engineering.

ALEXANDER MASTER

Alexander Master did not have far to travel to pursue his future in 2009 when he graduated from Culver Military Academy in Culver, Indiana. He headed straight to Purdue University, eighty miles to the south.

He was offered a national four-year ROTC scholarship from the Army and Air Force. The Army got back to him first, so he took that offer. He enrolled in the computer and information technology degree program in the College of Technology, now called Purdue Polytechnic Institute.

He got a great education at Purdue, and also learned servant leadership from Army ROTC. In the spring of 2013, he graduated, was commissioned as a second lieutenant, and his military career began.

After graduating from Purdue, Master went through basic officer training at Fort Sill, Oklahoma and then reported to his first duty assignment with the 101st Airborne Division at Fort Campbell, Kentucky. He quickly deployed overseas to Afghanistan as part of Operation Resolute Support under NATO.

When he returned from deployment, he was offered the opportunity to become a cyber warfare officer in the Army, and he felt it was a perfect fit for his interests and the expertise he had acquired at Purdue. He was selected to change branches and attended one and a half years of technical training at Fort Gordon, Georgia. Master's next assignment was to U.S. Cyber Command at Fort Meade, Maryland. He spent three years conducting offensive and defensive cyber operations. He also earned a Master of Engineering degree in cybersecurity from the University of Maryland during nights and weekends.

At U.S. Cyber Command, Master met Purdue computer science professor Eugene Spafford. Spafford is executive director emeritus of CERIUS (Center for Education and Research in Information Assurance and Security) and was founder and director of the COAST (Computer Operations, Audit, and Security Technology) laboratory, both at Purdue. (Learn more in chapter 22.) Spafford is also an advisor to U.S. government agencies and industry.

Spafford was on a sabbatical at the U.S. National Security Agency when he met Masters. "He informed me about the interdisciplinary programs that Purdue has," Master says. "It sounded amazing. Purdue is my alma mater and it has a top-notch program—one of the best in the country. It's one of the few NSA-accredited universities. The Cyber Command will ultimately benefit from the research skills I have gained at Purdue in the long run."[40]

Spafford told people at PMRI that Master was interested in studying for a PhD at Purdue, and they contacted him. Master separately applied directly to Purdue with Army funding and was accepted. He decided to accept the Army funding.

"Dietz and I chatted about options, and it was a safer bet to take Army funding and let another person use PMRI funding," Master says. "PMRI called me a 'service fellow' in their circles, because they provided assistance to me in facilitating faculty and research programs, but [it] didn't come from their pool of funding."[41]

He began his doctoral studies in information security in the fall of 2020. His first semester was completely virtual due to the COVID-19 global pandemic. As the university began to slowly open back up, he was able to return to campus and work in lab spaces.

"I've been in the technology field for a while," Master says. "I studied computer and information technology at Purdue for my bachelor's degree. I have a master's degree in cybersecurity and am a cyber officer. I am also really interested in education and teaching. I've been a company commander and have done military leadership time. Now I am coming out with a PhD and think that I can make a larger positive difference for the next generation of leaders. My next position will be as a research scientist in the Army Cyber Institute at the United States Military Academy in West Point, New York. I'm excited to do research on the Army's hardest problems in the cyberspace domain, and to pass on what I can to undergraduate cadets in a professor role."[42]

Three years to a PhD is a fast track. "But Dr. Dietz actively finds faculty that are supportive of defense-adjacent research and helps to smooth out all of the edges," Master says. "And the whole administration has seemed to be really supportive of us too. Thirty-six months to complete a doctorate was an intimidating thought at first, but the PMRI faculty support makes a world of difference."[43]

The Army's approval of his PhD program came with an additional six-year service commitment. But Master already plans to make a career of his military service, so that works for him. He was promoted "below the zone," or one year earlier than his peers, to the rank of major in June 2023 at age thirty-two. The promotion ceremony was held on the Purdue Armory drill floor, and U.S. Army Lieutenant Colonel (Ret.) Dietz had the privilege of giving Master his oath of office renewal. Family, friends, faculty, and lab mates were able to join in the celebration.

The men and women in PMRI make strong connections with one another, and Master hopes to maintain those connections in his career.

"We can stay in touch and collaboratively do research," he says. "We can publish together. As the program grows and has this cohort of alumni, the alumni network is going to be really powerful. Inevitably some of the PMRI network will go on to be admirals and generals and influence national defense strategy."[44]

He loves Purdue. "I wouldn't trade the experience for anything," Master says. "It's great to come here, focus on research, get the degree, and not have to worry about a day job. And the support structure here has been amazing. I was talking to a soldier who is a prospective student. He has applied to several schools and came here for a symposium this week and was amazed. He told me he had two universities flat-out deny his application. They turned away a fully funded Army officer because they didn't think it was possible. And then he came to Purdue, and they said, 'We want you. We will figure out a way to get you here and get you through a computer science degree in thirty-six months.' That is so refreshing because there are other top graduate schools that are just not supportive of defense-related research like they are here."[45]

Master's wife Stephanie enjoyed being back in West Lafayette. They met at Purdue during their undergraduate years. It's especially nice since both of their families are in Indiana. She is a physical therapist assistant and had the opportunity to work as an early intervention specialist on campus at Purdue, promoting occupational safety and health to the staff.

Master said that Stephanie appreciated the employment opportunities that spouses have in the Greater Lafayette area, and the fact that, if they work at Purdue, they can even get a graduate degree tuition-free through Purdue Global.

"We had great options for family activities during graduate school," he says. "Purdue would bring in Broadway musicals, theater performances, and other events unavailable at most military bases. Indianapolis and Chicago are close by, there are lots of wineries to explore, and the state parks in Indiana are top-notch. PMRI also gave families free tickets to Big Ten football games each fall—we had a lot of fun with it."[46]

Spafford and Dietz were cochairs on Master's dissertation committee. His research involved modeling and characterization of Internet censorship technologies. Master successfully completed the interdisciplinary information security program on time: he defended his dissertation during the summer of 2023 and graduated with his PhD that August.

CASEY JONES

Dr. Casey Jones took a unique route to graduate school at Purdue. He earned an undergraduate degree in business at Washington State University, followed by a six-year enlistment in the Navy serving as a nuclear electronics technician.

When that ended in 2016, he enrolled at the University of Hawaii at Manoa on a three-year track to earn a bachelor's degree in mechanical engineering. While there, he took part in the Veterans to Energy Careers program based at California State University San Marcos. The program mentors students from many different schools, and he learned about PMRI through its representative at the

University of Hawaii. The Veterans to Energy Careers program works to move military veterans into sustainable energy careers.

Before he graduated from the University of Hawaii, Jones took part in a PMRI summer program that gave him experience in a research lab. He liked it so much that when he completed his degree in Hawaii, he came to Purdue. He received his PhD in aerospace engineering in the summer of 2023 and took a job in the energy industry.

"Originally my plan was to get an engineering degree at Hawaii, and then get a job in the shipyard at Hawaii. Originally, I wanted to stay in Hawaii for the rest of my life. But it was PMRI that got me to Purdue for the summer program. I was looking for something to do over the summer, looking for an internship or something, and they said, 'Do you want to go out to Purdue for a summer and do some research?' I heard Purdue is a really good engineering school, so I said, 'Sure, I'll go do that.' The summer went really well and I liked the professor that I worked for, and before I left I said I would be interested in coming back for grad school, and he said, 'Yeah, that sounds good. Just apply and I'll let you in.' So, it worked out pretty well for me."[47]

Since he is not active-duty military, he is not officially a part of PMRI in his graduate program, but he stays in contact with people running the program. He is a traditional graduate student, receiving tuition remission and some pay for his work as a research assistant.

Purdue has been great, Jones says.

"I've been given a lot of great opportunities," he says. "I never really thought that I'd be able to attend an engineering school like Purdue. I know it's one of the best. It's an opportunity I've gotten and it has been really awesome."[48]

BARRY SCOTT

Barry Scott enlisted in the Navy in 2005, several years after he graduated from the University of Oregon with a bachelor's degree in political science.

Growing up, he had always been interested in a military career and maybe even going to an academy. But his life plans changed, and he went to Oregon.

"After I graduated, I moved to Boulder, Colorado and helped start a small business there," Scott says. "I ran with that for a couple of years and then 9/11 happened and the invasion in Iraq happened. And I just felt like I had not fulfilled my commitment to serve. So, I decided to join the military."[49]

He was accepted into Navy Officer Candidate School in Newport, Rhode Island. He also attended the Naval Postgraduate School in Monterey, California and earned a master's degree in strategic studies.

"Then my advisor said, 'You know, you seem to like this academic work, you might look into doing a PhD someday. I think you would benefit from that,'" Scott says. "That was in 2013. The Navy then didn't have an option to get a PhD and it still doesn't today. The Army, Air Force, and Marines do. But not the Navy."[50]

He started looking for opportunities, and he found PMRI. "I spent about the next five years trying to convince my detailer to let me go, and they finally agreed," he says.[51]

He started at Purdue in January 2020 and finished his PhD in technology within three years.

"I wouldn't have been able to do it without the people at PMRI," Scott says. "Dr. Dietz, he really rolled out the red carpet for me when I first reached out to him to express an interest in coming to the program. I flew out for a day to tour the campus and he gave me the full walking tour, drove me around the campus, introduced me to a variety of professors to try to start identifying potential advisors [and] research advisors, and showed me all the different resources available on the campus. He really went out of his way to create an inviting atmosphere. I was considering other schools as well. But the support that PMRI was willing to provide was just really unmatched."[52]

After receiving his degree, he went to work in Washington, D.C., at DARPA. "That was a great transition back from academia into the Department of Defense with my PhD in technology," he says. "The research that I was doing is very relevant to the kind of work that DARPA does. DARPA is a science and technology organization in the military. I worked there as a fellow for three months, and now I will go back to my next assignment in the Navy in Virginia Beach."[53]

He is married and they have three young children. Due to the COVID-19 pandemic while he was studying at Purdue, Scott was able to do a lot of his work virtually from Virginia Beach, traveling back and forth to campus as needed. His wife and children remained in Virginia.

"Purdue was prepared for COVID more than most schools," Scott says. "It had all the infrastructure in place to go seamlessly with all the online learning systems."[54]

"At Purdue I learned a lot of really important skills that relate to professional research in general: how to formulate good questions, how to conduct research, how to find information, how to answer those questions, how to set up tests, how to collect information, how to evaluate information, both qualitative and quantitative analysis, and then how to communicate your results and your findings orally and in written forms."[55]

He also had an opportunity to teach a course at Purdue through a program titled FORCES. (See chapter 22 for more on the FORCES program.) The course was titled "Technology, Strategy, and War."

Scott had to make a five-year commitment to the Navy for the opportunity to be a PMRI fellow, but he plans a career in the service, so that works for him.

"The research I was doing at Purdue was very relevant to the military today," he says. "On all fronts, it was worth the time."[56]

Next: As PMRI offers active military officers incredible graduate opportunities, Purdue is expanding its national security technology research and has become a leading university in the United States in areas such as hypersonics, semiconductors, energetics, and more.

22

NATIONAL SECURITY TECHNOLOGY RESEARCH

To confront the challenges our nation faces today, we need people who understand the intersection of economics, diplomacy, emerging technology, and the sciences. We find these people at places like Purdue.

U.S. SECRETARY OF STATE ANTONY BLINKEN

In January 2013, Mitchell E. Daniels, Jr. ended his second term as governor of Indiana as one of the most popular public officials in the history of the state. Indiana governors can serve an unlimited number of years, but they can only serve two four-year terms consecutively.

Not yet sixty-four years old and still filled with ideas, enthusiasm, and goals, Daniels carefully considered his future as the end of his time as governor neared.

He considered running for President of the United States and picked up serious support, but in May 2011 decided against it. One year later, in June 2012, he was introduced as the next president of Purdue University, a school he called his "polestar" while serving as governor. His presidency would begin when his term as governor ended.

Mike Pence, who would be elected Vice President of the United States in 2016, succeeded Daniels as Governor of Indiana and was sworn into office in Indianapolis on January 14, 2013. That same afternoon, Daniels drove one hour north to West Lafayette and started work as the twelfth president of Purdue. One of his early initiatives began when he learned Purdue faculty did not have security clearances to do sensitive research with government entities. He set about to change that.

"Given the disciplines at which Purdue is excellent, I was surprised and puzzled that we weren't pursuing more and doing more research in national security,"

Daniels says. "It struck me as anomalous, given all our history, that we weren't doing more in this. When I got here, to my surprise, we had no security clearances, which is the first step toward doing any such work. So, we went to work on that."[1]

Dr. Daniel DeLaurentis, the director of Purdue's Institute for Global Security and Defense Innovation (i-GSDI), a professor of aeronautics and astronautics, and vice president for research institutes and centers in the Discovery Park District, was among those who proposed the national security clearances and has seen their impact on the university.

"Now when we need to do even more in hypersonics and energetic materials, we have the national security clearance and the ability to do these things," he says.[2] Much of the work is taking place in a multidisciplinary research area named Discovery Park launched in 2001 during the administration of former Purdue president Dr. Martin Jischke, and the Discovery Park District and Discovery Park Aerospace District expansions started by Daniels during his term as president.

Research, teaching, and partnerships at Purdue are a major part of the university's mission that reaches back to the Morrell Land Grant Act of 1862. The work impacts individual states, the nation as a whole, businesses, and industry. And students participating in these initiatives today will become leaders in research and development tomorrow, DeLaurentis says.

"It's the land-grant mission to produce the capabilities that are needed to defend the nation," he says. "When people approach us because of the unique capabilities we have to get the research done, with the left eye they're eyeing the research products and with the right eye, they're waiting for our students to graduate to get out there and do the magic.[3]

"As its mission to kick-start and accelerate Purdue defense and security activities came to a successful conclusion, the next steps are being picked up by PARI and the relevant research centers and institutes," DeLaurentis says.[4]

NEXT MOVES

As governor, Daniels launched programs and projects called "Major Moves," and at Purdue he launched initiatives called "Next Moves." Among the "Next Moves" announced in 2021 was an investment in a National Security and Technology Initiative. The national security clearances made the initiative possible. A Purdue announcement said, "U.S. leadership in advanced technology capabilities relative to its strategic rivals is narrowing, and swift action must be taken to reverse this trend to ensure long-term national security and economic competitiveness. Through the National Security and Technology Initiative, Purdue will work to address some of the greatest technology challenges facing the U.S. in four strategic areas: hypersonic and space vehicles; energetic materials and systems; cybersecurity; and secure microelectronics."[5]

Building on a long history of excellence in the four strategic areas, when Daniels stepped aside as president of Purdue on January 1, 2023, the University had already accomplished leadership among U.S. universities in national security research, education, and partnerships with industry, governments, and universities. Daniels was succeeded at Purdue by Dr. Mung Chiang who had served as Purdue's John A. Edwardson Dean of the College of Engineering and Executive Vice President for Strategic Initiatives. In his first months in office Chiang immediately addressed the University's progress in national security research, learning, and partnerships with governments, industry and other universities.

"We are located at the heart of the 'Silicon Heartland,' and Purdue has a long and proud tradition as a public land-grant institution in our country to serve students," Chiang said during a *Washington Post Live* interview on May 18, 2023. "We are now among the leading research universities in America, the largest undergrad STEM enrollment."[6]

One week earlier on the Purdue campus, Chiang had said that Purdue is the number one university in the nation in semiconductor research, education, and industrial partnerships.[7]

Chiang says Purdue's "Next Moves" will continue to guide the course of the University. "Part of my job as executive vice president for strategic initiatives was to work with many colleagues to help push strategic initiatives such as national security technologies," Chiang says. "We're very proud of what we've done with our students, faculty, and partners."[8]

PURDUE ENGINEERING

Much of the work in national security technology initiatives is being done in the College of Engineering, which marks its 150th anniversary in 2024.

"Purdue Engineering has had a history of military-related research for decades," says Dr. Arvind Raman, Purdue University's John A. Edwardson Dean of Engineering. "We started the Zucrow Labs [in 1948] that are very closely connected with a lot of needs in the defense sector and in many other areas. But I think what President Daniels's investments did was boost a few critical areas where we were world-class, where nobody could beat us. That helped us build teams that no one at the university level could compete with, such as our work in energetics, for example, which is all about explosives."[9]

The College of Engineering added more than one hundred faculty between 2012 and 2023. By 2023 the college had about 430 faculty. The hiring has been focused on building world-class teams. "We started hiring people in certain areas," Raman says. "We call them preeminent teams. Preeminent teams were funded from the engineering expansion that happened under President Daniels." The College of Engineering brought faculty to Purdue who were active leaders in some of the most exciting and promising areas of research. "Talent is everything," Raman says. "In hiring we make sure we have the best faculty. And I don't just mean paper-writing faculty. I mean it's people who are going to be the leaders who, when they see opportunities, they go out and get things, entrepreneurial people who are deep scholars, but also leaders. That has been key in our success."[10]

Nearly eleven thousand Purdue undergraduates major in engineering and nearly five thousand more students are studying for advanced degrees. Purdue has the largest college of engineering among top programs in the nation. In the 2023–24 *U.S. News & World Report* ranking of best engineering schools, Purdue was ranked fourth. It had more students than the first three schools– MIT, Stanford, and University of California, Berkeley—combined. Among its many accomplishments are the founding of the National Society of Black Engineers and the first School of Engineering Education.

"As we look ahead at national security technology, I can foresee there's going to be a lot happening," Raman says. "It all boils down to great people and creating opportunities for them. And we'll keep doing that."[11]

PURDUE SEMICONDUCTOR RESEARCH, EDUCATION, AND PARTNERSHIPS

Purdue has a long history in semiconductor research. Reaching back to the 1940s, Purdue University physicist Dr. Karl Lark-Horovitz was performing pioneering work in solid-state physics. His findings helped lead to invention of the transistor. In 1959, Purdue alumnus John (Mohamed) Atalla coinvented the MOSFET (metal–oxide–semiconductor field-effect transistor) at Bell Labs. Alumnus

George Scalise served as president of the Semiconductor Industry Association for fourteen years. In 1980, Mark Lundstrom received his PhD in electrical engineering from Purdue University and joined the university faculty. In 2024, he was the Don and Carol Scifres Distinguished Professor of Electrical and Computer Engineering and the inaugural Chief Semiconductor Officer. He has spent his career working in semiconductors.

The end of Daniels's term as Purdue's president and the first months of Chiang's presidency were filled with a head-spinning series of announcements in semiconductor research, education and partnerships.

- In May 2022, the university announced a Semiconductor Degrees Program, "a comprehensive set of innovative, interdisciplinary degrees and credentials in semiconductors and microelectronics."[12] It was the first comprehensive semiconductor degree program in the nation. Students rushed to sign up—almost twice as many as were expected for the first offerings.
- Also in May 2022, Purdue announced it was partnering with Indiana's Ivy Tech Community College to "provide collaborative educational opportunities for faculty and students in microelectronics and to explore ways to attract more talent to this area."[13]
- In June 2022, Purdue's College of Engineering announced it was partnering with Media Tek, Inc., and opening the company's first semiconductor chip design center on Purdue's West Lafayette campus.
- In July 2022, SkyWater Technology announced plans to open a $1.8 billion state-of-the-art semiconductor manufacturing facility in Purdue's Discovery Park District, with the goal of creating 750 new jobs within five years after opening the 600,000-square-foot facility. "SkyWater Technology is the only chip manufacturing company that's fully owned by the U.S., so it does a significant amount of work with the Department of Defense,"[14] Lundstrom said. In April 2024, SkyWater released its option on Purdue land, but said it remained "a valued partner with research opportunities in the works."[15]
- In April 2023, Purdue cosponsored the "CHIPS for America: Execute for Success 2023 Policy and Strategy Summit" in Washington, D.C. More than 250 participants from government, industry, and academia participated. The summit was continued in the spring of 2024.
- Also in April 2023, the university announced the "Purdue Computes" initiative, including a $100 million investment in semiconductor facilities. Phase

One was a $49 million upgrade to the twenty-year-old, 186,000-square-foot Birck Nanotechnology Center in Discovery Park. The center includes a 25,000-square-foot nanofabrication cleanroom. "Purdue is leading the charge in semiconductor research and education," Lundstrom said. "State-of-the-art facilities like the Birck Nanotechnology Center provide the foundation for new and exciting research in many facets of microelectronics and support our workforce development initiatives."[16] In 1962, Purdue created the first Department of Computer Science in the nation. Between 2023 and 2028, Computer Science, Computer Engineering, and related departments will add fifty new faculty. Moreover, as the U.S. government embraces AI as a national security tool, the Institute for Physical Artificial Intelligence will use Purdue's strengths in materials science, engineering, microelectronics, computer science, agriculture, and life sciences to solve some of the world's toughest challenges.

- In May 2023, Purdue entered into an international agreement with the government of India to advance workforce development, research and development, and industry partnerships in semiconductors.
- Also in May 2023, Purdue, the Indiana Economic Development Corporation, and imec, a Belgium-based research company working in the field of semiconductor development and applications, announced a five-year $10 million partnership. It will focus on semiconductor development and applications. An imec center will be opened in Purdue's Discovery Park District.
- And again in May 2023, Chiang went to Hiroshima, Japan, to a G7 Summit where he signed an international agreement with Micron, Tokyo Electron, and U.S. and Japanese universities to establish an UPWARDS Network for workforce advancement, research, and development in semiconductors. Micron and Tokyo Electron, the U.S. National Science Foundation, and the ten U.S. and Japanese universities together will invest more than $60 million in the five-year project. "Purdue is the leading American university in semiconductor talent, innovation and industry partnership," Chiang said during the signing ceremony. "We are excited to partner with the semiconductor companies and other institutions for semiconductor collaboration between the U.S. and Japan. We will also launch the Negishi Fellowship in addition to the UPWARDS Network program to strengthen such collaboration."[17] The fellowship is named for Ei-ichi Negishi, the late Purdue professor who won the 2010 Nobel Prize in chemistry. He was a Japanese citizen.

One of the biggest announcements came on April 3, 2024 when SK Hynix, Inc., announced plans to invest nearly $4 billion in an advanced packaging fabrication and research and development facility in the Purdue Research Park. "We are excited to build a state-of-the-art advanced packaging facility in Indiana," said SK Hynix CEO Kwak Noh-Jung. "We believe this project will lay the foundation for a new Silicon Heartland, a semiconductor ecosystem centered in the Midwest Triangle. This facility will create more than one thousand local, high-paying jobs and produce AI memory chips with unmatched capabilities, so that America can onshore more of its critical chip supply chain. We are grateful for the support of Gov. [Eric] Holcomb and the state of Indiana, of President Chiang at Purdue University, and of the broader community involved, and we look forward to expanding our partnership in the long run."[18]

"SK Hynix is the global pioneer and dominant market leader in memory chips for AI," Chiang said. "This transformational investment reflects our state and university's tremendous strength in semiconductors, hardware AI and development of the Hard-Tech Corridor. It is also a monumental moment for completing the supply chain of the digital economy in our country through the advanced packaging of chips. Located at Purdue Research Park, the largest facility of its kind at a U.S. university will grow and succeed through innovation."[19]

U.S. SENATOR TODD YOUNG AND THE CHIPS AND SCIENCE ACT OF 2022

United States Senator Todd Young (R-Indiana), a U.S. Naval Academy graduate, was an author of the federal 2022 CHIPS and Science Act. Among its provisions is $52 billion to increase domestic research and manufacturing of semiconductors in the United States. The CHIPS and Science Act was a combination of two efforts, funding for the previously enacted CHIPS for America Act and authorization included in the Endless Frontier Act which later merged with a number of other bills in the Senate and became known as the U.S. Innovation and Competition Act. Some of the initial ideas in the Endless Frontier Act were initiated by Keith Krach while serving as Under Secretary of State from 2019 to 2021. Krach was previously chairman of the Purdue Board of Trustees.

Young says the United States was a leader in semiconductor research and production but gave up that role when American companies began sending that work to other nations. The CHIPS and Science Act is focused on bringing production back to the United States.

"Not only is our modern economy dependent on these computer chips, just about everything with an on and off switch these days contains computer chips, many of which are made in Taiwan," Young says. "The highest end computer chips, those that have very high processing power and can be found in our military hardware like our weapons and systems including jets and radars, and on our nuclear missile submarines, those are made in Taiwan, and we need to be able to reshore that capability. The Koreans have also entered the market at the high end, and today the leading-edge producers are located in South Korea and Taiwan. Now [with the CHIPS and Science Act] we have an incentive to get some producers to locate on American soil. I think one of the things we have learned is that having the ability to manufacture high-value critical components like computer chips, which are necessary to run a modern economy, to assemble automobiles, to help make our pacemakers work and just about everything in addition to our weapon systems, you have to maintain that [manufacturing] ability. Otherwise, you risk a dependency on other countries, some of whom you cannot trust, or some of whom may see their manufacturing or distribution capacity interrupted during times of crisis, like a global pandemic."[20]

Young has been on the Purdue campus to see first-hand the University's work in semiconductors.

"I'm really excited about it," he says. "Since we passed CHIPS and Science, they've really enhanced the course offerings and souped up the dedicated program through their collaboration with various universities and they're unique interaction with Ivy Tech. Purdue is just critical to most of these activities because of the nature of the scholarship and the training that occurs at Purdue."[21] In September 2022, Young joined U.S. Secretary of State Antony J. Blinken and Secretary of Commerce Gina Raimondo in a visit to campus focusing on Purdue's research and workforce development to restore U.S. leadership in semiconductor manufacturing.

"To confront the challenges our nation faces today, we need people who understand the intersection of economics, diplomacy, emerging technology, and the sciences," Blinken said after the tour. "We find these people at places like Purdue which bring together academia and the private sector to ensure that we can remain the world's innovation leader and standard setter. The groundbreaking work here and at institutions around the country is rooted in the recognition that foreign, economic, and domestic policy are inextricably linked and that domestic competitiveness, national security, and a strong middle class are mutually reinforcing."[22]

Secretary of Commerce Raimondo said, "Purdue's cutting-edge research and workforce development are at the forefront of helping us shape the future of innovation in America's semiconductor manufacturing industry. I'm excited to learn about the workforce pipelines Purdue is creating, including opportunities at all levels of industry. I'm excited to have met the students who are future leaders of America's semiconductor industry. The graduates from these programs—from PhDs to associate degree holders—will be at the forefront of innovation as we revitalize American manufacturing."[23]

Lundstrom is also excited about the teaching, research, and partnerships at Purdue. "Over the years [in the U.S.] we've outsourced more and more of the manufacturing," he says. "So now we have only ten percent of the actual manufacturing of chips. We're still very strong in various aspects of it. We're strong in the design of chips, we're strong in the tools that are inside these factories that build chips. But in the actual factories that manufacture the chips, we've outsourced more and more of that. I think COVID was kind of a wake-up call or a Sputnik moment. We learned how dangerous it is."[24]

HYPERSONIC RESEARCH

Hypersonic research at Purdue expands on work that started on campus in the 1980s and 1990s. Hypersonics refers to flight at or exceeding five times the speed of sound.

Chiang says Purdue has become the "epicenter" for hypersonic research and testing in the United States.

"It's important because hypersonics has been marked off as the number one priority in national security today," Daniels says. "Distressingly no one believes that we are qualitatively stronger than our adversaries in this area. So, we better get busy. And that's one reason that we've emphasized it here because we have some of the best people in the world. We've decided to have more of these people and add facilities and contribute where apparently it can matter most."[25]

Dr. Steven Schneider came to Purdue in 1989 after finishing his PhD at California Institute of Technology (Caltech). His research focus is in hypersonic and supersonic laminar-turbulent transition and low-disturbance wind tunnels and associated instrumentation.

During the Cold War between the United States and the Soviet Union, there was a great deal of research in hypersonics, sponsored mostly by the government. But with the end of the Cold War in the 1990s, that funding was cut.

"The budget at NASA and at the Defense Department for most research was cut by a factor of three at the end of the Cold War," Schneider says. "So, two-thirds of the work disappeared everywhere. It was hard everywhere. Companies were downsizing, everybody was downsizing, jobs were going away everywhere."[26]

Schneider was able to continue his work through some funding from the Air Force Office of Scientific Research and from Boeing. It was used to build a Mach 6 quiet wind tunnel.

"I had money from the Air Force Office of Scientific Research continuously. Actually, I still do," Schneider says. "It was never a lot of money. And I worked at least a couple of weeks almost every summer for free because there wasn't enough money."[27]

Some people advised him to get out of this research. But others, experienced people with a longer vision, told him the country would need this one day. The word "hypersonic" even fell out of use for a time and was replaced by "high speed."

"Hypersonics is in Purdue's DNA," Chiang says. "Leaders such as Steve Schneider—he's been doing hypersonics research in our Mach 6 wind tunnel throughout the past decades, even when it was not a hot topic."[28]

Finally, the U.S. realized it trailed Russia and China in hypersonic research, and funding began again. The university has added researchers in hypersonics and Schneider has moved into a senior technical expert role.

In 2021, China tested a weapon flying 15,000 miles an hour "that could reach anywhere on earth in less than an hour," according to *The Wall Street Journal*. "[Hypersonic] weapons can attack with extreme speed, be launched from great distances, and evade most air defenses," the *Journal* reported. "They can carry conventional explosives or nuclear warheads. China and Russia have them ready to use. The U.S. doesn't. For more than sixty years, the U.S. has invested billions of dollars in dozens of programs to develop its own version of the technology. Those efforts have either ended in failure or been canceled before having a chance to succeed."[29]

In 2016 Dr. Mark Lewis, a former U.S. deputy undersecretary of defense, was part of a National Academies panel warning that Russia and China were developing hypersonic weapons. In response, the Army, Navy, and Air Force stepped up work in hypersonics.

"We are in a race," Lewis told the *Journal.*

In 2021, the university established the Purdue Applied Research Institute (PARI) as part of its Next Moves initiative. The center has a particular focus on national security as well as economic and food security. Among accomplishments since its founding, the institute has launched the Hypersonics Advanced Manufacturing Technology Center (HAMTC), as well as Infrastructure Research and Innovative Solutions (IRIS), "which focuses on advanced infrastructure and building systems for defense, civil and energy applications," according to a Purdue news release.[30] In April 2023, Mark Lewis was named chief executive officer of the Purdue Applied Research Institute.

"Mark Lewis is one of the most prominent leaders in defense research in our country," Chiang says. "He brings the perfect combination of academia excellence, industry experience and government leadership. With this transformational hire, PARI is ready to grow rapidly to become the most impactful emergent organization for national security and defense in the United States. Hundreds of researchers will be recruited in the coming years to win dozens of crucial projects, substantially elevating excellence at scale at Purdue."[31]

"As part of Purdue Next Moves, we've put together some brand-new facilities including facilities for hypersonics," says Dr. Karen Plaut, Purdue's executive vice president for research. "We also have the energetics group and some specialized equipment there we put together and then the refresh of the Birck Nanotechnology Center specifically for microelectronics and quantum science. So, there have been many improvements worth hundreds of millions of dollars between all those facilities that we've invested in to really have the cutting-edge tools to meet the needs."[32]

During several years before and after announcing the "next moves" for national security technology, Purdue made a number of announcements focusing on advances in hypersonic research.

WORLD'S FIRST MACH 8 QUIET WIND TUNNEL

In February 2020, Purdue announced it had received a $5.9 million contract from the Air Force Research Laboratory to develop the world's first Mach 8 quiet wind tunnel.

"This award is one of a growing number of large-scale research programs enabled by Purdue's ongoing commitment to national security research and the efforts of its Institute for Global Security and Defense Innovation," said Dr. Theresa Mayer, at that time Purdue's executive vice president for research and partnerships. "Purdue has a long track record as a university leader in national defense and is establishing itself as a hub of hypersonic capabilities research."[33]

At the time of the announcement, Purdue was home to one of only two Mach 6 wind tunnels in the United States.

HYPERSONICS AND APPLIED RESEARCH FACILITY

Purdue announced plans for a $41 million, 65,000-square-foot Hypersonics and Applied Research Facility in July 2021. The facility will be home to the world's only Mach 8 quiet wind tunnel and a hypersonic pulse shock tunnel.

According to a Purdue news release, "The tunnels recreate different scenarios such as spacecraft reentry or missile flight through the atmosphere as well as replicating unique engine conditions for extremely high-speed propulsion."[34]

The hypersonic pulse shock tunnel is a donation from the Northrop Grumman corporation. The facility is in Purdue's Discovery Park Aerospace District.

HYPERSONICS ADVANCED MANUFACTURING TECHNOLOGY CENTER

In February 2022, Purdue expanded its hub of hypersonic research with a new center focused on developing high-temperature materials and creating new manufacturing processes to build and join these materials.

Hypersonic speeds create extremely hot temperatures, causing surface-level reactions that break down materials.

"The Hypersonics Advanced Manufacturing Technology Center will be a single location at Purdue for industry partners, including GE Additive, Dynetics, Lockheed Martin, Aerojet Rocketdyne, GE Edison Works, Boeing, and several small businesses, to work on materials and manufacturing innovations and provide access to testing capabilities that would enable the U.S. to overtake near-peer adversaries in the field," according to a Purdue news release.[35]

HIGH-SPEED PROPULSION LABORATORY

In April 2022, the Purdue Board of Trustees approved a high-speed propulsion laboratory that outpaces every other university in the nation, "putting Purdue's testing capabilities on scale with large defense contractor facilities," according to a news release.[36] The lab, in the Discovery Park District, has testing capabilities at extreme temperature and pressure conditions.

The $73 million, 55,000-square-foot lab will enable testing for the Hypersonics Advanced Manufacturing Technology Center.

"With the Purdue faculty and significant input from industry and government partners, we designed the High-Speed Propulsion Lab to fill a testing capability gap that exists between fundamental research and test and evaluation at full-scale," said Scott Meyer, managing director of Maurice J. Zucrow Laboratories. "We are essentially expanding the scale and capacity of research and development experiments to actual flight systems."[37]

Concurrent with announcement of the High-Speed Propulsion Laboratory, Purdue announced a ten-year, $75 million research and testing agreement with Rolls-Royce.

"Purdue has become the epicenter of hypersonic research and testing in the U.S.," Chiang said at the announcement. "We are excited across three tracks: first, our own investment for federal and industry projects, such as the wind tunnel and manufacturing facility announced in 2021, and the high-speed propulsion facility in 2022 that Rolls Royce will be able to use; second, the private sector's investment to grow its presence in the Discovery Park District at Purdue; and third, a nonprofit consortium of industry members for ground testing hosted at Purdue."[38] The testing and research agreement focuses on gas turbine technology and electrical and digital technology.

STRATOLAUNCH ADVANCED PROGRAMS OFFICE

Stratolaunch LLC and Purdue announced in January 2023 a partnership to accelerate the time needed to design, build, test, and fly hypersonic vehicles. The company established the Stratolaunch Advanced Programs Office in the Convergence Center in the Discovery Park District.

According to a University news release, "Stratolaunch and Purdue will leverage the University's world-class multidisciplinary hypersonic design methods, ground test facilities, faculty, staff, and students to anchor ground simulations. By combining this capability with Stratolaunch's paid prototyping fabrication, flight test service, as well as hypersonic flight test data from the Talon-A, the integrated team will develop methodologies to accelerate the design to fly time of hypersonic systems."[39] Stratolaunch is a Mojave, California company with a mission to accelerate hypersonic technology.

MAURICE ZUCROW LABS

Founded in 1948 by Purdue professor Maurice Zucrow and later named for him, the Zucrow Labs twenty-four-acre campus, part of Purdue's Discovery Park District, is the world's largest academic propulsion lab, featuring world-class research in combustion, turbines, compressors, energetic materials, hypersonics, aerodynamics, fluid mechanics, and more.

Zucrow was born in Kiev, Russia in 1899, four years before the Wright brothers' first successful flight at Kitty Hawk, North Carolina. His family fled violent antisemitism and in 1915 arrived in the United States. He studied at Harvard University where he graduated magna cum laude in 1922 with the school's first bachelor's degree in engineering. He received Purdue's first PhD in engineering in 1928. The entire faculty was present for his oral exam. With his new degree, he went to work in private industry focusing on gas turbines and rocket propulsion.

He played a key role in the development of the first U.S. gas turbine, built by the Elliott Company in 1942. Zucrow worked at Aerojet during World War II and helped develop the JATO (jet-assisted take-off) rocket that was used by seaplanes taking off in adverse conditions. He also taught a course in jet propulsion theory to aircraft industry engineers.[40]

In 1946, Purdue recruited him back to campus to lead jet propulsion education and research.

In his book *The Rocket Lab, Maurice Zucrow, Purdue University, and America's Race to Space*, Purdue history professor Michael G. Smith calls Zucrow "a true pioneer of rocket engineering. . . . He taught the country's first university courses in jet propulsion during the Second World War and was the first leading engineer afterward to confirm the possibilities of rocket travel beyond Earth. He established the first university laboratory in the U.S. dedicated to education and research in jet propulsion and rocketry. He published the world's first textbook on jet propulsion and rocketry. . . .In 1952 after five years of serving on the Pentagon's Panel on Propulsion and Fuels, he joined an official committee to advocate for the Atlas intercontinental ballistic missile."[41]

Zucrow retired from Purdue in 1966. Purdue's then president Dr. Frederick Hovde, himself named "Rocket Man" by *Time* magazine in 1946, called Zucrow one of the nation's leading rocket engineers. Zucrow died in 1975.

In 2023, Dr. Robert Lucht, Purdue's Ralph and Bettye Bailey Distinguished Professor of Mechanical Engineering, serves as director of Zucrow Laboratories. Lucht says research funded by agencies such as the Air Force Office of Scientific Research and the Office of Naval Research takes place at Zucrow.

"There's a variety of research projects here by different faculty members that are associated with the military or national security," he says. "There's a lot of research on energetic materials, which is almost all funded by the military, and there's work on advanced propulsion concepts, which is funded by different companies. Some of the companies are more interested in commercial applications, but there are other companies that are interested in advanced engines and propulsion concepts that would have military applications."[42]

RAY W. HERRICK LABORATORIES

Founded in 1957, Purdue's 83,000-square-foot Ray W. Herrick Laboratories supports world-class mechanical engineering research with a focus on sustainable buildings and transportation, perception-based engineering, clean water, and indoor air quality. Researchers from more than forty countries do their work at the Herrick Labs.

Dr. Jeffrey Rhoads was director of Herrick Labs from 2019 to 2022, when he became the inaugural executive director of the Purdue Institute for National Security. While at Purdue he helped forge partnerships between the university and the Department of Defense, including studying energetic materials with the Army and becoming a regional research hub for the Air Force Research Laboratory.

Dr. Gregory Shaver became director of Herrick Labs in 2022. He has received the Purdue Spira Award for fostering excellence in commercial or defense product realization. Research conducted at Herrick Labs for the Department of Defense includes the exploration of refrigerants that are sustainable and safe to operate in combat conditions.

PURDUE ENERGETICS RESEARCH CENTER

With a university history in energetic materials that reaches back to the mid-twentieth century, the Purdue Energetics Research Center (PERC) is a world leader in the development of superior explosives, propellants, and pyrotechnics. Its mission statement is "To drive the field of energetic materials forward through our ideas, our students, and our partnerships."[43]

In late spring of 2023, it hosted its third biennial summit, hosting more than one hundred experts in energetic materials from government, industry, and academia. Attendees came from eight universities, fifteen government or military agencies, and twenty-one companies. Three Department of Defense laboratories and the Office of the Under Secretary of Defense for Acquisition and Sustainment showcased their energetics research agendas at the event.[44]

ENHANCED OIL RECOVERY (EOR) LABORATORY

While advancement in new energy sources and technologies progresses, more than eighty percent of today's global energy supply originates from reliable and venerable fossil fuels, including more than a third from oil alone.[45] Throughout the twenty-first century, oil will continue to be a significant source of energy and chemical feedstocks for other evolving industries in a dynamic global economy. With the continuing endeavor of identifying and securing new petroleum reserves, maximizing hydrocarbon recovery from known reservoirs is crucial for energy security.

Since 2014, Purdue's Enhanced Oil Recovery (EOR) laboratory, in partnership with Pioneer Oil Company of Vincennes, Indiana, has been addressing this economic growth need through advanced research. This multidisciplinary group of faculty, staff, and students utilize Purdue's chemical, mechanical, and materials engineering expertise while also leveraging resources in the Department of Chemistry and the Department of Earth, Atmospheric and Planetary Sciences to develop targeted chemical and computational solutions to be directly implemented in a safe and environmentally conscious manner in the Illinois Basin and across the greater United States. Dr. Cliff Johnston was the inaugural director of the EOR laboratory before Chemical Engineering's Dr. Nate Schultheiss became the director in 2017.

The EOR laboratory was established at Purdue University because a need existed for oil and gas operators to have access to fundamental research coupled with applied understanding to produce field-deployable solutions. This need continues to this day, and the EOR Laboratory is an excellent example of Purdue's Deliberate Innovation initiative that utilizes institutional expertise to solve complex industrial problems, Schultheiss says. The EOR Laboratory provides technical services for Illinois Basin companies and conducts research projects that bring the latest technology to hydrocarbons as feedstocks and bridge energy for the future generations.

PURDUE CENTER FOR EDUCATION AND RESEARCH IN INFORMATION ASSURANCE AND SECURITY

Purdue's Center for Education and Research in Information Assurance and Security (CERIAS) formed in 1998, is "the world's foremost interdisciplinary academic center for cyber and cyber-physical systems; [with] more than a hundred researchers addressing issues of security, privacy, resiliency, trusted electronics, autonomy, and explainable artificial intelligence."[46] CERIAS involves researchers from multiple Purdue campuses, seven colleges and twenty-five departments.

"CERIAS has been in operation for twenty-five years, and the field has advanced considerably in that time, in no small part as a result of efforts by our students, faculty, and partners," said Dr. Eugene Spafford, director emeritus of CERIAS and professor of computer science. "We're now looking ahead to what's next—to make computing even safer for everyone."[47]

INSTITUTE FOR GLOBAL SECURITY AND DEFENSE INNOVATION

The Institute for Global Security and Defense Innovation [i-GSDI] was launched in December of 2016—before the "Next Moves" national security technologies initiative was announced. "The institute works with Purdue's other centers and institutes to research areas such as advanced instrumentation, nanotechnology, social and behavioral sciences, big data analytics, and simulations to deliver integrated systems solutions to the nation's security and defense community," according to a university news release.[48] Its mission is "to bring timely, responsive and transformative solutions to the most pressing security and defense challenges facing the nation and the world."[49]

"We live in a dangerous world in which we must continuously invent more, discover more, and innovate more than those who oppose us, and be able to deliver those technologies quickly into the hands of the people who use them to protect the rest of us," then President Daniels said in announcing the institute. "Purdue is well-positioned to do this. We are accomplished at not only discoveries in science, engineering, and technology, but delivering those discoveries to the market quickly. We think we can do the same for national security and defense."[50]

PURDUE HOMELAND SECURITY INSTITUTE

The Purdue Homeland Security Institute was established following the terrorist attacks of September 11, 2001, as an interdisciplinary center within Discovery Park. Its charter is to "help our nation prevent, protect, respond, and recover from any threat or action taken against our homeland." Dr. Alok Chaturvedi became the founding director in 2003. Under his leadership, the center developed a novel software for researchers, called Synthetic Environment for Analysis and Simulation (SEAS), which has had a national impact through its annual Measured Response exercises.

Today, the Purdue Homeland Security Institute is part of the Purdue Polytechnic Institute, with Dr. J. Eric Dietz serving as its director. He is also the director of the Purdue Military Research Institute and a professor of computer and information technology. The Institute adheres to "the principles outlined in the National Response Framework," working daily to identify and address the myriad homeland security challenges our nation faces. Utilizing the power of interdisciplinary discovery, learning, and engagement at Purdue University, the Institute applies this knowledge across the state of Indiana and the nation, according to its website.

GRAHAM COOKS AND PUBLIC SAFETY RESEARCH USING MASS SPECTROMETRY

Dr. Graham Cooks is one of the world's one hundred most highly cited chemists.[51] He has been doing research at Purdue since 1971, and during that time he has served as major professor to 156 PhD graduates. His research group works on mass spectrometry, an instrumental method that is widely used for chemical analysis across the fields of environmental science, drug discovery, fundamental biology, earth and atmospheric science, and space science. Highlights of the work of this group include building new types of mass spectrometers, introducing new methods of making ions and of characterizing them, performing accelerated chemical synthesis in microdroplets, and softly landing and collecting ions to make new compounds and new materials.[52]

This work was driven by the desire to simplify and speed up chemical analysis, a passion Graham developed during his PhD work in South Africa in the 1960s, where he extracted chemicals from trees and then performed months of tedious separation before obtaining tiny amounts of impure chemicals. The desire for speed and simplicity led to tandem mass spectrometry (MS/MS), a method in which complex samples are ionized, separated using a first stage of MS, then a second stage is used to characterize fragment ions generated after the first separation stage. This methodology for complex mixture analysis, now very widely used throughout mass spectrometry, was first described in Purdue publications in the mid-1970s, as summarized in the journal *Analytical Chemistry*.[53]

Increased speed of analysis is achieved by examining complex materials directly without prior work-up. Most real-world samples are complex mixtures of compounds, such as environmental samples, forensic residues, biofluids, and bioagents. Concerns regarding public health and public safety concerns are best met by identification of such materials quickly at the site of need, whether this be the scene of an accident, a crime scene, or materials used in a terrorist attack. Immediate action requires fast on-site analysis, and mass spectrometry is the preferred choice for its sensitivity, universal applicability, and the specificity of the chemical information that it provides. On-site analysis requires a portable system. The first MS/MS instrument featured a half-ton magnet and an array of electronics and vacuum equipment that filled a small room. It was definitely not portable! This led to two decades of work building smaller instruments, culminating in the creation of a battery-operated system which weighed 4 kg and had MS/MS capabilities.[54]

Along the way to this development, several companies were spun out of the research group, most notably Griffin Analytical Systems, later part of FLIR and currently part of Teledyne but still in West Lafayette, employing some fifty people and building mass spectrometers under government contracts.

More recent work in the Cooks group has involved ionization from small paper triangles, known as paper spray ionization,[55] a method that works well for point-of-care analysis of single drops of blood to quantify therapeutic drugs as well detect overdose cases. In another ambient ionization method, known by the acronym DESI, one simply sprays droplets of solvent onto the sample in the open air to form ions which are sucked into the mass spectrometer for analysis.[56] This method is well-suited to the study of large numbers of samples in times of less than one second per sample. For example, 6,144 samples of nanogram size can be examined in an hour. This high throughput method is being commercialized because it provides analytical information, but can also be used to generate new compounds and test the biological activity of these new compounds. These are key steps in pharmaceutical drug discovery: they transform the mass spectrometer from an instrument for analysis to an instrument for synthesis. Examples of interest include the chemical modification of existing compounds—for example, the opioid rescue medicine naloxone—to increase the analgesic function and decrease the tendency to addiction. Finally, the combined synthesis and analysis capabilities of the mass spectrometer extend to the detection of chemical agents and well as research aimed at discovering antidotes to nerve agents.

ADVANCING ARMY MODERNIZATION PRIORITIES THROUGH COLLABORATIVE ENERGETIC MATERIALS RESEARCH

In August 2020, the U.S. Army announced an $8 million joint project with Purdue in sustainable energetic materials research. The funds were authorized by Congress with a potential investment of up to $24 million.

An Army news release stated, "The project includes research in the area of modeling and simulations, energetic materials synthesis and scale-up, additive manufacturing, environmental sustainment and novel characterization methods for energetic materials."[57]

EXPANSION OF ROLLS-ROYCE IN PURDUE AEROSPACE DISTRICT

An agreement between Rolls-Royce, Purdue University, and the Purdue Research Foundation to expand Rolls-Royce's presence and work in the Aerospace District was announced in August 2021.

"The new test facilities will be used to develop high-altitude and hybrid-electric engines to power the next generation of U.S. military aircraft," according to a Purdue news release. "Rolls-Royce West Lafayette will be developed through a multimillion-dollar investment from the research foundation, Purdue, and Rolls-Royce North America."[58]

In April 2022, Rolls-Royce announced it would spend $204 million to build two new facilities at Purdue and to expand another. "This is an exciting story," Chiang says. "In fact, it's three stories. One is that Rolls Royce has decided to expand substantially its own facilities here in the Discovery Park District at Purdue. That's their own facilities, their own resources, and their own employees. We're very grateful for that. Many other companies these days are choosing us. Two, they are working with us on research. They actually also signed a ten-year agreement, which is the largest we've ever had in Purdue history with a single company to do research and testing with our professors and students. And third, they are a leading partner with us in creating a national nonprofit consortium in a hypersonic ground test center. So, there are actually three different stories going on. They are all involving Rolls-Royce as a great partner."[59]

SAAB

In May 2019, the Sweden-based global defense and security company Saab announced that Purdue's Discovery Park Aerospace District would be the location for its expansion in the U.S. aerospace sector. Saab's $37 million facility opened in the fall of 2021 and is the site for domestic production of the company's contribution to the Boeing T-7A Red Hawk trainer program. It also supports Saab's collaboration with Purdue in research and development in autonomy, artificial intelligence, and advanced manufacturing.

The U.S. Air Force plans to purchase 351 jets from Boeing in a first phase. Saab is a partner and supplier to Boeing in the project. The Boeing T-7A will help train Air Force pilots for generations. Saab is expected to hire up to three hundred employees for the facility including assemblers, engineers, system administrators, and more.

When the facility was announced in 2019, Daniels said, "Purdue's strong history in aircraft research and development makes Saab's choice a natural fit. But the even tighter fit is with our Discovery Park District concept. Saab's investment will bring more cutting-edge research partnerships for our faculty, more high-value employment and internship opportunities for our graduates, and more jobs and economic vitality for our neighbors."[60] Daniels said that by 2021, Saab and Purdue had at least five research projects on campus.

The T-7A Red Hawk is named to honor the Tuskegee Airmen, African American Army aviators who fought in World War II. They painted their planes with a red tail.

"Saab and Rolls-Royce are among our most important corporate partners in advancing manufacturing [and] in advancing aerospace," Chiang says.[61]

PURDUE PARTNERS WITH AIR FORCE RESEARCH LABORATORY (AFRL)

Purdue was also recently named the lead Midwest partner in a research and development pilot initiative with the Air Force Research Laboratory.

The announcement in February 2022, naming Purdue the Air Force Research Lab Regional Research Hub—Midwest, means the university will be involved in developing a science and technology ecosystem in fifteen states. It involves at least fifteen universities and about fifty industrial partners. Cornell University leads the mid-Atlantic regional research hub and will work together with Purdue on associated projects.

According to an Air Force Research Lab news release, "The Regional Hub Network at Purdue is dedicated to developing strong relationships between Air Force Research Lab scientists and engineers and partners to address defense-related issues—a collaboration that will provide access to valuable resources as well as seedling funding for projects. The regional research hubs will also integrate stakeholders, encouraging science and technology exchanges and driving innovation. [The] Air Force Research Lab will then gain access to new technologies and ideas that lets it accelerate the translation of science and technology to the warfighter and commercial markets. This brings significant benefits to Air Force Research Lab, the Air Force [AFRL], and the Defense Department."[62]

The Hub officially opened in April 2023. "Purdue is proud to play a lead role in this unique program by the AFRL," Chiang says. "This network headquartered at our university will serve the entire Midwest region and bring together universities, industry, and government in innovating hypersonic, energetics, and microelectronics. Together, these efforts will make our country safer and stronger through impactful research."[63]

KRACH INSTITUTE FOR TECH DIPLOMACY

On April 5, 2022, government, business, academic, and civil society leaders attended a ceremony officially opening Purdue's Krach Institute for Tech Diplomacy. It was cofounded by Keith Krach, a 2022 Nobel Peace Prize nominee and past Chairman of the Purdue Board of Trustees, along with Purdue's president Mung Chiang.

"The nonpartisan Krach Institute for Tech Diplomacy is the world's first and only institution focused on Tech Statecraft, a new model of transformational diplomacy that integrates high-tech strategies with foreign policy tools and national security to ensure trusted technology is used to advance freedom," according to a Purdue news release. "The Krach Institute for Tech Diplomacy leverages Purdue University's strength in innovation, deep expertise in technology, and global prowess in educating transformational leaders, combined with its members' track record of building market-leading high-tech companies, onshoring strategic supply chains, and building global trust networks."[64]

"My focus will be on harnessing our three most powerful areas of competitive advantage by strengthening our partnerships with friends and allies, leveraging the innovation and resources of the private sector, and amplifying the moral high ground of our democratic trust principles to advance peace and prosperity," Krach said.[65]

In Washington, D.C., Krach asked Chiang to join his team and they created the "Trust Principle" doctrine "to defend against technological authoritarianism, safeguard global economic security, preserve democracy in Taiwan, and protect human rights."[66] A 2022 *Forbes* article explained: "Krach's 'Trust Principle' is based on democratic values. These include respect for the rule of law, property, press, human rights, national sovereignty, labor and the environment, and standards for transparency, integrity, and reciprocity. The 'Trust Principle' is the new basis for twenty-first century international relations. It stands as a peaceful alternative and antidote to Russia's and China's 'Power Principle,' a geopolitical framework rooted in brute power, coercion, and intimidation."[67]

NSWC CRANE AND PURDUE SIGN EDUCATIONAL PARTNERSHIP AGREEMENT AMENDMENT

The Naval Surface Warfare Center, Crane Division (NSWC Crane) in Crane, Indiana states its mission "is to deliver innovative solutions and readiness to the nation and its warfighters through application of our technical capabilities." It has 3,800 employees and 2,500 of them are scientists, engineers, and technicians.

Purdue has a long and active partnership with NSWC Crane. On February 21, 2023, Purdue and NSWC signed a partnership to ease and encourage even more collaborations. The Educational Partnership Agreement amendment "is a technology transfer agreement between a defense laboratory and an educational institution to encourage and enhance study in scientific disciplines at all levels of education," according to an NSWC Crane news release.[68]

"At no point in NSWC Crane's eighty-two-year history has there been greater collaboration with Purdue University; today our collaborations cover the full breadth of NSWC Crane's mission areas: strategic missions, electronic warfare and expeditionary warfare," said Dr. Kyle Werner, NSWC Crane Deputy Technical Director. "It is our aim to further expand this strategic partnership in support of emerging technologies central to our National Defense Strategy. This Educational Partnership Agreement aligns with the Department of Defense mission to inspire, cultivate, and develop exceptional STEM talent through a continuum of opportunities to enrich our current and future DoD workforce poised to tackle evolving defense technological challenges."[69]

Purdue will benefit from the facilities, expertise, and research opportunities at NSWC Crane. "Purdue and NSWC Crane are building an enduring partnership focused on national security," said Plaut, Executive Vice President for Research at Purdue. "This educational partnership agreement enables us to work together in new ways and mobilizes the strengths of both NSWC Crane and Purdue for the national good."[70]

An example of the agreement is "NSWC Crane designating a liaison to Purdue to collaborate specifically on National Security Innovation Network opportunities. NSWC Crane personnel can teach science courses or assist in the development of courses and materials, and NSWC Crane can involve Purdue faculty and students in its research projects," according to the NSWC Crane news release.[71]

"The amendment of the Educational Partnership Agreement empowers us to work together in new ways, allowing Purdue University increased awareness of DoD challenges and enabling us to share resources to enhance student and faculty opportunities through NSWC Crane and [the] National Security Innovation Network," said Glenn Berger, NSWC Crane's Purdue liaison. "Through this agreement, we're able to leverage the goodness of both organizations to help us each achieve our organizational goals."[72]

In 2023 NSWC Crane had five active Cooperative Research and Development Agreements with Purdue. Three members of the Purdue faculty were acting as temporary faculty at NSWC Crane. NSWC Crane is a Purdue Cyber Apprenticeship provider.[73]

In September 2023, officials from Purdue, the Purdue Applied Research Institute, and the Purdue Research Foundation announced a permanent presence at WestGate Academy in Odon, Indiana, adjacent to NSWC Crane, focusing on national security, defense, and semiconductors. Purdue@Crane is focusing on hypersonics, energetic materials, and trusted microelectronics.

"Today marks a momentous milestone and turns a new chapter in the collaboration between Purdue and Crane," said Purdue University president Mung Chiang. "This new strategic partnership with the most important defense presence in our state brings excellence at scale to deliver solutions for national security research. With one of the nation's largest and highly ranked STEM programs, Purdue is excited to become a permanent neighbor and dedicated partner with NSWC Crane. As America's leading university in semiconductor workforce and innovation, we are also looking forward to the new semiconductor ecosystem at WestGate Foundry 1."[74]

U.S. Representative Jim Baird, from Indiana's Fourth Congressional District (in which West Lafayette is located) called it an important step. "This kind of thing with Purdue, with the (Purdue Applied) Research Institute . . . all of that ties with America and the importance of protecting this country," Baird said.[75]

PURDUE@DC

In April 2023, Chiang announced an initiative to bring the University's strengths in national security, tech development, semiconductor talent, and the C-SPAN Archives to Washington, D.C.

"As the most consequential public university in America, Purdue has a special responsibility to bring all that Boilermakers have to offer to the capital," Chiang said. "Through Purdue@DC, we will both strengthen the impact of existing programs in D.C. and deploy new ones that bring many more faculty and students to national public service."[76]

Purdue@DC will be the D.C. home to Purdue's semiconductor and microelectronics program, the Krach Institute for Tech Diplomacy at Purdue, Purdue Policy Research Institute, and Purdue's federal relations team.

"In addition, to building a stronger talent pipeline from Purdue to the nation's capital, the C-SPAN Boilers Go to D.C. program will grow in scale and in scope, connecting D.C.-based alumni, as well as government and agency partners, with current students and faculty, providing internship, networking, and engagement opportunities. The program is designed to help students prepare for a successful career after graduation. All colleges, schools, departments, institutes, and centers at Purdue West Lafayette will be able to propose activities in our nation's capital," a Purdue news release said.[77]

C-SPAN was founded by Purdue graduate and Lafayette native Brian Lamb. The Purdue Brian Lamb School of Communications is named in his honor.

FORCES

- "A comprehensive overview of the U.S. Strategic Petroleum Reserve located on the Texas and Louisiana Gulf Coasts."
- "Does International Trade Lead to Conflict?"
- "World War II teaches us that the Ukraine war may continue for some time."

These are just a few examples of reports coming from the Purdue University FORCES initiative, housed in the College of Liberal Arts and created in collaboration with Discovery Park and the Institute for Global Security and Defense Innovation (i-GSDI).

FORCES is a play on the four "s" words at the heart of the initiative: security, strategy, and social systems.

It was founded by Dr. Sorin Adam Matei, associate dean for research and graduate education in Purdue's College of Liberal Arts and a professor of communication in the Brian Lamb School of Communication. It was started with the support of the Justin S. Morrill Dean of the College of Liberal Arts, David A. Reingold.

"FORCES is a research accelerator created in the College of Liberal Arts to combine social science, data science, and military science in new and exciting ways to produce new analytic tools, visualization tools, and simulation tools that can help us better understand military operations past, present, and future," Matei says. "This is at the heart of the project. It's a data-centric project, and its goal is to gain new insights on how military operations are conducted, flow, succeed, or fail."[78]

FORCES was started in 2019, and advances the national security and technology initiative named as one of the "Next Moves" in Purdue research. "We've aligned ourselves with it," Matei says. "We thought that this would be a good opportunity for those of us in liberal arts to do new work in this space."[79]

While FORCES works with both graduate and undergraduate students, there is a focus on undergraduates. "We've involved up to twenty undergraduate students so far, combining a variety of talents," Matei says. "Some of them are computer scientists, some of them are engineers, some of them are virtual-reality builders. Some of them are political scientists. Without the talent of our undergraduate students, we wouldn't have gotten as far as we did."[80]

During its first academic year, FORCES created a speaker series for undergraduate and graduate students; a course for undergraduate and graduate students focused on technology, war, and strategy; funding opportunities for research and learning in strategy, security, and social systems; and interdisciplinary partnerships around strategy, security, social systems research, scholarship, and instruction.

The central project in 2023 is called BattleFlow. "It's a simulation engine," Matei says. "You input the initial conditions of a battle and then you can predict the outcome."[81]

According to the BattleFlow website, "The method can simulate any military conflict between military units of a defined size and force. The model predicts where all units will go, both as individual units but also as members of greater units. The model estimates how much offensive or defensive power the units will use and with what effect on the opposing force, while considering physical [terrestrial, maritime, or air] obstacles or adverse phenomena. Furthermore, the model depletes the opposing forces proportional to their force projection abilities. The model applies to all combatants engaged in an operation, equally, regardless of side."[82]

It can be used to analyze historic or future battles. Historical battles it has been used to analyze include General George Pickett's charge at Gettysburg during the U.S. Civil War and the D-Day landing at Omaha Beach during World War II.

"It can be a planning aid or a training aid," Matei says, "You arrange what the actual problem will be, arrange the forces on the map, you give orders, and then you press the button and the results will say—your solution is correct; you have a fifty or sixty percent chance of winning. Or—no, your solution is incorrect; you have a ten percent chance of winning."[83]

The outreach director and the history research expert for FORCES is Robert Kirchubel, who earned a PhD in modern European history at Purdue and is a retired Army Lieutenant Colonel who served across eighteen time zones as an armor officer during the Cold War. He teaches numerous courses on world wars and defense and security policy at Purdue.

"We began working together on BattleFlow with the World War II 'Eastern Front' battle of Smolensk, USSR, summer 1941," Kirchubel says. "We wanted to depict military operations as a continuous motion [flow], not just one line that's a three-inch-long arrow on a page of paper representing one hundred miles over a week, or not a map-per-day booklet like what you used to flip from a Cracker Jack prize. With this information digitized, scholars could also apply research tools to it, plus double-check our data."[84]

Jonathan Poggie is the FORCES director of military analytics and computational conflict dynamics. As a professor in Purdue's School of Aeronautics and Astronautics, he is the innovation lead for hypersonics at Purdue's Institute for Global Security and Defense Innovation.

Matei says FORCES collaborates with professional military education institutions such as the Air War College, the Air University School of Advanced Strategic Studies, the U.S. Army Training and Doctrine Command, the Space Force, and the Naval Postgraduate School.

THE DEFENSE CIVILIAN TRAINING CORPS AT PURDUE

Beginning in the fall semester of 2023, twenty Purdue juniors were the first students in Purdue University's Defense Civilian Training Corps. The Corps is a pilot program that gives students a direct pathway to civilian careers with the Department of Defense. Purdue is just one of four universities selected for the program "preparing [students] to work on diverse, innovative teams within the defense ecosystem."[85]

"The program is the latest and broadest example of us stepping up to the plate in workforce development," said Dr. Daniel DeLaurentis, the principal investigator for the Purdue program. "We consider it an honor but also are aware of the heavy responsibility we have to ensure success of the pilot."[86]

THERE IS MORE TO COME

President Mung Chiang is committed to continuing and expanding Purdue University's focus on national security technology education, research, outreach, and partnerships. He is working to tell the Purdue story around the nation and the world.

"I think it's only natural that the outstanding work by our professors and students and our partners is getting attention," he says. "And we hope that more and more people will recognize the outstanding work here at Purdue. We're proud to work alongside many Department of Defense labs and academies and many partners, Saab and Rolls Royce being two prime examples. I am immensely proud and honored to be part of this family that's doing so much to protect our freedom and advance the land-grant mission in America. As an innovative university, we are always open-minded to possibilities to advance the mission of this land-grant institution. Across the decades and across many dimensions, including new ones recently, we are growing very rapidly. Boilermakers are very proud to be able to work alongside ROTC students, Purdue Military Research Institute students, and veterans, and to work on topics that are important to the safety and the freedom of all Americans.

"Purdue is a very special place."[87]

Navy captain and Purdue graduate Michael Christian was captured in 1967 when his plane was shot down over North Vietnam. As a prisoner of war held in brutal conditions, he handcrafted a small U.S. flag. When it was found, he was severely beaten and returned to his cell, where he made another U.S. flag. Image courtesy of the U.S. Navy.

Purdue astronaut Michael McCulley reaches out to shake hands with fellow Boilermaker engineer K. O. Johnson at the groundbreaking for Neil Armstrong Hall in 2004. McCulley graduated from Purdue on a Navy program for enlisted men and women. Also in photo are Purdue astronauts Mark Brown (next to McCulley), Guy Gardner (behind McCulley) and Don Williams (in knit cap, back left). Image courtesy of Purdue University.

Purdue Army ROTC graduate Lieutenant General (ret.) Karen Gibson became the Sergeant of Arms of the United States Senate on March 22, 2021. Photograph by Dan Rios, U.S. Senate Photographic Studio.

Joseph Alford was in Purdue NROTC and served in Vietnam after graduation. He then began a career with Eli Lilly and Company where he became a leader in bioprocess automation, batch process control, computer system validation, online data analysis, alarm management, process analytical technologies, and applications of artificial intelligence, all of which involved use of computer systems. Image courtesy of the Joseph Alford family.

Theresa Carter joined Air Force ROTC while a student at Purdue. When she retired from the Air Force after thirty-one years of service, she had been the first female civil engineer promoted to brigadier general and then to major general, two stars. Image courtesy of the U.S. Air Force.

Purdue graduate Lieutenant General (ret.) Christopher Weggeman. Image courtesy of the U.S. Air Force.

Purdue Military Research Institute, March 2023. Image courtesy of Purdue University.

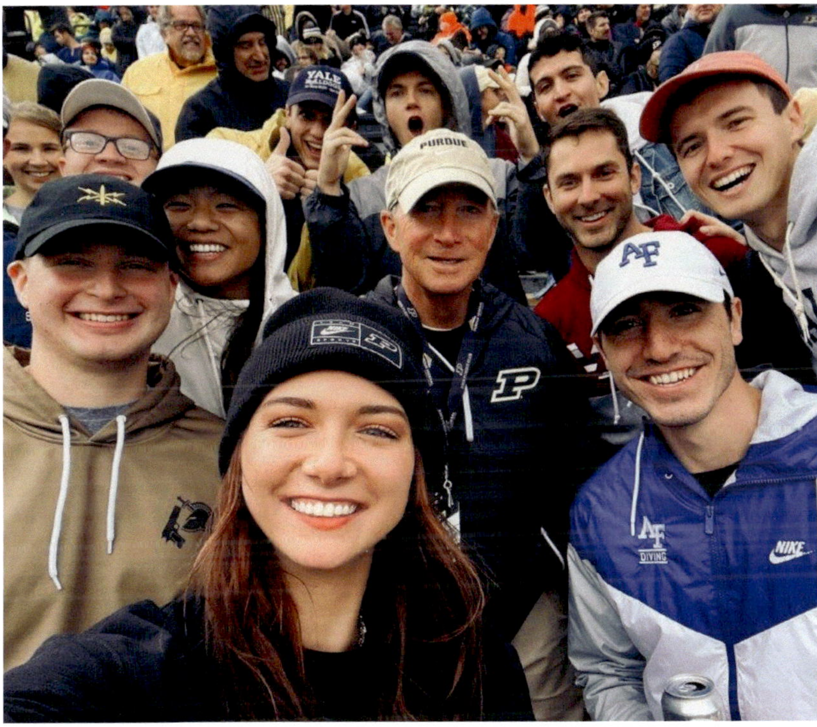

Purdue Military Research Institute students at a football game with then President Mitchell E. Daniels, Jr. PMRI students include Ryan Schneider, Winnie Chen, Dominick DeFazio, Taylor Schorlemmer, Andrew Jariga, Harmont Grenier, Neal Ottinger, Rob Pekarek, and Jack Zocher. The students hail from the U.S. Air Force, Naval, and Military Academies as well as Purdue and Yale Air Force ROTC. Photo courtesy of Gabrielle Trent.

Purdue President Mung Chiang. Image courtesy of Purdue University.

Daniel DeLaurentis, the director of Purdue's Institute for Global Security and Defense Innovation (i-GSDI). DeLaurentis is a professor of aeronautics and astronautics, and also serves as vice president for research institutes and centers in the Discovery Park District at Purdue. Image courtesy of Purdue University.

Arvind Raman, the John A. Edwardson Dean of Engineering at Purdue University. Image courtesy of Purdue University.

Purdue's inaugural Chief Semiconductor Officer, Mark Lundstrom. Image courtesy of Purdue University.

Purdue President Mung Chiang and U.S. Senator Todd Young (R-IN). Image courtesy of Purdue University.

Karen Plaut, Purdue University's Executive Vice President for Research. Image courtesy of Purdue University/Purdue Agriculture.

NOTES

CHAPTER 1

1. *Purdue Alumnus* 7, no. 1 (October 1919): 12.
2. Harvey Wiley, *Harvey W. Wiley: An Autobiography* (Indianapolis: Bobbs-Merrill, 1930), 127.
3. Sean A. Gainey, "Our History," Army ROTC, https://armyrotc.army.mil/history/.
4. Michael David Cohen, "Schools for Soldiers," *New York Times*, July 3, 2012.
5. Speech by the Honorable Justin S. Morrill of Vermont in the House of Representatives, June 6, 1862, accessed via HathiTrust, https://babel.hathitrust.org/cgi/pt?id=hvd.hnyplb&seq=5.
6. Wiley, *An Autobiography*, 57–58.
7. Wiley, *An Autobiography*, 40.
8. Wiley, *An Autobiography*, 58.
9. Wiley, *An Autobiography*, 58.
10. Wiley, *An Autobiography*, 59
11. Wiley, *An Autobiography*, 63.
12. Wiley, *An Autobiography*, 52.
13. Wiley, *An Autobiography*, 127.
14. Robert C. Kriebel, "Old Lafayette: The Forgotten Stein Family," *Journal and Courier* (Lafayette, IN), September 2, 2016.
15. George W. Munro, "The Purdue Army," *The New Purdue* (unpublished, 1946). George W. Munro papers, Virginia Kelly Karnes Archives and Special Collections Research Center, Purdue University, West Lafayette, Indiana.
16. Wiley, *An Autobiography*, 128.
17. *Annual Register of Purdue University, Lafayette, Indiana, 1877–1878* (Indianapolis: Indiana Journal Company, 1878), 39. In Purdue University Annual Registers, 1876–86, Virginia Kelly Karnes Archives and Special Collections Research Center, Purdue University, West Lafayette, Indiana.
18. Wiley, *An Autobiography*, 131.
19. Wiley, *An Autobiography*, 132.
20. Wiley, *An Autobiography*, 157.

21. Wiley, *An Autobiography*, 157, 158.
22. Wiley, *An Autobiography*, 29.
23. Robert W. Topping, *A Century and Beyond, The History of Purdue University* (West Lafayette, Ind.: Purdue University Press, 1988), 109.
24. Lindsey Beckley, "Dr. Harvey "Old Borax" Wiley and His Poison Squad," *Untold Indiana* (blog), Indiana Historical Bureau, June 13, 2016, https://blog.history.in.gov/dr-harvey-wiley-and-his-poison-squad/.
25. Wiley, *An Autobiography*, 281.
26. Wiley, *An Autobiography*, 128.
27. Wiley, *An Autobiography*, 128.
28. Wiley, *An Autobiography*, 128.

CHAPTER 2

1. John Norberg and Kathy Matter, *Heart of the University: 125 Years of Purdue Bands* (West Lafayette, Ind.: Purdue University Press, 2011), 33.
2. Norberg and Matter, *Heart of the University*, 12.
3. Norberg and Matter, *Heart of the University*, 12–34.
4. Norberg and Matter, *Heart of the University*, 33.
5. Norberg and Matter, *Heart of the University*, 33.
6. *Seventh Annual Report of Purdue University for the College Year Ending June 30, 1881* (Indianapolis: William Burford, 1882), 19–20. In Purdue University Annual Reports, 1–9 (1874–83), Virginia Kelly Karnes Archives and Special Collections Research Center, Purdue University, West Lafayette, Indiana.
7. *The Ninth Annual Register of Purdue University, Lafayette, Ind., 1882–83* (Indianapolis: William Burford, 1883), 9. In Purdue University Annual Registers, 1876–86, Virginia Kelly Karnes Archives and Special Collections Research Center, Purdue University, West Lafayette, Indiana.
8. "Bugle Notes," *The Purdue* (West Lafayette, Ind.), November 1, 1882, 12.
9. "Bugle Notes."
10. "Bugle Notes."
11. *The Purdue* (West Lafayette, Ind.), November 1, 1882, 12.
12. "City News," *Journal* (Lafayette, Ind.), April 23, 1883.
13. *The Purdue* (West Lafayette, Ind.), April 1883, 82, 83.
14. *The Tenth Annual Register, Purdue University, Lafayette, Ind. 1883–84*. In Purdue University Annual Registers, 1876–86, Virginia Kelly Karnes Archives and Special Collections Research Center, Purdue University, West Lafayette, Indiana.
15. As estimated by the Inflation Calculator at https://www.in2013dollars.com/.

16. Purdue University, "The Military Department of Purdue," *Debris* (1916), 176.
17. *The Annual Register of Purdue University, Lafayette, Ind., 1888–90*, 80. In Purdue University Annual Registers, 1886–93, Virginia Kelly Karnes Archives and Special Collections Research Center, Purdue University, West Lafayette, Indiana.
18. Purdue University, "The Infantry," *Debris* (1889), n.p.
19. Purdue University, "The Infantry," *Debris* (1889), n.p.
20. Purdue University, "The Infantry," *Debris* (1889), n.p.
21. Purdue University, "The Artillery," *Debris* (1889), n.p.
22. Purdue University, "The Coed Cadet Corps," *Debris* (1889), n.p.
23. Purdue University, "The Coed Cadet Corps," *Debris* (1889), n.p.
24. *The Annual Register of Purdue University, Lafayette, Ind., 1889–91*, 76. In Purdue University Annual Registers, 1886–93, Virginia Kelly Karnes Archives and Special Collections Research Center, Purdue University, West Lafayette, Indiana.
25. *The Annual Register of Purdue University, Lafayette, Ind., 1889–91*, 99.
26. *The Thirty-Seventh Annual Catalogue of Purdue University, 1910–1911* (Lafayette, Ind.: Purdue University, 1911), 46, https://earchives.lib.purdue.edu/digital/collection/ua175/id/37053/rec/28.
27. "Voluntary ROTC OK'd By Purdue University Faculty," *Journal and Courier* (Lafayette, Ind.), March 16, 1965, 1.
28. Purdue University, *Debris* (1891), 59.
29. *The Annual Register of Purdue University, Lafayette, Ind., 1889–91*, 76.
30. Purdue University, *Debris* (1900), 238.
31. Purdue University, *Debris* (1895), 78.
32. Purdue University, *Debris* (1891), 90.
33. Purdue University, *Debris* (1898), 44–45.
34. Purdue University, "The Military," *Debris* (1899), 296 (online pagination).
35. Purdue University, "The Military," *Debris* (1899), 296 (online pagination).
36. Purdue University, *Debris* (1906), 68.
37. Purdue University, *Debris* (1916), 176.
38. Scrapbook in the possession of Purdue Army ROTC.
39. Purdue University, *Debris* (1916), 176.
40. Purdue University, *Debris* (1891), 59.
41. Purdue University, *Debris* (1913), 68.
42. Purdue University, *Debris* (1913), 68.
43. Kevin Cullen, "Purdue in '13: 'We Had Fun,'" *Journal and Courier* (Lafayette, Ind.), April 22, 1978, 1.
44. Cullen, "Purdue in '13: 'We Had Fun,'" 1.

45. Cullen, "Purdue in '13: 'We Had Fun,'" 2.
46. Gordon Graham, "Graham Crackers" column, *Journal and Courier* (Lafayette, Ind.), June 18, 1958, 24.
47. "Purdue's Greatest Athlete Sketched by Chicago Paper," Purdue *Exponent* (West Lafayette, Ind.), January 15, 1916, 1.
48. "Elmer Oliphant Still Most Colorful Athlete," *Purdue Alumnus* 38, no. 9, June 1, 1951, 22.
49. "Outdoing the Merriwells, Starring Elmer Oliphant," *Journal and Courier* (Lafayette, Ind.), February 3, 1931, 10.
50. "Officials Cancel Army-Navy Game," *New York Times*, January 8, 1928, 179.
51. The Dwight D. Eisenhower Library in Abilene, Kansas includes Eisenhower's pre-presidential papers, 1916–1952. Box 88 includes personal correspondence between Eisenhower and his "West Point football friend" Elmer Oliphant.
52. "Elmer Q. Oliphant Dead at 82; Legendary West Point Athlete," *New York Times*, July 6, 1975, 35.
53. "Purdue Armory Fire Brings New Mystery," *Indianapolis Star*, February 25, 1916, 4.
54. "Historic Armory at University is Victim of Flames," *Courier* (Lafayette, Ind.), February 24, 1916, 1, 6.
55. "Historic Armory at University is Victim of Flames," 6.
56. "Historic Armory at University is Victim of Flames," 6.

CHAPTER 3

1. "Purdue May Have Artillery Battery," *Purdue Exponent* (West Lafayette, Ind.), October 18, 1914, 1.
2. J. Holmes Martin, "The Men of Battery B," article from unnamed magazine. In J. Holmes Martin Battery B papers, folder 11 "Published Magazine Article Battery B Service," Virginia Kelly Karnes Archives and Special Collections Research Center, Purdue University, West Lafayette, Indiana.
3. "Battery Equipment Placed in Armory," *Purdue Exponent* (West Lafayette, Ind.), December 18, 1914, 1.
4. "Camp Llano Grande Historical Marker Dedication is Scheduled," McAllen (Tex.) *Monitor*, March 20, 1988, 13A, 16A.
5. "Pancho Villa, Mexican revolutionary," *Encyclopedia Britannica*, April 12, 2024, https://www.britannica.com/biography/Pancho-Villa-Mexican-revolutionary.
6. C. A. Gustafson, "Infamy Sparks Columbus History," in Joyce Reynolds, *Pancho Villa & Columbus, NM 1891 to Early 1920s* (Deming, N. Mex: JReynolds Photo

& Computer Works, 2012), 18.

7. Clifford K. Berryman, "I've Had About Enough of This" (political cartoon), *Washington Evening Star*, March 10, 1916, https://catalog.archives.gov/id/6011165.
8. Mitchell Yockelson, "The United States Armed Forces and the Mexican Punitive Expedition: Part 1," *Prologue Magazine* 29, no. 3 (Fall 1997), https://www.archives.gov/publications/prologue/1997/fall/mexican-punitive-expedition-1.html#main-col.
9. Glenn Williams, "CMH Remembers National Defense Act of 1916," *CMH News and Features*, U.S. Army Center of Military History, May 2016, https://history.army.mil/news/2016/160500a_natDefAct1916.html.
10. "No Battery Call," *Purdue Exponent* (West Lafayette, Ind.), March 31, 1916, 1.
11. "Battery B May Not Go to Summer Camp," *Purdue Exponent* (West Lafayette, Ind.), May 14, 1916, 1.
12. "Lafayette Gives Big Send-Off to Purdue Organization," Indianapolis *Star*, June 24, 1916, 1.
13. "Camp Llano Grande Historical Marker Dedication is Scheduled," 13A, 16A.
14. "Camp Llano Grande Historical Marker Dedication is Scheduled," 13A, 16A.
15. Edwin L. McMahan, letter to J. Holmes Martin, March 31, 1967, in Folder 7, J. Holmes Martin Battery B Papers, Virginia Kelly Karnes Archives and Special Collections Research Center, Purdue University, West Lafayette, Indiana.
16. "Camp Llano Grande Historical Marker Dedication is Scheduled," 13A, 16A.
17. "Camp Llano Grande Historical Marker Dedication is Scheduled," 13A, 16A.
18. "Battery B Receives Warm Welcome Back to Purdue," *Purdue Exponent* (West Lafayette, Ind.), September 29, 1916, 1.
19. "Battery B Receives Warm Welcome Back to Purdue," *Purdue Exponent* (West Lafayette, Ind.), September 29, 1916, 1.
20. "Purdue Battery is Mustered Out with Ceremonies," *Purdue Exponent* (West Lafayette, Ind.), January 13, 1917, 1.

CHAPTER 4

1. Purdue University, *Debris* (1917), 78.
2. William Murray Hepburn and Louis Martin Sears, *Purdue University: Fifty Years of Progress* (Indianapolis: Hollenbeck Press, 1925), 156.
3. James Byron Manson, World War I diary, 129. Identifier 2022-075, James Byron Manson World War I Diary, Box 1, Folder 1, Virginia Kelly Karnes Archives and Special Collections Research Center, Purdue University, West Lafayette,

Indiana.

4. Maxwell E. McDowell, "Letters from France," September 20–November 13, 1917, 13. Identifier MSD 256, Maxwell E. McDowell diary, Box 1, Folder 1, Virginia Kelly Karnes Archives and Special Collections Research Center, Purdue University, West Lafayette, Indiana.
5. Julius L. Born, letter to parents, November 25, 1917. In Julius L. Born correspondence, Virginia Kelly Karnes Archives and Special Collections Research Center, Purdue University, West Lafayette, Indiana.
6. Charles Brouse, "My Army Experiences in the World War from May 1917 to January 1919," 79. In Charles R. Brouse collection, Box 1, Folder 1, Virginia Kelly Karnes Archives and Special Collections Research Center, Purdue University, West Lafayette, Indiana.
7. Winthrop E. Stone, 1917 diary. In Winthrop E. Stone papers, Box 30, Virginia Kelly Karnes Archives and Special Collections Research Center, Purdue University, West Lafayette, Indiana.
8. Stone, 1917 diary.
9. Hepburn and Sears, *Purdue University: Fifty Years of Progress*, 142.
10. Purdue University, *Debris* (1917), 342–43.
11. Purdue University, *Debris* (1917), 20.
12. Purdue University, *Debris* (1917), 21.
13. H. B. Knoll, *The Story of Purdue Engineering* (West Lafayette, Ind.: Purdue University Studies, 1963), 63.
14. Hepburn and Sears, *Purdue University: Fifty Years of Progress*, 143.
15. Hepburn and Sears, *Purdue University: Fifty Years of Progress*, 147.
16. Winthrop E. Stone, "Patriotism Through Sacrifice," May 27, 1917. In Winthrop E. Stone papers, Box 30, Virginia Kelly Karnes Archives and Special Collections Research Center, Purdue University, West Lafayette, Indiana.
17. Winthrop E. Stone, "Address Before the University," speech May 30, 1917. In Winthrop E. Stone papers, Box 30, Virginia Kelly Karnes Archives and Special Collections Research Center, Purdue University, West Lafayette, Indiana.
18. Stone, "Address Before the University."
19. Hepburn and Sears, *Purdue University: Fifty Years of Progress*, 143.
20. Brouse, "My Army Experiences in the World War from May 1917 to January 1919," 1.
21. Hepburn and Sears, *Purdue University: Fifty Years of Progress*, 143.
22. Born, letter to parents, November 25, 1917.
23. Hepburn and Sears, *Purdue University: Fifty Years of Progress*, 144–45.

24. Hepburn and Sears, *Purdue University: Fifty Years of Progress*, 147.
25. Hepburn and Sears, *Purdue University: Fifty Years of Progress*, 147.
26. Hepburn and Sears, *Purdue University: Fifty Years of Progress*, 148.
27. McDowell, "Letters from France," September 30, 1917, 21.
28. Manson, World War I diary, 163, 196–87.
29. Hepburn and Sears, *Purdue University: Fifty Years of Progress*, 148.
30. "Purdue's New Armory Is Formally Dedicated," *Indianapolis News*, April 26, 1918, 14.
31. Hepburn and Sears, *Purdue University: Fifty Years of Progress*, 147.
32. Purdue University, *Debris* (1919), 55.
33. Purdue University, *Debris* (1919), 55.
34. Hepburn and Sears, *Purdue University: Fifty Years of Progress*, 149–50.
35. Hepburn and Sears, *Purdue University: Fifty Years of Progress*, 151.
36. Hepburn and Sears, *Purdue University: Fifty Years of Progress*, 151.
37. John M. Barry, *The Great Influenza: The Story of the Deadliest Pandemic in History* (New York: Penguin Books, 2005), 4.
38. U.S. Centers for Disease Control and Prevention, "The 1918 Flu Pandemic: Why it Matters 100 Years Later," https://blogs.cdc.gov/publichealthmatters/2018/05/1918-flu/.
39. "War—Its Bearing Upon Local Community Affairs," *Tippecanoe County Democrat*, (Lafayette, Ind.), October 11, 1918, 1.
40. "Many Celebrate Discovery Day," *Lafayette Journal* (Lafayette, Ind.), October 12, 1918, 6.
41. Hepburn and Sears, *Purdue University: Fifty Years of Progress*, 153.
42. Hepburn and Sears, *Purdue University: Fifty Years of Progress*, 153–54.
43. "Lafayette Celebrates the World's Greatest Victory With Two Giant Parades," *Lafayette Journal* (Lafayette, Ind.), November 12, 1918, 1.
44. "30,000 People In Big Celebration," *Lafayette Journal* (Lafayette, Ind.), November 12, 1918, 4.
45. James Byron Manson, World War I diary, 381–83.
46. James Byron Manson, World War I diary, 381–83.
47. Purdue University, *Debris* (1919), 203.
48. Purdue University, *Debris* (1919), 195.
49. Maxwell E. McDowell, "Letters from France," September 30, 1917, 36.
50. Hepburn and Sears, *Purdue University: Fifty Years of Progress*, 154.
51. Hepburn and Sears, *Purdue University: Fifty Years of Progress*, 157.
52. Hepburn and Sears, *Purdue University: Fifty Years of Progress*, 160–63.

53. "Remembering and Honoring Our Purdue World War I Veterans Who Gave Their Lives – Lest We Forget," *Memoirs & Memories: Tales from Purdue Archives and Special Collections* (blog), November 11, 2016, https://blogs.lib.purdue.edu/asc/2016/11/11/remembering-and-honoring-our-purdue-world-war-i-veterans-who-gave-their-lives-lest-we-forget/.
54. Purdue *Debris* (1915), 104.
55. "Purdue Day-by-Day, Oct. 18," *Purdue Alumnus News Letter and War Bulletin*, Vol. 6, No. 2 (December 1918), 5. In *Purdue Alumnus* Vol. 6-7, November to July 1918–20, Virginia Kelly Karnes Archives and Special Collections Research Center, Purdue University, West Lafayette, Indiana.
56. Purdue *Debris* (1915), 104.
57. Knoll, *The Story of Purdue Engineering*, 65.

PROFILE: CHARLES R. BROUSE

1. Charles Brouse, "My Army Experiences in the World War, May 1917 to January 1919," 2. In Charles R. Brouse collection, Box 1, Folder 1, Virginia Kelly Karnes Archives and Special Collections Research Center, Purdue University, West Lafayette, Indiana.
2. Brouse, "My Army Experiences in the World War," 3–4.
3. Brouse, "My Army Experiences in the World War," 5.
4. Brouse, "My Army Experiences in the World War," 6–7.
5. Brouse, "My Army Experiences in the World War," 12–18.
6. Brouse, "My Army Experiences in the World War," 26–27.
7. Brouse, "My Army Experiences in the World War," 28–29.
8. Brouse, "My Army Experiences in the World War," 41.
9. Brouse, "My Army Experiences in the World War," 58–61.
10. Brouse, "My Army Experiences in the World War," 64–65.
11. Brouse, "My Army Experiences in the World War," 67.
12. Brouse, "My Army Experiences in the World War," 71–72.
13. Brouse, "My Army Experiences in the World War," 81.
14. Brouse, "My Army Experiences in the World War," 94.
15. Brouse, "My Army Experiences in the World War," 94–96.
16. Brouse, "My Army Experiences in the World War," 100–1.

CHAPTER 5

1. K. W. Huffine and Dorothy Clark, *Debris* (1920), 36.
2. Purdue University, *Debris* (1919), 42.

3. Purdue University, *Debris* (1919), 41.
4. John Norberg, *Wings of Their Dreams: Purdue in Flight*, 2nd ed. (West Lafayette, Ind.: Purdue University Press, 2019), 106.
5. George Haskins Jr., interviewed by author John Norberg, March 15, 2003.
6. "Purdue Alumni Are Coming in Airplanes," *Purdue Exponent* (West Lafayette, Ind.), June 8, 1919, 4.
7. "Alumnus Comes By Aerial Route," *Lafayette Morning Journal* (Lafayette, Ind.), June 9, 1919.
8. Norberg, *Wings of Their Dreams*, 108.
9. Lt. George W. Haskins, "Aeronautics," *The Purdue Engineering Review* 15 (1920): 9.
10. Norberg, *Wings of Their Dreams*, 113.
11. "History: Origin of the Purdue Memorial Union," Purdue Memorial Union, https://union.purdue.edu/about/history.html.
12. "History," Purdue Memorial Union.
13. *Purdue Exponent* (West Lafayette, Ind.), "Students Go Over the Top with $326,335," November 12, 1920, 1.
14. "History," Purdue Memorial Union.
15. "History," Purdue Memorial Union.
16. "History," Purdue Memorial Union.
17. Purdue University, *Debris* (1919), 187.
18. Sean A. Gainey, "Our History," Army ROTC, accessed January 2, 2024, https://armyrotc.army.mil/history/.
19. Purdue University, "The Military," *Debris* (1929).
20. H. B. Knoll, *The Story of Purdue Engineering* (West Lafayette, Ind.: Purdue University Studies, 1963), 346.
21. Norberg, *Wings of Their Dreams*, 114.
22. *Purdue Engineering Review* (May 1920), 24–37.
23. George Haskins Jr., interviewed by author John Norberg, March 15, 2003.
24. George Haskins Jr., interviewed by author John Norberg, March 15, 2003.
25. Norberg, *Wings of Their Dreams*, 115.

CHAPTER 6

1. H. B. Knoll, *The Story of Purdue Engineering* (West Lafayette, Ind.: Purdue University, 1963), 348–49.
2. Knoll, *The Story of Purdue Engineering*, 348.
3. Knoll, *The Story of Purdue Engineering*, 348–49.
4. Knoll, *The Story of Purdue Engineering*, 347–48.

5. Knoll, *The Story of Purdue Engineering*, 346.
6. Knoll, *The Story of Purdue Engineering*, 347.
7. Knoll, *The Story of Purdue Engineering*, 348.
8. Knoll, *The Story of Purdue Engineering*, 339.
9. Angie Klink, *The Deans' Bible: Five Purdue Women and Their Quest for Equality* (West Lafayette, Ind.: Purdue University Press, 2014), 57.
10. Klink, *The Deans' Bible*, 88.

CHAPTER 7

1. "Grove Webster: Biographical Information, Virginia Kelly Karnes Archives and Special Collections Research Center, Purdue University, West Lafayette, Indiana, https://archives.lib.purdue.edu/agents/people/184.
2. Grove Webster, "The Civilian Pilot Training Program," *Aerospace Historian Magazine* 26, no. 1 (March 1979): 34–39. https://www.jstor.org/stable/44524918.
3. National Museum of the United States Air Force, "Civilian Pilot Training Program," https://www.nationalmuseum.af.mil/Visit/Museum-Exhibits/Fact-Sheets/Display/Article/196137/civilian-pilot-training-program/.
4. John Norberg, *Wings of Their Dreams: Purdue in Flight*, 2nd ed. (West Lafayette, Ind.: Purdue University Press, 2019), 216.
5. "Training of Fifty Flyers under U.S. Plan Begun at Purdue," *Journal and Courier* (Lafayette, Ind.), February 17, 1939, 1.
6. "Training of Fifty Flyers under U.S. Plan Begun at Purdue," *Journal and Courier* (Lafayette, Ind.), February 17, 1939, 9.
7. "Purdue Leads Nation in the Training of Young Aviators," *Journal and Courier* (Lafayette, Ind.), June 16, 1939, 3.
8. Walker M. Mahurin, *Honest John: The Autobiography of Walker M. Mahurin* (New York: G. P. Putnam's Sons, 1962), 113.
9. Mahurin, *Honest John*, 109.
10. Mahurin, *Honest John*, 112.
11. Mahurin, *Honest John*, 113.
12. Mahurin, *Honest John*, 118–24.
13. "Walker Melville Mahurin," American Air Museum in Britain, https://www.americanairmuseum.com/archive/person/walker-melville-mahurin.
14. Dennis McLellan, "Flyer Was First World War II Double Ace in Europe," *Los Angeles Times*, May 14, 2010, AA6.
15. Webster, "The Civilian Pilot Training Program," 34–39.
16. Webster, "The Civilian Pilot Training Program," 34–39.

17. Roger Guillemette, "Civilian Pilot Training Program," U.S. Centennial of Flight Commission, https://www.centennialofflight.net/essay/GENERAL_AVIATION/civilian_pilot_training/GA20.htm.
18. "Civilian Pilot Training Program (CPTP)," U.S. Centennial of Flight Commission, https://www.centennialofflight.net/essay/GENERAL_AVIATION/civilian_pilot_training/GA20.htm.
19. Guillemette, "Civilian Pilot Training Program."
20. "Civilian Pilot Training Program (CPTP)."
21. "'Cap' Aretz, Pioneer of Aviation, Dies," *Journal and Courier* (Lafayette, Ind.), February 29, 1968, 6.
22. National Museum of the United States Air Force, "Civilian Pilot Training Program," https://www.nationalmuseum.af.mil/Visit/Museum-Exhibits/Fact-Sheets/Display/Article/196137/civilian-pilot-training-program/.
23. "Young Women to Join Ranks of Purdue Flying Students," *Journal and Courier* (Lafayette, Ind.), October 21, 1939, 5.
24. "Federal - New Air Commerce Regulations Relating to Customs, Immigration, Entry and Clearance, and Public Health," *Journal of Air Law and Commerce* 12 , no. 4 (1941): 371, https://scholar.smu.edu/cgi/viewcontent.cgi?article=3287&context=jalc.
25. Office of the Registrar, Purdue University, interview with author John Norberg, November 29, 2022.
26. "Aviation Banquet Draws Notables to the University," *Journal and Courier* (Lafayette, Ind.), May 27, 1940, 4.

CHAPTER 8

1. Pvt. Benjamin Hal, "Remembering Pearl Harbor," U.S. Army, December 6, 2023, https://www.army.mil/article/272241/remembering_pearl_harbor.
2. Al Blackburn, *Aces Wild: The Race for Mach 1* (Wilmington, Del.: Scholarly Resources, 1999) 91.
3. "G. S. Welch, Del. War Hero, Dies in Crash," *Wilmington* (Del.) *Morning Journal*, October 13, 1954, 8 (continued from page 1).
4. Blackburn, *Aces Wild*, 91.
5. "Delta Upsilon," Purdue University, *Debris* (1938), 367; "Delta Upsilon," Purdue University, *Debris* (1939), 379.
6. "State, City Acclaim Welch for Deed at Pearl Harbor," *Wilmington* (Del.) *News Journal*, May 26, 1942, 1, 9.
7. "'I'm Not a Good Shot,' Says Pacific Ace," *Journal and Courier* (Lafayette, Ind.),

May 12, 1944, 1.

8. Blackburn, *Aces Wild*, 94.
9. Ken Taylor, interviewed by author John Norberg, May 15, 2003.
10. "State, City Acclaim Welch for Deed at Pearl Harbor," *Wilmington* (Del.) *News Journal*, May 26, 1942, 1, 9.
11. Gordon Prange, *At Dawn We Slept: The Untold History of Pearl Harbor* (New York: McGraw-Hill Book Company, 1981), 89.
12. John Norberg, *Wings of Their Dreams: Purdue in Flight*, 2nd ed. (West Lafayette, Ind.: Purdue University Press, 2019), 124.
13. Norberg, *Wings of Their Dreams*, 133, 134.
14. Norberg, *Wings of Their Dreams*, 140, 141.
15. Prange, *At Dawn We Slept*, 89, 91.
16. Prange, *At Dawn We Slept*, 91.
17. F. L. Martin and P. N. L. Bellinger, "Joint Estimate Covering Joint Army and Navy Air Action in the Event of Sudden Hostile Action against Oahu or Fleet Units in the Hawaiian Area," March 31, 1941, https://www.ibiblio.org/pha/timeline/410331apw2.html.
18. Norberg, *Wings of Their Dreams*, 244.
19. Gordon Prange, *December 7th, 1941: The Day the Japanese Attacked Pearl Harbor* (New York: McGraw-Hill Book Company, 1988), 216, 217.
20. Prange, *December 7th, 1941*, 214.
21. Prange, *At Dawn We Slept*, 521.
22. Blackburn, *Aces Wild*, 147.
23. John Chamberlin, "Pearl Harbor and Purdue University: Pioneer Aviators 'Seek What Lies Before,'" *Air Power History* 67, no. 1 (Spring 2020), 28, https://www.jstor.org/stable/26907206.

CHAPTER 9

1. Purdue University Board of Trustees minutes, June 8, 1940, 73, https://earchives.lib.purdue.edu/digital/collection/bot/id/11379/rec/404.
2. "4,000 Students Attend Opening 'Fitness' Convo," *Purdue Exponent* (West Lafayette, Ind.), September 12, 1940, 1.
3. E. F. Bruhn, *A History of Aeronautical Engineering and Research at Purdue for Period 1937 to 1950* (West Lafayette, Ind.: Purdue University, 1968), 15.
4. H. B. Knoll, *The Story of Purdue Engineering* (West Lafayette, Ind.: Purdue University, 1963), 105.
5. Arthur Shak, interview with author John Norberg, February 27, 2024.

6. Kathlyn Clore, "Character. Duty. Honor," *Generations* Magazine (Dec 2020–January 2021), https://generations808.com/character-duty-honor/.
7. Arthur Shak, interview with author John Norberg, February 27, 2024.
8. Clore, "Character. Duty. Honor."
9. Clore, "Character. Duty. Honor."
10. Rich Rhodes [the nephew of Harry Michael], interview with author John Norberg, May 23, 2003.
11. William Moffat, interview with John Norberg as cited in *A Force for Change: The Class of 1950* (West Lafayette, IN: Purdue Research Foundation, 1995), 185.
12. Norberg, *A Force for Change: The Class of 1950*, 91–92.
13. "Pilot Son of Noted Father May Leave Purdue, Join Army," *Journal and Courier* (Lafayette, Ind.), January 23, 1941, 1.
14. John Traugott, "Believe U.S. Faces Long, Hard Battle," *Purdue Exponent* (West Lafayette, Ind.), December 9, 1941, 1.
15. Traugott, "Believe U.S. Faces Long, Hard Battle."
16. Edward Elliott, "Unity, Loyalty, Good Sense—Elliott To the Students of Purdue," *Purdue Exponent*, (West Lafayette, Ind.), December 9, 1941, 1.
17. "Exponent War Platform (An Editorial)," *Purdue Exponent* (West Lafayette, Ind.), December 9, 1941, 1.
18. *Journal and Courier* (Lafayette, Ind.), December 8, 1941, 1.
19. "Our Community Duty," *Journal and Courier* (Lafayette, Ind.), December 8, 1941, 1.
20. Ken Klosson, "Students Meet in Music Hall to Learn Their Part in War," *Purdue Exponent* (West Lafayette, Ind.), 1.
21. Klosson, "Students Meet in Music Hall."
22. Klosson, "Students Meet in Music Hall."
23. Andrew J. DeKever, *Here Rests in Honored Glory: Life Stories of Our Country's Medal of Honor Recipients* (Bennington, Vt.: Merriam Press, 2008), 202.
24. Knoll, *The Story of Purdue Engineering*, 106.
25. Ruth Freehafer, *R. B. Stewart and Purdue University* (West Lafayette, Ind.: Purdue Research Foundation, 1983), 88.
26. Angie Klink, *The Dean's Bible: Five Purdue Women and Their Quest for Equality* (West Lafayette, Ind.: Purdue University Press, 2014), 114.
27. John Norberg, *Ever True: One Hundred Fifty Years of Giant Leaps at Purdue University*, (West Lafayette, Ind.: Purdue University Press, 2019), 119–20.
28. "AWS Conference Stresses Training For Vital Jobs," *Purdue Exponent* (West Lafayette, Ind.), October 29, 1942, 1.

29. As quoted in Klink, *The Dean's Bible*, 144.
30. "About Dorothy Stratton," Dorothy Stratton Veteran and Military Success Center, Purdue University, https://www.purdue.edu/veterans/about/dorothy.html.
31. "Who Was the First Female General Officer in the U.S. Army?" United States Center of Military History, January 31, 2021, https://history.army.mil/faq/faq-femgo.htm.
32. "Navy's First Female Admiral, Arlene Duerk, Passes Away," Naval History and Heritage Command, July 25, 2018, https://www.history.navy.mil/news-and-events/news/2018/navy-s-first-female-admiral--alene-duerk--passes-away.html.
33. H. B. Knoll, ed., *1941–1945: A Record of a University in the War Years* (West Lafayette, Ind.: Archives of Purdue, 1947), 194.
34. Freehafer, *R. B. Stewart and Purdue University*, 85.
35. DeKever, *Here Rests in Honored Glory*, 203.
36. DeKever, *Here Rests in Honored Glory*, 206.
37. As quoted in DeKever, *Here Rests in Honored Glory*, 209.
38. Norberg, *A Force for Change: The Class of 1950*, 185–86.
39. Purdue University, *Debris* (1942), 217.
40. Bill Hoskins, "Dotty Lamour Attracts 20,000 to War Bond Rally in Stadium," *Purdue Exponent* (West Lafayette, Ind.), September 25, 1942, 1.
41. As quoted in Knoll, ed., *1941–1945: A Record of a University in the War Years*, 43–44.
42. Purdue University, *Debris* (1943), 159–60.
43. "University Provides Training for 3,000 Students in Service," *Purdue Patrol* (Purdue Alumni Association) 1, no. 1 (August 1943): 1.
44. "6,787 Students in University for Term Which Started November 8," *Purdue Patrol* (Purdue Alumni Association) 1, no. 4 (November 1943): 1.
45. "Purdue Man, Leading European Ace, Gets DSC from Lieut. Gen. Ira Eaker," *Purdue Patrol* (Purdue Alumni Association) 1, no. 5 (December 1943): 1.
46. "Navy Cross Awarded Missing Purdue Flyer," *Purdue Patrol* (Purdue Alumni Association) 1, no. 5, (December 1943): 1.
47. Freehafer, *R. B. Stewart and Purdue University*, 79–80.
48. Freehafer, *R. B. Stewart and Purdue University*, 88–89.
49. "Scenes of Naval Electronics Training at Purdue," *Purdue Patrol* (Purdue Alumni Association) 1, no. 1 (August 1943): 3.
50. Knoll, *The Story of Purdue Engineering*, 107.
51. Knoll, *The Story of Purdue Engineering*, 354.

52. Freehafer, *R.B. Stewart and Purdue University*, 81.
53. Freehafer, *R.B. Stewart and Purdue University*, 90.
54. Freehafer, *R.B. Stewart and Purdue University*, 106–7.
55. "Marines, Sailors on Summer Squad Boost Purdue Grid Hopes," *Purdue Patrol* (Purdue Alumni Association) 1, no. 1 (August 1943): 4.
56. Bob Collins, *Boilermakers: A History of Purdue Football* (Lafayette, Ind.: Haywood Printing Company, 1976), 89.
57. Mark Davis, "How a Philadelphia Man Reshaped the Marines," *Philadelphia Inquirer*, August 1, 1997, 25.
58. Davis, "How a Philadelphia Man Reshaped the Marines," 34.
59. Mike Burton, "To The Corps: As Marines They Fought the Enemy, Integrated the Corps, and Changed Their Country," *Philadelphia Inquirer*, July 30, 1995, 13–17.
60. Davis, "How a Philadelphia Man Reshaped the Marines," 34.
61. Davis, "How a Philadelphia Man Reshaped the Marines," 34.
62. Matt Schudel, "Frederick C. Branch; Was First Black Officer in U.S. Marine Corps," *Washington Post*, April 13, 2005, B06.
63. "6,787 Students in University for Term Which Started November 8," 1.
64. Bruhn, *A History of Aeronautical Engineering and Research*, 15.
65. A. F. Grandt Jr., W. A. Gustafson, and L. T. Cargnino, *One Small Step: The History of Aerospace Engineering at Purdue University*, 2nd ed. (West Lafayette, Ind.: Purdue University School of Aeronautics and Astronautics, 1995), 39.
66. "Enrollment of 4,024 Includes 1,574 Civilian Students," *Purdue Patrol* (Purdue Alumni Association) 2, no. 1 (August 1944).
67. Esther Conelley Boonstra, "The Way It Was At Purdue, 1941-1945," MSA 57, Esther Conelley Boonstra collection, Virginia Kelly Karnes Archives and Special Collections Research Center, Purdue University, West Lafayette, Indiana, https://archives.lib.purdue.edu/repositories/2/resources/679.
68. Robert Topping, *A Century and Beyond: The History of Purdue University*, (West Lafayette, Ind.: Purdue Research Foundation, 1988), 240.
69. "Engineering, Science, and Management War Training," Wikipedia, https://en.wikipedia.org/wiki/Engineering,_Science,_and_Management_War_Training.
70. Knoll, *The Story of Purdue Engineering*, 108.
71. Knoll, *The Story of Purdue Engineering*, 108.
72. "Research Starters: Women in World War II," The National World War II Museum, New Orleans, https://www.nationalww2museum.org/students-teachers/student-resources/research-starters/research-starters-women-world-war-ii.

73. "Biography of Lillian Mollar Gilbreth," Rosen Center for Advanced Computing, Purdue University, https://www.rcac.purdue.edu/knowledge/gilbreth/bio.
74. Klink, *The Dean's Bible*, 112.
75. Freehafer, *R. B. Stewart and Purdue University*, 87.
76. Knoll, ed., *1941–1945, A Record of a University in the War Years*, 212–13.
77. Knoll, ed., *1941–1945, A Record of a University in the War Years*, 195.
78. "Doolittle's Son, 38, Found Dead at Base," *New York Times*, April 10, 1958.
79. DeKever, *Here Rests in Honored Glory*, 210.
80. DeKever, *Here Rests in Honored Glory*, 214.
81. DeKever, *Here Rests in Honored Glory*, 218.
82. DeKever, *Here Rests in Honored Glory*, 220–21.
83. DeKever, *Here Rests in Honored Glory*, 222.
84. DeKever, *Here Rests in Honored Glory*, 224.
85. War Department, Bureau of Public Relations, Press Branch, SIS Release C-454.
86. DeKever, *Here Rests in Honored Glory*, 216, 220.

PROFILE: JOHN F. BABBITT

1. John F. Babbitt, interview with author John Norberg, August 10, 2022.
2. "Worthy Instructor Leaves Many Friends to Mourn His Death—Loved By Students," Purdue *Exponent* (West Lafayette, Ind.), November 26, 1907, 1.

CHAPTER 10

1. H. B. Knoll, ed., *1941–1945: A Record of a University in the War Years* (West Lafayette, Ind.: Archives of Purdue, 1947), 127.
2. "Dean A. A. Potter Accepts Award," *Purdue Exponent* (West Lafayette, Ind.), September 16, 1944, 1.
3. "Dean A. A. Potter Accepts Award," 1.
4. Purdue University U.S. Army Ordnance Experiment Station, Small Arms Division Report no, 200, May 1947, confidential, declassified in 1956. In Purdue University College of Engineering Records, Box 1, Folder 10, Virginia Kelly Karnes Archives and Special Collections Research Center, Purdue University, West Lafayette, Indiana.
5. H. B. Knoll, *The Story of Purdue Engineering* (West Lafayette, Ind.: Purdue University, 1963), 217.
6. Knoll, ed., *1941–1945: A Record of a University in the War Years*, 122.
7. Knoll, *The Story of Purdue Engineering*, 218.
8. Purdue University U.S. Army Ordnance Experiment Station, Small Arms

Division Report no, 200, May 1947, confidential, declassified in 1956, Part II: "History of the Ranges and Other Structures, 3. In Purdue University College of Engineering Records, Box 1, Folder 10, Virginia Kelly Karnes Archives and Special Collections Research Center, Purdue University, West Lafayette, Indiana.

9. Purdue University U.S. Army Ordnance Experiment Station, Small Arms Division Report no, 200, Part II, 5.
10. Purdue University U.S. Army Ordnance Experiment Station, Small Arms Division Report no, 200, Part II, 11.
11. Knoll, ed., *1941–1945: A Record of a University in the War Years*, 126.
12. Knoll, ed., *1941–1945: A Record of a University in the War Years*, 126.
13. Purdue University U.S. Army Ordnance Experiment Station, Small Arms Division Report no, 200, May 1947, confidential, declassified in 1956, Part IV: "Hazards of The Ordinance Project," 1. In Purdue University College of Engineering Records, Box 1, Folder 10, Virginia Kelly Karnes Archives and Special Collections Research Center, Purdue University, West Lafayette, Indiana.
14. Purdue University U.S. Army Ordnance Experiment Station, Small Arms Division Report no, 200, Part IV, 1.
15. Purdue University U.S. Army Ordnance Experiment Station, Small Arms Division Report no, 200, Part IV, 1–2.
16. Purdue University U.S. Army Ordnance Experiment Station, Small Arms Division Report no, 200, Part IV, 3.
17. Purdue University U.S. Army Ordnance Experiment Station, Small Arms Division Report no, 200, Part IV, 3, 7.
18. Knoll, *The Story of Purdue Engineering*, 217.
19. Fred C. Kelly, *David Ross, Modern Pioneer: A Biography* (New York: Alfred A. Knopf, 1946), 111.
20. Knoll, ed., *1941–1945: A Record of a University in the War Years*, 69.
21. Knoll, ed., *1941–1945: A Record of a University in the War Years*, 70.
22. Knoll, ed., *1941–1945: A Record of a University in the War Years*, 77-83.
23. Knoll, *The Story of Purdue Engineering*, 109.
24. Knoll, ed., *1941–1945: A Record of a University in the War Years*, 74.
25. Knoll, ed., *1941–1945: A Record of a University in the War Years*, 85.
26. Knoll, ed., *1941–1945: A Record of a University in the War Years*, 84, 86.
27. Knoll, *The Story of Purdue Engineering*, 109.
28. Knoll, ed., *1941–1945: A Record of a University in the War Years*, 72.
29. Knoll, ed., *1941–1945: A Record of a University in the War Years*, 72, 73.
30. Knoll, ed., *1941–1945: A Record of a University in the War Years*, 91.

31. Knoll, ed., *1941–1945: A Record of a University in the War Years*, 92–98.
32. Knoll, ed., *1941–1945: A Record of a University in the War Years*, 98.
33. Knoll, ed., *1941–1945: A Record of a University in the War Years*, 100–5.
34. Knoll, *The Story of Purdue Engineering*, 334.
35. Knoll, *The Story of Purdue Engineering*, 106.
36. Knoll, *The Story of Purdue Engineering*, 114.
37. Knoll, *The Story of Purdue Engineering*, 114–18.
38. Knoll, *The Story of Purdue Engineering*, 109.
39. Knoll, *The Story of Purdue Engineering*, 109.
40. Knoll, ed., *1941–1945: A Record of a University in the War Years*, 166.
41. Knoll, ed., *1941–1945: A Record of a University in the War Years*, 167.
42. Knoll, ed., *1941–1945: A Record of a University in the War Years*, 167–69.
43. Knoll, ed., *1941–1945: A Record of a University in the War Years*, 173–75.
44. Knoll, ed., *1941–1945: A Record of a University in the War Years*, 213.

CHAPTER 11

1. John Norberg, *A Force for Change: The Class of 1950* (West Lafayette, Ind.: Purdue Research Foundation, 1995), 225.
2. Norberg, *A Force for Change*, 225–26.
3. "Servicemen's Readjustment Act (1944)," Milestone Documents, National Archives, https://www.archives.gov/milestone-documents/servicemens-readjustment-act.
4. "Servicemen's Readjustment Act (1944)."
5. H. B. Knoll, *The Story of Purdue Engineering* (West Lafayette, Ind.: Purdue University, 1963), 112.
6. Knoll, *The Story of Purdue Engineering*, 123.
7. "Servicemen's Readjustment Act (1944)."
8. Knoll, *The Story of Purdue Engineering*, 123–24.
9. Ruth Freehafer, *R. B. Stewart and Purdue University* (West Lafayette, Ind.: Purdue Research Foundation, 1983), 100.
10. R. B. Stewart, interview by Robert Eckles, September 29, 1969, Box 2, Folder 15, Purdue University Office of Publications Oral History Program collection, Virginia Kelly Karnes Archives and Special Collections Research Center, Purdue University, West Lafayette, Indiana.
11. Stewart, interview by Eckles, September 29, 1969.
12. Freehafer, *R. B. Stewart and Purdue University*, 102.
13. R. B. Stewart had received an honorary PhD from Butler University in

Indianapolis in 1943.

14. Freehafer, *R. B. Stewart and Purdue University*, 103.
15. John Norberg, "Local Man's Aid to Japanese Still Remembered," *Journal and Courier* (Lafayette, Ind.), August 14, 1983, 1.
16. Norberg, "Local Man's Aid to Japanese Still Remembered," 1.

CHAPTER 12

1. Neil Armstrong, interview by author John Norberg, June 2003.
2. Neil Armstrong, interview by author John Norberg, June 2003.
3. Neil Armstrong, interview by author John Norberg, June 2003.
4. Neil Armstrong, interview by author John Norberg, June 2003.
5. Eugene Cernan and Don Davis, *The Last Man on the Moon: Astronaut Eugene Cernan and America's Race in Space* (New York: St. Martin's Press, 1999), 23–24.
6. Eugene Cernan, interview by author John Norberg, June 2003.
7. Eugene Cernan, interview by author John Norberg, June 2003.
8. C. Donald Chrysler and Donald L. Chaffee, *On Course to the Stars: The Roger B. Chaffee Story* (Grand Rapids, Mich.: Kregel Publications, 1968), 51.
9. John Norberg, *Wings of Their Dreams: Purdue in Flight*, 2nd ed. (West Lafayette, Ind.: Purdue University Press, 2020), 337.
10. John Norberg, *A Force for Change: The Class of 1950* (West Lafayette, Ind.: Purdue Research Foundation, 1995), 336–37.
11. John Blaha, interview with author John Norberg, January 20, 2023.
12. A. F. Grandt Jr., W. A. Gustafson, and L. T. Cargnino, *One Small Step: The History of Aerospace Engineering at Purdue University*, 2nd ed. (West Lafayette, Ind.: Purdue University School of Aeronautics and Astronautics, 1995), 174.
13. Grandt Jr., Gustafson, and Cargnino, *One Small Step*, 175.
14. Grandt Jr., Gustafson, and Cargnino, *One Small Step*, 175–76.
15. Roy Bridges Jr., interview with author John Norberg, January 20, 2023.
16. Roy Bridges Jr., *An Improbable Astronaut: How a Georgia Farm Boy Wound Up Flying the Space Shuttle* (Camano Island, Wash.: Heart Ally Books, 2022), 89.
17. John Blaha, interview with author John Norberg, January 20, 2023.
18. John Blaha, interview with author John Norberg, January 20, 2023.
19. John Blaha, interview with author John Norberg, January 20, 2023.
20. John Casper, interview with author John Norberg, January 26, 2023.
21. John Casper, interview with author John Norberg, January 26, 2023.
22. John Casper, *The Sky Above: An Astronaut's Memoir of Adventure, Persistence, and Faith* (West Lafayette, Ind.: Purdue University Press, 2022).

23. John Norberg, *Wings of Their Dreams*, 1st ed. (West Lafayette, Ind.: Purdue University Press, 2003), 103.
24. Norberg, *Wings of Their Dreams*, 1st ed., 103.
25. Jerry Ross, *Spacewalker: My Journey in Space and Faith as NASA's Record-Setting Frequent Flyer* (West Lafayette, Ind.: Purdue University Press, 2013), xvii.
26. Jerry Ross, interview with author John Norberg, January 20, 2023.
27. Jerry Ross, interview with author John Norberg, January 20, 2023.
28. Mark Brown, interview with author John Norberg, April 26, 2023.
29. Mark Brown, interview with author John Norberg, April 26, 2023.
30. Mark Brown, interview with author John Norberg, April 26, 2023.
31. Mark Brown, interview with author John Norberg, April 26, 2023.
32. Mark Brown, interview with author John Norberg, April 26, 2023.
33. Mark Polansky, email with author John Norberg, January 30, 2024.
34. Norberg, *Wings of Their Dreams*, 2nd ed., 407.
35. Mark Polansky, email with author John Norberg, January 2024.
36. "Purdue in Space: Scott Tingle," Purdue University, https://www.purdue.edu/space/astronaut/scott-tingle/.
37. NASA, "Meet Artemis Team Member Scott Tingle," YouTube, December 9, 2020, https://www.youtube.com/watch?v=GqAheEDtWK4.

CHAPTER 13

1. William G. Holder, *The Purdue Drill Team: A Multimedia Legacy Scrapbook, 1947–1970; Purdue's Finest!* (2009), chapter 5, page 2. Purdue History Collection, Virginia Kelly Karnes Archives and Special Collections Research Center, Purdue University, West Lafayette, Indiana.
2. Wayne Henderson, interview with author John Norberg, December 13, 2022.
3. Wayne Henderson, interview with author John Norberg, December 13, 2022.
4. Wayne Henderson, interview with author John Norberg, December 13, 2022.
5. Wayne Henderson, interview with author John Norberg, December 13, 2022.
6. Wayne Henderson, interview with author John Norberg, December 13, 2022.
7. Purdue ROTC Hall of Fame induction citation for Wayne Henderson.
8. Holder, *The Purdue Drill Team*, chapter 1, page 2.
9. Holder, *The Purdue Drill Team*, chapter 1, page 2.
10. Holder, *The Purdue Drill Team*, chapter 1, page 2.
11. Holder, *The Purdue Drill Team*, chapter 1, page 2.
12. Marcus Clarke, interview with author John Norberg, December 16, 2022.
13. Holder, *The Purdue Drill Team*, chapter 6, page 2.

14. Marcus Clarke, interview with author John Norberg, December 16, 2022.
15. "Cornell McCullom Jr. 1957," West Point Association of Graduates, https://alumni.westpointaog.org/memorial-article?id=e2f1a399-6226-4725-b4a5-073b9f9e5cd5.
16. "Cornell McCullom Jr. 1957."
17. John Whiteclay Chambers II, *The Oxford Companion to American Military History*, (Oxford: Oxford University Press, 1999), 8.
18. Joseph Lelyveld, "Navy ROTC at Negro School Graduates Its First Thirteen Officers," *New York Times*, May 18, 1970, 1.
19. Chambers, *The Oxford Companion to American Military History*, 9
20. Holder, *The Purdue Drill Team*, chapter 6, page 2.
21. Holder, *The Purdue Drill Team*, chapter 6, page 3.
22. Holder, *The Purdue Drill Team*, chapter 6, page 8.
23. Holder, *The Purdue Drill Team*, chapter 6, page 9.
24. Holder, *The Purdue Drill Team*, chapter 6, page 9.
25. Marcus Clarke, interview with author John Norberg, December 16, 2022.
26. Marcus Clarke, interview with author John Norberg, December 16, 2022.
27. John Trott, interview with author John Norberg, December 8, 2022.
28. John Trott, interview with author John Norberg, December 8, 2022.
29. John Trott, interview with author John Norberg, December 8, 2022.
30. John Trott, interview with author John Norberg, December 8, 2022.
31. Darrell J. Katovsich, "1LT Daniel Walter Jordan—US Army," in "Purdue Alumni/Student Casualties on the Vietnam Veterans Memorial," (Purdue University, 2019), 22, https://earchives.lib.purdue.edu/digital/collection/msa395/id/25/rec/1.
32. Ron Neubauer, interview with author John Norberg, December 9, 2022.
33. Ron Neubauer, interview with author John Norberg, December 9, 2022.
34. Associated Press, "President Kennedy On Purdue Drill Team," *Journal and Courier* (Lafayette, Ind.), April 7, 1961, 1.
35. Ron Neubauer, interview with author John Norberg, December 9, 2022.
36. Holder, *The Purdue Drill Team*, chapter 9, page 1.
37. Nancy Trott, interview with author John Norberg, December 8, 2022.
38. Bonnie Graham Rabert, interview with author John Norberg, December 14, 2022.
39. Holder, *The Purdue Drill Team*, chapter 9, page 71.
40. Holder, *The Purdue Drill Team*, chapter 10, page 1.
41. Holder, *The Purdue Drill Team*, chapter 10, page 5.

CHAPTER 14

1. "Purdue Not Entering ROTC Tiff," *Journal and Courier* (Lafayette, Ind.), February 12, 1960, 28.
2. "Purdue Not Entering ROTC Tiff," 28.
3. "Purdue Not Entering ROTC Tiff," 28.
4. "Purdue Not Entering ROTC Tiff," 28.
5. Ron Harley, "Senate Approves ROTC Bill," *Purdue Exponent* (West Lafayette, Ind.), Friday February 10, 1961, 1.
6. Harley, "Senate Approves ROTC Bill," 1.
7. Harley, "Senate Approves ROTC Bill," 6.
8. "Student Vote Favors Voluntary ROTC," *Journal and Courier* (Lafayette, Ind.), April 22, 1961, 1.
9. Purdue Board of Trustees minutes, June 3, 1961, https://earchives.lib.purdue.edu/digital/collection/bot/id/24564.
10. Purdue Board of Trustees minutes, June 3, 1961.
11. Purdue Board of Trustees minutes, June 3, 1961.
12. Purdue Board of Trustees minutes, June 3, 1961.
13. Purdue Board of Trustees minutes, June 3, 1961.
14. Associated Press, "Conant Off to Head War Science Study," *New York Times*, February 16, 1941, 7.
15. Robert W. Topping, *The Hovde Years: A Biography of Frederick L. Hovde* (West Lafayette, Ind.: Purdue University Research Foundation, 1980), 118.
16. Topping, *The Hovde Years*, 160, 163.
17. Topping, *The Hovde Years*, 163.
18. Walter Waggoner, "Frederick Lawson Hovde, Former President of Purdue," *New York Times*, March 2, 1983, B7.
19. Atomic Heritage Foundation, "Timeline," (2022), https://ahf.nuclearmuseum.org/ahf/nuc-history/timeline/.
20. Topping, *The Hovde Years*, 164.
21. Michael G. Smith, *The Rocket Lab: Maurice Zucrow, Purdue University, and America's Race to Space* (West Lafayette, Ind.: Purdue University Press, 2023), 129–30.
22. "Purdue's Rocket Man," *Time*, September 3, 1945.
23. Frederick Hovde, interview with R. B. Eckles, June 1, 1972, tape number 4, page 114, Purdue University Office of Publications Oral History Program Collection, Purdue University Archives and Special Collections, Purdue University Libraries, West Lafayette, IN, https://earchives.lib.purdue.edu/digital/collection/ms02/id/4410/rec/5.

24. Frederick Hovde, interview with R. B. Eckles, June 1, 1972, tape number 4., page 117, https://earchives.lib.purdue.edu/digital/collection/ms02/id/4413/rec/5.
25. Frederick Hovde, interview with R. B. Eckles, June 1, 1972, tape number 4, page 120, https://earchives.lib.purdue.edu/digital/collection/ms02/id/4413/rec/5.
26. Frederick Hovde, interview with R. B. Eckles, June 1, 1972, tape number 4, pages 120–21, https://earchives.lib.purdue.edu/digital/collection/ms02/id/4413/rec/5.
27. "Frederick L. Hovde: Biographical Information," Virginia Kelly Karnes Archives and Special Collections Research Center, Purdue University, West Lafayette, Indiana, https://archives.lib.purdue.edu/repositories/2/resources/1109.
28. Lyndon B. Johnson, "Statement by the President Upon Approving the Reserve Officers' Training Corps Vitalization Act," October 14, 1964. Accessed online at John Woolley and Gerhard Peters, The American Presidency Project, https://www.presidency.ucsb.edu/node/242286.
29. "Voluntary ROTC OK'd by Purdue University Faculty," *Journal and Courier* (Lafayette, Ind.), March 16, 1965, 1.
30. "Voluntary ROTC OK'd by Purdue University Faculty," 1.
31. "Voluntary ROTC OK'd by Purdue University Faculty," 1.
32. "Voluntary ROTC OK'd by Purdue University Faculty," 1, 8.
33. "Voluntary ROTC OK'd by Purdue University Faculty," 8.
34. "Voluntary ROTC OK'd by Purdue University Faculty," 8.
35. "Purdue Trustees OK $765,957 in Construction," *Journal and Courier* (Lafayette, Ind.), June 7, 1965, 9.
36. Western Society of Engineers, "The Washington Award: Recipients; 1960s" (2024), https://www.washingtonaward.com/directory/1960s/.
37. Western Society of Engineers, "The Washington Award: Recipients" (2024), https://www.washingtonaward.com/recipients/.
38. John Norberg, *Ever True: One Hundred Fifty Years of Giant Leaps at Purdue University*, (West Lafayette, Ind.: Purdue University Press, 2019), 249.
39. "Hovde First College Chief to Get Top Defense Medal," *Journal and Courier* (Lafayette, Ind.), May 16, 1970, 10.
40. "Hovde First College Chief to Get Top Defense Medal," 10.
41. Richard M Nixon, "Remarks at a Dinner Honoring Dr. Frederick L. Hovde on His Retirement as President of Purdue University," June 24, 1971. Accessed online at John Woolley and Gerhard Peters, The American Presidency Project, https://www.presidency.ucsb.edu/documents/remarks-dinner-honoring-dr-frederick-l-hovde-his-retirement-president-purdue-university.

CHAPTER 15

1. Sally Watlington, interview with author John Norberg, January 11, 2023.
2. Sally Watlington, interview with author John Norberg, January 11, 2023.
3. Sally Watlington, interview with author John Norberg, January 11, 2023.
4. Sally Watlington, interview with author John Norberg, January 11, 2023.
5. Sally Watlington, interview with author John Norberg, January 11, 2023.
6. Danielle DeSimone, "Over Two Hundred Years of Service: The History of Women in the U.S. Military," USO.org, February 28, 2023, https://www.uso.org/stories/3005-over-200-years-of-service-the-history-of-women-in-the-us-military.
7. "Progressing Toward Equity and Inclusion: The 75th Anniversary of the Women's Armed Services Integration Act," Naval History and Heritage Command, June 5, 2023, https://www.history.navy.mil/browse-by-topic/diversity/women-in-the-navy/WASIA/WASIA-at-75.html.
8. Katrine M. Waterman, "A Brief History of the Female Military Pilot," *Aerospace Power Chronicles* (Summer 2001), https://www.airuniversity.af.edu/Portals/10/ASPJ/journals/Chronicles/waterman.pdf.
9. Cheryl Pellerin, Department of Defense News, "Carter Opens All Military Occupations, Positions to Women," December 3, 2015, https://www.defense.gov/News/News-Stories/Article/Article/632536/carter-opens-all-military-occupations-positions-to-women/.
10. "Air Force ROTC Unit to Open Four-Year Program to Women," *Journal and Courier* (Lafayette, Ind.), June 27, 1970, 6.
11. "Air Force ROTC Unit to Open Four-Year Program to Women," *Journal and Courier* (Lafayette, Ind.), June 27, 1970, 6.
12. "Air Force ROTC Unit to Open Four-Year Program to Women," *Journal and Courier* (Lafayette, Ind.), June 27, 1970, 6.
13. "Two ROTC Units Enroll At Least Six Coeds," *Journal and Courier* (Lafayette, Ind.), September 15, 1970, 52.
14. "Purdue's First," *Journal and Courier* (Lafayette, Ind.), June 15, 1971, 7.
15. R. W. Kennedy, "Navy Blue and Blonde," *Proceedings* (U.S. Naval Institute) 99, no. 8 (August 1973), https://www.usni.org/magazines/proceedings/1973/august/navy-blue-and-blonde.
16. Jan Fitzpatrick, "Ships May Never Be the Same," *Journal and Courier* (Lafayette, Ind.), January 4, 1973, 24.
17. Fitzpatrick, "Ships May Never Be the Same," 24.
18. "Slight Dip in Rosters for ROTCs," *Journal and Courier* (Lafayette, Ind.),

August 27, 1974, 53.

19. Purdue News Service, "Navy Life Appeals to Coeds," *Journal and Courier* (Lafayette, Ind.), February 25, 1975, 12.
20. Purdue News Service, "Navy Life Appeals to Coeds," 12.
21. James Hagerty, "Rosemary Mariner, Spurned by Airline Executive, Led the Way for Female Pilots in the U.S. Navy," *Wall Street Journal*, February 15, 2019, https://www.wsj.com/articles/rosemary-mariner-spurned-by-airline-executive-led-way-for-female-pilots-in-u-s-navy-11550244600.
22. Kevin Cullen, Robert Krizek, Donald Petrin, Manoj S. Patankar, and Thomas Q. Carney, *A Passion for Excellence: The History of Aviation Education at Purdue* (West Lafayette, Ind.: Purdue University Press, 2020), 10.
23. After her father's death, her mother remarried a man named Harold Merims, and for a time Rosemary took his last name.
24. Cullen et al., *A Passion for Excellence*, 10.
25. USS Midway Museum, "Celebrating Fifty Years of Women in Naval Aviation," *Midway Currents* (Spring 2023), https://midwaycurrents.org/spring-2023/celebrating-50-years-of-women-in-naval-aviation/.
26. Cullen et al., *A Passion for Excellence*, 10.
27. Hagerty, "Rosemary Mariner."
28. Cullen et al., *A Passion for Excellence*, 45.
29. Cullen et al., *A Passion for Excellence*, 45.
30. "First All-Women Missing (Wo)man Formation," Women in the Navy, March 29, 2023, https://www.navy.mil/Women-In-the-Navy/Past/Display-Past-Woman-Bio/Article/2959685/first-all-woman-missing-woman-formation/.
31. Vivian Leonard Turnbull, interview with author John Norberg, February 8, 2023.
32. Vivian Leonard Turnbull, interview with author John Norberg, February 8, 2023.
33. Vivian Leonard Turnbull, interview with author John Norberg, February 8, 2023.
34. Lucy Young, interview with author John Norberg, February 21, 2023.
35. Lucy Young, interview with author John Norberg, February 21, 2023.
36. Lucy Young, interview with author John Norberg, February 21, 2023.
37. Lucy Young, interview with author John Norberg, February 21, 2023.
38. Lucy Young, interview with author John Norberg, February 21, 2023.
39. Lucy Young, interview with author John Norberg, February 21, 2023.
40. Colleen Nevius, interview with author John Norberg, January 25, 2023.
41. Colleen Nevius, interview with author John Norberg, January 25, 2023.
42. Colleen Nevius, interview with author John Norberg, January 25, 2023.
43. Colleen Nevius, interview with author John Norberg, January 25, 2023.

44. Colleen Nevius, interview with author John Norberg, January 25, 2023.
45. Colleen Nevius, interview with author John Norberg, January 25, 2023.
46. "CAPT Colleen Nevius, USNR (Ret.): First USN Female Test Pilot," Naval Helicopter Association Historical Society (1997), https://www.nhahistoricalsociety.org/capt-colleen-nevius-usnr-ret-biography/.
47. Carol Pottenger, interview with author John Norberg, January 21, 2023.
48. Carol Pottenger, interview with author John Norberg, January 21, 2023.
49. Carol Pottenger, interview with author John Norberg, January 21, 2023.
50. Carol Pottenger, interview with author John Norberg, January 21, 2023.
51. Carol Pottenger, interview with author John Norberg, January 21, 2023.
52. Erika Covington Steuterman, interview with author John Norberg, February 9, 2023.
53. Erika Covington Steuterman, interview with author John Norberg, February 9, 2023.
54. Erika Covington Steuterman, interview with author John Norberg, February 9, 2023.
55. Erika Covington Steuterman, interview with author John Norberg, February 9, 2023.
56. Erika Covington Steuterman, interview with author John Norberg, February 9, 2023.
57. Erika Covington Steuterman, interview with author John Norberg, February 9, 2023.
58. Erika Covington Steuterman, interview with author John Norberg, February 9, 2023.
59. Erika Covington Steuterman, interview with author John Norberg, February 9, 2023.
60. Erika Covington Steuterman, interview with author John Norberg, February 9, 2023.
61. Erika Covington Steuterman, interview with author John Norberg, February 9, 2023.
62. Erika Covington Steuterman, interview with author John Norberg, February 9, 2023.
63. Erika Covington Steuterman, interview with author John Norberg, February 9, 2023.
64. Erika Covington Steuterman, interview with author John Norberg, February 9, 2023.

PROFILE: MAJOR (RET.) HEATHER PENNEY

1. Heather Penney, interview with author John Norberg, April 24, 2023.
2. Tanya G. Brown, "Heather Penney, An American Air[wo]man," *Purdue Alumnus*, (November/December 2012), 53.
3. Brown, "Heather Penney," 53.
4. Brown, "Heather Penney," 53.
5. Andrew Skoia, "Young Female Purdue Pilots Find Fulfillment in the Venerable Air Race Classic," *Purdue Exponent*, July 1, 1995, 19.
6. Skoia, "Young Female Purdue Pilots Find Fulfillment," 19.
7. Skoia, "Young Female Purdue Pilots Find Fulfillment," 19.
8. Skoia, "Young Female Purdue Pilots Find Fulfillment," 19.
9. Heather Penney, "9/11 and Every-day Heroism," TEDxChelseaPark, June 2019, https://www.ted.com/talks/heather_lucky_penney_9_11_and_every_day_heroism.
10. David Ching, "Fighter Pilot, A Purdue Alumna, Was Prepared to Sacrifice Her Life on 9/11," Purdue News Release, September 9, 2021, https://stories.purdue.edu/fighter-pilot-a-purdue-alumna-was-prepared-to-sacrifice-her-life-on-9-11/.
11. Heather Penney, "F-16 Fighter Pilot Presents at Museum Speaker Series," EAA (Experimental Aircraft Association) Aviation Museum Adventure Speaker Series, November 30, 2022, https://heatherpenney.com/highlights or https://www.eaa.org/videos/6316358160112.
12. Heather Penney, interview with author John Norberg, April 24, 2023.
13. Heather Penney, interview with author John Norberg, April 24, 2023.
14. Heather Penney, interview with author John Norberg, April 24, 2023.
15. Wings Club Foundation, Inc., "The Wings Club Foundation Announces Heather Penney as 2017 Outstanding Aviator Award Recipient," March 9, 2017, https://www.prnewswire.com/news-releases/the-wings-club-foundation-announces-heather-penney-as-2017-outstanding-aviator-award-recipient-300419961.html.
16. Ching, "Fighter Pilot."
17. Ching, "Fighter Pilot."
18. Penney, "9/11 and Every-day Heroism."
19. Penney, "9/11 and Every-day Heroism."

CHAPTER 16

1. Senator John McCain (R-Arizona), as quoted in Leo K. Thorness, "The Michael Christian Story," https://www.purdue.edu/uns/html3month/020517.Christian.bio.html. This is condensed from a speech by Colonel Leo K. Thorness, USAF (Ret.) and a recipient of the Medal of Honor, given at the ROTC Hall of Fame induction ceremony for Michael Christian.
2. Thorness, "The Michael Christian Story."
3. Lieutenant Commander Clint D. Sadler (Ret.), as quoted in Thorness, "The Michael Christian Story."
4. Thorness, "The Michael Christian Story."
5. McCain, as quoted in Thorness, "The Michael Christian Story."
6. Silver Star citation for Michael Christian, as accessed at the Hall of Valor Project, https://valor.militarytimes.com/hero/23363.
7. Dan Kasperick, "NESP: A Scientific Education," *All Hands: The Bureau of Naval Personnel Career Publication* 611 (December 1967), 10, https://media.defense.gov/2019/Jul/25/2002162222/-1/-1/1/AH196712.PDF.
8. "Navy Enlisted Scientific Education Program," Elmore Family School of Electrical and Computer Engineering, https://engineering.purdue.edu/ECE/Alums/NESEP.
9. "Science Alumni and Navy Veterans Reunited After Forty Years," Purdue College of Science, https://www.purdue.edu/science/about/news_and_publications/articles/Science-NESEP.html
10. "Science Alumni and Navy Veterans Reunited After Forty Years."
11. "Navy Enlisted Scientific Education Program."
12. Kasperick, "NESP: A Scientific Education," 10.
13. Homepage for United Space Alliance, the Space Operations Company, http://www.unitedspacealliance.com/.
14. Michael McCulley, interview with author John Norberg, January 20, 2023.
15. Michael McCulley, interview with author John Norberg, January 20, 2023.
16. Michael McCulley, interview with author John Norberg, January 20, 2023.
17. Michael McCulley, interview with author John Norberg, January 20, 2023.
18. Michael McCulley, interview with author John Norberg, January 20, 2023.
19. Michael McCulley, interview with author John Norberg, January 20, 2023.
20. John Norberg, *Wings of Their Dreams: Purdue in Flight* (West Lafayette, Ind.: Purdue University Press, 2020), 324.
21. Henry Davis, interview with author John Norberg, January 21, 2023.
22. Henry Davis, interview with author John Norberg, January 21, 2023.

23. Henry Davis, interview with author John Norberg, January 21, 2023.
24. Henry Davis, interview with author John Norberg, January 21, 2023.
25. Henry Davis, interview with author John Norberg, January 21, 2023.
26. Henry Davis, interview with author John Norberg, January 21, 2023.
27. Henry Davis, interview with author John Norberg, January 21, 2023.
28. Henry Davis, interview with author John Norberg, January 21, 2023.

CHAPTER 17

1. Angela Lange, interview with author John Norberg, March 10, 2023.
2. Mac Hathaway, e-mail interview with John Norberg, May 1, 2024.
3. Erik Namestnik, e-mail interview with John Norberg, May 1, 2024.
4. Mathias Sutton, e-mail interview with John Norberg, April 30, 2024.
5. Angela Lange interview with author John Norberg, March 10, 2023.
6. Seth Bretscher interview with author John Norberg, February 10, 2023.
7. Mathias Sutton, interview with author John Norberg, February 2, 2023.
8. Kevin White, interview with author John Norberg, February 1, 2023.
9. Kevin White, interview with author John Norberg, February 1, 2023.
10. Angela Lange, interview with author John Norberg, March 10, 2023.
11. Angela Lange, interview with author John Norberg, March 10, 2023.
12. Angela Lange, interview with author John Norberg, March 10, 2023.
13. Cody Crawford, interview with author John Norberg, March 9, 2023.
14. Cody Crawford, interview with author John Norberg, March 9, 2023.
15. Cody Crawford, interview with author John Norberg, March 9, 2023.
16. Cody Crawford, interview with author John Norberg, March 9, 2023.
17. Karen Gibson, interview with author John Norberg, April 18, 2023.
18. Karen Gibson, interview with author John Norberg, April 18, 2023.
19. Karen Gibson, interview with author John Norberg, April 18, 2023.
20. Karen Gibson, interview with author John Norberg, April 18, 2023.
21. Karen Gibson, interview with author John Norberg, April 18, 2023.
22. Karen Gibson, interview with author John Norberg, April 18, 2023.
23. Karen Gibson, interview with author John Norberg, April 18, 2023.
24. Karen Gibson, interview with author John Norberg, April 18, 2023.
25. Christopher Nelson, interview with author John Norberg, January 31, 2023.
26. Christopher Nelson, interview with author John Norberg, January 31, 2023.
27. Christopher Nelson, interview with author John Norberg, January 31, 2023.
28. "Leaders: Biography; Captain Chris Nelson," America's Navy, https://www.surfpac.navy.mil/Leaders/Biography/Article/2502734/capt-chris-nelson/.

29. Christopher Nelson, interview with author John Norberg, January 31, 2023.
30. Christopher Nelson, interview with author John Norberg, January 31, 2023.
31. Myers Hogan, interview with author John Norberg, March 9, 2023.
32. Myers Hogan, interview with author John Norberg, March 9, 2023.
33. Myers Hogan, interview with author John Norberg, March 9, 2023.
34. Myers Hogan, interview with author John Norberg, March 9, 2023.
35. Myers Hogan, interview with author John Norberg, March 9, 2023.
36. Myers Hogan, interview with author John Norberg, March 9, 2023.
37. Myers Hogan, interview with author John Norberg, March 9, 2023.
38. Joseph Alford, interview with author John Norberg, April 1, 2023.
39. Joseph Alford, interview with author John Norberg, April 1, 2023.
40. Joseph Alford, interview with author John Norberg, April 1, 2023.
41. Joseph Alford, interview with author John Norberg, April 1, 2023.
42. Joseph Alford, email exchange with author John Norberg, April 24, 2024.
43. Joseph Alford, interview with author John Norberg, April 1, 2023.
44. Joseph Alford, interview with author John Norberg, April 1, 2023.
45. Joseph Alford, interview with author John Norberg, April 1, 2023.
46. Joseph Alford, interview with author John Norberg, April 1, 2023.
47. Joseph Alford, interview with author John Norberg, April 1, 2023.
48. Ken Callahan, interview with author John Norberg, December 15, 2022.
49. Adrian Flores, interview with author John Norberg, February 27, 2023.
50. Adrian Flores, interview with author John Norberg, February 27, 2023.
51. Adrian Flores, interview with author John Norberg, February 27, 2023.
52. Nathan Ganti, interview with author John Norberg, March 9, 2023.
53. Nathan Ganti, interview with author John Norberg, March 9, 2023.
54. Nathan Ganti, interview with author John Norberg, March 9, 2023.
55. Nathan Ganti, interview with author John Norberg, March 9, 2023.
56. Theresa Carter, interview with author John Norberg, January 30, 2023.
57. "Biographies: Major General Theresa C. Carter," U.S. Air Force, https://www.af.mil/About-Us/Biographies/Display/Article/108561/theresa-c-carter/.
58. Theresa Carter, interview with author John Norberg, January 30, 2023.
59. Theresa Carter, interview with author John Norberg, January 30, 2023.
60. Theresa Carter, interview with author John Norberg, January 30, 2023.
61. Theresa Carter, interview with author John Norberg, January 30, 2023.
62. Theresa Carter, interview with author John Norberg, January 30, 2023.
63. Theresa Carter, interview with author John Norberg, January 30, 2023.
64. Theresa Carter, interview with author John Norberg, January 30, 2023.

65. Theresa Carter, interview with author John Norberg, January 30, 2023.
66. Theresa Carter, interview with author John Norberg, January 30, 2023.

PROFILE: LIEUTENANT GENERAL (RET.) CHRISTOPHER P. WEGGEMAN

1. Christopher Weggeman, interview with author John Norberg, October 3, 2023.
2. Christopher Weggeman, interview with author John Norberg, October 3, 2023.
3. Christopher Weggeman, interview with author John Norberg, October 3, 2023.
4. Christopher Weggeman, interview with author John Norberg, October 3, 2023.
5. Neil Armstrong, Aeronautical Engineering '55, fall of 2004 interview with Raymond Cubberley, broadcast media senior producer, Purdue Marketing Photo and Video.
6. Christopher Weggeman, interview with author John Norberg, October 3, 2023.
7. Christopher Weggeman, interview with author John Norberg, October 3, 2023.
8. Christopher Weggeman, interview with author John Norberg, October 3, 2023.
9. Christopher Weggeman, Air Force CEA RM Tech Talk, February 2023. Text provided to John Norberg by Christopher Weggeman.
10. Weggeman, Air Force CEA RM Tech Talk.
11. Weggeman, Air Force CEA RM Tech Talk.
12. Weggeman, Air Force CEA RM Tech Talk.
13. Weggeman, Air Force CEA RM Tech Talk.
14. Weggeman, Air Force CEA RM Tech Talk.
15. Weggeman, Air Force CEA RM Tech Talk.

CHAPTER 18

1. Morgan Torres, interview with author John Norberg, January 17, 2023.
2. Morgan Torres, interview with author John Norberg, January 17, 2023.
3. Morgan Torres, interview with author John Norberg, January 17, 2023.
4. Morgan Torres, interview with author John Norberg, January 17, 2023.
5. Morgan Torres, interview with author John Norberg, January 17, 2023.
6. Morgan Torres, interview with author John Norberg, January 17, 2023.
7. Jamie Richards, interview with author John Norberg, February 12, 2023.
8. Jamie Richards, interview with author John Norberg, February 12, 2023.
9. Jamie Richards, interview with author John Norberg, February 12, 2023.
10. David Hankins, interview with author John Norberg, September 15, 2023.
11. Dale Whittaker interview with author John Norberg, September 14, 2023.
12. David Hankins interview with author John Norberg, September 15, 2023.
13. Dan Carpenter, interview with author John Norberg, February 1, 2023.

14. Purdue Military Family Research Center, "Our Mission," https://www.mfri.purdue.edu/about/mission/.
15. Shelley McDermott Wadsworth, interview with author John Norberg, January 27, 2023.
16. Shelley McDermott Wadsworth, interview with author John Norberg, January 27, 2023.
17. Shelley McDermott Wadsworth, interview with author John Norberg, January 27, 2023.
18. Shelley McDermott Wadsworth, interview with author John Norberg, January 27, 2023.
19. Shelley McDermott Wadsworth, interview with author John Norberg, January 27, 2023.
20. Shelley McDermott Wadsworth, interview with author John Norberg, January 27, 2023.
21. Shelley McDermott Wadsworth, interview with author John Norberg, January 27, 2023.
22. Shelley McDermott Wadsworth, interview with author John Norberg, January 27, 2023.
23. Shelley McDermott Wadsworth, interview with author John Norberg, January 27, 2023.
24. Purdue Military Family Research Institute, "Family Support," https://www.mfri.purdue.edu/programs/outreach/.
25. Shelley McDermott Wadsworth, interview with author John Norberg, January 27, 2023.

CHAPTER 19

1. Kelvin Gumbs, interview with author John Norberg, March 20, 2023.
2. Kelvin Gumbs, interview with author John Norberg, March 20, 2023.
3. Frank Dooley, interview with author John Norberg, January 26, 2023.
4. Frank Dooley, interview with author John Norberg, January 26, 2023.
5. Frank Dooley, interview with author John Norberg, January 26, 2023.
6. Alex Giberson, interview with author John Norberg, February 7, 2023.
7. Alex Giberson, interview with author John Norberg, February 7, 2023.
8. Jeff Smith, interview with author John Norberg, February 7, 2023.
9. Alex Giberson, interview with author John Norberg, February 7, 2023.
10. Frank Dooley, interview with author John Norberg, January 26, 2023.
11. Frank Dooley, interview with author John Norberg, January 26, 2023.

12. Kelvin Gumbs, interview with author John Norberg, March 20, 2023.
13. Christopher Martin, email with author John Norberg, April 3, 2023.
14. Andrea Pluckebaum, director, analytics, Purdue Institutional Data, Analytics, and Assessment, interview with author John Norberg, April 3, 2023.
15. "New Military Advisory Board to Boost Purdue's Online Learning 2.0 Initiative," Purdue News, September 26, 2023, https://www.purdue.edu/newsroom/releases/2023/Q3/new-military-advisory-board-to-boost-purdues-online-learning-2.0-initiative.html.
16. Christopher Martin, interview with author John Norberg, April 3, 2023.
17. Christopher Martin, interview with author John Norberg, April 3, 2023.
18. Ethan Sneider, interview with author John Norberg, May 15, 2023.
19. Ethan Sneider, interview with author John Norberg, May 15, 2023.
20. Ethan Sneider, interview with author John Norberg, May 15, 2023.
21. Ethan Sneider, interview with author John Norberg, May 15, 2023.
22. Ethan Sneider, interview with author John Norberg, May 15, 2023.

CHAPTER 20

1. "AAE Graduate Student, Coast Guard Helicopter Pilot Awarded Distinguished Flying Cross," Purdue School of Aeronautics and Astronautics Spotlights, November 8, 2019, https://engineering.purdue.edu/AAE/spotlights/2019/2019-1101CarrilloDFC.
2. "AAE Graduate Student, Coast Guard Helicopter Pilot Awarded Distinguished Flying Cross."
3. Alten F. "Skip" Grandt Jr., "Summary of The Purdue School of Aeronautics and Astronautics Contribution to the Graduate Education of Armed Services Personnel," compiled November 2021.
4. Adrian Morrison, interview with author John Norberg, January 17, 2023.
5. RAAF Air Commodore and Director General Aircraft Engineering E. J. Whitehead letter to Prof. Alten F. Grandt Jr., chairman of the graduate student selection board for School of Aeronautics and Astronautics, March 16, 1984.
6. Alten F. Grandt Jr., interview with author John Norberg, November 17, 2022.
7. Alten F. Grandt Jr., interview with author John Norberg, November 17, 2022.
8. D. E. Tindal, Air Commodore, Director General Technical Airworthiness—Australian Defence Force, letter to Alten F. Grandt Jr., July 20, 2010.
9. Adrian Morrison, interview with author John Norberg, January 17, 2023.
10. Adrian Morrison, interview with author John Norberg, January 17, 2023.
11. Adrian Morrison, interview with author John Norberg, January 17, 2023.

12. Adrian Morrison, interview with author John Norberg, January 17, 2023.
13. Kevin Walker, interview with author John Norberg, November 17, 2022.
14. Kevin Walker, interview with author John Norberg, November 17, 2022.
15. Kevin Walker, interview with author John Norberg, November 17, 2022.
16. Kevin Walker, interview with author John Norberg, November 17, 2022.
17. Alten F. Grandt Jr., interview with author John Norberg, November 17, 2022.
18. Kevin Walker, interview with author John Norberg, November 17, 2022.

CHAPTER 21

1. Glenn R. Peterson, interview with author John Norberg, March 24, 2023.
2. Mung Chiang, interview with author John Norberg, July 12, 2022.
3. Mitch Daniels, interview with author John Norberg, February 6, 2023.
4. "2023-2024 Best Engineering Schools," *U.S. News and World Report*, https://www.usnews.com/best-graduate-schools/top-engineering-schools/eng-rankings.
5. Arvind Raman, interview with author John Norberg, February 2023.
6. Arvind Raman, interview with author John Norberg, February 2023.
7. Joe Pekny, interview with author John Norberg, June 20, 2022.
8. Dulcy Abraham, interview with author John Norberg, April 4, 2023.
9. Dulcy Abraham, interview with author John Norberg, April 4, 2023.
10. Joe Pekny, interview with author John Norberg, June 20, 2022.
11. Joe Pekny, interview with author John Norberg, June 20, 2022.
12. Joe Pekny, interview with author John Norberg, June 20, 2022.
13. J. Eric Dietz, interview with author John Norberg, June 20, 2022.
14. Joe Pekny, interview with author John Norberg, June 20, 2022.
15. J. Eric Dietz, interview with author John Norberg, June 20, 2022.
16. J. Eric Dietz, interview with author John Norberg, June 20, 2022.
17. Joe Pekny, interview with author John Norberg, June 20, 2022.
18. David Hankins, interview with author John Norberg, March 27, 2023.
19. J. Eric Dietz, interview with author John Norberg, June 20, 2022.
20. Joe Pekny, interview with author John Norberg, June 20, 2022.
21. Joe Pekny, interview with author John Norberg, June 20, 2022.
22. Purdue Engineering, "Purdue Military Research Institute," YouTube, October 6, 2021, https://www.youtube.com/watch?v=r33qUOyHtZI.
23. Joe Pekny, interview with author John Norberg, June 20, 2022.
24. David Hankins, interview with author John Norberg, March 2, 2023.
25. Shreyas Sundaram, interview with author John Norberg, April 12, 2023.

26. Shreyas Sundaram, interview with author John Norberg, April 12, 2023.
27. Charles E. Anklam III, email exchange with author John Norberg, May 21, 2023.
28. Charles E. Anklam III, email exchange with author John Norberg, May 21, 2023.
29. Charles E. Anklam III, email exchange with author John Norberg, May 21, 2023.
30. Charles E. Anklam III, email exchange with author John Norberg, May 21, 2023.
31. Charles E. Anklam III, email exchange with author John Norberg, May 21, 2023.
32. Charles E. Anklam III, email exchange with author John Norberg, May 21, 2023.
33. Charles E. Anklam III, email exchange with author John Norberg, May 21, 2023.
34. Glenn Peterson, interview with author John Norberg, March 24, 2023.
35. Glenn Peterson, interview with author John Norberg, March 24, 2023.
36. Glenn Peterson, interview with author John Norberg, March 24, 2023.
37. Glenn Peterson, interview with author John Norberg, March 24, 2023.
38. Glenn Peterson, interview with author John Norberg, March 24, 2023.
39. Glenn Peterson, interview with author John Norberg, March 24, 2023.
40. Alexander Master, interview with author John Norberg, March 31, 2023.
41. Alexander Master, interview with author John Norberg, March 31, 2023.
42. Alexander Master, interview with author John Norberg, March 31, 2023.
43. Alexander Master, interview with author John Norberg, March 31, 2023.
44. Alexander Master, interview with author John Norberg, March 31, 2023.
45. Alexander Master, interview with author John Norberg, March 31, 2023.
46. Alexander Master, interview with author John Norberg, March 31, 2023.
47. Casey Jones, interview with author John Norberg, April 3, 2023.
48. Casey Jones, interview with author John Norberg, April 3, 2023.
49. Barry Scott, interview with author John Norberg, March 30, 2023.
50. Barry Scott, interview with author John Norberg, March 30, 2023.
51. Barry Scott, interview with author John Norberg, March 30, 2023.
52. Barry Scott, interview with author John Norberg, March 30, 2023.
53. Barry Scott, interview with author John Norberg, March 30, 2023.
54. Barry Scott, interview with author John Norberg, March 30, 2023.
55. Barry Scott, interview with author John Norberg, March 30, 2023.
56. Barry Scott, interview with author John Norberg, March 30, 2023.

CHAPTER 22

1. Mitchell E. Daniels, interview with author John Norberg, February 6, 2023.
2. Daniel DeLaurentis, interview with author John Norberg, February 17, 2023.
3. Daniel DeLaurentis, interview with author John Norberg, February 17, 2023.
4. Daniel DeLaurentis, email with author John Norberg, May 20, 2024.

5. "Purdue Launches Next Moves Initiatives," Purdue News Release, April 9, 2021, https://www.purdue.edu/newsroom/releases/2021/Q2/purdue-launches-next-moves-initiatives.html.
6. Ann Caldwell, "Bringing It Home: Jobs," *Washington Post* Live interview, May 18, 2023, https://www.washingtonpost.com/washington-post-live/2023/05/18/transcript-bringing-it-home-jobs/.
7. Mung Chiang and Keith Krach, "Krach Institute for Tech Diplomacy at Purdue Fireside Chat," May 11, 2023, https://www.youtube.com/watch?v=1btP5OUeU60.
8. Mung Chiang, interview with author John Norberg, July 12, 2022.
9. Arvind Raman, interview with author John Norberg, February 27, 2023.
10. Arvind Raman, interview with author John Norberg, February 27, 2023.
11. Arvind Raman, interview with author John Norberg, February 27, 2023.
12. "Purdue University Partners With Leading Global Chipmaker on Semiconductor Design Center," Purdue News Release, June 28, 2022, https://www.purdue.edu/newsroom/releases/2022/Q2/purdue-university-partners-with-leading-global-chipmaker-on-midwests-first-semiconductor-design-center.html.
13. "Purdue, Ivy Tech Partner on Next-Generation Microelectronics Workforce," Purdue News Release, May 5, 2022, https://www.purdue.edu/newsroom/releases/2022/Q2/purdue,-ivy-tech-partner-on-next-generation-micro electronics-workforce.html.
14. Mark Lundstrom, interview with author John Norberg, July 20, 2023.
15. Marlee Thomas, "Original Microchip Plant No Longer Coming to West Lafayette," WLFI-TV, West Lafayette, Indiana, April 5, 2024, https://www.wlfi.com/news/local/original-microchip-plant-no-longer-coming-to-west-lafayette/article_3d14e17a-f382-11ee-af52-ef8451cfa877.html.
16. "Purdue Announces 3-Pronged 'Purdue Computes' Initiative: Propel Computer Science to the Nation's Top 10, Launch the Institute of Physical AI and Expand Semiconductor Facilities," Purdue News Release, April 14, 2023, https://www.purdue.edu/newsroom/releases/2023/Q2/purdue-announces-3-pronged-purdue-computes-initiative-propel-computer-science-to-the-nations-top-10-launch-the-institute-of-physical-ai-and-expand-semiconductor-facilities.html.
17. "Purdue Signs Landmark U.S.-Japan Agreement in Semiconductors at G7 Summit," Purdue News Release, May 22, 2023, https://www.purdue.edu/newsroom/releases/2023/Q2/purdue-signs-landmark-u.s-japan-agreement-in

-semiconductors-at-g7-summit.html.

18. "SK Hynix Announces Semiconductor Advanced Packaging Investment in Purdue Research Park," Purdue News Release, April 3, 2024, https://www.purdue.edu/newsroom/releases/2024/Q2/sk-hynix-announces-semiconductor-advanced-packaging-investment-in-purdue-research-park.html.
19. "SK Hynix Announces Semiconductor Advanced Packaging Investment in Purdue Research Park."
20. Senator Todd Young interview with author John Norberg, July 20, 2023.
21. Senator Todd Young interview with author John Norberg, July 20, 2023.
22. "Secretaries of State, Commerce Discuss Efforts to Build a US Microelectronics Ecosystem," Purdue News Release, September 13, 2022, https://www.purdue.edu/newsroom/releases/2022/Q3/secretaries-of-state,-commerce-discuss-efforts-to-build-a-u.s-microelectronics-ecosystem.html.
23. "Secretaries of State, Commerce Discuss Efforts to Build a US Microelectronics Ecosystem."
24. Mark Lundstrom, interview with author John Norberg, February 20, 2023.
25. Mitchell E. Daniels, interview with author John Norberg, February 6, 2023.
26. Steven Schneider, interview with author John Norberg, April 20, 2023.
27. Steven Schneider, interview with author John Norberg, April 20, 2023.
28. Mung Chiang, interview with author John Norberg, July 12, 2023.
29. Sharon Weinberger, "Hypersonic Missiles Are Game-Changers, and America Doesn't Have Them," Wall Street Journal, September 18, 2023, https://www.wsj.com/politics/national-security/hypersonic-missiles-america-military-behind-936a3128.
30. "Mark Lewis Named Inaugural CEO of Purdue Applied Research Institute," Purdue News Release, April 11, 2023, https://www.purdue.edu/newsroom/releases/2023/Q2/mark-lewis-named-inaugural-ceo-of-purdue-applied-research-institute.html.
31. "Mark Lewis Named Inaugural CEO of Purdue Applied Research Institute."
32. Karen Plaut, interview with author John Norberg, March 10, 2023.
33. "Purdue to Develop World's First Mach 8 Wind Tunnel," Purdue News Release, February 4, 2020, https://www.purdue.edu/newsroom/releases/2020/Q1/purdue-to-develop-worlds-first-mach-8-quiet-wind-tunnel.html.
34. "New Purdue Research Building Will Offer a World's First in Hypersonic Testing, Materials Development," Purdue News Release, July 27, 2021, https://www.purdue.edu/newsroom/releases/2021/Q3/new-purdue-research-building

-will-offer-a-worlds-first,-and-hypersonic-testing,-materials-development.html.

35. "Purdue Hypersonics Combines Industry, Academia in New Materials and Manufacturing Center," Purdue News Release, February 7, 2022, https://www.purdue.edu/newsroom/releases/2022/Q1/purdue-hypersonics-combines-industry,-academia-in-new-materials-and-manufacturing-center.html.
36. "Purdue Strengthens National Security Focus with New Propulsion Lab," Purdue News Release, April 8, 2022, https://www.purdue.edu/newsroom/releases/2022/Q2/purdue-strengthens-national-security-focus-with-new-propulsion-lab.html.
37. "Purdue Strengthens National Security Focus with New Propulsion Lab."
38. "Purdue, Rolls-Royce Sign 10-Year, $75 Million Strategic Alliance Agreement," Purdue News Release, May 25, 2022, https://www.purdue.edu/newsroom/releases/2022/Q2/purdue,-rolls-royce-sign-10-year,-75-million-strategic-alliance-agreement.html.
39. "Stratolaunch Creates Advanced Program Office at Discovery Park District and Collaborates with Purdue University on Hypersonic Design and Test," Purdue News Release, January 23, 2023, https://www.purdue.edu/newsroom/releases/2023/Q1/stratolaunch-creates-advanced-program-office-at-discovery-park-district-and-collaborate-with-purdue-university-on-hypersonic-design-and-test.html.
40. "Maurice Zucrow," Virginia Kelly Karnes Archives and Special Collections, Purdue University, West Lafayette, Indiana, https://archives.lib.purdue.edu/agents/people/772.
41. Michael G. Smith, *The Rocket Lab: Maurice Zucrow, Purdue University, and America's Race to Space* (West Lafayette, Ind.: Purdue University Press, 2023), 2.
42. Robert Lucht, interview with author John Norberg, April 17, 2023.
43. "PERC Mission Statement," Purdue Energetics Research Center, https://engineering.purdue.edu/Energetics.
44. "PERC Hosts Energetics Experts across Academia, Industry, and Government at PEMS '23," Purdue Energetics Research Center, https://engineering.purdue.edu/Energetics/news/pems23-hosts-energetics-experts-across-academia-industry-and-government.
45. Hannah Ritchie and Pablo Rosado, "Energy Mix," Our World in Data, January 2024, https://ourworldindata.org/energy-mix.
46. Purdue University Department of Computer Science, "History of Information

Security at Purdue," https://www.cs.purdue.edu/graduate/professional/about/history.html.

47. "U.S. Cybersecurity Leaders to Examine Lessons Learned and Set Strategies for Future Risk," Purdue News Release, February 20, 2023, https://www.purdue.edu/research/features/stories/u-s-cybersecurity-leaders-to-examine-lessons-learned-and-set-strategies-for-future-risk/.
48. "Global Defense and Security Institute Launched at Purdue," Purdue News Release, December 1, 2016, https://www.purdue.edu/newsroom/releases/2016/Q4/global-defense-and-security-institute-launched-at-purdue.html.
49. As quoted in "Booz Allen Hamilton, Purdue collaborate to stop cyber criminals, address other national defense challenges," Purdue News Release, March 21, 2019, https://www.purdue.edu/newsroom/releases/2019/Q1/booz-allen-hamilton-purdue-collaborate-to-stop-cyber-criminals,-address-other-national-defense-challenges.html.
50. As quoted in "Booz Allen Hamilton."
51. Thomson ISI Web of Science Ranking, 2023.
52. R. Graham Cooks and Xin Yan, "Mass Spectrometry for Synthesis and Analysis," *Annual Review Of Analytical Chemistry* 11 (2018): 1–28, https://doi.org/10.1146/annurev-anchem-061417-125820.
53. R. W. Kondrat and R. G. Cooks, "Direct Analysis of Mixtures by Mass Spectrometry," *Analytical Chemistry* 50, no. 1 (1978): 81–92, https://pubs.acs.org/doi/abs/10.1021/ac50023a781.
54. Linfan Li, Tsung-Chi Chen, Yue Ren, et al., "Mini 12, Miniature Mass Spectrometer for Clinical and Other Applications—Introduction and Characterization," *Analytical Chemistry* 86, no. 6 (2014): 2909–16, https://doi.org/10.1021/ac403766c.
55. He Wang, Jiangjiang Liu, R. Graham Cooks, Zheng Ouyang, "Paper Spray for Direct Analysis of Complex Mixtures Using Mass Spectrometry," *Angewandt Chemie* 49, no. 5 (2010): 877–880, https://doi.org/10.1002/anie.200906314.
56. Zoltán Takáts, Justin M. Wiseman, Bogdan Gologan, and R. Graham Cooks, "Mass Spectrometry Sampling Under Ambient Conditions with Desorption Electrospray Ionization," *Science* 306, no. 5695 (2004): 471–73, https://doi.org/10.1126/science.1104404.
57. U.S. Army CCDC Army Research Laboratory Public Affairs, "Army Partners with Purdue University for Futuristic Materials Research," August 31, 2020, https://www.army.mil/article/238634/army_partners_with_purdue_university_for_futuristic_materials_research.
58. "Purdue Welcomes the Largest Economic Development Project to West

Lafayette from Rolls-Royce and Invests in Aerospace Engineering Epicenter," Purdue News Release, August 2, 2021, https://www.purdue.edu/newsroom/releases/2021/Q3/purdue-welcomes-the-largest-economic-development-project-to-west-lafayette-from-rolls-royce-and-invests-in-aerospace-engineering-epicenter.html.

59. Mung Chiang, interview with author John Norberg, July 12, 2023.
60. "Saab's Global Defense and Security Company Lands in Indiana, To Open Site Near Purdue University," Purdue News Release, May 8, 2019, https://www.purdue.edu/newsroom/releases/2019/Q2/saabs-global-defense-and-security-company-lands-in-indiana,-to-open-site-near-purdue-university.html.
61. Mung Chiang, interview with author John Norberg, July 12, 2023.
62. Air Force Research Laboratory, "AFRL Regional Network – Midwest," https://afresearchlab.com/lablife/afrl-regional-network-midwest/.
63. Air Force Research Laboratory, "AFRL Regional Network – Midwest."
64. "Purdue University Opens Krach Institute for Tech Development in Honor of 2022 Nobel Peace Prize Nominee Keith Krach," *Business Wire*, April 5, 2022, https://www.businesswire.com/news/home/20220405006267/en/Purdue-University-Opens-Krach-Institute-for-Tech-Diplomacy-in-Honor-of-2022-Nobel-Peace-Prize-Nominee-Keith-Krach.
65. "Purdue University Opens Krach Institute."
66. "Purdue University Opens Krach Institute."
67. Roslyn Layton, "2022 Nobel Peace Prize Nominee Keith Krach's 'Trust Principle" Is Antidote to Authoritarianism," *Forbes*, May 23, 2022.
68. NSWC Crane Corporate Communications, "NSWC Crane, Purdue University Sign Educational Partnership Agreement Amendment to Advance Partnership," February 22, 2023, https://www.purdue.edu/research/features/stories/nswc-crane-purdue-university-sign-educational-partnership-agreement-amendment-to-advance-partnership/.
69. NSWC Crane Corporate Communications, "NSWC Crane, Purdue University Sign Educational Partnership Agreement."
70. NSWC Crane Corporate Communications, "NSWC Crane, Purdue University Sign Educational Partnership Agreement."
71. NSWC Crane Corporate Communications, "NSWC Crane, Purdue University Sign Educational Partnership Agreement."
72. NSWC Crane Corporate Communications, "NSWC Crane, Purdue University Sign Educational Partnership Agreement."

73. NSWC Crane Corporate Communications, "NSWC Crane, Purdue University Sign Educational Partnership Agreement."
74. "Purdue Establishes Permanent Presence Next to NSWC Crane for Future of National Defense and Semiconductors," Purdue News Release, September 6, 2023, https://www.purdue.edu/newsroom/releases/2023/Q3/purdue-establishes-permanent-presence-next-to-nswc-crane-for-future-of-national-defense-and-semiconductors.html.
75. "Purdue Establishes Permanent Presence Next to NSWC Crane."
76. "Purdue@DC to Amplify Boilermaker Presence in Nation's Capital," Purdue News Release, April 28, 2023, https://www.purdue.edu/newsroom/releases/2023/Q2/purdue@dc-to-amplify-boilermaker-presence-in-nations-capital.html.
77. "Purdue@DC to Amplify Boilermaker Presence in Nation's Capital."
78. Sorin Adam Matei, interview with author John Norberg, April 12, 2023.
79. Sorin Adam Matei, interview with author John Norberg, April 12, 2023.
80. Sorin Adam Matei, interview with author John Norberg, April 12, 2023.
81. Sorin Adam Matei, interview with author John Norberg, April 12, 2023.
82. FORCES, "Battle Flow," https://www.cla.purdue.edu/research/forces-initiative/research-outreach/battleflow.html.
83. Sorin Adam Matei, interview with author John Norberg, April 12, 2023.
84. Robert Kirchubel, email exchange with author John Norberg, May 9, 2023.
85. "Defense Civilian Training Corps at Purdue Creates Path to Service," Purdue News Release, September 1, 2023, https://www.purdue.edu/newsroom/releases/2023/Q3/defense-civilian-training-corps-at-purdue-creates-path-to-service.html.
86. "Defense Civilian Training Corps at Purdue Creates Path to Service."
87. Mung Chiang, interview with author John Norberg, July 12, 2023.

INDEX

ABOUT THE AUTHOR

JOHN NORBERG IS AN INDIANA JOURNALISM HALL OF FAME WRITER WHO IS RETIRED FROM Purdue University and the Lafayette (IN) *Journal and Courier*, where he wrote a newspaper column for more than forty-one years and was an award-winning news and feature reporter, receiving more than fifty state and national awards. This is his ninth book. He has written articles for the *Saturday Evening Post*, *USA Today*, the *Christian Science Monitor*, and *Time* magazine. He was interviewed on CBS News Sunday Morning, NPR's Big Picture Science, and many newspapers, radio, and TV shows. He received the Purdue for Life Foundation Special Boilermaker Award and the Block P Award from Purdue Bands and Orchestras.